College Reading
and Study Skills

College Reading and Study Skills

FOURTH EDITION

Kathleen T. McWhorter
Niagara County Community College

SCOTT, FORESMAN AND COMPANY

Glenview, Illinois   Boston   London

LIBRARY OF CONGRESS
Library of Congress Cataloging-in-Publication Data

McWhorter, Kathleen T.
  College reading and study skills / Kathleen T. McWhorter.—4th
  ed.
  p.   cm.
  Bibliography: p.
  Includes index.
  ISBN 0-673-39664-9
  1. Reading (Higher education)   2. Study, Method of.   I. Title.
LB2395.3.M386   1989
428.4'07'11— dc19   88-23975
                                                           CIP

1 2 3 4 5 6 7 8 9 10—MKN—94 93 92 91 90 89 88

Printed in the United States of America

Hugh D. Barlow, *Introduction to Criminology*. Copyright © 1984 by Little, Brown and Company (Inc.). Reprinted by permission.

Lois Berman and J. C. Evans, *Exploring the Cosmos*. Copyright © 1986 by Little, Brown and Co. (Inc.). Reprinted by permission.

Sissela Bok, "To Lie or Not to Lie—The Doctor's Dilemma." Copyright © 1978 by The New York Times Company. Reprinted by permission.

Mary Calderone, "It's Really the Men Who Need Liberating." Guest Editorial, *Life 69*, September 4, 1970. Copyright © 1970 by Time, Inc. Reprinted by permission.

Bernard C. Campbell, *Humankind Emerging*. Copyright © 1985 by Little, Brown and Co. (Inc.). Reprinted by permission.

Roger Chisholm and Marilu McCarty, *Principles of Economics*. Copyright © 1987 by Scott, Foresman and Co., Inc. Reprinted by permission of the publisher.

James C. Coleman et al., *Abnormal Psychology and Modern Life*. Copyright © 1984 by Scott, Foresman and Co., Inc. Reprinted by permission of the publisher.

Elliott Currie and Jerome H. Skolnick, *America's Problems: Social Issues and Public Policy*. Copyright © 1984 by Little, Brown and Co. (Inc.). Reprinted by permission.

Helena Curtis, *Biology*, 4th ed., Worth Publishers, New York, 1983.

Bowman O. Davis et al., *Conceptual Human Physiology*. 1985. Columbus, OH: Charles E. Merrill.

Douglas Ehninger et al., *Principles and Types of Speech Communication*. Copyright © 1986 by Scott, Foresman and Co., Inc. Reprinted by permission of the publisher.

Robert B. Ekelund, Jr., and Robert D. Tollison, *Economics*. Copyright © 1986 by Little, Brown and Co. (Inc.). Reprinted by permission.

James Geiwitz, *Looking at Ourselves: An Introduction to Psychology*. Copyright © 1976 by Little, Brown and Company (Inc.). Reprinted by permission of the author.

Paul B. Hewitt, *Conceptual Physics*. Copyright © 1985 by Little, Brown and Co. (Inc.). Reprinted by permission.

T. H. Holmes and R. H. Rahe, "The Social Readjustment Rating Scale." *Journal of Psychosometic Research* 11, 1967, pp. 213–218. Reprinted by permission of Pergamon Press, Inc.

Michael C. Howard, *Contemporary Cultural Anthropology*. Copyright © 1986 by Little, Brown, and Co. (Inc.). Reprinted by permission.

Paul M. Insel and Walton T. Roth, *Core Concepts in Health*. By permission of Mayfield Publishing Company. Copyright © 1988, 1985, 1982, 1979, 1976 by Mayfield Publishing Co.

Walter S. Jones, *The Logic of International Relations*. Copyright © 1985 by Little, Brown and Co. (Inc.). Reprinted by permission.

Thomas C. Kinnear and Kenneth L. Bernhardt, *Principles of Marketing*. Copyright © 1986 by Scott, Foresman and Co., Inc. Reprinted by permission of the publisher.

Robert L. Lineberry, *Government in America*. Copyright © 1986 by Little, Brown and Co., (Inc.). Reprinted by permission.

D. Meichenbaum, "A Self-Instructional Approach to Stress Management: A Proposal for Stress Innoculating Training." In D. C. Spielberger and I. G. Sarason, *Stress and Anxiety*, Vol. 1, pp. 237–263. 1975. Reprinted by permission of Hemisphere Publishing Corporation.

Charles D. Miller and Vern H. Heeren, *Mathematical Ideas*. Copyright © 1986 by Scott, Foresman and Co., Inc. Reprinted by permission of the publisher.

Robert C. Nickerson, *Fundamentals of Structured COBOL*. Copyright © 1984 by Little, Brown and Co. (Inc.). Reprinted by permission.

Hal B. Pickle and Royce L. Abrahamson, *Introduction to Business*. Copyright © 1986 by Scott, Foresman and Co., Inc. Reprinted by permission of the publisher.

continued on page 435

For Thomas and Brette

Preface

Beginning college students require a foundation in reading and study skills that will enable them to handle college-level work. *College Reading and Study Skills*, fourth edition, presents the basic techniques for reading comprehension and efficiency, study, note-taking, written assignments and research papers, and taking exams. The reading and study skills I have chosen to present are those most vital to students' success in college. Each unit teaches skills that are immediately usable—all have clear and direct application to students' course work.

More than twenty years of teaching reading and study courses in both two- and four-year colleges have demonstrated to me the need for a text that covers *both* reading and study skills and provides for *both* instruction and application. This text was written to meet those needs.

Reading and study skills are inseparable. A student must develop in both areas in order to successfully handle college work. With this goal in mind, I have tried to provide complete coverage of both skills throughout the text and to show their relationship and interdependency. In doing so, my emphasis has been on direct instruction. My central aim is to teach reading and study through a "how-to" approach.

The units of the text are interchangeable, enabling the instructor to adapt the material to a variety of instructional sequences. Part One provides an introduction to the college experience and presents skills, habits, and attitudes that contribute to college success. Topics include active learning, demands and expectations of college, time management, and organizational skills. This section also establishes the theoretical framework of the text by discussing the learning and memory processes and the principles on which many of the skills presented throughout the text are based. Part Two encourages students to be aware of and control the reading process. They are shown how to cope with factors such as poor concentration and stress which block comprehension. Reading as a thinking process is emphasized. Topics include prereading, activating background knowledge, formulating guide questions, and monitoring comprehension. Part Three focuses on the development of comprehension skills. Sentence and paragraph structure are described and recognition of thought patterns introduced. Part Four teaches textbook reading skills: how to use textbook organization, how to underline and mark a textbook, how to organize a system of study for various academic disciplines, and how to organize information for efficient learning. Part Five helps students improve their ability to perform in the classroom by describing how to take notes in lectures, how to prepare for and take exams, how to participate in class activities and projects, and how to prepare written class assignments and research papers. Because vocabulary development is critical for improved reading and mastery of course content, Part Six focuses on improving vocabulary. The final section, Part Seven, discusses reading efficiency, reading flexibility, and skimming and scanning.

The text format was chosen to provide ample practice as well as instruction. Explanation of each new technique is followed by exercises illustrating the use of that technique and allowing the student to test its effectiveness. Students are thus guided in their understanding of the techniques presented and then in trying out each new skill. Many exercises quote excerpts from a wide range of college texts, providing realistic examples of college textbook reading. A second type of exercise is based on a unique feature of this book—the sample textbook chapters included in the appendixes. Portions of the sample chapters are used throughout the book so that the student can practice skills with actual textbook material. A last type of exercise requires the student to apply each skill in his or her own course work.

Several features make this book well suited to the needs of beginning college students. First, the book approaches both reading and study as active processes in which the student assesses the task, selects appropriate strategies, monitors his or her performance, and takes any necessary actions to modify and improve it. Second, the text focuses on reading as a cognitive process, applying the findings from the research areas of metacognition and prose structure analysis to encourage students to approach reading as an active mental process of selecting, processing, and organizing information to be learned. Third, the text emphasizes the necessity of adapting skills and techniques to suit the characteristics and requirements of specific academic disciplines, as well as accommodating the student's particular learning style. Fourth, the sample textbook chapters described above provide an essential link, or intermediate step, between in-chapter practice and independent application of new techniques. Finally, the level of writing and of practice exercises has been carefully controlled, and the sample textbook chapters are selected to be representative of college textbook reading assignments.

A partial Answer Key is included to make the text adaptable to self-instruction and to provide immediate feedback for students as they work through the practice exercises. An Instructor's Manual gives the instructor a detailed description of the text and specific suggestions for classroom use. The manual also contains chapter review quizzes, a complete answer key, and a set of overhead projection materials to enhance and supplement classroom instruction.

The fourth edition of this text includes changes and additions that reflect current emphases and directions in research on adult learning processes. A major focus of the text is on active reading. A new chapter on strategies for active reading is primarily concerned with metacognition—monitoring, evaluating, and improving students' level of cognitive functioning. Specifically, students are taught to activate their background knowledge, to establish purposes for reading through the use of guide questions, and to select appropriate reading strategies. Positive and negative comprehension signals are described, and specific monitoring techniques are suggested. Steps to follow when comprehension is poor or incomplete are emphasized.

Across many academic disciplines there is also a growing interest in collaborative learning—learning through structured group activities in which students exchange ideas and view one another's thinking and learning processes. Students who are accustomed to formal classroom situations are often less familiar with this form of instruction; consequently, a new chapter has been added on participating in class activities and projects.

Revisions in the fourth edition also reflect changes in the college student population. Because many students enter college with little knowledge of what academic work and college life involves, the text contains a new section on academic demands and expectations. A section on managing and coping with stress has been added to help beginning students find other aspects of college less frustrating. (One of the sample textbook chapters also deals with this topic.) Revisions furthermore address the topic of procrastination and add a new section on listening skills. Listening is approached as an active information-intake process requiring a deliberate focus and intention. Finally, the two sample textbook chapters included in this edition add flexibility and diversity in both content and format, providing an opportunity for students to adapt reading and learning strategies to suit particular academic disciplines.

In preparing this edition, I appreciate the excellent ideas, suggestions, and advice provided by my reviewers: Esther M. Eddy, Greater Hartford Community College; Rosemary Wolfe, Anne Arundel Community College; Paulette C. Babner, Cape Cod Community College; Gloria Tribble, Youngstown State University; Suzanne Parrott, Delaware State College. I am particularly indebted to Joseph Opiela, my editor at Scott, Foresman/Little, Brown College Division, for his insight, guidance, and support in preparing this fourth edition.

K.T.M.

Contents

**College Reading
and Study Skills**

PART ONE

Succeeding in College

Many students find their first few weeks in college a confusing and frustrating period. Even excellent students who achieved high grades in high school discover that college is a difficult and challenging experience.

Getting started in college may be difficult for you because it is a completely new situation. The physical surroundings are new and it is easy to feel lost. Many times, too, you don't have many friends with whom to share experiences and ask questions. Also, college classes are conducted differently from high school classes. Your professors may not act like high school teachers, and they may seem to expect different things from you. Finally, you find that you have not only a lot more work and responsibility, but also a lot more freedom. You find that the amount of reading, writing, and studying required is much greater than you expected, and you realize you have a lot of choices and decisions to make. You choose your own courses, your own time schedule, and even whether or not to attend class.

The purpose of Part One is to give you some tips on how to minimize the frustration and confusion that most students experience as they begin college. This part includes specific suggestions that will help you start your courses in an effective and organized way.

Each chapter discusses particular aspects of getting started in college. Chapter 1 offers many specific suggestions on how to approach college learning and study and how to get organized to become a successful student. You will also learn how to get information, how to become familiar with policies and procedures that affect you, how to get help with problems, and how to take advantage of services available on campus. Chapter 2 is concerned with time efficiency and is designed to help you handle the extra demands of the heavy work load required in most of your courses. Chapter 3 identifies the ability to learn as the key to academic success, describes how learning occurs, and presents the basic principles of learning. It also explains how these principles are behind many of the techniques presented throughout this text.

1

How to Succeed

> **Use this chapter to:**
> 1. *Learn what is expected of you in college.*
> 2. *Become an active learner.*
> 3. *Get off to the right start.*
> 4. *Learn about campus facilities and resources.*

To be successful in a new part-time job, you must learn quickly what the job involves and how to perform specific tasks. You are expected to be organized and to work effectively and efficiently. You must also become familiar with other personnel and with the facilities in which you will be working. You must learn where items are kept and how to get things done. Similarly, as you begin college, you must learn what is expected of you and how to accomplish it. College is a new experience, and to be successful you must learn what it involves and what is expected of you. Learning through reading and studying is your primary task, and you must learn to handle this task efficiently. It is also important that you get started in an organized manner, thereby making the learning easier and more effective. Finally, you must become familiar with the facilities and resources available on your campus.

COLLEGE: NEW DEMANDS AND EXPECTATIONS

College is a unique learning experience. Whether you have just completed high school or are returning to college with a variety of work experience or family responsibilities, you will face new demands and expectations in college. The following sections describe these demands and discuss how to cope with each.

Set Your Own Operating Rules

College is very different from your other educational experiences and from jobs you may have held because there are few clear limits, rules, or controls. There are no defined work hours. Except for scheduled classes, your time is your own. Often there are no penalties for missing classes or failing to complete assignments. You do what you want, when you want, if you want to at all. For many students, this new freedom requires some adjustment. Some students feel they should spend all of their free time studying; others put off study or never quite find the right time for study.

One of the best ways to handle this freedom is to establish your own set of operating rules. For example, you might decide to attend all classes, regardless of whether attendance is taken. Here are other examples of rules successful students have set for themselves.

> Study at least three hours each day or evening.
> Start studying for a major examination at least a week before the exam.
> Complete all homework assignments regardless of whether you get credit for them.
> Make review a part of each study session.
> Read all assigned chapters before the class in which they are discussed.

Write your rules on paper and post them above your desk as a constant reminder. Consider these as goals and work toward accomplishing each.

EXERCISE 1 _____

Directions: *Analyze the assignments and requirements of each of the courses you are taking this semester. Make a list of five to ten operating rules you intend to follow this term or semester. Include at least one rule that applies to each of your courses. Monitor the effectiveness of these rules during the next two weeks and make any needed changes.*

To read better & spell better.

English

Drafting

Take Responsibility for Your Own Learning

In college, learning is mainly up to you. Instructors function as guides. They define and explain what is to be learned, but you do the learning. Class time is far shorter than in high school; time is often insufficient to provide numerous drills, practices, and reviews of factual course content. Instead, college class time is used primarily to introduce content that is to be learned and to discuss ideas. Instructors expect you to learn the material and to be prepared to discuss it in class. *When, where,* and *how* you learn are your decisions. This text will help you in making these decisions: Throughout you will be presented with numerous learning strategies and how to apply them.

Focus on Concepts: Each course you take will seem to have an endless amount of facts, statistics, dates, definitions, formulas, rules, and principles to learn. It is easy to become convinced that these are enough to learn and to become a robot learner—memorizing facts from texts and lectures, then recalling them on exams and quizzes. Actually, factual information is only a starting point, a base from which to approach the real content of a course. Most college instructors expect you to go beyond facts to analysis: to consider what the collection of facts and details *means*. Many students "can't see the forest for the trees"; they get caught up in specifics and fail to see the larger, more important concepts. Be sure to keep these questions in mind as you read and study:

Why do I need to know this?
Why is this important?
What principle or trend does this illustrate?
How can I use this information?
How does this fit with other course content?

Focus on Ideas, Not Right Answers: Through previous schooling, many students have come to expect their answers to be either right or wrong. They assume that learning is limited to a collection of facts and that their mastery of the course is measured by the number of right answers they have learned. When faced with an essay question such as the following, they become distraught:

Defend or criticize the arguments that are offered in favor of capital punishment. Refer to any readings that you have completed.

There is no one right answer: You can either defend the arguments or criticize them. The instructor who asks this question expects you to think and to provide a reasoned, logical, consistent response using information acquired through your reading. Here are a few more examples of questions for which there are no single correct answers.

Do animals think?
Would you be willing to reduce your standard of living by 15 percent if the United States could thereby eliminate poverty? Defend your response.
Imagine a society in which everyone has exactly the same income. You are the manager of an industrial plant. What plans, policies, or programs would you implement that would motivate your employees to work?

Evaluate New Ideas: Throughout college you will continually meet new ideas; you will agree with some and disagree with others. Don't make the mistake of accepting or rejecting a new idea, however, until you have really explored it and have considered its assumptions and implications. Ask questions such as:

What evidence is available in support of this idea?
What opposing evidence is available?
How does my personal experience relate to this idea?
What additional information do I need in order to make a decision?

BECOMING AN ACTIVE LEARNER

A freshman who had always thought of himself as a B student was getting low Cs and Ds in his business course. The instructor gave weekly quizzes; each was a practical problem to solve. Each week the student memorized his lecture notes and carefully reread each assigned chapter in his textbook. When he spoke with his instructor about his low grades, the instructor told him his study methods were not effective and that he needed to become more active and involved with the subject matter. Memorizing and rereading are passive, inactive approaches. Instead the instructor suggested that he think about content, ask questions, anticipate practical applications, solve potential problems, and draw connections between ideas.

Active Versus Passive Learning

How did you learn to ride a bike, play racquetball, or change a tire? In each case you learned by doing, by active participation. College learning requires similar active involvement and participation. Active learning, then, is expected in most college courses and can often make the difference between earning barely average grades and top grades. Table 1-1 lists common college learning situations and shows the difference between active and passive learning.

The examples in Table 1-1 show that passive learners do not carry the learning process far enough. They do not go beyond what instructors tell them to do. They fail to think about, organize, and react to course content.

TABLE 1-1   Characteristics of Passive and Active Learners

	Passive Learners	*Active Learners*
Class lectures	Write down what the instructor says	Decide what is important to write down
Textbook assignments	Read	Read, think, ask questions, try to connect ideas
Studying	Reread	Make outlines and study sheets, predict exam questions, look for trends and patterns
Writing class assignments	Only follow the professor's instructions	Try to discover the significance of the assignment, look for the principles and concepts it illustrates
Writing term papers	Do only what is expected to get a good grade	Try to expand their knowledge and experience with a topic and connect it to the course objective or content

Active Learning Strategies

When you study, you should be thinking and reacting to the material in front of you. This is how you make it happen.

1. Ask questions about what you are reading. You will find that this helps to focus your attention and improve your concentration.
2. Discover the purpose behind assignments. Why might a sociology assignment require you to spend an hour at the monkey house of the local zoo, for example?
3. Try to see how each assignment fits with the rest of the course. For instance, why does a section titled "Amortization" belong in a business mathematics textbook chapter titled "Business and Consumer Loans"?
4. Relate what you are learning to what you already know from the course and from your background knowledge and personal experience. Connect a law in physics with how your car brakes work, for example.
5. Think of examples or situations in which you can apply the information.

EXERCISE 2 _____

Directions: *Review each of the following learning situations. Answer each question by suggesting active learning approaches.*

1. Having a graded exam returned to you by your history professor. How could you use this as a learning device?

   _____

2. Being assigned "Letter from Birmingham Jail" by Martin Luther King, Jr., for your English composition class. What questions would you try to answer as you read?

   _____

3. Completing a biology lab. How would you prepare for it?

   _____

4. Reading an article in *Newsweek* on crime in major U.S. cities assigned by your sociology instructor. How would you record important ideas?

   _____

GETTING STARTED

Many college students begin their first semester feeling rushed and confused. Being a successful student requires careful planning and organization. Here are some suggestions that will help make your first term or semester less hectic and will get you off to a good start in college.

Attend Information and Orientation Sessions

If the college offers any orientation activities, such as campus tours, a get-acquainted-with-the-college workshop, or a back to school social event, try to attend. The activity will give you a chance to meet faculty and students and pick up useful information about the college.

Get Your Life Organized

Arrange your housing, transportation, finances, and part-time job schedule as soon as possible. Unless these are settled and organized, you will find it difficult to concentrate on your courses. Problems with any of these can disrupt your life and take valuable time to solve once you are involved with the semester.

Attend the First Class

Attending the first class of a course is crucial to surviving in that course. Attend it at all costs, even if you are late. Many students think that nothing is taught the first day. They may be correct in that the instructor does not present the first lecture, but they fail to realize that something much more important occurs. It is during the first meeting that the instructor introduces the course, discusses its organization, and explains requirements (tests, exams, papers).

Get to Know Someone in Each Class

During the first week, try to get to know someone in each of your classes. You will find it helpful to have someone to talk to, and you will feel you are part of the class. In case you miss a class, you will have someone from whom you can get the assignment and borrow notes. Also, this person may be able to explain ideas or assignments that are unclear, or you may be able to study with him or her.

Purchase Your Textbooks

As soon as possible after the instructor assigns the text, go to the bookstore and buy it. Do this even if you do not have an assignment to complete right away. Then you'll have the book and can begin an assignment as soon as it is given.

Get Materials for Each Course Organized

You should have a notebook for each class—either spiral bound or loose leaf. You will use it to take lecture notes and to record outlines or summary-study sheets you might prepare from the text or lecture. Be sure to keep the instructor's course outline, or syllabus, as well as the course assignment and/or requirement sheets in a place where you can readily refer to them. The syllabus is particularly useful because it specifies course objectives and provides an overall picture of the course. Also, date and organize day-to-day class handouts; these are important when studying and reviewing for an exam. Be sure to organize and date all of your class homework assignments and to keep returned quizzes, exams, and written assignments.

Organize an Assignment Notebook or Pocket Calendar

College instructors frequently give long-term assignments and announce dates for papers, assignments, and exams much in advance. They frequently do not feel it is their responsibility to remind students as the dates approach. Consequently, you will need to develop some system for keeping track of what assignments need to be done and when each is due.

Many students keep small notebooks in which they record all their assignments as they are given. If you keep one, you can see at a glance what particular assignments, tests, and quizzes are coming up. Crossing assignments off as they are completed will give you a sense of accomplishment and help you feel you are getting things done. Other students use a pocket calendar and record due dates in the appropriate date blocks. Most useful are the monthly calendars that display a full month on one page. These allow you to see upcoming due dates easily without flipping pages. Both assignment notebooks and pocket calendars will eliminate the problem many students experience—realizing at the last moment that an assignment is due and then frantically trying to meet the deadline.

Learn the Early Warning Signals of Academic Difficulty

Because some instructors give only two or three exams per semester, you cannot rely solely on exam grades to determine if you are doing well in each of your courses. Here are a few questions that will tell you whether you are on the right track in a course:

1. Are you getting behind on assignments?
2. Do you feel lost or confused about the course?
3. Have you missed several classes already?
4. Do you have to force yourself to go to class?

If you answer yes to one or more of these questions, you may be heading for academic difficulty. Take action as soon as possible by talking to your instructor to find out how you can catch up.

Get to Know Your Adviser

Most colleges assign each student an adviser to help the student plan his or her academic program. Your adviser can help you with more than just selecting courses and being certain you meet curriculum requirements for graduation. He or she can tell you whom to see to solve a particular problem, give you advice on how to handle certain courses, and provide a perspective on jobs within his or her field or refer you to someone who has more information. Many advisers consider it the student's responsibility to read the college catalog, so before you make an appointment with your adviser, be sure that you are familiar with the information the catalog contains.

Attend Classes Regularly

Instructors vary in their attendance policy. Some require regular attendance and penalize students who exceed a specified number of absences. Others do not have a specific limit on absences and leave it to students' discretion whether or not to attend class. You should not assume that regular attendance is not important just because an instructor does not require it. Classes provide new information, interpretation, and discussion of information presented in the text, as well as vital synthesis, review, and repetition necessary for learning. Studies have indicated that successful students attend class regularly, while unsuccessful students do not.

Get to Know Your Instructors

It is important for you and your instructors to get to know each other. You will find that your instructors are better able to help you if they know something about your background, your career goals, or your special difficulties with the course. You can get to know an instructor by stopping to ask a question after class or by talking with him or her during office hours.

Use Instructors' Office Hours

Each college instructor usually posts a list of several hours per week during which he or she will be available in his or her office to meet individually with students. It is usually not necessary to make an appointment to see an instructor during these times, but if you feel uncomfortable just walking in, you might mention to the instructor after class that you'd like to talk with him or her during office hours.

You can talk with the instructor during office hours about anything related to the course—how you are doing, trouble you are having with the course, difficulty you have encountered with a particular assignment—or to get further information or explanation about a topic.

Make Good Impressions

Based on how you act and react (how much you participate in class, how alert and interested you seem, how serious you are about learning), your instructors will form lasting impressions of you. They are naturally more willing to help a serious, conscientious student than one who seems not to care about learning.

Keep Up with Daily Assignments

Because many instructors do not check or require you to complete assignments as they are given, it is very easy to let things go and, as a result, have work accumulate as the semester progresses. There is danger in allowing work to pile up as the semester goes on; you may get so far behind that you'll become discouraged and will not want or be able to spend the time required to catch up. Many students drop or withdraw from a course for this exact reason. One excellent way to be sure you will keep up with your courses is to follow a study-time schedule. Developing this schedule is discussed in the next chapter of this part of the text.

Directions: *Read each of these situations and offer possible solutions to each problem.*

1. Because of an error in his class schedule, Sam missed the first class meeting of his criminal justice course. What should he do?

    _____

2. Suppose that you are confused about what is expected of you for a term paper assignment given by your biology instructor. You decide to talk to your instructor but discover that you have other classes scheduled during each of his office hours. What should you do?

    _____

3. Suppose you are taking a course in sociology. The instructor assigns several textbook chapters each week and has recommended that you outline each chapter. She conducts class discussions on brief readings distributed in class that relate to chapter topics. Weekly quizzes and class assignments are given, evaluated, and returned to students. How would you organize these various course materials?

    _____

4. Suppose your business management professor distributes study guides for each unit on which he lectures. There is no text—only his lectures and a book of readings on topics related to the lectures. He gives the class twenty essay questions before each exam and tells you that four will be on the test. How would you organize the materials and prepare for these exams?

    _____

LEARNING YOUR WAY AROUND

The expression *learning your way around,* means several things. First, it means learning the location of various buildings, offices, and classrooms on campus. Second, and most important, it means knowing where to go for things you need, what policies affect you, whom to talk to, and how and where to get information you need. Finally, it means being aware of what is going on around you—such as new courses being offered, a new sports team forming, a freshman class picnic on a Sunday afternoon, visiting lecturers on campus, and the schedule for free movies.

There is substantial evidence that students who are active and involved with the college scene around them are more likely to be successful than those who participate only by attending class and returning home. In order to get involved, however, you have to learn your way around. It is important to become familiar with the various offices, services, and student activities on campus. It is equally important to be fully familiar with the rules and policies that may affect you.

Information Sources

The college provides several sources of general information for all students. These are described below.

The College Catalog: The college catalog contains official information about your college, including its rules and policies and course and curriculum information. It explains which courses are required for the degree you seek and the amount and type of credit each course carries. The catalog also explains course numbering systems and indicates what courses must be taken before others (prerequisites). Important deadlines are also listed in the catalog. For example, most catalogs will indicate the last date on which you can withdraw from a course, when you must file for a pass/fail grade, and when to file for graduation. Catalogs usually explain how semester averages, often called grade or quality point averages, are computed and give the minimum averages required at various times during enrollment.

The Student Newspaper: Most colleges subsidize, or financially support, a student newspaper published at least weekly during the academic semester. In addition to feature articles about issues and events on campus, you will find notices of upcoming activities sponsored by various student groups, announcements about changes in college policies, and information on important dates and deadlines. The student paper is usually free. Pick up a copy each time it is issued and look through it.

Brochures and Pamphlets: Pick up and read brochures and pamphlets that you see. They provide a quick way of learning about some of the new and unusual groups or events on campus. Some offices that offer services to students—such as the counseling center, financial aid office, and learning labs—prepare and distribute brochures to make students aware of their services.

Bulletin Boards: On bulletin boards near or outside various department offices, you will find several types of important information. Last-minute information, such as room changes and class cancellations, may be posted. Department information, such as faculty office hours, course changes, and student adviser assignment lists, may also be up.

College Services/Offices

A large portion of every college's budget goes toward providing a variety of support services for students. Some of the most common student service offices are listed below, along with a brief description of what they offer. Try to locate each of these offices on your campus and become familiar with the specific services offered by each.

The Counseling and Testing Center: This office provides useful information and advice on establishing a major, choosing a career, and handling personal problems. If you are undecided about which degree or major to choose, you are not alone. About 60 to 70 percent of college students change their majors at least once. If you make a change, it is most important to make the change that is best for you, and the counseling center can often help you make this decision. Many centers also offer vocational testing that may help identify career areas that are suited to your interests. At community colleges, this office often provides information on and assistance with transferring to four-year colleges.

The Financial Aid Office: Because obtaining tuition assistance awards, loans, and scholarships is sometimes quite complicated, most colleges have a special office whose primary function is to help students receive all possible financial assistance. Smaller colleges sometimes designate one staff member in the counseling center to help with financial aid. In any case, find out who is responsible for financial aid at your college and visit that person's office. Do not be one of the many students who finds out too late, after the deadline for application, that he or she was eligible for some type of aid.

The Library: Most students think of the library only as a place where books are stored, but a library also offers many valuable services. The library may loan records or films; it often houses coin-operated photocopying machines; it may provide listening rooms, typing rooms, and study rooms. Many libraries operate an interlibrary loan system through which you can borrow books from other libraries.

The people who work in a library are perhaps more important than any particular thing that is kept there. While you may think of librarians as people who check out and shelve books, you will find that college librarians are valuable to talk to. They can help you locate information, suggest a focus and direction for approaching a topic, and help you organize your research. Even though librarians always look busy, do not hesitate to ask them questions. There is always at least one librarian, usually located in the reference area, whose primary responsibility is to assist students.

Visit the library, look around, and be ready to use it effectively when you get your first class assignment this semester. Take a tour, and obtain a copy of the library's floor plan if one is available.

The Placement Office: Although you are not looking for a full-time job right now, it is wise to learn what services the placement office offers. (At small colleges this office may be part of the counseling center.) Placement offices maintain a listing of current full- and part-time job openings. Some placement offices also, upon request, establish a placement file containing a student's background information, transcripts, and references. While at the college a student can use this service to collect and organize job-related information. Later, when applying for a job, the student can request that his or her file be sent to potential employers.

The Student Health Office: Most colleges have some type of health clinic or office to help students who become ill or injured while on campus. Find out what particular services your clinic offers. Does it dispense medicines? Make referrals to area physicians? Offer free tests?

The Reading-Learning Lab: Most colleges now a have a center that offers students help with reading, learning, and studying for their college courses. While the services offered by learning labs vary greatly from college to college, check to see if the lab at your college offers tutorial services, self-instructional learning modules, or minicourses at any time during the semester. Some labs offer brushup courses in skills like spelling, puncutation, and usage; basic math computation (percentages, fractions, and so forth); and term paper writing. Check to see if your college's lab offers anything that could help you become a more successful student.

The Student Center: This building or area houses many of the social and recreational services available to students. Snack bars, theaters, game rooms, lounges, and offices for student groups are often located there. The Student Center is a good place to meet people and to find out what is happening on campus.

The Registrar's (Student Records) Office: This office keeps records on courses you take as well as grades you receive and mails your grades to you at the end of each semester. These records keep track of when you graduate and what degree you receive.

The Bursar's (Student Accounts) Office: All financial records are kept by this office. The people who work there send tuition bills and collect tuition payments.

Department Offices: Each discipline or subject area usually has a department office that is located near the offices of the faculty members who are in that department. The department secretary works there, and the department chairman's office is usually in the same location.

The Student Affairs Office: The Student Affairs (or Student Activities) Office plans and organizes extracurricular activities. This office can give you information on various athletic, social, and religious functions that are held on campus.

EXERCISE 4 _____

Directions: *If you have learned your way around your campus, you should be able to answer the following questions:*

1. Beyond lending books, what services does your library offer? List as many other library services as you were able to discover. Also list the hours the library is open.

   _____

   _____

2. List at least five student activities (clubs, teams) that the college sponsors.

   _____

3. How would you request a transcript to be sent to an employer?

   _____

4. Does the college allow you to take courses on a pass/fail or satisfactory/unsatisfactory basis instead of receiving a letter grade? When and how may you elect to take this type of grade?

   _____

5. Where is the student health office located?

   _____

6. How often is the student newspaper published? Where is it available?

   _____

7. What is the last day that you can withdraw from a course this semester?

   _____

8. Where would you go to change from one curriculum to another?

   _____

9. What is meant by grade point or quality point average and how is it computed?

   _____

10. Does the college offer any brushup courses in skills such as spelling, punctuation, or basic math computation?

   _____

11. Does your department office have a bulletin board or other ways to communicate information to its students?

   _____

SUMMARY

College is a new experience. To be successful you must learn what is expected of you and how to approach new learning and study demands. This chapter presented numerous practical suggestions for achieving success in college. You must set your own operating rules, take responsibility for your own learning, and focus on and evaluate ideas. Active learning is essential; you must become actively involved with reading assignments, lectures, and class activities. Getting the right start in college is important. You should get to know other students, your instructor, and your advisor and get organized for each of your courses. As a new student you should learn your way around campus and become familiar with the services the college offers and the activities it sponsors. Identify information sources and the services your college offers.

2

Managing Your Time

Use this chapter to:

1. *Analyze how you currently use your time.*
2. *Find out how much time is needed for reading and study.*
3. *Learn how to manage your time more effectively.*

Managing your time is a skill that directly affects your success in college. It also determines whether college becomes a nightmare of pressures, deadlines, and overdue assignments or an enjoyable experience in which you work hard and also have fun and take advantage of the social life it offers. Let's look at how a few students are handling the heavy work load of college courses.

John is at a ball game with Susan. They both have difficult majors and have exams and papers due that week. They are enjoying the game and are not even thinking about their studies.

Sam and Pat are also at the ball game, but they are not having as much fun. Sam has an exam on Monday and Pat has a term paper due soon. Sam feels guilty that he's taking time away from studying, and Pat finds that she keeps thinking about her paper. Because both are worrying about something, neither is much fun to be with.

What is the difference between the two couples? Why are John and Susan having a good time despite the pressures of their studies, while Sam and Pat are not? The answer lies in how each has managed his or her time. John and Susan are keeping up with their work and can afford the "time off" from study to go to the game. Also, they have set aside sufficient time for study and know they will get their work done. Sam and Pat, on the other hand, have not organized their time. They haven't reserved specific times for study and do not plan ahead in getting their assignments done. They often find themselves short on time with work piling up. As a result, they feel guilty about time used for anything but study. Even when they are not studying, they are thinking or worrying about studying.

Throughout this chapter you will learn how to manage your time effectively so you can avoid these problems and get the most out of college both academically and socially.

ESTABLISHING YOUR PRIORITIES

One of the first steps in getting organized and succeeding in college is to set your priorities—to decide what is and is not important to you. For most college students, finding enough time to do everything they *should* do and everything they *want* to do is nearly impossible. They face a series of conflicts over the use of their time and are forced to choose between a variety of activities. Here are a few examples:

Want to: *Should do:*
1. Watch late movie   *vs.*   get good night's sleep
2. Go to hockey game   *vs.*   work on term paper
3. Go out with friends   *vs.*   finish psychology reading assignment

These day-to-day choices can be frustrating and use up valuable time as you weigh the alternatives and make decisions. Often, these choices can be narrowed down to wanting to take part in an enjoyable activity while knowing you should be studying, reading, or writing a paper. At other times, it may be a conflict between two things you need to do, one for your studies, another for something else important in your life.

One of the best ways to handle these frequent conflicts is to identify your priorities. Ask yourself, What is most important to me? What activities can I afford to give up? What is least important to me when I am pressured for time? For many students, studying is their first priority. For others with family responsibilities, caring for a child is their first priority with attending college next in importance.

By clearly establishing and following your priorities, you will find that much worry and guilt are eliminated. Instead, you'll feel that you are on target, working steadily toward the goals you have established.

EXERCISE 1 _____

Directions: *Consider your plans for the next several days. List as many "want to" activities as you can with their corresponding "should do" activities.*

_____

_____

_____

ANALYZING YOUR TIME

Once you've established your priorities, the next step in managing your time is relatively easy. This step—analyzing and planning your time—will enable you to reserve time for both leisure activities and college course work. You can reserve enough time to study for an exam in psychology, time for library research, and time for reading biology assignments. To do this, you must determine how much time is available and then decide how you will use it.

Let's begin by making some rough estimates. First, estimate the number of reading and study hours you need per week. For each course that you are taking, estimate how many hours per week you would need to spend, outside of class time, in order to get the grade you want to earn. Be honest; indicate what grade you can realistically achieve. When estimating time, consider how much time you need to study, how many assignments there are, how fast you normally read, and how difficult the subject is for you. As a general rule of thumb, many instructors expect you to spend two hours of preparation, study, or review for each hour spent in class. This figure, however, is just an estimate; some students will need to spend more time, while others can spend less. Once you are well into each of your courses and begin to see how you are doing, you can modify your estimates on the chart in Figure 2-1. When you are finished, add up the hours and fill in the total.

Now, let's see if you have enough time available each week to earn the grades you indicated on the chart. To find out, analyze your actual time commitments. Fill in Figure 2-2, estimating the time you need for each activity. Remember to indicate how much time each actually takes. Do not indicate an hour for lunch if you usually take only ten or fifteen minutes for a quick sandwich. When you have completed the chart, total the hours per week to discover your actual weekly time commitment.

Now that you know your total committed time per week, it is easy to see how much time you have left to divide between, on the one hand, reading, and study for your courses and leisure activities on the other. Each week has 168 hours. Just copy your total committed time from Figure 2-2 and subtract:

$$\begin{array}{r} 168 \text{ hours in one week} \\ - \underline{\hspace{1cm}} \text{ total committed time} \\ \hline \underline{\hspace{1cm}} \text{ hours available} \end{array}$$

Name of Course	Desired Grade	Hours per Week Needed

Total Hours _____

FIGURE 2-1   Estimated Study Time per Course

	Hours per Day	Hours per Week
Sleep	_____	_____
Breakfast	_____	_____
Lunch	_____	_____
Dinner	_____	_____
Part- or full-time job	_____	_____
Time spent in classes	_____	_____
Transportation time	_____	_____
Personal care (dressing, shaving, etc.)	_____	_____
Household/family responsibilities (cooking dinner, driving mother to work, etc.)	_____	_____

Total committed time per week _____

FIGURE 2-2   Weekly Time Commitment

Are you surprised to see how many hours per week you have left? Look back to Figure 2-1 and see how many hours you estimated you needed to earn a particular grade in each course and write the hours on the first blank. Now answer this question: Do you have enough time available for reading and study to achieve the grades you want?

Estimated hours needed for grades ____ hours
Actual study hours available ____ hours

If your answer to the question was no, one of two things is probably true. Either you were unrealistic in your estimate of committed time, or you really are committed to such a point that it is unrealistic to take as many courses as you are taking and aim toward the grades you indicated. There are several alternatives to consider if your time is overcommitted. Can any activity be dropped or done in less time? Can you reduce the number of hours you work, or can another family member split some time-consuming responsibilities with you? If you are unable to reduce your committed time, consider taking fewer college courses or adjusting your expected grades to more achievable levels.

If your answer to the question was yes, you are ready to begin to develop a schedule that will help you use your available time most effectively. You are probably concerned at this point, however, that the above time analysis did not take into account social and leisure activities. That omission was deliberate up to this point.

While leisure time is essential to everyone's well-being, it should not take precedence over college course work. Most students who develop and follow a time schedule for accomplishing their course work are able to devote reasonable amounts of time to leisure and social activities. They also find time to become involved with campus groups and activities—an important aspect of college life.

BUILDING YOUR TIME SCHEDULE

A study-time schedule is a weekly plan of when and what you will study. It identifies specific times for studying particular subjects as well as times for writing papers, conducting library research, and completing homework assignments for each course.

The major purpose in developing a study-time schedule is to allow you to decide in advance how you will divide your available time between study and leisure activities. A schedule will eliminate the need to make frustrating last-minute choices between "should" and "want to" activities.

The sample study-time schedule in Figure 2-3 was developed by a freshman student. Read it carefully.

Your Own Schedule

Now that you have seen a sample schedule, you can begin to build your own schedule. Fill in the blank schedule shown in Figure 2-4, following steps 1–7:

1. Write *class* in all the time blocks that you spend attending class and labs.
2. If you have a part-time job, write *work* in the appropriate time blocks.
3. Write *trans.* in those portions of the time blocks in which you travel around or to and from campus and to and from work.
4. Block off with an X realistic amounts of time for breakfast, lunch, and dinner.
5. Also block off and write P in blocks of time committed to personal, family, and household responsibilities.
6. Block out reasonable amounts of time, especially on weekends, for having fun and relaxing. For example, mark off the time when your favorite television show is on or for going to see a movie.
7. Include any appointments, such as with the doctor or dentist or for a haircut.

The empty time blocks are those available for study and for leisure activities. Look through the following hints before you attempt to decide which subject you will study at what time.

1. Study difficult subjects first. It is tempting to get easy things and short assignments out of the way beforehand, but do not give in to this approach. When you start studying, your mind is fresh and alert and you are at your peak of concentration. This is the time you are best equipped to handle difficult subjects. Thinking through complicated problems or studying complex ideas requires all the brain power you have, and you have most at the beginning of a study session.
2. Leave the routine and more mechanical tasks for last. Activities like recopying papers or alphabetizing a bibliography for a research paper do not require a high degree of concentration and can be left until you are tired.
3. Schedule study for a particular course close to the time when you attend class; that is, plan to study the evening before the class meets or at a time after the class meeting. If a class meets on Tuesday morning, plan to study Monday evening, or Tuesday afternoon or evening. If you place study time and class time close together, it will be easier to relate class lectures and discussions to what you are reading and studying.

	Monday	Tuesday	Wednesday	Thursday	Friday	Saturday	Sunday
7:00							
8:00	TRANSPORTATION TIME						
9:00	History class	Psychology class	History class	Psychology class	History class		
10:00	review History notes; read assignment	study	review History notes; read assignment	TRANSPORTATION	review History notes	type Chemistry Lab report	revise English paper
11:00	Math class	Psychology	Math class	study Psychology	Math class	(other typing)	review history assignment
12:00	LUNCH	LUNCH	English Composition class	LUNCH	English Composition class		
1:00	Math homework	review lab procedures		Math homework		draft English paper	
2:00	Chemistry class		LUNCH	read Chemistry	LUNCH	read Psychology chapter	Math homework
3:00	TRANSPORTATION	Chemistry Lab	TRANSPORTATION		TRANSPORTATION		read and study Chemistry
4:00						review Psychology notes	
5:00	DINNER	TRANSPORTATION DINNER	DINNER	DINNER	DINNER		
6:00	WORK	Write lab report; start reading new Chemistry chapter; type	WORK	read English assignment	WORK		plan next week's study
7:00							
8:00		English Composition		revise returned Composition			
9:00							
10:00							
11:00							

FIGURE 2-3   Example of a Study-Time Schedule

	Monday	Tuesday	Wednesday	Thursday	Friday	Saturday	Sunday
7:00							
8:00							
9:00							
10:00							
11:00							
12:00							
1:00							
2:00							
3:00							
4:00							
5:00							
6:00							
7:00							
8:00							
9:00							
10:00							
11:00							

FIGURE 2-4   Study-Time Schedule

4. Build into your schedule a short break before you begin studying each new subject. Your mind needs time to refocus—to switch from one set of facts, problems, and issues to another.

5. Short breaks should also be included when you are working on just one assignment for a long period of time. A 10-minute break after 50–60 minutes of study is reasonable.

6. When reading or studying a particular subject, try to schedule two or three short, separate blocks of time for that course rather than one long, continuous block. As will be explained in the next chapter on principles of learning, you are able to learn more by spacing or spreading out your study time than you are by completing it in one sitting.

7. Schedule study sessions at times when you know you are usually alert and feel like studying. Do not schedule a study time early on Saturday morning if you are a person who does not really wake up until noon, and try not to schedule study time late in the evening if you are usually tired by that time.

8. Plan to study at times when the physical surroundings are conducive to study. If the dinner hour is a rushed and confusing time, don't attempt to study then if there are alternative times available.

9. Set aside a specific time each week for analyzing the specific tasks that need to be done, planning when to do them, and reviewing your prior week's performance.

Using the suggestions above, plan a tentative study-time schedule for the week, using the blank schedule in Figure 2-4. First, identify only the times when it would be best to study. Then decide what subjects you will study during these times and in what order you will study them. You will need to refer to Figure 2-1 to check the total number of hours per week that each course requires. Try to be as specific as possible in identifying what is to be done at particular times. If you know, for example, that there is a weekly homework assignment in math due each Wednesday, reserve a specific block of time for completing that assignment.

Now that you have identified study times, the remaining time can be scheduled for additional leisure and social activities. Analyze this remaining time to determine how it can best be used. What things do you enjoy most? What things do you do just because you have nothing else to do? Plan specific times for activities that are most important to you.

USING YOUR TIME SCHEDULE

Using your schedule will be a challenge because it will mean saying no in a number of different situations. When friends call or stop by and ask you to join them at a time when you planned to study, you will have to refuse, but you could let them know when you will be free and offer to join them then. When a friend or family member asks you to do a favor—like driving him or her somewhere—you will have to refuse, but you can suggest some alternative times when you will be free. You will find that your friends and family will accept your restraints and may even respect you for being conscientious. Don't you respect someone who gets a lot done and is successful in whatever he or she attempts?

Try out the schedule that you have built for one week. Be realistic and make adjustments where they are obviously needed. Mark these changes on the schedule itself. Do not stop to decide if you should follow or change each block on the schedule. Doing so forces you back into the "want to" versus "should" conflict that the schedule was designed to eliminate.

After using the schedule for one week, evaluate it by asking yourself the following questions:

1. Did you over- or underestimate the amount of time you needed for each course? (The time will vary, of course, from week to week, so be sure to allow enough for those heavy times of the semester—midterm and final exam weeks.)
2. Did you find some conflicts? Can they be resolved?
3. Did you find some scheduled study times particularly inconvenient? Can they be rearranged?
4. Did it help you to get more work done?

Revise your schedule and then try the revised schedule for the next week. Within a week or two you will have worked out a schedule that will carry you through the remainder of the semester. You will be using your time effectively and getting the grades that you have decided you want. Best of all, frustrating day-to-day conflicts over time will be eliminated.

TIME-SAVING TIPS FOR STUDENTS WITH BUSY SCHEDULES

Here are a few suggestions that will help you to make the best use of your time. If you are an older student with family responsibilities who is returning to college, or if you are trying both to work and to attend college, you will find these suggestions particularly valuable.

1. *Use the telephone*. When you need information or must make an appointment, phone rather than visit the office. To find out if a book you've requested at the library has come in, for example, phone the circulation desk.
2. *Set priorities*. There may be days or weeks when you cannot get every assignment done. Many students work until they are exhausted and leave remaining assignments unfinished. A better approach is to decide what is most important to complete immediately and which assignments could, if necessary, be completed later.
3. *Use spare moments*. Think of all the time that you spend waiting. You wait for a class to begin, for a ride, for a friend to call, for a pizza to arrive. Instead of wasting this time, you could use it to review a set of lecture notes, work on review questions at the end of a chapter, or review a chemistry lab setup. Always carry with you something you can work on in spare moments.
4. *Learn to combine activities*. Most people think it is impossible to do two things at once, but busy students soon learn that it is possible to combine some daily chores with routine class assignments. Some students, for example, are able to go to a laundromat and, while there, outline a history chapter or work on routine assignments during breaks. Others review formulas for math or science courses or review vocabulary cards for language courses while walking to classes.
5. *Use lists to keep yourself organized and to save time*. A daily "to do" list is helpful in keeping track of what daily living/household tasks and errands as well as course assignments need to be done. As you think of things to be done, jot them down. Then look over the list each morning

and try to find the best way to get everything done. You may find, for instance, that you can stop at the post office on the way to the bookstore, thus saving yourself a trip.

6. *Do not be afraid to admit you are trying to do too much.* If you find your life is becoming too hectic or unmanageable, or if you are facing pressures beyond your ability to handle them, consider dropping a course. Don't be too concerned that this will put you behind schedule for graduation. More than half of all college students take longer than the traditional time expected to earn their degrees. Besides, you may be able to pick up the course later during a summer session or carry a heavier load another semester.

PROCRASTINATION

Have you ever felt that you should work on an assignment, and even wanted to get it out of the way, but could not get started? If so, you may have been a victim of procrastination—putting off tasks that need to be done. Although you know you should review your biology notes this evening, for instance, you procrastinate and do something else instead. Tedious, difficult, or uninteresting tasks are often those that we put off doing. It is often these very tasks, however, that are essential to success in college courses. The following suggestions can help you to overcome or control a tendency to procrastinate and put you on track for success.

Give Yourself Five Minutes to Start

If you are having difficulty beginning a task, say to yourself that you will work on it for just five minutes. Often, once you start working, motivation and interest build and you will want to continue working.

Divide the Task into Manageable Parts

Complicated tasks are often difficult to start because they are long and seem unmanageable. Before beginning such tasks, spend a few minutes organizing and planning. Divide each task into parts, and then devise an approach strategy. In other words, list what needs to be done and in what order. In devising an approach strategy for a one-hour biology exam on the topic of cells, one student wrote the following list of subtopics to review:

atoms and molecules	cell organization
organic molecules	cell functioning
cell theory	cell division

She then decided the order in which she would study these topics, the study strategy she would use, and the time she would devote to each.

Clear Your Desk

Move everything from your desk except materials for the task at hand. With nothing else in front of you, you are more likely to start working and less likely to be distracted from your task while working.

Start Regardless of What You Do

If you are having difficulty getting started, do something rather than sit and stare, regardless of how trivial it may seem. If you are having trouble writing a paper from rough draft notes, for example, start by recopying the notes. Suddenly you'll find yourself rearranging and rephrasing them, and you'll be well on your way toward writing a draft.

Recognize When You Need More Information

Sometimes procrastination is a signal that you lack skills or information. You may be avoiding a task because you're not sure how to do it. You may not really understand why you use a certain procedures to solve a type of math problem, for example, so you feel reluctant to do math homework. Or selecting a term paper topic may be difficult if you aren't certain of its purpose or expected length. Overcome such stumbling blocks by discussing them with classmates or with your professor.

Think Positively

As you begin a task, send yourself positive messages such as "I'll be able to stick with this," or "It will feel great to have this job done." Avoid negatives such as "This is so boring" or "I can't wait to finish."

Recognize Escape Routes

Some students escape work by claiming they haven't enough time to get everything done. Close analysis of their time usage often reveals they are wasting valuable time by following one or more escape routes. One route is to needlessly spend time away from your desk—returning library books, going out to pick up take-out food, dropping off laundry, and so on. Another escape route is to overdo routine tasks: meticulously cleaning your room, pressing clothing, or polishing the car. Doing things by hand also consumes time: copying a friend's notes rather than photocopying them, or balancing your checkbook by hand rather than using a calculator. Analyze your time carefully to detect and avoid any escape routes such as these.

Avoid "The Great Escape"—Television

For some students television poses the greatest threat to keeping to their study-time schedule, and certainly it is often the cause of procrastination. If a TV set is on, it is tempting to watch whatever is showing. To overcome this temptation, turn it on and off at specific times for particular programs you want to see. Don't leave it on between programs you intend to watch; you'll probably continue watching.

EXERCISE 2 _____

Directions: *Read each situation described, and then answer the questions that follow. Discuss your responses with another student or write your answers in the spaces provided.*

1. In analyzing his amount of committed time, George Andrews filled in a chart as follows:

Sleep	56
Breakfast, lunch, dinner (total)	14
Job	35
Time in classes	23
Transportation	10
Personal care	15
Household/family	20
Total	173

George has to have at least a part-time job in order to pay for school. He is enrolled in science lab technology, so he must spend a lot of class hours in lab. He estimates that he needs 30 hours per week to maintain a high B average this semester. If he schedules this amount of time, he will have virtually no time for leisure and recreation. Look at his chart again. What could he do? What are his choices? Try to find as many alternatives as you can.

_____

_____

2. Susan is a serious student but is having difficulty with her accounting course. She has decided to spend all day Sunday studying accounting. She plans to lock herself in her room and not come out until she has reviewed four chapters. What is wrong with her approach? What study plan would be more effective?

_____

_____

3. Mark realizes that he has three assignments that have to be completed in one evening. The assignments are to revise an English composition, to read and underline ten pages in his anatomy and physiology text, and to recopy a homework assignment for sociology. He decides to get the sociology assignment out of the way first, then do the English composition (because English is one of his favorite subjects), and read the anatomy and physiology text last. Evaluate Mark's plan of study.

_____

_____

4. You are taking a course in music appreciation, and your instructor often asks you to listen to a certain part of a concert on FM radio or to watch a particular program on television. Since you cannot predict when these assignments will be given or at what time you need to complete them, what could you do to include them in your weekly study schedule?

_____

_____

5. Sam Smith is registered for the following courses, which meet at the times indicated:

Business Management 905	T–Th 12–1:30 P.M.
English 101	M–W–F 11 A.M.–12 NOON
Math 201	T–Th 9–10:30 A.M.
Biology 601	Class M–W–F, 2–3 P.M.; lab W, 3–5 P.M.
Psychology 502	M–W–F 9–10 A.M.

The work load for each course is as follows:

English	One 250-word essay per week
Math	A homework assignment for each class, which takes approximately one hour to complete; a quiz each Thursday
Biology	Preparation for weekly lab; one chapter to read per week; a one-hour exam every three weeks
Business Management	Two chapters assigned each week; midterm and final exams; one term paper due at the end of the semester
Psychology	One chapter to read per week; one library reading assignment per week; four major exams throughout the semester

Because Sam has a part-time job, he has the following times available for study:

between his classes
evenings: Tuesday, Wednesday
afternoons: Monday, Thursday, and Friday
weekends: Saturday morning, all day and evening Sunday

What study schedule would you recommend for Sam? Indicate the times he should study each subject and what tasks he should work on.

SUMMARY

The ability to use time effectively greatly increases a student's degree of success in college. This chapter presented specific suggestions for analyzing and organizing your time. You began the chapter by analyzing your current time commitments and determining how much time you have available to meet college course demands. Next you were asked to estimate the amount of time each course requires per week to earn a certain grade and to determine the total amount you need to spend on course work each week. The chapter then offered steps in planning and using a weekly study-time schedule and making necessary adjustments to meet the course load you have assumed. Finally, the chapter presented some time-saving tips for busy students and discussed the problem of procrastination.

3

Becoming a More Successful Learner: Principles of Learning and Memory

Use this chapter to:

1. *Find out how forgetting, learning, and memory work.*
2. *Learn principles that will help you learn.*

Now that you are involved with your courses and have become familiar with your campus, it is time to consider how to be successful in your courses.

Think of the courses you are taking this semester and why you are taking them. Most likely, some are required courses, and others you have elected on the basis of interest, convenience, advice, or need. Now think of what you want from each course. At the very minimum, of course, you want to pass. To do so, you must *learn* enough to complete assignments, to pass exams, and to write acceptable papers. You are probably taking certain courses to *learn* a skill, such as math, writing, accounting, or data processing. In others you are *learning* a new academic discipline, such as anthropology, psychology, ecology, or sociology. Regardless of the type of course you are taking, you have one overall goal—to learn.

FORGETTING

Have you ever wondered why you cannot remember what you have just read? Have you noticed students in your classes who seem to remember everything? Do you wonder why you can't? The answer is not that these other students are brighter than you are or that they have studied twice as long as you have. Instead, they have learned *how* to learn and to remember; they have developed techniques for effective learning.

Forgetting, defined as the loss of information stored in memory, is a normal, everyday occurrence. It happens because other information interferes with or prevents you from recalling the desired information. Psychologists have extensively studied the rate at which forgetting takes place.

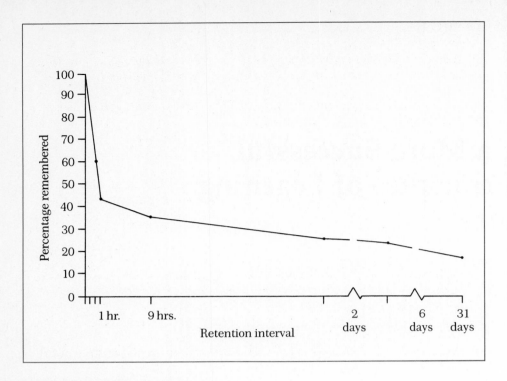

FIGURE 3-1   The Retention Curve

For most people, forgetting occurs very rapidly immediately after learning and then levels off over time. Figure 3-1 demonstrates just how fast forgetting normally occurs and how much information is lost. The figure depicts what is known as the retention curve, and it shows how much you are able to remember over time.

The retention curve has serious implications for you as a learner. Basically, it suggests that unless you are one of the lucky few who remember almost everything they hear or read, you will forget a large portion of the information you learn unless you do something to prevent it. For instance, the graph shows that your recall of learned information drops to below 50 percent within an hour and to about 30 percent within two days.

Fortunately, there are specific techniques to prevent or slow down forgetting. These techniques are what the remainder of this book is all about. Throughout the book you will learn techniques to enable you to identify what to learn (pick out what is important) and to learn it in the most effective way. Each technique is intended to help you remember more and to slow down your rate of forgetting. For instance, in Chapter 14 you will learn how taking notes during class lectures can help you learn and remember what the lecture is about. In Chapter 12 you will learn a system for reading to learn and remember more.

Before we go on to present these specific techniques, however, it is useful that you understand a little about the learning and memory process and why forgetting occurs. Once you know how learning occurs, you will be able to see why and how the various techniques suggested throughout the book are effective. Each reading and study technique is based on the learning and memory process and is designed to help you learn in the most efficient way.

Directions: *Apply the information you have learned about the rate of forgetting to each of the following reading-study situations. Refer to Figure 3-1.*

1. How much information from a textbook chapter can you expect to recall two days after you read it?

   _____

2. How much information presented in a lecture last week can you expect to remember this week if you do not take any notes on the lecture?

   _____

3. What do you think your level of recall would be if you took notes on a particular lecture but did not review your notes for two weeks?

   _____

4. Why would it be necessary to take notes on a film shown in class if you have to write a reaction paper on it that evening?

   _____

HOW PEOPLE LEARN AND REMEMBER

Three stages are involved in the memory process: encoding, storage, and retrieval. First, information enters the brain from a variety of sources. This process is known as *encoding*. In reading and study situations, information is entered primarily through reading or listening. This information lingers briefly in what is known as *sensory storage* and is then either *stored* or discarded. Momentary or brief storage is called *short-term memory*. Next, information in your short-term memory is either forgotten or transferred into more permanent storage. This permanent storage is called *long-term memory*. Anything you want to remember for more than a few seconds must be stored in your long-term memory. To place information in long-term memory it must be learned in some way. Finally, information can be brought back or remembered through a process known as *retrieval*. Figure 3-2 is a visual model of the learning and memory processes. Refer to it frequently as you read the sections that explain each stage.

How Encoding Works

Every waking moment your mind is bombarded with a variety of impressions of what is going on around you. Your five senses—hearing, sight, touch, taste, and smell—provide information about the world around you. Think for a moment of all the signals your brain receives at a given moment. If you are reading, your eyes transmit not only the visual

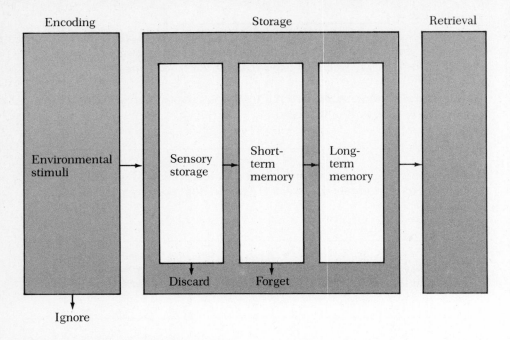

FIGURE 3-2   A Model of Memory

patterns of the words, but also information about the size and color of the print. You may hear a door slamming, a clock ticking, a dog barking. Your sense of smell may detect perfume or cigarette smoke; your sense of touch or feeling may signal that a pen you are using to underline will soon run out of ink or that the room is chilly. When you listen to a classroom lecture, you are constantly receiving numerous stimuli—from the professor, from the lecture hall, from students around you. All these environmental stimuli are transmitted to your brain for a very brief sensory storage and interpretation.

How Sensory Storage Works

Information received from the sense organs is transmitted through the nervous system to the brain, which accepts and interprets it. The information lingers briefly in the nervous system for the brain to interpret it; this lingering is known as sensory storage.

How does your mind handle the barrage of information conveyed by your senses? Thanks to what is known as *selective attention,* your brain automatically sorts out the more important signals from the trivial ones. Trivial signals, such as insignificant noises around you, are ignored or discarded. Through skills of concentration and attention, you can train yourself to ignore other more distracting signals, such as a dog barking or people talking in the background.

Although your sensory storage accepts all information, data is kept there only briefly, usually less than a few seconds. Then the information either fades or decays or is replaced with incoming new stimuli. The function, then, of sensory storage is to retain information long enough for you to selectively attend to it and transmit it to your short-term memory.

How Short-Term Memory Works

Short-term memory holds the information acquired from your sensory storage system. It is used to store information you wish to retain for only a few seconds. A telephone number, for example, is stored in your short-term memory until you dial it. A lecturer's words are retained until you can record them in your notes. Most researchers agree that short-term memory lasts much less than one minute, perhaps 20 seconds or less. Information can be kept or maintained longer if you practice or rehearse the information (repeating a phone number, for example). When you are introduced to someone, then, unless you repeat or rehearse the person's name at the time of introduction, you will not be able to remember it. New incoming information will force it out of your short-term memory.

Your short-term memory is limited in capacity as well as in time span. Research conducted by the psychologist George Miller suggests that we have room in our short-term memories to store from five to nine bits (or pieces or sets) of information at a time—that is, an average of seven. If you try to store more than seven, earlier items are "bumped out." The size of each bit, however, is not limited to a single item. You can group items together to form a longer bit or piece. Known as the Number Seven Theory, this finding is useful in both daily and academic situations.* When you read a textbook chapter or listen to a lecture, for example, your short-term memory is unable to retain each piece of information you receive. It is necessary to rearrange the information into groups or sets—ideas or topics. To retain information beyond the limitations of short-term memory, it must be transferred to long-term memory for more permanent storage.

EXERCISE 2

Directions: *Use your knowledge of the memory process to answer the following questions.*

1. Observe and analyze the area in which you are sitting. What sensory impressions (sights, sounds, touch sensations) have you been ignoring due to selective attention?

   _____

2. Can you remember what you ate for lunch three weeks ago? If not, why not?

   _____

3. Use your knowledge of the Number Seven Theory to explain why dashes are placed in your Social Security number after the third and fifth numbers and after the area code and the first three digits of your phone number.

   _____

*George Miller, "The Magic Number Seven plus or minus two; Some limits on our capacity for processing information," *Psychological Review*, 63 (1956): 81–97.

4. Explain why two people are able to carry on a deep conversation at a crowded, noisy party.

_____

5. Explain why someone who looks up a phone number and then walks into another room to dial it might forget the number.

_____

Learning: The Transfer from Short- to Long-term Memory

To retain information beyond the brief moment you acquire it, it must be transferred to long-term memory for permanent storage. There are several processes by which to store information in long-term memory: rote learning, rehearsal, and recoding.

Rote Learning: Rote learning involves repetition of information in the form in which it was acquired in sensory storage. Learning the spelling of a word, memorizing the exact definition of a word, or repeating a formula until you can remember it are examples. Material learned through this means is often learned in a fixed order. Rote learning is usually an inefficient means to store large quantities of information.

Elaborative Rehearsal: Used at this stage, rehearsal involves much more than simple repetition or practice. Elaborative rehearsal is a thinking process. It involves connecting new material with already learned material, asking questions, and making associations. It is a process of making the information meaningful and "fitting" it into an established category or relating it to existing memory stores. This form of rehearsal is discussed in more detail later.

Recoding: Recoding is a process of rearranging, rephrasing, changing, or grouping information so that it becomes more meaningful and easier to recall. Expressing ideas in your own words is a form of recoding, or you might recode information from a reading assignment by outlining it. Taking notes in lectures is also a form of recoding, as is writing a term paper that summarizes several reference sources.

Rehearsal and recoding are the underlying principles on which many learning strategies presented later in this book are based. Chapter 11, for example, discusses textbook underlining and marking. Underlining is a form of rehearsal. In deciding which information to underline, you review the information and sort the important from the unimportant. When you make marginal notes, you recode the information by classifying, organizing, labeling, or summarizing it.

EXERCISE 3 _____

Directions: *Decide whether each of the following activities primarily involves rote learning, elaborative rehearsal, or recoding.*

1. Learning a formula in economics for computing the rate of inflation.

_____

2. Relating the ideas and feelings expressed in a poem read in your English literature class to your personal experience.

_____

3. Making a chart that compares three political action groups.

_____

4. Learning metric equivalents for U.S. units of volume and weight.

_____

5. Drawing a diagram that shows the processes by which the Constitution can be amended.

_____

EXERCISE 4 ─────────────────

Directions: *Use your knowledge of the memory process to answer the following questions.*

1. Two groups of students read the same textbook chapter. One group underlined key ideas on each page; the second group paraphrased and recorded the important ideas from each page. Explain why the second group received higher scores on a test based on the chapter than did the first group.

_____

2. On many campuses, weekly recitations or discussions are scheduled for small groups to review material presented in large lecture classes. What learning function do these recitation sections provide?

_____

3. After lecturing on the causes of domestic violence, a sociology instructor showed her class a videotape of an incident of domestic violence. What learning function(s) did the film provide? How would the tape help students remember the lecture?

_____

4. A text that contains photographs is often easier to learn from than one without them. What learning function do the pictures perform?

_____

How Long-term Memory Works

Long-term memory is your permanent store of information. Unlike short-term memory, long-term memory is nearly unlimited in both span and capacity. It contains hundreds of thousands of facts, details, impressions, and experiences that you have accumulated throughout your life.

Once information is stored in your long-term memory, you recall or pull it out through a process known as retrieval. Academic tasks requiring you to retrieve knowledge include math or science problems, quizzes and exams, and papers. Retrieval is integrally tied to storage. The manner in which information is stored in your memory affects its availability and the ease with which you can retrieve it. For example, suppose you have studied a topic but find that on an exam you are unable to remember much about it. There are several possible explanations: (1) you never completely learned (stored) the information in the first place; (2) you did not study (store) the information in the right way; (3) you are not asking the right questions or using the right means to retrieve it; or (4) you have forgotten it. Later in this chapter you will learn principles that will enable you to store information effectively to retard forgetting.

EXERCISE 5 _____

Directions: *For each of the following activities, decide whether it involves encoding, storage, and/or retrieval.*

1. Taking an essay exam. _____

2. Listening to a lecture. _____

3. Taking notes on a film shown in class. _____

4. Solving a homework problem in mathematics. _____

5. Balancing a ledger in accounting. _____

EXERCISE 6 _____

Directions: *Use your knowledge of how memory works to explain each of the following situations.*

1. A student spends more time than anyone else in her class preparing for the midterm exam, yet she cannot remember important definitions and concepts at the time of the exam. Offer several possibilities that may explain her dilemma.

   _____

2. Try to recall the sixth number of your Social Security number without repeating the first five. What does this show about how you learned (rehearsed) your number?

   _____

3. A computer science instructor begins a class session by handing out a quiz. One student is surprised and says he did not know there would be a quiz. All the other students recall the instructor announcing the quiz the week before. The student has never been absent or late for class. Why does he not know about the quiz?

   _____

4. A business instructor plans to lecture on the process of job-stress analysis. Before class she draws a diagram of this process on the chalkboard. During the lecture she refers to it frequently. Why did the instructor draw the diagram?

    _____

5. A student is studying a difficult chapter in biology. Her roommate asks her a question, but she does not answer. The roommate assumes she is angry at her for interrupting her study and storms out of the room. What is the cause of the misunderstanding?

    _____

6. Suppose you are reading a section of your history text. You come across an unfamiliar word and so look up its meaning. Once you have looked up the word, you find that you must reread the section. Why?

    _____

7. A political science instructor is discussing an essay on world terrorism. He begins the discussion by asking his students to recall recent terrorist acts and how they were resolved. How is the instructor helping his students learn the content of the essay?

    _____

8. A sociology instructor asks her students to read and write a summary of a journal article she has placed on reserve in the library. How is she helping her students learn the material?

    _____

PRINCIPLES OF LEARNING

Now that you know how the memory process works, it is appropriate to consider ways in which you can learn most effectively. This section presents a summary of principles of learning. Each has specific applications for learning material contained in college texts or presented in class lectures.

Principle 1: Intent to Remember

What were you wearing seventeen months ago at this time? What did you eat for lunch on March 18, 1988? Why can't you answer these questions? The answer, of course, is simple: because you did not store the information; there was no need to remember what you were wearing or eating. One of the most obvious principles related to memory is that you remember only what you intend to remember—that which you identify as worth remembering.

To further illustrate this principle, draw the face side of a one-dollar bill in the space provided below before you read any more.

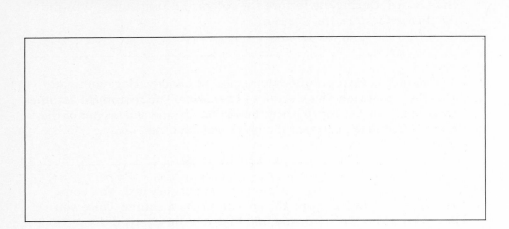

Now, did you include each of the following: the face of George Washington, the seal of the Department of the Treasury, the Federal Reserve Bank seal, the signature of the treasurer of the United States, the signature of the secretary of the Treasury, the words *Federal Reserve Note*, serial numbers, the series date, the words *UNITED STATES OF AMERICA*, and so on? Did you put all of these things in the right places? Most likely you were not able to reproduce a dollar bill accurately, and just think of how often you have looked at one. You did not remember the details on the bill because, whenever you looked at one, you had no *intention* of remembering it.

Application: Intent to remember has direct applications to both textbook reading and lecture note-taking. As you read or listen, you should select what you intend to remember by sorting out the important ideas from those that are relatively unimportant.

This principle also provides the basis for the techniques of prereading and active reading (presented in Chapters 5 and 6). You will learn that prereading is a method of getting an overview, or advance picture, of what is important and worth remembering in a textbook chapter before you read it completely. Prereading really tells you, in advance of a complete reading, what material you should intend to remember. Suppose you discover through prereading a chapter in an astronomy text that the chapter discusses the location, physical properties, and appearance of eight planets. Then you can establish an intent to remember. As you read, you will plan on identifying and remembering the name, location, properties, and appearance of each planet. The technique of active reading involves forming questions to guide your reading. It requires that, for each dark print (or boldface) heading within a textbook chapter, you form a question; as you read, you then try to find the answer to the question. The answer to your question is what you intend to remember.

Principle 2: Meaningfulness

Material that is meaningful, or makes sense, is easier to learn and remember than meaningless information. If would be easier to learn a list of meaningful words than a list of nonsense words. Try the following experiment to test the accuracy of this statement.

EXPERIMENT _____

Directions:

1. *Read through list 1 below, spending a maximum of 15 seconds.*
2. *Now, cover list 1 with your hand or a piece of scrap paper, and write down in the space provided on the next page as many items as you can remember.*
3. *Follow steps 1 and 2 for each of the other three lists.*
4. *Check to see how many items you had correct on each of the four lists.*

List 1	*List 2*	*List 3*	*List 4*
KQZ	BLT	WIN	WAS
NLR	TWA	SIT	THE
XOJ	SOS	LIE	CAR
BTK	CBS	SAW	RUN
YSW	NFL	NOT	OFF

List 1	*List 2*	*List 3*	*List 4*
____	____	____	____
____	____	____	____
____	____	____	____
____	____	____	____
____	____	____	____

Did you recall more items on list 2 than on list 1? Why? Did you remember more items on list 4 than on list 3? As you must now realize, after list 1, each list became more meaningful than the one before it. The lists progressed from nonsense syllables to meaningful letter groups to words and, finally, to words that, when strung together, produced meanings. This simple experiment demonstrates that you are able to remember information that is meaningful more easily than information that has no meaning.

Let's look at some other examples of the principle of meaningful learning. Consider phone numbers. Some are easy to remember; others are not. Would it be easy to remember the phone number of your local take-out pizza shop if the phone number were 825-3699? Probably not. Would it be easier to remember if you realized that the digits in the phone number correspond to letters on the phone dial that spell *take-out*? Yes. The word *take-out* has a particular meaning to you because you are using the phone number to order a take-out item.

Application: The principle of meaningful learning is critical in all textbook reading situations. It affirms the necessity of understanding (comprehending) what you read. If you do not understand a concept or idea, it is not meaningful and you will not be able to remember it. As you read, to be sure that you are comprehending, try to explain what you have read in your own words. If you cannot, you probably have not understood the material.

Several of the reading and study techniques presented in this text are, in part, based on the principle of meaningfulness. The technique of pre-reading, in which you become acquainted with the overall organization and content of a selection before you begin to read it, makes the reading process more meaningful. Active reading also makes reading more meaningful: You are reading to find specific information. The techniques of underlining and marking textbooks and taking lecture notes also give further meaning and organization to the materials to be studied.

Now suppose that, while learning vocabulary for an astronomy course, you discover you have to learn the terms for the lower, middle, and upper layers of the atmosphere. The terms are *troposphere, mesosphere,* and *exosphere*. One way to learn these words would be to memorize each word and its corresponding meaning. A better way would be to recognize that the root *sphere* in each refers to a three-dimensional object—in this case, the earth. The prefix, or beginning part of each word, in some way describes the atmosphere in relation to the earth. *Tropo-* means "change," and it is in this lower layer of the earth's atmosphere that the temperature changes with increasing altitude. The prefix *meso-* means "center or middle," so *mesosphere* is the center layer of the atmosphere. The prefix *exo-* means "outside or external," so it is the exosphere that is the uppermost or outer layer of the atmosphere (See Figure 3-3). It is by learning the meanings of the root *sphere* and the prefixes as well as connecting them with specific astronomical meanings that the terms become more meaningful and are easier to remember.

Principle 3: Categorization and Labeling

Categorization is the restructuring, or reorganizing, of information into meaningful groups for easier recall. Suppose you had to remember to

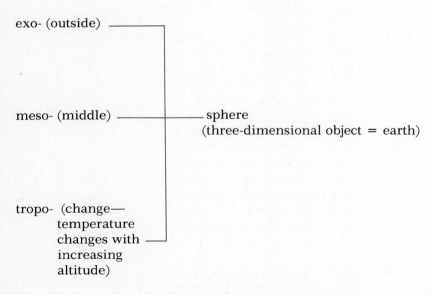

FIGURE 3-3 **Word Meaning as a Memory Aid**

buy the following items at the supermarket and couldn't write them down: apples, milk, toothpaste, eggs, pepperoni, shampoo, celery, deodorant, salami, cheese, pork chops, and onions. What could you do to make recall of the items easier? One thing you could do is classify the items by organizing them in the categories shown in these headings:

Toiletries	Dairy	Meat	Fruits/ Vegetables
toothpaste	milk	pepperoni	apples
deodorant	cheese	salami	onions
shampoo	eggs	pork chops	celery

By classifying the items in these categories, you are, first of all, making the information meaningful—it is organized according to aisles or departments within the store. Second, you have placed a label on each group of items. The labels "Toiletries," "Dairy," and so forth can serve as "memory tags" that will help you to remember to buy the items you classified under each category. Using memory tags may be compared to knowing which cupboard door to open in your kitchen when you are looking for something. If you know which door to open, locating a can of soup is relatively easy. But if you do not know where the canned items are stored, locating the soup could be difficult. In trying to remember your list of supermarket shopping items, if you can remember the category "Dairy," recalling the particular items you want to buy becomes a simpler task.

Application: Try to categorize information as you read it—either in your mind or on paper. In the following passage, you could classify the information into the two categories indicated by the headings in the diagram that follows.

Responsibility for the administration and enforcement of immigration laws rests primarily with the Secretary of State and the Attorney General.

The Secretary of State discharges most of his responsibilities through the Bureau of Security and Consular Affairs authorized by the 1952 act. This bureau embraces the Passport Office and Visa Office. These, in turn, carry on their work with the aid of American diplomatic and consular officers abroad, who, since 1924, have been charged with primary responsibility for selecting immigrants before they embark.

The Attorney General performs most of his functions in this field through the Immigration and Naturalization Service, which has a staff in all sections of the country and at important ports of entry. A board of appeals, established by the Attorney General and responsible to him, reviews appeals from orders and actions of agents of the Immigration and Naturalization Service. Hearing officers are not bound, however, to observe the standards of fairness prescribed by the Administrative Procedures Act.

–Ferguson and McHenry, *The American System of Government,* p. 213

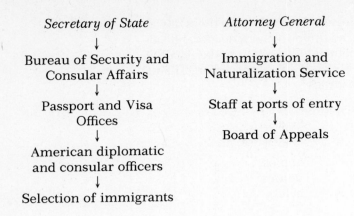

Several reading-study techniques suggested in this book employ the principle of categorization. As you take lecture notes (Chapter 14), for example, you arrange, classify, and categorize information. As you use the recall clue system for studying those lecture notes, you continue to apply the principle of labeling and grouping—categorizing information. As you underline and mark a textbook (Chapter 11), you perform a similar task.

Principle 4: Association

New information is easier to learn and remember if you can connect it with previously learned or familiar information. For instance, it is easy to remember your new license plate if it is 1776 US. You can associate, or connect, the new license plate with an already well-learned date and event, in this case the date the United States became independent. Or you can remember and recognize the shape of Italy on a map if you associate it with a boot.

In an American history course, it would be easier to understand and recall various battles in the Civil War if you had visited the cities in which they occurred and could form associations between the details of the battles and specific geographic points that you recall from your visits.

Application: As you read, always try to make connections between the new material and what you already know. You will see that the recall clue system for studying your notes (Chapter 14) relies heavily upon the principle of association. As you read each recall clue written in the margins of your notes, you attempt to relate, or associate, the clue with the corresponding facts in the notes.

Principle 5: Spaced Study

The length of time and spacing between reading-study lessons directly affects how much you learn. Generally, it is more effective to space or spread out study sessions rather than to study in one or two large blocks of time. In fact, research has shown that when periods of study are divided into units separated by breaks, the total time necessary to memorize information is significantly reduced.

Spaced learning and study has several advantages. First, it is likely that by spacing out your study you are reducing the possibility of becoming fatigued—both physically and mentally. Second, there is some evidence that, even when you stop studying and take a break, a certain amount of rehearsal continues to take place.

Finally, dividing your study time into small blocks is psychologically rewarding. When you finish a block, you will feel that you have made progress and are accomplishing something.

Application: The most direct application of this principle occurs as you organize daily and weekly study schedules, as discussed in Chapters 2 and 4. In addition, the use of the study card system described in Chapter 16 will also help you apply this learning principle to your work.

Principle 6: Consolidation

As you learn new information, your mind organizes that information and makes it fit with existing stored information. This process is called *consolidation*. Think of it as a process in which information settles, gels, or takes shape. Consolidation occurs when you briefly hold information in your memory, as you make notes, outline, or summarize what you read or hear in lecture. Consolidation also seems to occur once you've stopped studying: Your mind continues to mull over—sift, sort, and organize—what you have just learned. Often this consolidation occurs subconsciously while you are doing something else. Consolidation lends strong support to the principle of spaced study. Since consolidation occurs following a study session, if you schedule several short sessions rather than one long one, you are allowing consolidation to occur several times, rather than only once.

Application: You can facilitate consolidation by reviewing material shortly after your initial learning. For example, review your lecture notes shortly after taking them, or review your textbook underlining the day after reading the chapter. The techniques of underlining, summarizing, outlining, and mapping discussed in Chapters 12 and 13 employ the principle of consolidation.

Principle 7: Mnemonic Devices

Mnemonics are memory tricks, or aids, that you can devise to help you remember information. Mnemonics include rhymes, anagrams, words, nonsense words, sentences, or mental pictures that aid in the recall of facts. Do you remember this rhyme: "Thirty days hath September,/ April, June, and November./ All the rest have thirty-one/ except February, alone,/ which has twenty-eight days clear/ and twenty-nine in each leap year"? The rhyme is an example of a mnemonic device. It is a quick and easy way of remembering the number of days in each month of the year. You may have learned to recall the colors in the spectrum by remembering the name *Roy G. Biv;* each letter in this name stands for one of the colors that make up the spectrum: *R*ed, *O*range, *Y*ellow, *G*reen, *B*lue, *I*ndigo, *V*iolet.

The Chicago Police Department once developed an anagram to help officers remember what steps to follow when called to the scene of a crime. The officers' responsibility is to make a *preliminary* investigation by following the procedure below. Notice the word that is spelled by the first letters of the steps in the procedure.

P — Proceed to the scene.
R — Render assistance to the injured.
E — Effect the arrest of the perpetrator.
L — Locate and identify witnesses.
I — Interview complainant and witnesses.
M — Maintain the scene and protect evidence.
I — Interrogate suspects.
N — Note all conditions, events, and remarks.
A — Arrange for collection of evidence.
R — Report the incident fully and accurately.
Y — Yield responsibility to detectives.

–Wilson and McLaren, *Police Administration*, p. 353

Application: Mnemonic devices are useful when you are trying to learn information that has no inherent organization of its own. You will find the principle useful in reviewing texts and lecture notes as you prepare for exams.

Principle 8: Visualization

Recent research indicates that the brain's functions are divided between the left and right brain. The left brain handles verbal learning and the logical processing of information, while the right brain controls visual processes and more creative and insightful thought. Reading and writing are primarily left brain processes. However, if you can engage your right brain as well as your left in learning, you will increase the number of channels through which learning can occur, thereby enhancing learning effectiveness.

Visualization involves creating a mental or visual picture to be learned; it engages your right brain in the learning process. You might visualize the events in a short story for a literature class by imagining events, characters, or setting. Or for an American history class, you might visualize the panic on the day of the 1929 stock market crash. Drawing diagrams, charts, or graphs is also a form of visualization. In biology, for example, you might draw a diagram that shows how mitosis occurs. In a social problems class you might construct a chart listing types and impacts of military spending.

Application: As you read, attempt to create mental pictures of events and processes. Chapter 14 discusses how to construct visual and organizational charts and diagrams.

Principle 9: Elaboration

You have learned that information is transferred from short- to long-term memory through rehearsal. In most situations, rehearsal should involve more than mere repetition of material to be learned; rather, it must incorporate *elaboration*—thinking about and reacting to content. You might think of elaboration as expansion, evaluation, or application of ideas. Elaboration can involve asking questions, or thinking about implications, exceptions, similarities, or examples. You may look for relationships or connect the material to other course content. For a business marketing course, a student was studying discount pricing structures in which she learned various types of discounts a seller may give. To elaborate on this material the student

> thought of real-life situations in which she had seen or received these discounts;
>
> considered the impact of discounts on profit objectives (a topic previously studied); and
>
> compared the various types of discounts and identified when and by what type of business each might be used.

Through the above processes, the student actively worked with the concept of discount pricing.

Application: Elaboration is a useful means of study and review. It may occur as you read, as well. Outlining and textbook marking require elaboration, since you must discover and describe relationships among ideas. Elaboration is particularly useful in preparing for essay exams. It is also an excellent means of reviewing material in preparation for a class discussion or for generating ideas for writing assignments.

Principle 10: Periodic Review

The retention curve shown in Figure 3-1 demonstrates how quickly and dramatically forgetting occurs. Periodic review is useful to combat forgetting. Periodic review means returning to and quickly reviewing previously learned material on a regular basis. Suppose you have learned the material in the first three chapters of your criminology text during the first two weeks of the course. Unless you review that material you are likely to forget it and have to relearn it by the time your final exam is given. You might establish a periodic review schedule in which every three weeks or so you quickly review these chapters.

Numerous studies have documented that review immediately following learning increases retention. In fact, review done right after learning is more valuable than an equal amount of time spent reviewing several days later.

Application: Periodic review of previously learned material is difficult and time-consuming unless the material is reduced and organized. Techniques such as underlining, outlining, mapping, and summarizing make periodic review easier to accomplish.

EXERCISE 7 ——————————————

Directions: *Apply your knowledge of the memory process and principles of learning in answering the following questions.*

1. You are studying the principal causes of war in a political science course. Your textbook identifies fourteen such causes. What learning principles would you use to learn this material?

   —————————————————————————

2. A student is taking a chemistry course. Each week the instructor assigns two textbook chapters. In addition, a weekly lab and lab

[Handwritten margin note:]

10 Principles of Learning
1) Intent to Remember
2) Meaningfulness
3) Categorization + Labeling
4) Association
5) Spaced Study
6) Consolidation
7) Mnemonic devices
8) Visualization
9) Elaboration
10) Periodic Review

report are required. In class the instructor performs experiments, solves sample problems, and explains basic principles and laws. Suggest a periodic review plan for the student.

_____

3. How would you use the principle of association when studying the essential features of effective speaking styles for a speech communication course? The features are accuracy, simplicity, coherence, and appropriateness.

_____

4. The psychologist Abraham Maslow classified fundamental human needs into five categories, now known as Maslow's hierarchy. How would you use the principle of elaboration in learning this hierarchy? From most to least basic, the five levels are physiological needs, safety needs, belongingness and love needs, esteem needs, and self-actualization (self-fulfillment) needs.

_____

5. How would you use the principle of visualization in learning the law of demand in an economics class? The law states that the price of a product and the amount purchased are inversely related: If the price rises, the quantity demanded falls; if the price falls, the quantity demanded increases.

_____

6. For the first time, you are required to learn the metric system—the metric equivalents for measures of volume, weight, and temperature. How could you make this learning task as meaningful as possible?

_____

7. Vanessa is taking a business mathematics course. She does well on homework and weekly quizzes that deal with one specific type of problem. However, on one-hour exams in which she faces several different types of problems, she scores poorly. How might she improve her performance on exams?

_____

8. The textbook for your English class is an anthology (collection) of essays, each by a different author. For each class session your instructor assigns and discusses one essay. You have been reading each essay and taking notes on your instructor's discussion. Now a midterm exam has been announced which will consist of only one question. What principle(s) of learning would be useful in preparing for this exam?

_____

9. A nursing student is studying the various life stages (infant, toddler, adolescent, and so on) and the cognitive, physiological, and psychological developments at each stage. What principles of learning would be useful to her?

_____

10. Decide how you could organize (categorize) each of the following sets of information.

a. pollutants and their environmental effects
b. problems faced by two-career families
c. effects of terrorism
d. causes of the Vietnam War

a. _____

b. _____

c. _____

d. _____

SUMMARY

This chapter presented an overview of learning and memory processes and offered practical ways to learn more efficiently. Forgetting occurs very rapidly unless specific steps are taken to retain information.

To prevent forgetting, it is necessary to understand how learning and memory work. Three stages are involved in the memory process: encoding, storage, and retrieval. Encoding is the process through which information enters your brain through your various senses. This information lingers briefly in sensory storage, where it is interpreted. Next, the information is either stored briefly in short-term memory or discarded and forgotten. Then you must either transfer information into the more permanent long-term memory or allow it to be forgotten. Transferring facts from short- to long-term memory involves rote learning, elaborative rehearsal, and recoding. A number of learning principles influence how well information is stored in long-term memory. These include the intent to remember, meaningfulness, categorization, association, spaced study, consolidation, mnemonic devices, visualization, elaboration, and periodic review.

Handwritten marginal notes:
Memory Process
3 Stages
Encoding
Storing in Memory
Transferring

Short- To-Long-Term Memory
1) rote learning
2) elaborative rehearsal
3) recoding

PART TWO

Techniques for Effective Reading

Most college students have a basic competence in reading. They have acquired a core vocabulary and developed an understanding of language structure that allows basic understanding (comprehension) of units of written expression. Yet many students frequently complain that they have difficulty getting through the required reading in a course, that they cannot keep their minds on what they read, or that they cannot remember what they have read.

This seeming contradiction can be explained by the fact that most students have not developed (or have not been taught) necessary reading and study techniques that can influence and greatly alter their ability to read and retain textbook material. The primary purpose of this part of the book is to discuss reading habits and strategies that can enhance your ability to concentrate and to read and learn more effectively.

Chapter 4 presents techniques for improving your level of concentration by eliminating distractions and focusing your attention on the task at hand. It also discusses stress and how to manage it. Chapter 5 presents the technique of prereading, which provides a means of becoming familiar with the content and organization of a chapter before beginning to read it. Chapter 6 describes strategies for becoming a more active, involved reader. You will learn how to activate your background knowledge, define purposes for reading, select appropriate reading strategies, and monitor your comprehension.

3

A. Excluding Distractions

PAC
MP
NP

1 Place
2 Establish Area
3 Clutter
4 Materials
5 Peak Period
6 Noise
7 physical state

B. Focus Your Attention

1
2
3
4
5
6
7

C. Managing Stress Symptoms

How To reduce Stress

4

Improving Your Concentration and Managing Stress

Use this chapter to:

1. *Learn how to exclude distractions.*
2. *Develop skill in focusing your attention.*
3. *Learn to manage stress.*

Do these comments sound familiar?

"I just can't concentrate!"
"I've got so much reading to do; I'll never be able to catch up!"
"I try to study, but nothing happens."
"I waste a lot of time worrying or just thinking about things."

Many students find it difficult to concentrate—to keep their minds on what they are reading or studying. Many, too, feel pressured to get things done and to earn good grades. They may feel overwhelmed by the number of assignments and the amount of required reading. This kind of pressure and work load often produces stress.

Your ability to concentrate and to manage stress are critical to your success in college. Regardless of your intelligence or the skills and talents you possess, unless you can keep your mind on your work and maintain a balanced, focused approach, you won't succeed. This chapter presents two methods of improving your concentration—excluding distractions and focusing your attention. In addition, you will also learn to recognize the symptoms of stress and find out how to reduce or manage stress.

EXCLUDING DISTRACTIONS

It is impossible to eliminate all the sources of distraction and interruption, but if you can control several of the factors that interfere with concentration you will improve your ability to concentrate. Effective ways of controlling, if not eliminating, distractions are discussed in this section.

Choose a Place with Minimum Distraction

The place or physical location you choose for reading and study determines, in part, the number of distractions or interruptions you will have. If you try to read or study in a place where there is a lot of activity (doors slamming, people talking, a radio playing, machines running, and so forth), you will probably find that your mind wanders.

Choose a place where there is a minimum of distraction. If your home or dorm is too busy and noisy, study in a quiet place on campus. Try various student lounge areas, or check out study areas in the library. Empty classrooms are also good possibilities.

Establish a Study Area

Try to read and study in the same place rather than wherever it seems convenient at the time. There is a psychological advantage to working in the same place regularly. As with many other activities, you build a mental association, or connection, between an activity and the place where it occurs. If you sit down at a table set for dinner, for example, you expect to eat dinner. If you always sit in the same comfortable chair to watch television, eventually you expect to relax and watch television every time you sit in that chair. This psychological expectation also applies to reading and studying. If you become accustomed to working at a particular desk, you build up an association between the place—your desk—and the activity— reading and studying. Eventually, when you sit down at the desk, you expect to read or study. Your expectation makes the tasks at hand much easier; you do not have to convince yourself to work. Instead, you are almost automatically ready to read or study when you sit down at the desk.

In choosing a regular place to read, be sure you do not select a place you already associate with a different activity. Don't try to read in your TV chair or stretched out across your bed; you have already built associations with your chair and bed as places to relax or sleep.

Eliminate Distracting Clutter

Once you've organized a study area, keep it clear of possible distractions. Don't keep bills to be paid or letters to be answered on the desk where you study. Also, do not keep photos, mementos, or interesting magazines that may draw your mind away from study near or on your desk.

Have Necessary Materials Available

When you sit down to read or study, be sure that all the materials you need are readily available. These might include a dictionary, pens, pencils, paper, a calculator, index cards, a calendar, a clock, and so on. Surrounding yourself with these materials will also help to create a psychological readiness for reading or studying. Furthermore, if you have to get up to locate any of these items, you break your concentration and take the chance of being distracted from the task at hand.

Study at Peak Periods of Attention

The time of day or night when you read or study may influence how easy or difficult it is to shut out distractions. Most people have a time limit for how long they can keep their minds on one thing. This is called *attention span*. Attention span changes from subject to subject, from book to book, from lecturer to lecturer, and from one time of day to another. People experience peaks and valleys in attention span at different times of the day. Some people are very alert in the early morning; others find they are most alert at midday or in the early evening. To make concentration easier, try to read and study during the peaks of your attention span. Choose the times of day when you are most alert and when it is easiest to keep your mind on what you are doing. If you are not aware of your own peaks of attention, do a quick analysis of your effectiveness. Over a period of several days, keep track of when you read and studied and how much you accomplished each time. Then look for a pattern.

Control Noise Levels

Some students find it difficult to concentrate in a completely quiet room. Others need some background noise in order to concentrate. Most students find some middle ground, or compromise, between total silence and a loud, noisy background. Research suggests that the volume of background music that interferes with concentration varies with individuals. A noise level that is distracting to one student may not disturb another. To find out how much background noise you can take, try different levels and see which seems best suited for you.

Pay Attention to Your Physical State

How you feel physically greatly influences how well you can concentrate. If you are tired or sleepy, concentration will be difficult. If you are hungry, you will find that your thoughts drift toward what you'll have to eat when you're finished. If you feel sluggish, inactive, and in need of exercise, concentration will also be difficult. Try to schedule reading or studying at times when your physical needs are not likely to interfere. Also, if while reading, you find that you are hungry, tired, or sluggish, stop and try to correct the problem. Take a break, have a snack, or get up and walk around. If you are physically or mentally exhausted, however, it is usually best to stop and find a better time to complete the assignment.

EXERCISE 1 _____

Directions: *Decide what might interfere with studying in each of the following situations. Write your answer in the space provided.*

1. You are studying while stretched out on your bed.

_____

2. You begin studying immediately after you get home from a vigorous basketball team practice.

   _____

3. You are studying while playing a tape that you just purchased.

   _____

4. You are studying in an easy chair in front of the television.

   _____

5. You are studying on campus in the snack bar or cafeteria at noon, between your eleven o'clock and one o'clock classes.

   _____

6. You are studying at a table in the library and some friends decide to join you.

   _____

7. You are studying at your friend's house while you wait for her to get ready to go shopping.

   _____

EXERCISE 2 _____

Directions: *As you read an assignment this evening, be alert for distractions. Each time you lose your concentration, try to identify the cause. List below the items that distracted you and, if possible, describe a way to eliminate the distraction.*

1. _____

2. _____

3. _____

4. _____

FOCUSING YOUR ATTENTION

Focusing your attention on what you are reading or studying will improve your concentration. By directing your attention to what you are reading or studying, you will find that your mind wanders less often, and that you are able to complete reading and study assignments more efficiently.

Establish Goals and Time Limits

Psychologically, establishing and achieving goals are positive, rewarding experiences. It makes you feel good and proves that you are accomplishing something. Use this psychological principle to help focus on what you are reading or studying. For each reading assignment you have to do, give yourself a goal to work toward. Instead of just sitting down and beginning, first figure out how much you can accomplish in a specific amount of time. Set a time limit and work toward meeting it. Working under time pressure will help you focus your attention because you will be aware that distractions and daydreaming cost you time and delay you in meeting your goal. Then when you meet your goal, you will feel positive and know that you have accomplished something worthwhile.

Begin by establishing long-range goals. In Figure 4-1, you can see how one student set up study goals for the week. In Figure 4-2, the student has made his weekly goals more specific and detailed by setting time goals, day by day, for completing each assignment.

In setting goals and time limits, be as realistic and as specific as possible. For example, instead of deciding to study economics for two hours, set three more specific goals: review Chapter 2—½ hour; read and underline Chapter 3—1 hour; review lecture notes—½ hour.

EXERCISE 3 _____

Directions: *Review your class assignments, reading assignments, quizzes, and papers, including exams, for the next week of classes. Write a set of weekly reading/study goals that list what you hope to accomplish in each of your courses.*

EXERCISE 4 _____

Directions: *Using the weekly reading/study goals you prepared for Exercise 3, develop a set of daily reading/study goals that specify when you will complete each assignment and how much time you expect to spend on each.*

Data Processing	Review Chapters 2 + 3
	Edit and review 3 sets of class notes
English	Type paper due Wed.
	Do draft of ideas for next paper.
Ecology	Prepare for Lab on friday.
	Read and understand Chapter 6
	Review Chapter 5.
Psychology	Start research for 1st project.
	Review for quiz # 1 on friday
Speech Comm.	Do draft of ideas for Speech #2
	Write reaction paper to film
	shown on Tues.

FIGURE 4-1   Weekly Readings/Study Goals

Mon.	Read Data Processing Chap. 2	1 hr.
	Edit Monday's class notes (D.P.)	15 mins.
	Draft ideas for Speech reaction paper	½ hr.
	Read Economics Chap. 6	1½ hr.
Tues.	Type English composition	½ hr.
	Proofread composition	15 mins.
	Review Chaps. 2 & 3 Psychology for quiz	2 hrs.
Wed.	Read Data Processing Chap. 3	1½ hr.
	Edit Wed. class notes in D.P.	10 mins
Thurs.	Draft ideas - English composition	½ hr.
	Read Lab manual p. 152-160 and list procedures	45 min.
	Review Chapters 4 & 5 for Psychology quiz	2 hrs.
Fri.	Edit Fri's class D.P. notes	10 min.
Sat.	Review Economics Chap. 5	½ hr.
	Write and revise reaction paper for speech	1½ hr.
Sun.	Go to library - start Psychology research	2 hrs.

FIGURE 4-2   Daily Reading/Study Goals

Reward Yourself

Setting and meeting goals within a time limit is one type of reward that can help you focus your attention. Other types of rewards can be used to help you keep your mind on what you are doing: daily activities you enjoy—such as watching television, eating, making phone calls—can be used as rewards if you arrange them to follow periods of reading and studying. You might, for example, plan to call a friend after you finish working on your math problems. In this situation, calling a friend becomes a reward for finishing your math assignment. Or, if you plan to rewrite your English composition before watching a favorite television program, the program becomes a reward for finishing your revision of the written assignment.

Get Interested in the Subject

Interest is a major factor in keeping your attention focused. Hardly anyone has difficulty concentrating on a magazine article that is highly interesting or keeping his or her mind on a film or television show he or she wants to see. It is when the subject matter is not extremely interesting that the problem of daydreaming occurs. Although you cannot change a dull subject to make it interesting, there are a few things you can do to create or develop your interest in the subject. Try the following suggestions:

1. Read critically. As you read, look for ideas that you can question or disagree with. Look for points of view, opinions, statements that are not supported.
2. Try to predict or anticipate the author's thoughts. See if you can predict what the author is leading up to or what point he or she will make next.
3. Try to connect, or see the relationship between, new material and information you already have learned. Does the new material expand, alter, or contradict ideas you had before?

Use Writing to Focus Your Attention

Physical activities—such as writing and underlining—when combined with the mental activities of reading, reviewing, and memorizing, will help you focus your attention. By underlining, marking, outlining, or taking notes, you keep your mind active and involved. By deciding whether each idea is important enough to underline or write down, you are forced to think about, or pay attention to, each idea. To test the value of writing as you learn, try the following:

EXPERIMENT _____

Directions: *Below are listed two sets of words, which you will try to memorize. Follow each of the three steps right after you read the step. Do* not *read through all three steps before beginning.*

1. Read the words in set A once. Then reread them. Without looking, write down as many of the words as you can remember on a separate piece of paper.
2. Read the words in set B once. Then copy the words on a piece of paper. Without looking at the words or your copy of them, write down as many words as you can remember.
3. Check to see how many words you have correct on each list.

Set A			Set B		
MOM	COP	MOP	CAT	TAR	PAT
FAT	TAP	ARE	SAM	DAD	HOP
RAM	FAR	LAP	MAT	CAR	HAS
	RAM			RAT	

Most likely, you were able to remember more words in set B. Although you spent approximately the same amount of time learning the words in sets A and B, writing the words in B improved your ability to remember. This experiment demonstrates the value of combining writing with reading and remembering.

Vary Your Activities

Ability to focus on a particular subject will improve if you try not to force your concentration on only one type of activity for a long period of time. You might plan your study schedule so that you read sociology for a while, then work on math problems, and finally switch to writing an English paper. This plan would be much more effective than one with all reading activities—reading sociology, then reading chemistry, then reading an essay for English. As you vary the type and nature of your study activities, you are using different mental processes and different skills. The change from one skill or mental process to another will be refreshing and make concentration easier.

Keep a Distractions List

As you are reading or studying, often you will think of something you should remember to do. For example, a dental appointment you've scheduled for the next afternoon may flash through your mind. Although this flash does help you remember, it interferes with your concentration. To overcome these mental reminders flashing through your mind as you study, keep a distractions list. Have a separate sheet of paper nearby. Each time one of these mental reminders occurs, jot it down. You will find that by writing it down on paper, you will temporarily eliminate it from your memory. Use the same paper to record other ideas and problems that distract you. A distractions list might look like this:

Dentist - Tues. 2 p.m.
call Sam
buy Mother's Day Card
return library books

Use the Tally System to Build Your Attention Span

As mentioned earlier, your attention span is the length of time you can keep your mind focused on a particular subject without interference or distraction. An easy way to increase your attention span is to monitor, or keep track of, how many times you are distracted during a specified period of time (half an hour). Make a tally, or count, of distractions. Each time you think about something other than what you are studying, make a mark on the paper. Total your marks at the end of the specified time. Check yourself again, and try to reduce the number of distractions by 10 percent. Do not keep this tally every time you read or study anything, or you will rely on the technique to force your concentration. Instead, use it once every few days until you have sufficiently increased your concentration.

Directions: *Over the next week, try to build your attention span using the tally system suggested above. Record the results below.*

	Reading/Study Assignment	Time Period	Number of Distractions
1.	_____	_____	_____
2.	_____	_____	_____
3.	_____	_____	_____
4.	_____	_____	_____

MANAGING STRESS

Do you ever feel as though you just can't handle everything—your class work, your part-time job, the demands of family and friends? If so, you are probably feeling pressured or are under stress. Stress often results when you face new or difficult situations. Stress is a common problem for college students because college represents a dramatic change in life-style—socially, economically, or academically—and changes in life-style may affect you psychologically, emotionally, and even physically. Many college students feel pressure to perform well and to earn good grades. This pressure also contributes to stress. Finally, minor annoyances, often caused by living or functioning in a new and unfamiliar environment, produce stress. For example, the roommate who is always playing his stereo when you want to study, or a group of people talking at the next table in the library, becomes upsetting.

Although limited amounts of stress keep us active and alert, too much stress is harmful and produces negative psychological and physical effects. Stress can also interfere with concentration and often affects academic performance. If you are worried about getting good grades, you may feel stressed when taking quizzes and exams and, as a result, may not score as well as you normally would.

Symptoms of Stress

Although individuals react to stress and pressure differently, some common symptoms of stress are

short-temperedness	listlessness
feeling rushed	headaches
difficulty concentrating	queasiness, indigestion
weight loss	worn-out feeling, fatigue

At other times stress manifests itself in irrational thinking; small problems are seen as overwhelming; minor annoyances are exaggerated into serious confrontations. A disagreement with a roommate may become a major conflict or argument, or receiving an order of cold French fries from the snack bar seems more important than it is.

How to Reduce Stress

How you manage your life can reduce or prevent stress. Here are a few suggestions:

Manage Your Time Effectively: Time management can significantly reduce stress by allowing you to feel in control and certain that you will have time to accomplish necessary tasks. Refer to Chapter 2 for specific time management strategies.

Eliminate Stressors: Once you've identified a source of stress, eliminate it if possible. If, for instance, a part-time job is stressful, quit it or find another that is less stressful. If a roommate is causing stress, attempt to rearrange your living conditions. If a math course is creating stress, take action: Go to the learning lab or math lab for assistance or inquire about tutoring.

Accentuate Your Accomplishments: When you feel pressured, stop and review what you have already accomplished that day and that week. This review will give you confidence that you can handle the work load. A positive attitude goes a long way in overcoming stress.

Get Involved with Campus Activities: Some students become so involved with their course work that they do little else but study or worry about studying. In fact, they feel guilty or stressed when they are not studying. Be sure to allow some time in each day to relax and have fun. Campus activities provide a valuable means of releasing tension and taking your mind off your work.

Avoid Simultaneous Life Changes: College is a major change in lifestyle and is stressful in itself. Therefore, try to avoid additional major changes, such as marriage, initiating a conflict about religion with parents, or starting a new job.

Establish a Daily Routine: To eliminate daily hassles and make daily tasks as simple as possible, establish a daily routine. A routine eliminates the need to make numerous daily small decisions and, thereby, gives you a sense of "smooth sailing."

Seek Knowledgeable Advice: If stress becomes an insurmountable problem, seek assistance from the student counseling center. The office may offer workshops in stress reduction techniques such as relaxation or biofeedback training.

Get Physical Exercise: Exercise often releases tension, promotes a general feeling of wellness, and improves self-concept. Many students report that as little as 30 minutes of exercise produces immediate relaxation and helps them to place daily events into perspective.

Eat Nutritious Meals: Strength and endurance are affected by diet. When you feel rushed, eating available snacks rather than taking time to buy or prepare lunch or dinner or going to the dining hall may be tempting. Consuming large amounts of snack food may produce fluctuations in your blood sugar level, which can cause headaches or queasiness. During rushed, stressful times, such as exam days, nutritious food can help you keep calm and think more clearly. In general, try to eat fruits, vegetables, and protein; avoid refined sugar, large amounts of caffeine, and high-calorie, low-nutrient snacks.

Get Adequate Amounts of Sleep: Sleep allows the body time to replenish energy and to recover from the daily demands placed upon it. The amount of sleep one needs is highly individual. Discover how much you need by noticing patterns. For several weeks, analyze how well your day went and consider how much sleep you had the night before. Soon you will recognize patterns: You may notice irritability or "bad" days when you are short on sleep, or you might find you have caught a cold after a hectic weekend with little sleep. Try to respond to body signals rather than let work load or the expectations of others control your schedule.

EXERCISE 6 _____

Directions: *Analyze the following situations and answer the questions that follow.*

A student living in a dorm goes home for holidays and end-of-quarter breaks. Before each holiday or term end, she rushes to finish papers, catch up on reading, and study for exams or finals. She studies late each evening and pays little attention to her health. Each time she arrives home, she gets sick—once she had a severe cold, another time stomach flu, another time an ear infection. Her parents blamed dorm life, thinking she caught illnesses from other students.

1. How can you explain this student's pattern of illness?

    _____

2. Have you observed or experienced similar reactions to stress?

    _____

3. What would you suggest she do to overcome this pattern? Offer specific suggestions.

    _____

SUMMARY

Improving concentration involves two major skills or abilities—excluding distractions and focusing your attention. There are a number of ways to eliminate distractions. These include choosing a place with minimum distraction, reading in the same place, choosing an appropriate noise level, and paying attention to your physical state. To help you focus your attention, or concentrate, on the subject at hand, a variety of techniques were presented. Setting a goal and rewarding yourself when you achieve it is often an effective way of forcing yourself to keep your mind on your work. Getting yourself interested in the subject also aids in concentration. If you vary the subjects you study as well as the skills and abilities (both physical and mental) you use in studying, your mind will wander less. By keeping a distractions list on which you jot down appointments and other things you need to remember, you will keep them from interfering with your concentration. Concentration can also be improved by a concerted effort to build your attention span—the length of time you are able to focus on your subject without distraction.

Stress can interfere with your concentration and affect academic performance. Symptoms of stress include fatigue, short-temperedness, listlessness, indigestion, and irrational thinking. Stress can be reduced by exercising, eating nutritious meals, getting enough sleep, managing time, eliminating stressors, emphasizing accomplishments, avoiding life changes, maintaining a routine, and if necessary, seeking advice or counseling.

5

Prereading

Use this chapter to:

1. *Learn a way to get interested in what you are reading and to remember more.*

2. *Find out how to become familiar with what you are going to read before you begin.*

Do you check for traffic before crossing a street? Do you check the depth of a pool before diving in? What do you do to an article or chapter before you read it, before you "jump in"? In this section you will become acquainted with the technique of prereading—a useful way of checking any written material before you read it. Just as most people check traffic before crossing a street or water depth before diving, efficient readers check printed materials before reading to become generally familiar with the overall content and organinization.

HOW TO PREREAD

Your overall purposes in prereading are to identify the most important ideas in the material and to note their organization. You look only at specific parts and skip over the rest. The portions to look at in prereading a textbook chapter are described in the following paragraphs. Later you will learn how to adapt this procedure to other types of material.

Read the Title and Subtitle

The title provides the overall topic of the article or chapter; the subtitle suggests the specific focus, aspect, or approach toward the overall topic.

Read the Introduction or First Paragraph

The introduction, or first paragraph if there is no introduction, serves as a lead-in to the chapter. It gives you an idea of where the material is starting and where it is heading.

Read Each Boldface (Dark Print) Heading

The headings function as labels or topic statements for what is contained in the sections that follow them. In other words, a heading announces the major topic of each section.

Read the First Sentence Under Each Heading

The first sentence frequently tells you what the passage is about or states the central thought. You should be aware, however, that in some types of material or in certain styles of writing the first sentence does not function as a central thought. Instead, the opening sentence may function as a transition or lead-in statement, or may be written to catch your interest. If the first sentence seems unimportant, read the last sentence; often this sentence states or restates the central thought.

Note Any Typographical and Graphical Aids

Italics are used to emphasize important terms and definitions by using slanted (italic) type to distinguish them from the rest of the passage. Notice any material that is numbered 1, 2, 3, lettered a, b, c, or presented in list form. Graphs, charts, pictures, and tables are other means of emphasis and are usually meant to point out what is important in the chapter. Be sure to read the captions for pictures and the legends on graphs, charts, or tables. Notice words in italics or dark print—usually a definition follows.

Read the Last Paragraph or Summary

The summary or last paragraph gives a condensed view of the chapter and helps you identify key ideas. Often the summary outlines the key points in the chapter.

Read Quickly Any End-of-Article or End-of-Chapter Material

This might include references, study questions, vocabulary lists, or biographical information about the author. These materials will be useful later as you read and study the article or chapter, and it is important, as part of prereading, to note if such materials are included. If there are study questions, it is useful to read them through quickly since they will indicate what is important in the chapter. If a vocabulary list is included, rapidly skim through it to identify terms you will need to learn as you read.

DEMONSTRATION OF PREREADING

The textbook chapter excerpt seen in Figure 5-1 has been included to demonstrate what it is like to preread. This chapter excerpt is taken from an introductory text, *Psychology and Life*, by Philip G. Zimbardo (Glenview, Ill.: Scott, Foresman 1985). Features of this text are referred to frequently;

within communities and even across nations. The clearest example of this international concern for combating shared environmental stressors is the "acid rain" pollution that is harming the Canadian environment, in part caused by emissions from factories in the United States.

Coping Strategies

If living is inevitably stressful, and if too much stress can disrupt our lives, and even kill us, we need to learn how to cope so that we can survive. **Coping** refers to attempts to meet environmental demands in order to prevent negative consequences (Lazarus & Folkman, 1984). There are many different coping techniques, some of which will be more effective than others for a given person in a given situation.

Because animals in the wild must adapt biologically to their environment, their mechanisms for coping are coded in their genes and limited by the slow timetable of evolutionary processes. Human beings have a tremendous potential for adapting not only biologically, over generations, but psychologically, within a lifetime—even within a short period of time if they decide they want to change.

In this final section of the chapter, we will look at a variety of strategies that people use to reduce the amount of stress they experience and to lessen its harmful effects. Some strategies are ones that most of us use naturally and habitually, whereas others are special techniques that can be learned. Some strategies are individual ones, to be done "on one's own"; in contrast, social strategies depend on the presence of other people.

Problem-focused Versus Emotion-focused Coping

Coping strategies can be grouped into two main types, depending on whether the goal is to *deal with the problem* (problem-focused) or to *lessen the discomfort of it* (emotion-focused). Several subcategories of these two basic approaches are shown in **Table 14.5.**

The first main approach includes any strategy to deal *directly* with the stressor, whether through overt action or through realistic problem-solving mental activities. We face up to a bully or run away; we try to win him or her over with bribes or other incentives. Taking martial arts training or notifying the "proper authorities" are other approaches that may prevent a bully from continuing to be a threat. In all these strategies, our focus is on the *problem* to be dealt with and on the agent that has induced the stress. We acknowledge the "call to action," we appraise the situation and our resources for dealing with it, and we undertake a response that is appropriate for removing or lessening the threat.

In the second approach, we do not look for ways of changing the stressful situation; instead we try to change our feelings and thoughts about it. This coping strategy is called *emotion regulation*. It is a remedial, rather than a problem-solving strategy, because it is aimed at relieving the emotional impact of stress to make us feel better, even though the threatening or harmful stressor is not changed. Relying on this approach, people may take alcohol or tranquilizers—and these may work for a while. On occasion, haven't you dealt with an unpleasant event by using consciously planned distractions such as going to a party or watching TV? Some-

Table 14.5 *Taxonomy of Coping Strategies*

Problem-focused Coping Change stressor or one's relationship to it through direct actions and/or problem-solving activities	Fight (destroy, remove, or weaken the threat)
	Flight (distance oneself from the threat)
	Seek options to fight or flight (negotiating, bargaining, compromising)
	Prevent future stress (act to increase one's resistance or decrease strength of anticipated stress)
Emotion-focused Coping Change self through "activities" that make one feel better but do not change the stressor	Somatically focused activities (use of drugs, relaxation, biofeedback)
	Cognitively focused activities (planned distractions, fantasies, thoughts about oneself)
	Unconscious processes that distort reality and result in intrapsychic stress

(Lazarus, 1975)

FIGURE 5-1   Prereading

times, we confront our fears by "whistling a happy tune" or with laughter (see *Close-up,* p. 511). However, this approach to coping has its drawbacks.

> One research study compared depressed and nondepressed middle-aged people over a one-year period. It was found that those who were depressed were using appraisals and coping patterns that created problems and perpetuated their depression. They were just as likely as the nondepressed to feel that something could be done about the situations they faced, and even to focus on problem solutions, but they diverged in their tendency to accentuate the negative. They worried more about not being stronger, wished they could change themselves and/or the situation, kept putting off action until they had more information, and spent more time seeking emotional support for their feelings of distress. What emerged was an indecisive coping style that was likely to promote a sense of personal inadequacy—which, in turn, was a source of more depression. (Coyne et al., 1981)

The ego defense mechanisms discussed in chapter 12 (such as repression, denial of reality, and rationalization) are familiar emotion-regulating approaches. Undertaken unconsciously to protect us from the pain of inner anxieties, they enable us to appraise situations in less self-threatening ways. They lead to coping strategies that are essentially aimed at self-protection rather than at solving problems. At times, however, they cause us to distort reality and, when overused, can lead to maladaptive coping.

Altering Bodily Reactions

"Stress equals tension" for many people. This often means tight muscles, high blood pressure, constricted blood vessels in the brain, and chronic oversecretion of hormones. Fortunately, many of these tension responses can be controlled by a variety of techniques—some ages old, some quite new.

Relaxation

Relaxation through meditation has ancient roots in many parts of the world. For centuries in Eastern cultures, ways to calm the mind and still the body's tensions have been practiced. Today Zen discipline and Yoga exercises from Japan and India are part of daily life for many people both there and, increasingly, in the West. In our own culture, a growing number of people have been attracted to workshops and therapy in relaxation training and to various forms of meditation.

Just as stress is the nonspecific response of the body to any demand made on it, there is growing evidence that complete relaxation is a potent antistress response. The *relaxation response* is a condition in which muscle tension, cortical activity, heart rate, and blood pressure all decrease and breathing slows. There is reduced electrical activity in the brain, and input to the central nervous system from the outside environment is lowered. In this low level of arousal, recuperation from stress can take place. Four conditions are regarded as necessary to produce the relaxation response: (a) a quiet environment, (b) closed eyes, (c) a comfortable position, and (d) a repetitive mental device. The first three lower input to the nervous system, while the fourth lowers its internal stimulation (Benson, 1975).

Progressive relaxation is a technique that has been widely used in American psychotherapy. Designed by Edmund Jacobson (1970), the approach teaches people alternately to tense and relax their muscles. In this way they learn the experience of relaxation and discover how to extend it to each specific muscle. After several months of daily practice with progressive relaxation, people are able to achieve deep levels of relaxation. The relaxation response can also be produced by hypnosis. The beneficial effects of these relaxation training methods extend beyond the time when people are actively practicing them. For example, in one study hypertensive patients who learned to lower their blood pressure by relaxing continued to have lower blood pressure when they were asleep (Agras et al., 1980).

Biofeedback

Biological feedback, or *biofeedback,* was described briefly in chapter 8. Sophisticated recording devices and computers make it possible to provide this feedback by detecting small changes in a body process, amplifying them, and indicating they are present by means of a visual or auditory signal which is "on" whenever the change is occurring. Paradoxically, although individuals do not know how they do it, concentrating on the desired result in the presence of this signal produces change in the desired direction. Biofeedback is a self-regulatory technique being used for a variety of special applications, such as control of blood pressure, relaxation of forehead muscles (involved in tension headaches), and even overcoming extreme blushing. This method is also being used to induce nonspecific general relaxation (Birbaumer and Kimmel, 1979).

FIGURE 5-1 *(Continued)*

the complete chapter is included in Appendix A. To illustrate how pre-reading is done, these pages have been specially marked. Everything that you should look at or read has been shaded. Preread this excerpt now, reading only the shaded portions of each page.

Now that you have seen what it is like to preread, you are ready to test the technique and observe its benefits. Turn to the sample textbook chapter "Health, Stress, and Coping" in Appendix A (page 381). You have already preread two pages. Preread the entire chapter. You should not spend more than five minutes. When you finish, answer each question in the following exercise.

EXERCISE 1 ⸻⸻⸻⸻⸻

Directions: *Answer each of the following questions after you have preread the sample textbook chapter in Appendix A. Mark* T *after statements that are true and* F *after those that are false. Do not look back in the chapter to locate the answers. When you finish, check your answers in the answer key and write your score in the space indicated.*

1. Coping is the means of handling stress. ⸻⸻

2. All coping strategies are equally effective. ⸻⸻

3. Two kinds of coping strategies are the problem-focused and the solution-focused strategies. ⸻⸻

4. Emotion regulation is a coping strategy. ⸻⸻

5. Relaxation is a relatively newly discovered coping strategy. ⸻⸻

6. Stress equals tension. ⸻⸻

7. The relaxation response involves lowering blood pressure, breathing, and muscle tension. ⸻⸻

8. Relaxation techniques have been used in psychotherapy. ⸻⸻

9. Biofeedback is a means of eliminating sources of stress. ⸻⸻

10. A high level of stress can be physically dangerous. ⸻⸻

Score (number right): ⸻⸻

Look back at your score on the quiz in Exercise 1. Most likely you got at least half of the questions right, perhaps more. This quiz was a test of the main ideas that were presented in the chapter. You can see, then, that prereading does familiarize you with the chapter and enables you to identify and remember many of the main ideas it contains. Actually, each part of the chapter that you read while prereading provided you with specific information about the organization and content of the chapter. The following exercise emphasizes how each step in the prereading process provides you with useful information about the material to be read.

EXERCISE 2 _____

Directions: *Listed below are various parts of an actual textbook chapter or article to which you would refer in prereading. Read the parts; then answer the question that follows.*

1. *Sample text*
   Title: *Introductory Psychology*
   Subtitle: *Selected Case Studies and Readings*
   Question: What further information does the subtitle provide about the text content?

   _____

   _____

2. *Sample article*
   Title: "Psychologists Have Proof of ESP"
   Source: *Today's Women* magazine
   Question: Answer with yes or no. Would you expect this article to
   a. be technical?
   b. be highly factual with careful references?
   c. contain accounts of individuals with ESP?
   d. contain opinions?
   e. contain references for further study?

3. *Sample text*
   Section heading: Culture and Technology
   Subheadings: Historical Roots and Trends
   Recent Technological Changes
   Predicted Long-Range Effects
   Question: What clues do you have about how the author arranged ideas in this section of the text?

   _____

   _____

4. *Sample text*
   Title: *Business Management*
   Subtitle: *An Organizational Perspective*
   Copyright: 1974
   Question: What does this information tell you about the usefulness and limitations of the material contained in this text?

   _____

   _____

5. *Sample text*
   Title: *Biology*
   Chapter title: "The Human Animal: An Introduction"
   Chapter summary:
   We are vertebrates. As such, we have a bony, jointed supporting

endoskeleton that includes a skull and a vertebral column enclosing the central nervous system. Our bodies contain a coelom that is divided by a muscle, the diaphragm, into two major compartments, the abdominal cavity and the thoracic cavity.

Our bodies are organized into tissues and organs. Tissues are groups of cells that are structurally, functionally, and developmentally similar. Various types of tissues are grouped in different ways to form organs, and organs are grouped to form organ systems. The four principal tissue types of which our bodies are made are epithelial tissue, connective tissue, muscle, and nerve. Epithelium serves as a covering or lining for the body and its cavities. Glands are composed of specialized epithelial cells. Their secretions include mucus, perspiration, milk, saliva, hormones, and digestive enzymes. Connective tissues are characterized by their capacity to secrete substances, such as collagen and other fibers, that make up the intercellular matrix. They serve to support, strengthen, and protect the other tissues of the body. Muscle cells are specialized for contraction. Muscle is categorized as striated muscle or smooth muscle. In striated muscle, which includes cardiac and skeletal muscle, the striped pattern is due to regular assemblies of specialized proteins, actin and myosin. Smooth muscle, or involuntary muscle, is under the control of the autonomic nervous system, whereas striated muscle (with the exception of cardiac muscle) is under somatic control. Nerve cells, or neurons, are specialized for the conduction of an electrical impulse. Neurons consist of dendrites, a cell body, and an axon. Neurons are surrounded and supported by neuroglia or Schwann cells.

A multicellular animal processes nutrients to yield energy and structural materials. It regulates its internal environment, a process known as homeostasis. It coordinates the activities of its many tissues and organ systems in response to changes in both the internal and external environments. These integration and control systems characteristically function through negative feedback loops. Finally, as dictated by its genes, the organism reproduces itself.

–Curtis, *Biology*, p. 670

Question: The chapter will emphasize
    a. the human as a vertebrate
    b. the organization and functioning of the human body
    c. the four principal tissue types
    d. integration and control systems

6. *Sample text*
        Title: *Organizational Behavior and Performance*
    Chapter title: "Leadership"
Chapter introduction:
Leadership is one of the most important elements affecting organizational performance. For the manager, leadership is activity through which the goals and objectives of the organization are accomplished. Leadership has been the focus of attention of behavioral scientists because leaders have a significant effect on the behavior, attitudes, and performances of employees.

Leadership has been studied for a number of years, resulting in numerous theories and models. Like motivation, no universally

accepted theoretical framework of leadership has been developed.
This chapter will examine the development of leadership theory
from early studies to current situational approaches. We will first
examine the concept of influence as one foundation of leadership,
and then discuss the three main theoretical approaches to
leadership—trait, behavioral, and situational theories. Finally, we
will present some contemporary issues in leadership and combine
the presented material in an integrative model that stresses the
importance of a manager's developing the ability to *diagnose* a
situation and alter his or her style of leadership in the most effective
manner.

–Szilagyi and Wallace, *Organizational Behavior and Performance*, p. 317

Questions: a. Describe the chapter's organization.

_____

b. The chapter will focus primarily on
1. historical approaches to leadership
2. current problems in leadership
3. diagnosing a leadership style
4. theories of leadership

7. *Sample text*
Title: *Our Changing Economy*
Subtitle: *An Introduction to Economics*
Chapter title: "Why Are There Economic Systems?"
Graphic aids: The chapter includes the following graphic aids:
a. a graph showing the relationship between production of various types of goods and price
b. a "Beetle Bailey" cartoon that illustrates that choice is associated with cost
c. a picture of various objects that have been used as money in various cultures throughout the world
Question: What clues do the graph, cartoon, and picture give you about the chapter content?

_____

_____

8. *Sample text*
Title: *The World Today*
Subtitle: *Its Patterns and Cultures*
Chapter title: "The Orient"
Section headings: This chapter is divided into four major sections:
a. The Heritage of the Past in the Orient
b. How the People of the Orient Make a Living
c. New Directions for India, Pakistan, and Southeast Asia
d. The People's Republic of China, Democracy, and the Uncommitted Orient

Question: By noting the section titles within this chapter, what do you expect about the organization and content of the chapter?

_____

_____

HOW TO PREREAD ARTICLES AND CHAPTERS WITHOUT HEADINGS

Earlier in this chapter you learned that when prereading you should read boldface (dark print) headings. However, much material is written without these convenient labels of section content. In articles and chapters without headings, prereading becomes more time-consuming because you must read the first sentence of each paragraph. As you will see later in the text, by reading the first sentence of each paragraph, you are often reading the main idea of the paragraph. Articles or chapters without headings may still have introductory and concluding portions, graphic material, and questions at the end. You can also get ideas from the organization of the material. Is it a list of ideas on the topic? Is it a series of events? If you can see this, you will know what to expect in the rest of the article or chapter.

PREREADING SPECIFIC TYPES OF MATERIAL

Textbooks

Whenever you purchase a new textbook, it is useful to preread it before you begin to read specific assignments. If you are familiar with the overall organization, purpose, and content of the text, you will find that the individual chapters make more sense. You might think of individual chapters of a text as the pieces of a picture puzzle. When the pieces of the puzzle are put together, you can see the function of each piece, but each piece by itself has little meaning. Similarly, textbook chapters become more meaningful when seen as a functioning part of the entire text.

To preread a text, check the following:

1. _The title and subtitle._
2. _The author(s)._ In many cases, the name will be unfamiliar, but as you acquire knowledge in new fields of study, you will begin to recognize names of authorities.
3. _The publication or copyright date._ It is always useful to be aware of how up to date the text is. Especially in rapidly developing fields, a chapter written several years ago may be seriously outdated.
4. _The table of contents._ The table of contents provides a brief outline of the entire text. It lists all the major topics covered in the text and indicates how the text is organized.
5. _The preface or "Note to Students" at the beginning of the text._ This introductory portion of the text often contains important information about the text's organization and use.

6. *Learning aids.* Numerous learning aids are included within or at the end of each chapter and at the end of the text. Chapter 10, "Textbook Aids to Learning," discusses these aids in detail.

Textbook Chapters

This technique of prereading is highly effective when used in reading textbook chapters. When approaching a lengthy textbook chapter, first preread it entirely, noting only major groups of ideas. Then divide the chapter into smaller segments or sections and preread, then read, each section.

Articles and Selections

When prereading magazine articles, journal articles, or excerpts included within a book, in addition to the items listed earlier under the section "How to Preread," be sure to pay particular attention to:

1. *The title.* It often suggests the topic and author's focus, although sometimes it is intended to catch your interest.
2. *The author.* Check to see who wrote the material. If you are able to recognize the author's name, then you can form a set of expectations about the content of the article.
3. *The source.* When prereading material reprinted from another source, use the footnote or acknowledgment at the beginning or end to determine where the material was originally published. How much you accept of what is said depends on the type of publication the article appeared in. For example, you would expect an article on aggression published in the *Journal of Psychology* to be more research oriented than an article on the same topic published in a weekly news magazine.

Research and Reference Material

When you are collecting information for a class assignment or research paper, prereading is a valuable technique to use to identify sources that contain the information you need. When you have identified a book that appears to contain information on the topic you are researching, take a few moments to preread before checking it out of the library or using valuable time reading it unnecessarily. By prereading you may find that the source does not contain information you need, that it is too general or too detailed for your purpose, or that it only contains information you have already collected from another source.

To preread reference material, first check the index and table of contents. Then, if your topic is listed, quickly preread the appropriate sections or chapters to determine if they contain information that suits your purpose.

Newspapers

Information in newspaper articles is structured differently from most other types of writing. In contrast to most material in which the first few sentences are introductory, the opening sentences in news stories frequently carry the *most* important information. As the article progresses, the facts presented become more and more detailed, and you find more background information. To preread a news article, then, read the headline, the first few lines, and section headings; then glance through the rest of the article, picking up details such as names, dates, and places.

LIMITATIONS OF PREREADING

Prereading is used best with expository, factual material that is fairly well organized. Knowing this, you can see that prereading is not a good strategy to use when reading materials such as novels, poems, narrative articles, essays, or short stories. However, you will find it fairly easy to adapt the prereading technique to various types of writing you read.

DOES PREREADING WORK?

Research studies suggest that prereading does increase comprehension and improve recall. Several studies show that prereading is a useful technique for reading textbook chapters. In a study done by McClusky,* college students were divided into two groups. One group was taught how to use headings and summaries for prereading; the other group received no instruction. Both groups were given a selection to read and comprehension questions to answer. Results of the study indicated that the group who used headings and summaries read 24 percent faster and just as accurately as the students who did not preread.

WHAT DOES PREREADING ACCOMPLISH?

First, prereading helps you get interested in and involved with what you will read. It activates your thinking. Through prereading, you become familiar with the material or gain advance information about it. You become acquainted with the general subject of the material, you discover who wrote it, and you learn when and where it was published. You also become aware of the main subtopics and how they are organized. Because you know what to expect, then, reading the material completely will be easier.

Second, prereading helps bring to mind what you already know about the subject, thereby making the material more meaningful and interesting.

Third, prereading provides you with a mental outline of the material you are going to read. As you read the headings of a chapter, you are actually forming a mental outline of the chapter. You begin to anticipate the sequence of ideas; you see the relationships of topics to one another; you recognize what approach and direction the author has taken in writing

*H. Y. McClusky, "An Experiment on the Influence of Preliminary Skimming on Reading," *Journal of Educational Psychology*, 25 (1934): 521–29.

about his or her subject. With this outline in mind, the actual reading is a much simpler task. Reading the chapter becomes a matter of filling in the parts of the outline with the proper details.

Fourth, prereading is useful because it enables you to apply several principles of learning. Through prereading, you identify what is important, thus establishing an intent to remember. Prereading also facilitates meaningfulness by allowing you to become familiar with the basic content and organization of the material. Because prereading also provides an additional repetition of the major points, it functions as a type of rehearsal that enhances recall.

EXERCISE 3 ————————————————

Directions: *Select a chapter from one of your textbooks. To be practical, choose a chapter that you will be assigned to read in the near future. After prereading it, answer the following questions.*

1. What is the major topic of the chapter?

   _____

2. How does the author subdivide or break down this topic?

   _____

3. What approach does the author take toward the subject? (Does he or she cite research, give examples, describe problems, list causes?)

   _____

4. Can you construct a very general mental outline of the chapter?

   _____

SUMMARY

Prereading is a technique that allows the reader to become familiar with the material to be read before beginning to read it completely. The technique involves checking specific parts of an article or textbook chapter that provide the reader with a mental outline of the content of the material. Prereading makes the actual reading of the material easier and helps the reader understand and remember what he or she reads. In prereading, the reader should note items such as the following: title and subtitle; the author and source; publication or copyright date; introduction or first paragraph; each boldface (dark print) heading and the first sentence under it; typographical aids (italics, maps, pictures, charts, graphs); summary or last paragraph; and end-of-chapter or end-of-article materials.

6

Strategies for Active Reading

Use this chapter to:

1. *Activate your background knowledge.*
2. *Establish your purposes for reading.*
3. *Select appropriate reading strategies.*
4. *Monitor your comprehension.*

To those unfamiliar with the game, basketball might seem to be only a matter of placing a ball in a basket while preventing the opposing team members from doing the same. Similarly, football might appear to be a simple process of scoring field goals and touchdowns. Players of these games know, however, that each is a complex process involving skill, knowledge, and experience. Football players must develop skill in running, blocking, tackling, and passing; they must learn plays, rules, and penalties; they must practice and draw upon their past experience to anticipate the opposing team's actions.

Reading, too, may at first appear to be a simple physical process of moving one's eyes across lines of print. Like football, however, reading is a complex activity involving skill, knowledge, and experience. A reader must have skills in recognizing words, understanding main ideas and details, and following organizational development. Knowledge is required in understanding word meanings (you must know what an elephant is and looks like, for example, in order for the word *elephant* to be meaningful). Finally, experience is required to anticipate the author's ideas, decide what ideas are important, and evaluate and remember them.

The purpose of this chapter is to present several strategies that will improve your ability to handle the complex task of reading. The strategies are designed to improve your overall reading skill and efficiency. In subsequent units, you will then learn more specific comprehension and vocabulary skills.

ACTIVATE YOUR KNOWLEDGE AND EXPERIENCE

We have numerous sets of knowledge and experience that enable us to make sense of the world around us. You might think of these as blueprints or windows of experience that provide a structure to handle and interpret daily activities. You are familiar with general shapes, characteristics, or patterns of thousands of items, ideas, and actions. For example, you can recognize that a new four-wheel vehicle is a car, even if you've never seen that particular make or model before. You can recognize that a speaker is about to summarize his points even though you have not heard the speech before. You can recognize when a friend is about to ask for a favor. Each of these items has general characteristics with which you are familiar.

These sets of knowledge and experience are known as *schemata*. Schemata can greatly assist you in reading and study. First, they make content meaningful, and second, they enable you to tie or associate new information to previously learned material. Before you read or study a new topic, take a few moments to activate your schemata on the topic. Discover what you already know about the topic. Most students are surprised to find that there are very few topics about which they know nothing at all.

background knowelege

Suppose you are about to begin reading a chapter in a business textbook on advertising. Let's assume you have already preread it and you know that it covers three major topics: objectives of advertising, construction and design of ads, and production of ads. Before you begin reading the chapter, you should spend a minute or two recalling what you already know about these topics. You could activate your background information and experience with the topic by using one of the following techniques:

1. *Ask questions and try to answer them.* You might ask questions such as "What are the objectives of advertising?" In answering this question you will realize you already know several objectives: to sell a product, to introduce a new product, to announce sales or discounts, and so forth.
2. *Relate the topic to your own experience.* For a topic on the construction and design of ads, think about ads you have heard or read recently. What similarities exist? How do they begin? How do they end? Most likely, this process will lead you to realize that you already know something about how ads are designed.
3. *Free associate.* On a scrap sheet of paper, jot down everything that comes to mind about advertising. List facts and questions, or describe ads that you have recently heard or seen. This process will also activate your recall of information.

Activating your background knowledge on a topic before reading makes for effective learning because

1. It allows you to relate new information to information already stored in your memory. Learning will thus occur more easily and retrieval will be more efficient.
2. Topics become more interesting if you can connect them to your own experience.
3. Material that is meaningful is easier to learn and remember than that which is not.
4. Comprehension will be easier because you will have already thought about some of the ideas the assignment presents.

EXERCISE 1

Directions: *Preread the section "Health and Health Psychology" (pages 383–390) in the sample textbook chapter reprinted in Appendix A. Activate your background knowledge on the topic of prevention of illness by listing as many serious illnesses as you can think of, their causes, and how to prevent them.*

_____

_____

_____

EXERCISE 2 _____

Directions: *Assume you have just preread a chapter in a sociology text on domestic violence. Activate your knowledge of the topic using each of the techniques suggested above. Then answer the following questions.*

1. Did you discover you knew more about domestic violence than you initially thought?

   _____

2. Which technique worked best? Why?

   _____

3. Might the technique you choose depend on the subject matter with which you are working?

   _____

EXERCISE 3 _____

Directions: *Select a chapter from one of your textbooks. Preread it and then use one of the above techniques to discover what you already know about the topics covered in the chapter.*

ESTABLISH YOUR PURPOSES FOR READING

Have you ever read a complete page or more and then not remembered a thing you read? Have you wandered aimlessly through paragraph after paragraph, section after section, unable to remember key ideas you have just read, even when you were really trying to concentrate? If these problems sound familiar, you probably began reading without a specific purpose in mind. That is, you were not looking for anything in particular as you read. Perhaps the single most important thing to do to understand and remember more of what you read is to identify your purposes—to decide what facts and ideas you are looking for, and then read to find them.

By now, you are probably beginning to see the relationship of prereading, discussed in the last chapter, to identifying purposes for reading. Prereading helps you identify the topics that are included in the assignment. The next step is to develop guide questions that will focus your attention and lead you through the material.

Developing Guide Questions

Most textbook chapters use boldface headings to organize chapter content. The simplest way to establish a purpose for reading is to change each heading into one or more questions that will guide your reading. As you read, you then look for the answers. For a section with the heading "The Hidden Welfare System," you could ask the questions, What is the hidden welfare system? and How does it work? As you read that section, you would actively search for answers. Or for a section of a business textbook titled "Taxonomy of Organizational Research Strategies," you could pose such questions as, What is a taxonomy? or What research strategies are discussed and how are they used?

The excerpt printed below is taken from a psychology textbook chapter on sensation and perception. Before reading it, formulate several guide questions and list them here. Read to find the answers. After you have read the article, fill in the answers below.

Question 1: _____

_____

Answer: _____

_____

Question 2: _____

_____

Answer: _____

_____

CLASSIFYING THE SENSES

Most people learn quite early about the five basic senses: vision, audition, taste, smell, and touch. Few learn that this five-way classification dates to the Greek philosopher Aristotle, and just as few know that in fact there are many more than five senses and that Aristotle's classification is largely arbitrary. For example, touch (or the skin senses as they are more properly called) tells much more than how things "feel"; it also registers temperature, vibration, pain, and many other properties. Similarly, such perceptual experience of the world results from the senses working in close coordination. Locating an object often depends on eyes, ears, and touch working simultaneously. You will, for example, find it harder to tell where a sound originates with your eyes closed than with them open. Last, people sense the position of their limbs (the kinesthetic sense) and state of balance with respect to gravity (vestibular sense) without drawing on the five classical senses.

–Roediger et al., *Psychology*, p. 35

Most likely, you developed questions such as, What are the senses? and How are they classified? Then as you read the section, you found out that, in addition to the five basic senses, there are also kinesthetic and vestibular senses. You also discovered that the five-way classification of sensory perception, dating back to Aristotle, is not completely accurate as well as somewhat arbitrary. Did the guide questions help you focus your attention and make the passage easier to read?

Some students find it helpful to jot down their guide questions in the margins of their texts, next to the appropriate headings. These questions are then available for later study. Reviewing and answering your questions is an excellent method of review.

Formulating the Right Questions

Guide questions that begin with *What, Why,* and *How* are especially effective. *Who, When,* and *Where* questions are less useful because they can often be answered through superficial reading or may lead to simple, factual, or one-word answers. *What, Why,* and *How* questions, however, require detailed answers that demand more thought, and as a result, they force you to read in more depth in order to construct acceptable answers.

A section in a history text titled "The Fall of the Roman Empire," for example, could be turned into a question such as, When did the Roman Empire fall? For this question, the answer is merely a date. This question, then, would not guide your reading effectively. On the other hand, questions such as, How did the Roman Empire fall? What brought about the fall of the Roman Empire? or What factors contributed to the fall of the Roman Empire? would require you to recall important events and identify causes or reasons.

Here are a few examples of effective guide questions:

Heading	*Effective Guide Questions*
Management of Stress in Organizations	What types of stress occur?
	How is it controlled?
Theories of Leadership	What are the theories of leadership?
	How are they applied or used?
Styles of Leader Behavior	What are the styles of leader behavior?
	How do they differ?
	How effective are they?

EXERCISE 4 _____

Directions: *Assume that each of the following is a boldface heading within a textbook chapter and that related textual material follows. In the space provided, write questions that would guide your reading.*

1. Operating System Aids to Efficient Merging of Computer Files

   _____

   _____

2. Natural Immunity and Blood Types

   _____

   _____

3. Production of Electromagnetic Waves

_____

_____

4. Physical Changes in Adolescence

_____

_____

5. Sociological Factors Related to Delinquency

_____

_____

6. The Circular Flow of Spending, Production, and Income

_____

_____

7. Influence of "Experts" on Child-rearing Practices

_____

_____

8. Appraisal of Job Performance and Effectiveness

_____

_____

9. Inheritance of Physical Characteristics

_____

_____

10. Language Skills of Disadvantaged Children

_____

_____

Written Materials Without Headings

In articles and essays without headings, the title often provides a general overall purpose, and the first sentence of each paragraph can often be used to form a guide question about each paragraph. In the following paragraph, the first sentence could be turned into a question that would guide your reading.

Despite its recent increase in popularity, hypnotism has serious limitations that restrict its widespread use. First of all, not everyone is susceptible to hypnotism. Second, a person who does not cooperate with the hypnotist is unlikely to fall into a hypnotic trance. Finally, there are limits to the commands a subject will obey when hypnotized. In many cases, subjects will not do anything which violates their moral code.

From the first sentence you could form the question: What are the limitations of hypnotism? In reading the remainder of the paragraph, you would find three limitations: (1) Some people cannot be hypnotized; (2) the subject must cooperate or hypnosis will not occur; and (3) subjects will not follow commands to do what they believe is wrong.

EXERCISE 5 _____

Directions: *Assume that each of the following sentences is the first sentence of a paragraph within an article that does not contain boldface headings. Beside each sentence, write a guide question.*

First Sentence	Question
1. Historically, there have been three major branches of philosophical analysis.	_____ _____ _____
2. Scientists who are studying earthquakes attribute their cause to intense pressures and stresses that build up inside the earth.	_____ _____ _____
3. The way in which managers and employees view and treat conflict has changed measurably over the last fifty years.	_____ _____ _____
4. In the Marxist view, the government serves as an agent of social control.	_____ _____ _____
5. Perhaps it will be easier to understand the nature and function of empathetic listening if we contrast it to deliberative listening.	_____ _____ _____

6. The different types of drill presses for performing drilling and allied operations vary in design and specific function.

_____

_____

_____

7. To read data from a disk, the operating system has to know the sector and the track that contain the data.

_____

_____

_____

_____

8. In addition to the price of a good or service, there are dozens, perhaps hundreds, of other factors and circumstances affecting a person's decision to buy or not to buy.

_____

_____

_____

9. Although sometimes used interchangeably, poor nutritional states can be categorized as malnutrition, undernutrition, or overnutrition.

_____

_____

_____

10. Among the most important changes of the twentieth century is the rise of large governments.

_____

_____

_____

Are Guide Questions Effective?

A number of research studies have been conducted to test whether establishing purposes by forming guide questions improves understanding and recall of information. These studies confirm the effectiveness of guide questions and indicate that students who read with a purpose have a higher percentage of recall of factual information than students who read without a specific purpose.

In one experiment conducted by Frase and Schwartz,* for example, sixty-four college students were divided into two groups. Both groups were given a passage to read and study. One group (Group A) was directed to construct and write out questions based on the text; the other group (Group B) was simply directed to study the material. The results were as follows:

Group	Percentage of Recall
Group A	72%
Group B	53%

*L. T. Frase and B. J. Schwartz, "Effect of Question Production and Answering on Prose Recall," *Journal of Educational Psychology*, 67 (1975): 628–635.

The group that established a purpose for reading by forming questions recalled 19 percent more than the group that read without establishing a purpose.

Developing guide questions fulfills an essential principle of learning: the intent to remember. It focuses your attention on what is important—on what you are supposed to read and remember. Guide questions also force you to read actively—to sort out, process, and evaluate ideas to determine if they answer your guide question.

EXERCISE 6 _____

Directions: *Turn to the sample textbook chapter included in Appendix B (pages 412–423). Beginning with the heading "Homeotherms," form questions that would be useful in guiding your reading. Work through the next five pages, listing the questions you formed in the space provided below. Then read these pages and answer your questions on a separate sheet of paper.*

_____

_____

_____

_____

_____

EXERCISE 7 _____

Directions: *Choose a three-to-four-page selection from one of your textbooks. Select pages that have already been assigned or that you anticipate will be assigned. For each heading, form and record guide questions that establish a purpose for reading. Then read the selection and answer your questions.*

③ SELECT APPROPRIATE READING-STUDY STRATEGIES

Many students approach all their assignments in the same way, only to find out later that a different approach would have produced better results and saved valuable time. Here is an example:

> Jason was preparing for a midterm examination in human anatomy and physiology. As soon as the date of the exam was announced he began to prepare detailed outlines of each chapter. The night before the exam, while studying with a classmate, he discovered that a system of testing himself by drawing and labeling diagrams and making tables and function charts would have been a more active and effective means of learning.

This student approached his assignment mechanically and routinely. Instead, he should have analyzed the learning task and considered how to accomplish it most effectively.

Suppose you must review several chapters in your mass media and communications text in order to prepare for an essay exam. The first step is to analyze the assignment and then to select the strategy that will help you learn and remember as much as possible. Try to choose a strategy that fits the nature of the material to be reviewed and the type of exam you anticipate. Since an essay exam requires recall and written expression of ideas, you would predict possible essay questions and organize information to answer each.

Here are a few suggestions to use in deciding how to approach an assignment:

1. *Analyze the assignment.* Determine in as much detail as possible what you are expected to accomplish. Must you learn facts, dates, or formulas, understand theories, or solve problems? Is thorough, detailed recall required, or is your instructor concerned primarily with ideas and trends?

2. *Identify your options.* What strategies can you use? Consider several different ways to approach the task. For example, is thorough reading necessary? Can you afford to skim-read? Is note-taking needed or is underlining sufficient? Should you focus on details—dates, numbers, and facts, or concepts, trends, and patterns?

3. *Try to match the strategy to the material.* As you will see in later chapters, not all learning strategies are equally effective in all situations. To strike the best match, ask yourself questions such as:

1. What type of thinking and learning are required? For example, is the task primarily a problem-solving one, or does it require creative thought?
2. What level of recall is required—facts and details or just major concepts?
3. Am I expected to make applications?
4. Am I expected to evaluate and criticize?

EXERCISE 8 ———————————————

Directions: *On a separate sheet, analyze each of the following assignments. Decide what is expected in each assignment. Then suggest an approach that might be effective.*

1. Studying a chapter on probability in a math textbook.
2. Writing an analysis of a poem by John Donne for your English composition and introduction to literature class.
3. Reading a chapter in a criminology textbook in preparation for a class discussion and, eventually, an essay exam.

EXERCISE 9 ———————————————

Directions: *On a separate sheet, list all the assignments you have been given for this week in each of your courses. Then answer the following questions.*

1. Do the assignments differ in what is expected of you? If so, how?
2. How will you vary your approach to each assignment?

For many daily activities you maintain an awareness or "check" on how well you are performing them. In sports such as racquetball, tennis, or bowling, you know if you are playing a poor game; you actually keep score and deliberately try to correct errors and improve your performance. When preparing a favorite food, you often taste it as you work to be sure it will turn out as you want. When washing your car, you check to be sure that you have not missed any spots.

A similar type of checking should occur as you read. You should be aware of, or monitor, your performance. You need to "keep score" of how effectively and efficiently you are comprehending. However, since reading is a mental process, it is more difficult to monitor than bowling or cooking. There is very little clear, observable evidence to suggest whether you are on the right track when reading. Comprehension is also difficult to keep track of because it is not always either good or poor. You may understand certain ideas you read and be confused by others. At times, comprehension may be incomplete, you may miss certain key ideas and not know you missed them.

Recognizing Comprehension Signals

Think for a moment about what occurs when you read material you can understand easily and then compare this to what happens when you read complicated material that is difficult for you to understand. When you read certain material, does it seem that everything "clicks"—that is, do ideas seem to fit together and make sense? Is that "click" noticeably absent at other times?

Read each of the following paragraphs. As you read, be alert to your level of understanding of each.

PARAGRAPH 1

The two most common drugs that are legal and do not require a prescription are caffeine and nicotine. Caffeine is the active ingredient in coffee, tea, and many cola drinks. It stimulates the central nervous system and heart and therefore is often used to stay awake. Heavy use—say, seven to ten cups of coffee per day—has toxic effects, that is, acts like a mild poison. Prolonged heavy use appears to be addicting. Nicotine is the active ingredient in tobacco. One of the most addicting of all drugs and one of the most dangerous, at least when obtained by smoking, it has been implicated in lung cancer, emphysema, and heart disease.

–Geiwitz, *Psychology: Looking at Ourselves*, p. 276

PARAGRAPH 2

In the HOSC experiment, two variables were of sufficient importance to include as stratification (classification) variables prior to the random assignment of class sections to treatments. These two stratification variables were science subject (biology, chemistry, or physics) and teacher's understanding of science (high or low). Inclusion of these two variables in the HOSC design allowed the experimenter to make generalizations about the HOSC treatment in terms of science subject matter and the teacher's understanding of science. Even if the HOSC experiments had selected a completely random sample of American high school science teacher–class sections, generalizations regarding the effectiveness of the HOSC treatment would only be possible in terms of the factors included in the experimental design. . . .

–Lohnes and Cooley, *Introduction to Statistical Procedures*, p. 11

Did you feel comfortable and confident as you read paragraph 1? Did ideas seem to lead from one to another and make sense? How did you feel while reading paragraph 2? Most likely you sensed its difficulty and felt confused. Unfamiliar words were used and you could not follow the flow of ideas, so that the whole passage didn't make sense.

As you read paragraph 2, did you know that you were not understanding it? Did you feel confused or uncertain? Table 6-1 lists and compares common signals that may assist you in monitoring your comprehension. Not all signals appear at the same time, and not all signals work for everyone. As you study the list, identify those positive signals you sensed as you read paragraph 1 on common drugs. Then identify the negative signals that you sensed when reading about the HOSC experiment.

TABLE 6-1   Comprehension Signals

Positive Signals	*Negative Signals*
Everything seems to fit and make sense; ideas flow logically from one to another.	Some pieces do not seem to belong; the material seems disjointed.
You understand what is important.	Nothing or everything seems important.
You are able to see where the author is leading.	You feel as if you are struggling to stay with the author and are unable to predict what will follow.
You are able to make connections among ideas.	You are unable to detect relationships; the organization is not apparent.
You read at a regular, comfortable pace.	You often slow down or reread.
You understand why the material was assigned.	You do not know why the material was assigned and cannot explain why it is important.
You can express the main ideas in your own words.	You must reread and use the author's language to explain an idea.
You recognize most words or can figure them out from context.	Many words are unfamiliar.
You feel comfortable and have some knowledge about the topic.	The topic is unfamiliar, yet the author assumes you understand it.

EXERCISE 10 _____

Directions: *Read the section "Principles of Heat Balance" in the sample textbook chapter reprinted in Appendix B (pages 413–416). Monitor your comprehension as you read. After reading the section, answer the following questions.*

1. How would you rate your overall comprehension? What positive signals did you sense? Did you feel any negative signals?
2. Test the accuracy of your rating in question 1 by answering the following questions based on the material you read.
    a. Name and explain three means of heat transfer.
    b. Explain the difference between a poikilotherm and a homeotherm. Give an example of each.
    c. Identify the two primary sources of heat gain upon which living organisms depend.
    d. How does an organism's size affect heat transfer?
3. Check your answers in the Answer Key. In what sections was your comprehension strongest?
4. Did you feel at any time that you had lost or were about to lose comprehension? If so, go back to that section now. What made that section difficult to read?

EXERCISE 11 _____

Directions: *Select a three-to-four page section of a chapter in one of your textbooks. Read the section and then answer questions 1, 3, 4, in the above exercise.*

Monitoring Techniques

At times signals of poor comprehension do not come through clearly or strongly enough. In fact, some students think they have understood what they read until they are questioned in class or take an exam. Only then do they discover that their comprehension was incomplete. Other students find that they comprehend material on a surface, factual level, but do not recognize more complicated relationships and implied meanings, or do not see implications and applications. Use the following monitoring techniques to determine if you really understand what you read.

1. *Establish checkpoints.* Race car drivers make pit stops during races for quick mechanical checks and repairs; athletes are subject to frequent physical tests and examinations. These activities provide an opportunity to evaluate or assess performance and to correct any problems or malfunctions. Similarly when reading it is necessary to stop and evaluate.

As you preview a textbook assignment, identify reasonable or logical checkpoints: points at which to stop, check, and if necessary, correct your performance before continuing. Pencil a checkmark in the margin to designate these points. These checkpoints should be logical breaking points where one topic ends and another begins, or where a topic is broken down into several subtopics. As you reach each of these checkpoints, stop and assess your work using the techniques described below.

2. *Use your guide questions.* Earlier in this chapter, you learned how to form guide questions using boldface headings. These same questions can be used to monitor your comprehension while reading. When you fin-

ish a boldface-headed section, stop and take a moment to recall your guide question and answer it mentally or on paper. Your ability to answer your questions will indicate your level of comprehension.

3. *Ask connection questions.* To be certain that your comprehension is complete and that you are not recalling only superficial factual information, ask connection questions. Connection questions are those that require you to think about content. They force you to draw together ideas and to discover relationships between the material at hand and other material in the same chapter, in other chapters, or in class lectures. Here are a few examples.

What does this topic have to do with topics discussed earlier in the chapter?

How does this reading assignment fit with the topics of this week's class lectures?

What does this chapter have to do with the chapter assigned last week?

What principle do these problems illustrate?

Connection questions enable you to determine whether your learning is meaningful—whether you are simply taking in information or whether you are using the information and fitting it into the scheme of the course. The best time to ask connection questions is before beginning and after you have finished a chapter or each major section.

4. *Use internal dialogue.* Internal dialogue, mentally talking to yourself, is another excellent means of monitoring your reading and learning. It involves rephrasing to yourself the message the author is communicating or the ideas you are studying. If you are unable to express ideas in your own words, your understanding is very likely incomplete. Here are a few examples of its use.

Think as the Teacher Thinks

a. While reading a section in a math textbook, you mentally outline the steps to follow in solving a sample problem.
b. You are reading an essay that argues convincingly that the threat of nuclear war is real. As you finish reading each stage of the argument, you rephrase it in your own words.
c. As you finish each boldface section in a psychology chapter, you summarize the key points.

EXERCISE 12 _____

Directions: *Refer to the section "The Concept of Stress" (pages 390–403) in the sample textbook chapter reprinted in Appendix A. Write a list of guide and connection questions you could pose for this section.*

Guide Questions

_____

_____

_____

_____

_____

_____

_____

_____

EXERCISE 13 _____

Directions: *Choose a section from one of your own textbooks. Read it and monitor your comprehension using both guide and connection questions. List your questions on a separate sheet of paper.*

EXERCISE 14 _____

Directions: *Select another section from one of your textbooks and experiment with the technique of internal dialogue to monitor your comprehension. In the space provided below, describe the technique you used and evaluate its effectiveness.*

_____

_____

_____

_____

Strengthening Your Comprehension

You have learned how to recognize clues that signal strong or weak understanding of reading material and how to monitor your comprehension. This section will offer some suggestions to follow when you realize you need to strengthen your comprehension.

1. *Analyze the time and place in which you are reading.* If you've been reading or studying for several hours, mental fatigue may be the source of the problem. If you are reading in a place with numerous distractions or interruptions, lack of concentration may contribute to comprehension loss. (See Chapter 4 for suggestions on how to monitor and improve your concentration.)
2. *Rephrase each paragraph in your own words.* You might need to approach extremely complicated material sentence by sentence, expressing each in your own words.
3. *Read aloud sentences or sections that are particularly difficult.* The auditory feedback signals that oral reading provides often aid comprehension.
4. *Do not hesitate to reread difficult or complicated sections.* In fact, at times several readings are appropriate and necessary.

5. *Slow down your reading rate.* On occasion simply reading more slowly and carefully will provide you with the needed boost in comprehension.

6. *Write guide questions next to headings.* Refer to your questions frequently and jot down or underline answers.

7. *Write a brief outline of major points.* This will help you see the overall organization and progression of ideas. (See Chapter 13 for specific outlining techniques.)

8. *Underline key ideas.* After you've read a section, go back and think about and underline what is important. Underlining forces you to sort out what is important, and this sorting process builds comprehension and recall. (Refer to Chapter 11 for suggestions on how to underline effectively.)

9. *Write notes in the margins.* Explain or rephrase difficult or complicated ideas or sections.

10. *Determine if you lack background knowledge.* Comprehension is difficult, or at times impossible, if you lack essential information that the writer assumes you have. Suppose you are reading a section of a political science text in which the author describes implications of the balance of power in the Third World. If you do not understand the concept of balance of power, your comprehension will break down. When you lack background information, take immediate steps to correct the problem:

> consult other sections of your text, using the glossary and index
> obtain a more basic text that reviews fundamental principles and concepts
> consult reference materials (encyclopedias, subject or biographical dictionaries)
> ask your instructor to recommend additional sources, guidebooks, or review texts.

EXERCISE 15 _____

Directions: *The following two passages have been chosen for their difficulty. Monitor your comprehension as you read each, paying attention to both positive and negative signals. After you have read each passage, list the signals you received (refer to Table 6-1) and indicate what you could do to strengthen your comprehension.*

PARAGRAPH 1

Throughout the last quarter-century, the debate regarding international economic development has been conducted principally between the traditionalists (whose analyses focus on modernization strategies) and the radicals (who prefer to concentrate on the intrinsic characteristics of the international system that perpetuate dependency). More recently, however, a number of scholars have suggested new approaches to the problem. One, for example, has noted that neither of the two dominant theories can explain the late development of some countries because economic advancement is not necessarily tied to exclusively economic factors. This observation leads to the conclusion that disparate paths to development must consider such local sociological factors as traditions, motives, attitudes, and religious influences upon traditionalism and modernism.

–Jones, *The Logic of International Relations*, pp. 212–213

Positive signals: _____

Negative signals: _____

Strengthen comprehension by: _____

_____

PARAGRAPH 2

Any form of law has as its incentives a variety of normative, utilitarian and coercive sanctions. An individual may drive his automobile lawfully because he fears the consequences of wrongdoing (fear of coercive sanction), or as a matter of personal safety (utilitarian sanction) or a contribution to orderly social coexistance (normative sanction). Likewise among states, compliance with rules of law is rather consistent, and is grounded in normative and utilitarian motives. Governments do generally regard reciprocal behavior as mutually beneficial, and are often sensitive to international pressures. They wish to avoid reprisals and embarrassing declarations and resolutions brought on by improper behavior, except when perceived needs exceed the risk of external criticism.

–Jones, *The Logic of International Relations*, p. 495

Positive signals: _____

Negative signals: _____

Strengthen comprehension by: _____

_____

EXERCISE 16 _____

Directions: *Select three brief sections from your most difficult textbook. Choose three of the above suggestions for strengthening your comprehension and list them below. Try out each suggestion on one textbook section. Evaluate and describe the effectiveness of each.*

	Suggestion	*Evaluation*
1.	_____	_____
2.	_____	_____
3.	_____	_____

SUMMARY

Reading is an active process requiring skills, knowledge, and experience. To read most effectively, first discover what you already know about a topic by asking questions, drawing from your own experience, or free associating. Before reading, establish purposes for reading. Do this by developing guide questions based on boldface headings or topic sentences. Then, as you begin reading or studying, analyze the assignment and select strategies that suit the task and the material.

Comprehension monitoring is a means of checking or keeping track of your comprehension. As you read, you should pick up on positive and negative signals that indicate the level and quality of your comprehension. Four monitoring techniques are (1) establishing checkpoints, (2) using guide questions, (3) asking connection questions, and (4) using internal dialogue. Once you detect weak comprehension, take specific corrective action.

[Handwritten margin note:] skill knowlege experience

[Handwritten notes:]

Active Reading requires
1) skills
2) Knowledge
3) experience

Comprehension monitoring
1) establishing checkpoints
2) using guide questions
3) asking connections questions
4) using internal dialogue

PART THREE

Comprehension Skills

Can you remember how you were taught to read? Do you remember going to reading class or having reading groups in elementary school? Can you remember using readers (series of books with stories) and then answering questions on what you read? Did you use workbooks with drills and exercises that taught you about vowel sounds and syllables? You probably can remember some or all of these things because reading was a regular part of each day's instruction in elementary school.

Now, do you remember going to reading class in junior or senior high school? Probably not. Most secondary schools throughout the country do not offer reading classes as a regular part of each year's curriculum. In effect, then, reading instruction stopped for you at the end of grade six. This general practice of discontinuing reading instruction at the end of elementary school has serious implications and has directly affected how well you can read now, as you enter college.

When you finished sixth grade, you probably were reading at least at sixth-grade level. You achieved this level through the direct instruction and practice you received in grades one through six. Then, after you entered seventh grade, reading was no longer taught. Instead, it was left up to you to raise your reading skills to the seventh-grade level by the end of seventh grade, to the eighth-grade level by the end of eighth grade, and so forth. The assumption that you could improve your reading skills on your own continued throughout the remainder of your secondary education.

What occurs as a result of this lack of direct instruction is that some students are able to increase their own reading ability while others are not. Most students are able to make some improvement; that is, not many students still read at a sixth-grade level when in the twelfth grade. But on the other hand, a large percentage of students do not read at a twelfth-grade level at the end of twelfth grade.

continued

continued

More and more college students are not beginning college immediately after completing high school. Instead, they are returning to education after working, raising a family, or serving in the military. Many of these students have not read or studied textbook material for several years. As a result, their reading and study skills are "rusty" from lack of use.

The purpose of Part Three is to help you make up, or compensate, for the lack of reading instruction during secondary school or a time lapse in your educational experience. This part of your text will present some of the most important higher-level reading skills that should have been taught to all students as they began to read more complex and difficult assigned material. The chapters are primarily concerned with how to read better and how to remember more, most efficiently. Chapters 7, 8, and 9 will focus on common units of meaning—the sentence, the paragraph, and the textbook section and passage. Techniques for accurate and effective comprehension of each of these units are presented.

1) read better
2) remember
3) read efficiently

7

Understanding Sentences

Use this chapter to:

1. *Learn how to grasp quickly the meaning of a sentence.*
2. *Discover how to use punctuation as an aid to comprehension.*
3. *Learn how to approach complicated sentences.*

Along with words and phrases, sentences are basic units of meaning to consider when we try to improve reading rate and comprehension. Clear, accurate understanding of sentences is essential to all other comprehension skills and to the effective reading and study of textbook chapters.

A sentence is commonly defined as a group of words that express a complete thought or idea. A sentence must be about one thing—the *subject*—and some action that happens in relation to the subject—the *verb*. In some situations, instead of expressing action the verb links or connects two parts of the sentence. Together, the subject and verb form the *core parts* of the sentence and carry its essential meaning. Sentences can contain many other parts, however, and they can vary widely in pattern and complexity. To read a sentence effectively, it is necessary to develop the ability to recognize the structure of a sentence as well as to identify the core parts that convey the essential meaning of the sentence.

RECOGNIZING COMPLETE SENTENCES

Before beginning to develop skill in recognizing core parts of a sentence, you must understand the difference between complete and incomplete thoughts. A complete thought is one that supplies enough information to give you the full meaning that is being expressed by the writer. Incomplete thoughts give you only partial information. After reading an incomplete thought, you are left with a question about (1) what happened, or (2) to whom or what something happened. The following examples show the difference between groups of words that are complete sentences and those that are not complete sentences because they do not fully express the writers' meanings.

Example 1A: Slipped off the side of the road into the ditch during a winter storm.

In this sentence, you know what happened (something or someone slipped into the ditch), but you do not know what or who slipped. You do not know whether it was a truck, bus, car, or careless driver that went into the ditch.

Example 1B: The tractor-trailer slipped off the side of the road into the ditch during a winter storm.

Sentence 1B is complete. Now you know that what slipped off the road and went into the ditch was a tractor-trailer.

Example 2A: This chapter, an excellent summary of the current economic problems in Russia.

In this sentence, there is a subject, "chapter," and some information is given about the subject—"an excellent summary of current economic problems in Russia." The sentence is not complete because there is no action; nothing is happening in relation to the chapter. You do not know what is being said about the chapter—whether it is boring, or whether it is difficult to read.

Example 2B: This chapter, an excellent summary of the current economic problems in Russia, presents some very useful graphs.

Example 2B is a complete sentence because you now know what the chapter does—it presents useful graphs.

You can see that unless a group of words contains a subject and a verb, it does not express a complete thought.

EXERCISE 1 _____

Directions: *Read each of the following groups of words. Mark an* S *in the blank if the words form a sentence. Mark an* N *if they do not form a sentence.*

_S_ 1. Finance companies raise funds by selling commercial paper and by issuing stocks and bonds.[1]

_N_ 2. A second feature of the preoperational stage of child growth and development. *No Verb*

_N_ 3. Becoming less dependent on sensory-motor responses and more capable of processing language. *No Sub*

_S_ 4. A computer gets data from input devices and sends data to output devices.[2]

_N_ 5. The energy that is used in business and industry in the form of electricity. *No Verb*

____ 6. Added to the problem of racial unrest caused by court-ordered busing.

_S_ 7. In the rigid atmosphere created in many public schools by so many rules and regulations, creativity is often stifled.[3]

____ 8. Islands and peninsulas that are inhabited by fewer than one hundred people.

____ 9. Archimedes' principle states that an immersed body is buoyed up by a force that is equal to the weight of the fluid it displaces.

____ 10. Often a misplaced comma or other punctuation mark can change a sentence's meaning.

IDENTIFYING CORE PARTS

As you can see from the preceding examples and exercise, the two core parts of the sentence—the subject and the verb, or the subject and the action—must be present for a group of words to convey a complete thought. For a group of words to be considered a sentence in written English, three conditions must be met. The group of words must (1) contain a subject, (2) contain a verb, and (3) express a complete thought. To read and understand a sentence, you should be able to quickly identify these core parts. Read this sentence: The battleship sank. The sentence consists only of the core parts: the subject—*battleship*—and the verb or action—*sank*. Now read this sentence: After the battle, the ship sank. The core parts are still easy to identify—*ship* and *sank*. However, in addition to conveying the basic message that the ship sank, the sentence contains an additional piece of information—*when* it sank.

In each of the following examples, the core parts are underlined.

The <u>children lined up</u> according to height.

The <u>books fell</u> off the desk.

Most psychological <u>principles can be applied</u> by everyone.

The average <u>American consumes</u> six gallons of beer each year.

After her own illness, the <u>physician was</u> more sympathetic to her patients' concerns and fears.

In reading these examples, you probably noticed the words and phrases that were not core parts of the sentences and contained additional information that in some way described or further explained the chief thoughts in the sentences. In the last sentence, for example, the important thought is that the physician was sympathetic. The other parts of the sentence tell *when* she was more sympathetic (after her own illness), suggest *why* she was more sympathetic (due to her experience with illness), and tells to *whom* she was more sympathetic (to her own patients).

Objects

In some sentences, the verb has an object or thing it refers to that completes the meaning of the sentence. You might think of the object as the person, place, or thing upon whom or to which the action is performed. The object is often called the receiver of the action. Not all sentences have an object, however. Here are a few sentences in which the object is underlined.

The psychology instructor discussed a <u>theory of motivation</u>.
    –A theory of motivation is *what* the instructor discussed.

Accountants use <u>computerized programs</u> to complete routine computations.
    –Computerized programs are *what* accountants use.

Researchers have investigated the differences in communication styles.

    –Differences in communication styles are *what* researchers have investigated.

Sentence Modifiers

Once you have identified the core parts of a sentence, the next step is to determine how the meaning of those core parts is changed or modified by the remainder of the sentence. These remaining parts, called *modifiers,* provide you with further information about one of the core parts. Notice how each of the underlined modifiers expands, alters, or limits the meaning of the following sentences.

After showing the film, the instructor gave a quiz.

    –The modifier tells *when* the quiz was given.

Dr. Ling, my philosophy instructor, assigns one chapter per week.

    –The modifier indicates *who* Dr. Ling is.

Everyone except engineering majors is required to take a philosophy course.

    –The modifier limits by giving an exception.

Multiple Core Parts

Some sentences may have more than one subject or more than one verb. Read this sentence: The bookstore and library were closed. There are two subjects—*bookstore* and *library*. Next, consider the following sentence: The professor gave an assignment and canceled class. The instructor performed two actions—*gave* and *canceled*. Here are a few more examples of sentences that contain multiple core parts.

Diet and exercise both contribute to weight loss.

Quick weight loss schemes deceive consumers and discourage them from trying legitimate plans.

Local businesses and private citizens organized the scholarship fund and solicited donations throughout the community.

You should have noticed that sentence 1 contains two subjects, sentence 2 has two predicates, and sentence 3 contains both two subjects and two predicates.

To read a sentence accurately, you must notice and understand the relationship between the modifiers and the core parts. In some cases, modifiers provide relatively unimportant additional information to which you should pay little attention. At other times, modifiers qualify, limit, or restrict the meaning of the core parts and significantly alter their meaning, as in the following sentence:

Those congressmen hoping for a pay increase voted against the budget cut.

Here the underlined portion is essential; you would not fully understand the sentence unless you knew that not all congressmen, but only those hoping for a pay increase, voted against the cut.

EXERCISE 2 _____

Directions: *Read each of the following sentences, underline the subject and verb, and circle the object if present.*

1. My sister took her car to the garage for repairs.
2. The library was closed for the entire week due to a flu epidemic.
3. The textbook contains exercises intended to increase reading speed.
4. Most governments in today's world claim to be democratic.
5. Storage, processing, and retrieval are essential data processing functions.
6. Reports such as the check-and-earnings statement are essential to operating a business.
7. Some companies issue written warranties to induce consumers to purchase their products.
8. Life insurance needs are determined by subtracting the financial resources that will be available at death from the financial losses likely to result from the death.[4]
9. An audit, a procedure designed to increase the quality of health care, is required of all Joint Commission–accredited hospitals.[5]
10. Numerous authors have researched delinquency and offered subcultural theories.

RECOGNIZING COMBINED IDEAS

Many sentences that you read in textbooks and reference material express more than one idea. Often, a writer combines closely related ideas into one sentence to make the connection between them clearer and easier to understand.

There are two basic sentence patterns commonly used to combine ideas—coordinate and subordinate. Each type provides the reader with clues about the relationship and relative importance of the ideas.

Coordinate Sentences

Coordinate sentences express ideas that are equally important. They coordinate, or tie together, two or more ideas. This is done for three reasons: (1) to emphasize their relationship, (2) to indicate their equal importance, and/or (3) to make the material more concise and easier to read. In the following example notice how two related ideas are combined.

1. Marlene was in obvious danger.
2. Joe quickly pulled Marlene from the street.

   Combined sentence:
   Marlene was in obvious danger, and Joe quickly pulled her from the street.

In this case the combined sentence establishes that the two equally important events are parts of a single incident.

As you read coordinate sentences, be sure to locate two sets of core parts. If you do not read carefully or if you are reading too fast, you might miss the second idea. Often you can recognize a sentence that combines two or more ideas by its structure and punctuation. Although a later section of this chapter discusses punctuation in more detail, basically, coordinate ideas are combined by using either a semicolon or a comma along with one of the following words: *and, but, or, either-or, neither-nor*. Here are a few examples:

The students wanted the instructur to cancel the class, <u>but</u> the instructor decided to reschedule it.

The union members wanted to strike; the company did nothing to discourage them.

Some students decided to take the final exam, <u>and</u> others chose to rely on their semester average.

Subordinate Sentences

Subordinate sentences contain one key, important idea and one or more less important, or subordinate, ideas that explain the key idea. These less important ideas have their own core parts, but they depend on the base sentence to complete their meaning. For example, in the following sentence you do not fully understand the meaning of the underlined portion until you read the entire sentence.

Two forms
Subordinate   Key idea
Key idea   Subordinate

<u>Because Diane forgot to make a payment</u>, she had to pay a late charge on her loan.

In this sentence, the more important idea is that Diane had to pay a late charge. The reason for the late charge is presented as background information that amplifies and further explains the basic message.

As you read subordinate sentences, be sure to notice the relationship between the two ideas. The idea of lesser importance may describe or explain a condition, cause, reason, purpose, time, or place. Here are a few additional examples of sentences that relate ideas. In each the base sentence is underlined and the function of the less important idea is indicated in parentheses above it.

(*description*)
<u>My grandfather</u>, who is eighty years old, <u>collects stamps</u>.

(*time*)
<u>American foreign policy changed</u> when we entered the Vietnam War.

(*condition*)
Unless my class is dismissed early, <u>I'll be late for my dental appointment</u>.

(*reason*)
Since I failed my last history exam, <u>I decided to drop the course</u>.

EXERCISE 3 _____

Directions: *Read each of the following and decide whether it is a coordinate or a subordinate sentence. Mark C in the space to the right if the sentence is coordinate. Mark S if it is subordinate, and underline the more important, key idea.*

1. The personnel office eagerly accepted my application for a job, and I expect to receive an offer next week. _____C_____
2. Since it is difficult to stop smoking, the individual who wants to quit may find group therapy effective. _____S_____
3. Birth control is interference with the natural rhythms of reproduction; some individuals object to it on this basis. _____
4. Computers have become part of our daily lives, but their role in today's college classrooms has not yet been fully explored. _____S_____
5. Marriage consists of shared experiences and ambitions, and both are influenced by the values of each partner. _____C_____
6. As far as we can tell from historical evidence, humankind has inhabited this earth for several million years. _____
7. Because sugar is Cuba's main export, the Cuban economy depends upon the worldwide demand for and price of sugar. _____
8. The personnel manager who accepted my application is well known for interviewing all likely candidates. _____
9. Even though a feather and a brick will fall equally fast in a vacuum, they fall quite differently in the presence of air. _____S_____
10. We never learn anything in a vacuum; we are always having other experiences before and after we learn new material. _____

EXERCISE 4 _____

Directions: *Choose a page from one of your textbooks. Read each sentence and underline all coordinate sentences. Place brackets [ ] around all subordinate sentences.*

EXERCISE 5 _____

Directions: *Turn to the sample textbook chapter included in Appendix B of this text. Beginning with the section headed "Principles of Heat Balance" on page 416, read each sentence and underline the core parts of each. Continue reading and underlining until you finish the page. For coordinate sentences, underline both sets of core parts. For subordinate sentences, underline the core parts in the more important, key idea.*

EXERCISE 6 _____

Directions: *Select one page from a chapter in a textbook you are currently reading. After you have read each sentence, underline its core parts. For coordinate sentences, underline both sets of core parts. For subordinate sentences, underline the core parts in the more important, key idea.*

PAYING ATTENTION TO PUNCTUATION

Read the following paragraph.

some of the earliest philosophical speculations were concerned with what the material world is made of is each substance such as rock or wood infinitely divisible so that its subdivisions always yield the same properties as the whole substance or is there some level of structure below which the subdivisions will show new properties and forms the greek philosopher democritus 460 370 bc suggested that the material objects of our experience are actually made up of fundamental units.

–Berman and Evans, *Exploring the Cosmos*, p. 4

Reading this paragraph was awkward and difficult because all punctuation was deleted. None of the words were separated from each other; you had no clues as to what words belonged together. Paying attention to punctuation can make reading easier. It helps comprehension in several ways:

1. It separates different pieces of the sentence from one another.
2. It suggests thought or idea groupings.
3. It provides clues to the relative importance of ideas within the sentence.

Each type of punctuation mark has specific functions. Those punctuation marks most useful to sentence comprehension are described below.

The Comma

The comma has a number of different uses, but in each case it separates some type of information from other parts of the sentence. The different uses of the comma are explained below.

The Introductory Use: The comma can be used to separate introductory, beginning, or opening parts of a sentence from the main part of the sentence. These parts may connect what will be said in one sentence with what has already been said in a previous sentence, provide some background information, set the scene or time frame, or offer some qualifying information or considerations. These introductory comments are less important, and tend to explain or modify the sentence's main thought. The following examples show how commas can be used to separate introductory phrases from the main sentence.

Not surprisingly, it is not only the size of America's corporations that is at issue.

Use in Subordinate and Coordinate Sentences: Commas are used along with a conjunction (*and, or, but, nor, for*), to separate complete thoughts in coordinate sentences. In subordinate sentences, the comma may be used to separate the key idea from the less important idea that explains it.

When atoms interact with one another, new particles are formed.

The Parenthetical Use: The comma can be used to separate additional information from the main part of the sentence. Writers occasionally interrupt the core sentence to add some extra (parenthetical) information that is important but not crucial to the sentence meaning. They use a comma before and after this parenthetical information. This use of a comma helps you tell important from less important information and should aid you in identifying the sentence's core parts.

Like (----)

Each of the sentences in the following examples illustrates the parenthetical use of the comma.

Dolphins, as a matter of fact, are very friendly creatures that frequently come to the rescue of people.

Drugs and alcohol, experts warn, are an unsafe and dangerous combination.

The Coal Mine Safety Act, one of the first federal efforts to enforce safety standards, reduced worker productivity.

The Serial Use: Whenever several items are presented in a list, or series, in a sentence, they are separated by commas. In all cases, the items in a series are equal and consistent in how they are connected or related to the core parts of the sentence. Read each of the following sentences, which are examples of the serial use of the comma. Notice how the underlined items in the series have a parallel or equal relationship to one another.

Each state maintained its sovereignty, freedom, and independence.

Social adjustment requires that an individual maintain himself independently, be gainfully employed, and conform to the social standards set by the community.

Directions: *In each sentence that follows, cross out the part or parts that you identify as of lesser importance in the sentence based on the use and placement of commas.*

1. In the nineteenth century, industrialization made a strong impact on society.
2. That is, no member of the Congress should serve more than three years in any six.
3. How is it, then, that we perceive depth as a third dimension?
4. Perhaps even more important, when humans think, they know they are thinking.
5. Graphite, on the other hand, is made of carbon layers stacked one on top of the other, like sheets of paper.

The Semicolon

The primary use of the semicolon is to separate two very closely related ideas that have been combined into a coordinate sentence. Sentences 1 and 2 in the following examples can be combined using a semicolon to form sentence 3.

1. They bought the house at a very low price.
2. The former owner had to sell immediately and move to another city.
3. They bought the house at a very low price; the former owner had to sell immediately and move to another city.

When you are reading a sentence that contains a semicolon, be alert for two separate ideas and two sets of core parts. When a semicolon is used, you know that the two ideas have equal weight or importance. Each of the following sentences contains two ideas separated by a semicolon. The core parts of each sentence are underlined.

The fishermen caught fifteen trout; they cooked them over an open fire.

All objects radiate some form of electromagnetic radiation; the amount depends on their temperature and physical state.

Occasionally, a semicolon is used to separate sentence parts that, if divided by commas, would be confusing or difficult to read. To illustrate this use of the semicolon, the following example has been written in two versions.

1. Speakers at the conference included Dr. Frank, a biologist, Dr. Flock, a philosopher, and Professor Smich, a geneticist.
2. Speakers at the conference included Dr. Frank, a biologist; Dr. Flock, a philosopher; and Professor Smich, a geneticist.

As you read the first version of the sentence, you are not sure whether the speakers include Dr. Frank and a biologist or whether it was Dr. Frank who was being described as a biologist. The use of the semicolon in the second version makes it clear that Dr. Frank is the biologist.

The Colon

The colon is most often used to introduce a list, statement, or quotation. The colon tells you, the reader, that some type of additional information, which further explains the main idea of a sentence, is to follow. The colon also serves as a marker indicating that the sentence's core parts precede the colon.

The causes of the war can be divided into three categories: social, economic, and political. (Here the colon indicates that a list of categories will follow.)

Chomsky described two levels of language: One underlying or deep structure involved with meaning, and a surface level used in ordinary conversation. (The colon in this example signals that an explanation of the two levels of language is to follow.)

The Dash

The dash is most commonly used in a sentence to separate unessential or parenthetical elements from the core sentence, when using a comma would be confusing. This usage also assists the reader in separating core parts from supporting information.

At least three sports—basketball, football, and tennis—are continually gaining television fans.

EXERCISE 8 _____

Directions: *Using punctuation as a guide, underline the core parts of each sentence.*

1. Steel, for instance, is mostly iron, with various other metals added, such as chromium, nickel, vanadium, manganese, or zirconium.
2. Among the physical traits that, added together, separate humans from all other animals, there are three of overwhelming significance: a skeleton built for walking upright; eyes capable of sharp, three-dimensional vision in color; and hands that provide both a powerful grip and nimble manipulations.[6]
3. Unfortunately, though, despite recent medical advances, the cause of mental retardation cannot be determined in most cases.
4. For a hundred years, changes in the environment, caused by humans using fossil fuels, clearing large forest areas, and excavating the land, have rapidly accelerated.
5. Throughout history, man has been puzzled and exasperated by the strange duality of his nature—half animal, half angel—and much religious and philosophical teaching has been an attempt to understand and integrate these two sides of human nature.[7]
6. Poverty and mild retardation go hand in hand, yet the vast majority of individuals from poverty neighborhoods are not mentally retarded.[8]
7. Like horses, human beings have a variety of gaits; they amble, stride, jog, and sprint.[9]

8. Evolutionary biologists have made this much clear to us: each species is a product of its genes and its environment.[10]
9. Anthropologists have accumulated a vast store of evidence to support their theory: tools and artifacts, such as those unearthed in Choukoutien, and the bones of animals who were contemporaries.[11]
10. Infant apes and monkeys, as they grow up, must learn a code of behavior, much as a human child has to do; all the members of a group are linked by an elaborate system of communication that uses both sounds and gestures and shows considerable sophistication.[12]

DECIPHERING COMPLICATED SENTENCES

Many sentences are short, direct, and straightforward and, as such, are easy to comprehend. Others, however, are complicated by the addition of numerous facts and the expression of complex relationships. In the following example, a simple sentence is compared with a complicated one. Facts that explain and clarify the core meaning were added, resulting in a complicated second sentence.

Simple sentence: Abnormal behavior is the product of biochemical processes in the brain.

Complicated sentence: Many professionals in the field of psychology, especially those with medical backgrounds, believe that most, if not all, abnormal behavior is the product of biochemical processes in the brain of the affected individual.

The sentence is complicated by the addition of three pieces of information: (1) who believes abnormal behavior is biochemically caused—"many professionals in the field of psychology, especially with medical backgrounds"; (2) the qualifying statement "most, if not all"; and (3) whose brain—"of the affected individual."

The key to understanding a complicated sentence is to unravel it, identifying its core parts and analyzing how each additional piece (fact) modifies the meaning of the core. The following steps are useful.

Step 1: Locate the Core Parts. Establish what the sentence is about and what action is occurring. Be alert for compound subjects or verbs. Many complicated sentences may express more than one idea and have more than one set of core parts.

Step 2: Study the Modifiers. Identify how each remaining piece of the sentence alters its meaning. Does it describe the subject? Does it tell when, why, how, or where the action occurred?

Step 3: Paraphrase. Express the sentence's basic meaning in your own words without referring to the sentence. If necessary, split it into two or more basic sentences. This step provides the best test of whether you actually understand the sentence.

Step 4: Check Vocabulary. If step 3 fails, then difficult or technical vocabulary may be interfering with your comprehension. Check your text's glossary or consult the dictionary.

Here is an example of this four-step procedure:

Because of Washington's loss of world military superiority, the changing role of the Third World, the deterioration of American control over Western allies, and political changes in the United States affecting the conduct of foreign relations, the United States has, since the demise of détente, taken a militaristic stance.[13]

Step 1: Locate the Core Parts.

    (subject)   (verb)   (object)
The United States   has taken   a militaristic stance.

Step 2: Study the Modifiers. The first part of the sentence gives four reasons why the United States has taken a militaristic stance. The phrase "since the demise of détente" indicates when this action occurred.

Step 3: Paraphrase. The sentence might be paraphrased as follows:

The United States has taken a militaristic stance since the demise of détente.

    This statement expresses the key idea. Details include that this has occurred because of (1) U.S. loss of world power, (2) the changing role of Third World countries, (3) the breakdown of control over allies, and (4) political changes in the United States.

Step 4: Check the Vocabulary. If necessary, check the meaning of words such as "détente," "demise," and "militaristic."

EXERCISE 9 _____

Directions: *Read each of the following sentences, using the procedure suggested above. Paraphrase each sentence in the space provided.*

1.   Multiple personality is a <u>reaction</u>, usually caused by stress, in which the patient manifests two or more systems of personality, each of which has distinct, well-developed emotional and thought processes and represents a unique personality.

> *Stress causes Multiple personality. Each personality is well-developed emotional + thought processes. Each personality represents a unique personality*

2.   In trying to identify the causes of problem drinking, some researchers have stressed the role of genetic factors, while others

have viewed it as an inability to adjust to the stress of life or as a social phenomenon.

_____

_____

3. <u>Some individuals</u> do not go through the normal process of grieving, perhaps because of their personality makeup or as a consequence of the particular situation: the individual may, for instance, be stoical about his or her feelings or may have to manage the affairs of the family.[14]

_____

_____

4. <u>Policies</u> that encourage industries to pack up and move from one state to another, or out of the country, in search of lower labor costs, lighter taxes, and fewer regulations, are policies that, whatever their intention, ultimately <u>promote</u> racial inequality through their disproportionate impact on minority workers.[15]

Policies ^(that encourage industries to move,) promote racial inequality why lower labor costs, lighter taxes, fewer regulations

5. Beyond the volume and quality of arms transferred to troubled regions by the Soviet Union and the United States, the Soviet bloc has demonstrated a superior willingness to arrange deliveries [of arms] on schedules that could not be met by the West, thus enabling it to influence events in regional hotspots at critical junctions, while Western arms have generally been much slower to arrive.[16]

_____

_____

_____

EXERCISE 10 ――――――――――

Directions: _Select several pages from one of your more difficult textbooks. Quickly look through these pages and locate ten long or complicated sentences. Then paraphrase each._

Troublesome Types of Sentences

Sentences may be complicated because they are packed with information that modifies and explains the key idea. However, sentences can also be troublesome if they follow unusual or unfamiliar sentence patterns. As you learned earlier in the chapter, many sentences follow the subject-verb-object pattern. When this pattern is not followed or is modified, sentences become more difficult to read. Three types of difficult sentence patterns are described below.

Reversed Order of Events: Most sentences present ideas in chronological order—the order in which they occur, as in the following sentence:

After class, I went to the bookstore.

However, when the order of events presented in the sentence is presented differently from the way they actually occurred, the reader must make a mental switch or transformation, reversing the order of events in his or her mind, as in the following:

I went to the bookstore after class.

The above switch is easy to make. However, when the ideas become more complex and less familiar, the switch is more difficult, and sometimes easy to miss:

The industrial workers become proletarians where before they were serfs.[17]

Here you must transform the sentence by thinking, "the workers were serfs, then they became proletarians."

When reading reverse-order sentences, stop and establish the correct order of events before continuing to read.

EXERCISE 11 _____

Directions: *For each of the following sentences, list the events in correct chronological order.*

1. American intervention in the Vietnam War followed earlier French involvement.

   _____

2. Although it has subsequently been revised and extended, the Omnibus Crime Control and Safe Streets Act, when passed in 1968, was intended to establish a massive campaign against lawlessness.

   _____

3. In computing federal income tax owed, in order to consult a tax table, you must compute your adjusted gross income and taxable income.

   _____

4. In computing net cost, before you subtract cash discount, you must subtract trade discounts from the list price.

_____

5. Prior to a presidential review of the proposed federal budget, the Office of Management and Budget holds hearings and reviews its assessment of the economy.

_____

Distance Between Subject and Verb: In most sentences the verb (action) closely follows the subject, as in the sentence:

Effective <u>managers share</u> a number of common characteristics.

However, some writers place additional information between the subject and verb, as in the following:

<u>Chief executive officers</u> who are successful at acquiring considerable power and using it to control others <u>tend to share</u> a number of common characteristics.

When the subject and verb are split, the reader is forced to carry mentally an incomplete idea while he or she reads additional information about the subject before reaching the action of the sentence. For this type of sentence, make an effort to hold in mind the subject until you reach the verb. Reread if necessary.

EXERCISE 12 _____

Directions: _For each of the following sentences underline the subject and verb._

1. <u>Industry</u>, the second and more modern form of production, <u>displaced</u> feudalism.

_____

2. <u>Israel</u>, surrounded by boundaries easily crossed by hostile tanks and infantry and further limited by its tiny size, is severely <u>hindered</u> in national defense by its geography.

_____

3. <u>Crimes</u> committed in the course of one's occupation by those who operate inside business, government, or other establishments, in violation of their sense of loyalty to the employer or client, <u>are</u> among the most difficult to identify.

_____

4. A distinguished panel of educators and lawyers, which recently concluded that the only just system of punishment is one based on

retribution, proposed a maximum penalty for all crimes but murder of five years' imprisonment.[18]

_____

5. Currency and things that can be changed into currency very easily, such as bank accounts, stocks, bonds, Treasury bills, and the like, are termed liquid assets.[19]

_____

Inverted Sentence Order: As you learned earlier in the chapter, the most common, normal order of a sentence is subject-verb-object, as in the following:

Ted studied his chemistry textbook.

Occasionally, however, a writer will reverse this normal order, creating sentences such as

The chemistry textbook was studied by Ted.

The order is object-verb-subject. Sentences of this type use a verb form called the passive voice (and are often intended to focus the reader's attention on the object rather than the action). Reading such sentences requires a mental switch or transformation to place the sentence in normal order.
   Here is a more challenging example:

The twentieth century has seen a radical alteration in the world position of the United States.[20]

In this sentence, you must make a mental switch. The sentence might be paraphrased as follows:

The United States has experienced a severe change in its world position during the twentieth century.

EXERCISE 13 _____

Directions: *Paraphrase each of the following sentences, transforming the sentence to normal sentence order.*

1. Some of the most influential research linking mental illness to the state of the economy has been done by the sociologist M. Harvey Brenner.[21]

_____

2. A major reason for the fairly impressive gains in income by black women, as compared to Hispanic women, was found to be the much greater rate of employment.

_____

3. It has been argued that women's growing role in the work force has moved them toward economic equality with men, even if they have not yet attained that goal.

_____

4. It is suggested, for example, that the "love bonds" between parent and child are important to regulating the aggressive drive and that destructive behavior is prevented by the formation of stable human relationships in early childhood.[22]

_____

5. It is widely agreed that there has been a profound shift in the way Americans earn their livings in the twentieth century, especially during the last quarter.

_____

SUMMARY

The sentence, one of the basic units of meaning, is defined as a group of words that expresses a complete thought or idea. All complete sentences must have two essential components; these are called core parts. First, a sentence must have a subject; it must be about a person, thing, or idea. Second, a sentence must express some type of action; something must happen to or be done by the subject. To understand a sentence, the reader must be able to recognize these core parts. Many sentences combine two or more sets of core parts for the purpose of showing relationships between them.

Punctuation is an aid to the reader in comprehending sentence meaning and identifying the core parts of the sentence. Each type of punctuation mark gives the reader specific information about the relative importance of ideas and the location of core parts within the sentence.

Deciphering complicated sentences is a four-step process: Locate the core parts, study the modifiers, paraphrase, and check vocabulary. Types of complicated sentences include reversed order of events, split subject and verb, and inverted sentence order.

8

Understanding Paragraphs

> **Use this chapter to:**
> 1. *Find out what to look for as you read a paragraph.*
> 2. *Increase your recall of paragraph content.*

The *paragraph* can be defined as a group of related sentences about a single topic. Just as sentences have specific components—core parts—paragraphs also contain particular elements that are necessary for complete meaning to be conveyed.

THREE ESSENTIAL ELEMENTS OF A PARAGRAPH

The *topic*, the one thing the paragraph is about, is the unifying factor, and every sentence and idea contained in the paragraph relates to the topic. The *main idea*, what the author wants to communicate about the topic, is the central or most important thought in the paragraph. Every other sentence and idea in the paragraph is related to the main idea. The sentence that expresses this idea is called the *topic sentence*. *Details* are the proof, support, explanation, reasons, or examples that explain the paragraph's main idea.

Each of the following examples contains a group of sentences, but only one is a paragraph. Only that one has the three essential elements. Identify the paragraph.

> Cats frequently become aggressive when provoked. Some plants require more light than others due to coloration of their foliage. Some buildings, due to poor construction, waste a tremendous amount of energy.

> Some plants require more light than others due to coloration of their foliage. Some plants will live a long time without watering. Plants are being used as decorator items in stores and office buildings.

> Some plants require more light than others due to coloration of their foliage. Plants with shades of white, yellow, or pink in their leaves need more light than plants with completely green foliage. For example, a Swedish ivy plant with completely green leaves requires less light per day than a variegated Swed-

[handwritten margin note:]
3 parts
Topic
main Idea
Details

ish ivy that contains shades of white, yellow, and green in its leaves.

In the first example, the sentences were unrelated; each sentence was about a different thing, and there was no connection among them.

In the second example, each sentence was about plants—the common topic; however, the sentences together did not prove, explain, or support any particular idea about plants.

In the third example, each sentence was about plants, and all sentences were about one main idea—that some plants need more light than others due the coloration of their leaves. Thus, the third example is a paragraph; it has a topic—plants; a main idea—that plants require varying degrees of light due to coloration; and supporting details—the example of the Swedish ivy. The first sentence functions as a topic sentence.

In order to understand a paragraph, a reader must be able to identify the topic, main idea, and details easily. In the following paragraph, each of these parts is identified:

Topic sentence

As societies become industrialized, the distribution of workers among various economic activities tends to change in a predictable way. In the early stages, the population is engaged in agriculture and the collection of raw materials for food and shelter. But as technology develops, agricultural workers are drawn into manufacturing and construction.

Topic: distribution of workers

Details

HOW TO IDENTIFY THE TOPIC

The topic of a paragraph is the subject of the whole paragraph. It is the one thing that the whole paragraph is about. Usually, the topic of a paragraph can be expressed in two or three words. To find the topic of a paragraph, ask yourself this question: What is the one thing the author is discussing throughout the paragraph? Read the following example.

Inflation is a problem that involves everyone. *Inflation* is fairly easy to define: It is a general rise in the prices that people must pay for goods and services. Since the Great Depression of the 1930s, average prices in the United States have moved steadily upward, almost never downward. The rate of inflation was relatively modest during the 1940s and '50s, but in the 1960s and '70s prices increased at a faster rate. The cost of most goods and services today is about ten times higher than it was during the 1930s and '40s. Then a haircut cost about 75 cents and a dime tip was sufficient; a meal in a comfortable restaurant cost 50 cents; a pair of durable and stylish shoes cost about $4.95. Inflation in 1985 is about 4.1 percent, which is down significantly from the double-digit rate of 12 percent in 1981. But even at a 6 percent inflation rate, [the] prices, . . . will become a reality by 1990.

–Kinnear and Bernhardt, *Principles of Marketing*, p. 77.

In the example, the author is discussing one topic—inflation—throughout the paragraph. Notice how many times the word *inflation* is repeated in the paragraph. Frequently, ~~the repeated use of a word can~~ ~~serve as a clue to the topic of a paragraph.~~

EXERCISE 1 _____

Directions: *Read each of the following pragraphs and then select the topic of the paragraph from the choices given.*

1. The organization of both branches of Congress is based on political party lines. The *majority party* in each house is the one with the greatest number of members. Being the majority party is quite important because that party chooses the major officers of the branch of Congress, controls debate on the floor, selects all committee chairmen, and has a majority on all committees. For almost thirty years, the Democratic party was the majority party in both the House and the Senate; the Republicans were the minority party. In the 1980 elections the GOP ("Grand Old Party") won control of the Senate for the first time in twenty-eight years. Thus the Republicans became the majority party in the Senate, although the Democrats remained the majority party in the House.

   –Wasserman, *The Basics of American Politics*, pp. 94–95

   a. political parties
   b. majority parties in Congress
   c. the Republican majority
   d. branches of Congress

2. The total educational profile of the American population has been changing in recent years. By 1985 one person in five had a college degree, almost double the percentage in 1970. The percentage of adults with at least one year of college was 35 percent, and only 27 percent did not have a high school diploma. People aged 70 and older account for one-fourth of those who have less than a high school education. By 1990 it is expected that more than one adult in three will have had some college training. This trend is important because higher levels of education produce consumers who are more sophisticated in evaluating alternative product offerings, more receptive to new products, and more demanding of quality and performance.

   –Kinnear and Bernhardt, *Principles of Marketing*, p. 125

   a. consumer sophistication
   b. total population profile
   c. trend toward higher levels of education
   d. college degrees in America

3. Technological advancements in microcircuitry have enabled engineers to develop computers that can perform diagnostic and control functions in a host of conventional devices. For example, as you push the buttons of a microwave oven or photocopying machine, or even as you drive your car, it is likely that your actions are monitored and translated into action by an internal computer. The same can be said for dishwashers, refrigerators, sewing machines, lawn mowers, power hand tools, heating and cooling equipment, intrusion alarms, telephones, television, stereo systems, word processors, military vehicles and weapons, and industrial

robots. The computers in such applications are "special-purpose" computers, designed to perform a specific function in that particular device.

–Miller and Heeren, *Mathematical Ideas*, p. 629

a. diagnostic and control capabilities
b. monitoring functions
c. special-purpose computers
d. microcircuitry and control functions

4. The simple word "to" has caused a great deal of confusion in many areas of science. For example, consider the phrase, "Birds migrate southward to escape winter." The statement seems harmless enough, but if interpreted literally, it implies that the birds have a goal in mind, or that they are moving under the directions of some conscious force that compels them to escape winter. Philosophers have termed such assumptions *teleology*. (*Teleos* is Greek for *end* or *goal*.) It is commonly used in reference to ideas that go beyond what is actually verifiable and generally implies some inner drive to complete a goal or some directing force operating above the laws of nature.

–Wallace, *Biology: The World of Life*, pp. 31–32

a. forces operating above the laws of nature
b. confusion in language
c. literally interpreted statements
d. teleological assumptions

5. Pain sensations are generally classified by their sites of origin. Cutaneous pain originates from skin pain receptors and generally shows both fast and slow properties. In contrast, visceral pain comes from visceral organs and other deep tissues. This pain is generally of the slow, "aching" variety, which is difficult to localize. Frequently, visceral pain may be referred to other parts of the body supplied by the same spinal nerve (the dermatomal rule), known as *referred pain*. Also, visceral pain of the abdomen may cause overlying abdominal muscles to contract. This increased rigidity of the abdominal wall is called "guarding."

–Davis, Holtz, and Davis, *Conceptual Human Physiology*, pp. 195–196

a. classifying pain by site of origin
b. visceral organ pain
c. guarding in the abdominal wall
d. referred pain

6. Effective listening means listening with a third ear. By this I mean trying to listen for the meanings behind the words and not just to the words alone. The way words are spoken–loud, soft, fast, slow, strong, hesitating–is very important. There are messages buried in all the cues that surround words. If a mother says, "Come *in* now" in a soft, gentle voice, it may mean the kids have a few more minutes. If she says, "Come in NOW" there is no question about the meaning of the command. To listen effectively we have to pay attention to facial expressions and eye contact, gestures and body movement, posture and dress, as well as to the quality of the other person's voice, vocabulary, rhythm, rate, tone, and volume. These nonverbal cues are a vital part of any message. Listening with our third ear helps us to understand the whole message.

–Weaver, *Understanding Interpersonal Communications*, p. 117

a. meaning cues in listening
b. facial cues
c. the way words are spoken
d. listening techniques

7. Corporations may obtain short-term funds through the use of promissory notes, trade credit, etc. Long-term debt of the corporation is usually in the form of bonds issued by the corporation. *Bonds* are, in a sense, long-term promissory notes of the corporation. Bonds have a face value, which is usually in $1,000 denominations, and a maturity date, at which time the principal must be repaid. In addition, each certificate has a stated interest rate. The issuing corporation is obligated to pay the bondholder an amount of money equal to the interest percentage of the face value of the bond. For example, a bond with a face value of $1,000 and a 6 percent interest rate would require a payment of $60 a year until the bond matured.

     –Pickle and Abrahamson, *Introduction to Business*, p. 45

a. promissory notes
b. types of corporate debt
c. how bonds work
d. interest rates on bonds

8. To become part of the *official* data on crime, activites must be known to legal officials and must be appropriately labeled by them. Activities become known to the police, and hence become eligible for official labeling as crimes, in two ways. The most common way is for a member of the public to notify the police of a "crime" or "possible crime." The less common way is for the police to directly witness an activity that they then label crime. Police rely heavily on citizens bringing suspected crimes to their attention. This means that most actions that eventually become official crimes do so only because they have been evaluated as "crimes" or "possible crimes" by the public, who then bring them to the attention of the police. Here we see the importance of unofficial (public) evaluations and behavior in the production of *official* crime data.

     –Barlow, *Introduction to Criminology*, p. 99

a. evaluating possible crimes
b. criminal activity
c. collection of official crime data
d. direct witnessing of criminal behavior

9. The Bill of Rights is an inexhaustible source of potential conflicts over rights. Clearly, the Constitution meant to guarantee the right to a fair trial as well as a free press. But a trial may not be fair if press coverage inflames public opinion so much that an impartial jury cannot be found. In one famous criminal trial an Ohio physician, Sam Sheppard, was accused of the murder of his wife. The extent of press coverage rivaled that of a military campaign, and little of it sympathized with Dr. Sheppard. Found guilty and sent to the state penitentiary, Sheppard appealed his conviction to the Supreme Court. He argued that press coverage had interfered with his ability to get a fair trial. The Supreme Court agreed, claiming that the press had created a virtual "Roman circus," and reversed Sheppard's conviction.

     –Lineberry, *Government in America*, p. 142

a. the purpose of the Bill of Rights
b. conflicts between fair trials and the free press
c. rights of the free press
d. the Sheppard trial

10. A mixture of copper and tin in a molten state will cool to form a harder, stronger, and more durable solid than either copper itself or tin itself. This solid is bronze, historically the first of the materials we call *alloys*. Brass, a mixture of copper and zinc, is another alloy. Steels are alloys of iron with carbon, often with the addition of other elements for special purposes, like chromium for rustlessness and silicon for high permeability. Gallium arsenide is a newer alloy that is a semiconductor used in electronics for such solid-state devices as the light-emitting diodes in calculator readouts. All alloys are made by basically the same process, by mixing two or more molten metals in varying proportions and letting the mixture cool and solidify.

–Hewitt, *Conceptual Physics*, p. 169

a. manufacture of bronze alloys
b. uses of alloys
c. the process of cooling and solidifying metal alloys
d. production of alloys

EXERCISE 2 _____

Directions: *For each of the following paragraphs, read the paragraph and write the topic in the space provided. Be sure to limit the topic to two or three words.*

1. Energy conservation in the short run and long run will require creative solutions in all areas of business. A few innovative solutions have already surfaced which indicate that business understands the importance of saving energy. The makers of Maxwell House coffee developed a method to save natural gas. The first step in making instant coffee is to brew the coffee just as people do at home, except in 1000-gallon containers. The heat to brew the coffee had come from burning natural gas, and the process left Maxwell House with tons of coffee grounds. The company then had to use trucks (that burned gasoline) to cart the coffee grounds away. Maxwell House realized it could save most of the cost of the natural gas (and the gasoline cost) by burning the grounds to get the heat to brew subsequent batches of coffee. Natural gas is now used only to start the coffee grounds burning.

–Kinnear and Bernhardt, *Principles of Marketing*, pp. 79–81

Topic: _____

 2. What happens when your feelings about yourself are weak or negative? Since you tend to act consistently with the feelings you have about yourself, this can be a damaging or destructive situation. For example, what if you perceive yourself as a failure in school? This attitude may be a result of something as insignificant as misunderstanding directions for an assignment, or it may have developed over a long period of time: having to compete with a very successful brother or sister, having a string of unsympathetic

teachers, or not gaining enough positive reinforcement at home for schoolwork. Whatever the cause, it is likely that once you start thinking of yourself as a failure, you will begin to act the part. Because of poor study habits, inadequate reading, and lack of participation in class, a poor grade may result, reinforcing your feeling. Such negative feelings feed upon themselves and become a vicious cycle, a cycle that will begin to encompass all your thoughts, actions, and relationships.

–Weaver, *Understanding Interpersonal Communications*, p. 52

Topic: _____

3. A human being can handle only so much information at one time. This has to do not only with the capability of the human brain to decipher material but also with the various ways that emotions get bound to certain experiences. Often the root causes for conflict are closely tied to our emotional response pattern. In such cases, as sure as conflicts are bound to come up, so are the emotions that go along with them. If we are having an emotionally involving experience, it is difficult to take on and fully comprehend a new "load" of information at the same time. Our senses are preoccupied. If someone else tries to share some vital news with us while our feelings are thus tied up, interpersonal conflicts may result. We may experience this when we try to listen to a classroom lecture just after we've heard some upsetting news. The intensity of the emotional experience overshadows any material the teacher could offer. We simply don't have room for any more information.

–Weaver, *Understanding Interpersonal Communications*, p. 265

Topic: _____

4. One prominent theory in biological circles is that humans are by nature, or instinctively, aggressive. This argument has been helped along by influential studies of animal behavior. Konrad Lorenz's book, *On Aggression,* may be taken as a case in point. According to Lorenz, nature has armed animals with an instinct for aggression for three reasons: (1) to ensure that stronger animals succeed in mating the most desirable females of their kind, thus helping to perpetuate "good" qualities in future generations; (2) to ensure that each individual has sufficient physical space for securing food, raising young, and so on (defense of physical space is called *territoriality*); and (3) to maintain hierarchies of dominance, and through them a stable, well-policed society.

–Barlow, *Introduction to Criminology*, p. 147

Topic: _____

5. We can identify almost any object or event as a *pattern* or bundle of features. To define a dog, for example, we begin with a set of features: four legs, a hairy coat, a tail. Of course, this list so far describes a cat as well as a dog. So we add further features like round pupils (cats have vertical slits) and smooth tongues (cats' tongues are sandpapery). More features might distinguish a particular dog: a spot around the left eye, for example. Such features as antlers and flippers must be absent. Finally, we should

allow some leeway for features that might be *missing* in a particular dog, such as a tail that has been bobbed. When we think about it this way, we see that the category "dog" is itself a complex, abstract concept. Most theories of human pattern recognition hold that our visual system uses features of these sorts in recognizing objects.

–Roediger et al., *Psychology*, p. 129

Topic: _____

(6) Particularly after 1972, when Richard Nixon packed away so much extra money from his campaign that his staff was doling it out to Watergate burglars as "hush money," there has been grave concern about <u>money in politics</u>. One key aspect of this concern is the worry over the cost of elections. In 1984, our nation footed a bill of more than $1 billion for elections. (However, this included all elections— national, state, and local—and presidential expenditures are incurred only once every four years.) Horror stories about expensive campaigns have become a staple of American journalism.

–Lineberry, *Government in America*, p. 251

Topic: ___money in politics___

7. Although they can process and move information rapidly (sometimes at the speed of light), computers are passive electronic machines awaiting human commands. If a computer fails to understand the particular command, it will not work. If it receives an incorrect command, it will work incorrectly. Likewise, integrated software, word processors, electronic mail systems, dictaphones, and all other computerized devices used to speed the flow of information in the automated office cannot convert poor writing to good. Anyone with programming experience knows that instructions to a computer demand the same precise phrasing, logical organization, and exact punctuation required of any good letter, memo, or report. Otherwise, the message will not be understood by the recipient—machine or human.

–Dumont and Lannon, *Business Communications*, p. 8

Topic: _____

8. Unlike courtship, dating serves a number of important functions prior to and in addition to mate selection. For adolescents, as well as for increasing numbers of dating adults, dating is a form of recreation that allows people to enjoy not only a leisure activity but each other's company as well. For adolescents it is also a means of socialization in which young people learn the social and interpersonal skills that will allow them to interact meaningfully with one another throughout their lives. They also learn about sexuality and intimacy . . . , and through their dates establish status in their peer groups. . . . Girls tend to bring a person-centered orientation to dating, while boys bring a body-centered orientation, and within the dating context, both learn to integrate intimacy and sexuality . . .

–Fuhrmann, *Adolescence, Adolescents*, p. 114

Topic: _____

9. Since prices of goods and services have risen considerably during the twentieth century, the absolute dollar increase in government expenditures does not necessarily indicate whether government has grown bigger relative to the private sector. For this information, economists often look at government expenditures as a percentage of the *gross national product*, or GNP. The GNP is the aggregate value of all goods and services produced in the country over some period, usually a year. Using this measure, economists have found that while the government accounted for less than 10 percent of all purchases of goods and services as a percent of gross national product in 1929, by 1984 government purchases of goods and services were responsible for more than 20 percent of GNP. Since 1960, government's percentage of purchases of goods and services has remained fairly constant at 20 percent, but this constancy understates the growth of the government's role in the economy. The government's tax receipts at all levels in 1984 accounted for more than 30 percent of GNP. We can understand the discrepancy between expenditures and receipts and the expanding role of government by examining the kinds or distributions of expenditures at the various levels of government and then the ways the government collects revenues.

–Ekelund and Tollison, *Economics*, pp. 57–58

Topic: _____

10. Interestingly, it can take hours to digest a meal that required only minutes to eat. Obviously, we can eat food faster than we can digest it, so some degree of storage is needed within the digestive tract. The stomach is specialized to meet this need. The human stomach is a pouchlike enlargement of the gut tube that stores food as it is eaten and gradually releases it into the intestine for complete processing. . . . Because of its storage function, the tunica mucosa and tunica submucosa of the stomach are specialized for distention as food enters the stomach. These two layers of the stomach show longitudinal folds, or rugae, that can flatten as the stomach is stretched. The tunica muscularis of the stomach is also specialized for distention. The smooth muscle of this layer can be stretched without increasing its contraction strength, or tone. This allows the stomach to hold large quantities of food without increasing the pressure of its contents.

–Davis, Holtz, and Davis, *Conceptual Human Physiology*, p. 462

Topic: _digestion process_____

HOW TO FIND THE MAIN IDEA

The main idea of a paragraph tells you what the author wants you to know about the topic. The main idea is usually directly stated by the writer in one or more sentences within the paragraph. The sentence that states this main idea is called the *topic sentence*. The topic sentence tells what the rest of the paragraph is about. In some paragraphs, the main idea is not directly stated in any one sentence. Instead, it is left to the reader to infer, or reason out.

To find the main idea of a paragraph, first decide what the topic of the paragraph is. Then ask yourself these questions: What is the main idea—what is the author trying to say about the topic? Which sentence states the main idea? Read the following paragraph.

The Federal Trade Commission has become increasingly interested in false and misleading packaging. Complaints have been filed against many food packagers because they make boxes unnecessarily large to give a false impression of quantity. Cosmetics manufacturers have been accused of using false bottoms in packaging to make a small amount of their product appear to be much more.

In the preceding paragraph, the topic is false packaging. The main idea is that the Federal Trade Commission is becoming increasingly concerned about false or misleading packaging. The author states the main idea in the first sentence, so it is the topic sentence.

WHERE TO FIND THE TOPIC SENTENCE

Although the topic sentence of a paragraph can be located anywhere in the paragraph, there are several positions where it is most likely to be found. Each type of paragraph has been diagrammed to help you visualize how it is structured.

First Sentence

The most common placement of the topic sentence is first in the paragraph. In this type of paragraph, the author states the main idea at the beginning of the paragraph and then elaborates on it. For example:

The good listener, in order to achieve the purpose of acquiring information, is careful to follow specific steps to achieve accurate understanding. First, whenever possible the good listener prepares in advance for the speech or lecture he or she is going to attend. He or she studies the topic to be discussed and finds out about the speaker and his or her beliefs. Second, on arriving at the place where the speech is to be given, he or she chooses a seat where seeing, hearing, and remaining alert are easy. Finally, when the speech is over, an effective listener reviews what was said and reacts to and evaluates the ideas expressed.

Usually, in this type of paragraph, the author is employing a deductive thought pattern in which a statement is made at the beginning and then supported through the paragraph.

Last Sentence

The second most common position of the topic sentence is last in the paragraph. In this type of paragraph, the author leads or builds up to the main idea and then states it in a sentence at the very end. For example:

> Whenever possible, the good listener prepares in advance for the speech or lecture he or she plans to attend. He or she studies the topic to be discussed and finds out about the speaker and his or her beliefs. On arriving at the place where the speech is to be given, he or she chooses a seat where seeing, hearing, and remaining alert are easy. And, when the speech is over, he or she reviews what was said and reacts to and evaluates the ideas expressed. <u>Thus, an effective listener, in order to achieve the purpose of acquiring information, takes specific steps to achieve accurate understanding.</u>

The thought pattern frequently used in this type of paragraph is inductive. That is, the author provides supporting evidence for the main idea first, and then states it.

Middle of the Paragraph

Another common placement of the topic sentence is in the middle of the paragraph. In this case, the author builds up to the main idea, states it in the middle of the paragraph, and then goes on with further elaboration and detail. For example:

> Whenever possible, the good listener prepares in advance for the speech or lecture he or she plans to attend. He or she studies the topic to be discussed and finds out about the speaker and his or her beliefs. <u>An effective listener, as you are beginning to see, takes specific steps to achieve accurate understanding of the lecture.</u> Furthermore, on arriving at the place where the speech is to be given, he or she chooses a seat where it is easy to see, hear, and remain alert. Finally, when the speech is over, the effective listener reviews what was said and reacts to and evaluates the ideas expressed.

First and Last Sentences

Sometimes an author uses two sentences to state the main idea or state the main idea twice in one paragraph. Usually, in this type of paragraph, the writer states the main idea at the beginning of the paragraph, then explains or supports the idea, and finally restates the main idea at the very end. For example:

> <u>The good listener, in order to achieve the purpose of acquiring information, is careful to follow specific steps to achieve accurate understanding.</u> First, whenever possible the good listener prepares in advance for the speech or lecture he or she is going to attend. He or she studies the topic to be discussed and finds out about the speaker and his or her beliefs. Second, on arriving at the place where the speech is to be given, he or she chooses a seat where seeing, hearing, and remaining alert are easy. Finally, when the speech is over, he or she reviews what

was said and reacts to and evaluates the ideas expressed. <u>Effective listening is an active process in which a listener deliberately takes certain actions to ensure that accurate communication has occurred.</u>

EXERCISE 3

Directions: *Read each of the following paragraphs and underline the topic sentence.*

1. <u>At least four types of sensation are usually lumped together as the sense of touch: pressure, pain, warmth, and cold.</u> The skin contains various receptors that act together in ways that are still a bit mysterious, and it is not uniformly sensitive to all of these properties across its entire surface. When a small square of skin is touched with tiny needles that have been heated or chilled, some areas in the square sense only heat, some only cold, and some neither. Likewise, the skin is not uniformly sensitive to touch. If two pointed objects are pressed against the skin simultaneously, they often will be felt as one. The distance by which they must be separated to be experienced as two objects rather than one (a measurement called the *two-point threshold*) varies over the body as well; it is much greater on the back than on the fingertips, for instance.

   –Roediger et al., *Psychology*, p. 110

2. <u>Much of what we know about how consumers behave is based on theories and research from the field of psychology, the study of individual behavior.</u> In analyzing consumers' purchase decision processes, such psychological factors as motivation, perception, learning, personality, and attitudes are important to understand, since they can help explain the *why* behind consumer behavior. It is virtually impossible to directly determine the influence of these factors; thus, it must be inferred. It is impossible to observe directly what is going on in a buyer's mind. Often the consumers themselves do not know why they behave as they do. Other times they do know, but may not be willing to tell the researcher the true reasons for their behavior. So, marketers must study the psychological factors that are relevant to their products or services.

   –Kinnear and Bernhardt, *Principles of Marketing*, p. 149

3. The first all-electronic computer, ENIAC (Electronic Numerical Integrator and Calculator), was developed at the University of Pennsylvania in 1947 for a cost of $487,000. The device stood two stories high, covered fifteen thousand square feet, weighed some thirty tons, and contained 18,000 vacuum tubes (which failed at a rate of about one every seven minutes). Since that time, a revolution in miniaturization, mass production, and economic competition has brought about computers smaller than typewriters, twenty times faster than ENIAC, more powerful and much more reliable, and readily available to the average citizen. The cost of a million calculations is now measured in cents, rather than in tens of thousands of dollars. It is said that if the same rate of advancement had been possible in the automobile industry over the past thirty

years, a Rolls-Royce would now cost less than $3 and would go more than two million miles on a gallon of gasoline.

–Miller and Heeren, *Mathematical Ideas*, p. 628

4. An understanding of the eye's ability to form images of both near and distant objects requires a basic knowledge of certain principles of optics. Light travels through air at an incredibly fast rate, approximately 300,000 kilometers/second. Light also travels through other transparent media, such as water and glass, but more slowly. When light rays pass from one medium into another of a different density, the rays are bent unless they strike the surface of the second medium at a perfectly perpendicular angle. The extent of this bending, or refraction, of light varies with the angle between the light rays and the surface of the medium. . . .

–Davis, Holtz, and Davis, *Conceptual Human Physiology*, pp. 201–202

5. Business, labor, and farmers all fret over the impacts of government regulations. Even a minor change in government regulatory policy can cost industries large amounts or bring windfall profits. Tax policies also affect the livelihoods of farmers, firms, and workers. How the tax code is written determines whether people and producers pay a lot or a little of their incomes to the government. Because government often provides subsidies (to farmers, small businesses, railroads, minority businesses, and others), every economic group wants to get its share of direct aid and of government contracts. And in this day of the global economic connection, business, labor, and farmers alike worry about import quotas, tariffs (fees placed on imports), and the soundness of the dollar. In short, white-collar business executives, blue-collar workers, and khaki-collar farmers seek to influence government because regulations, taxes, subsidies, and international economic policy all affect their economic livelihoods. Let us take a quick tour of some of the major organized interests in the economic policy arena.

–Lineberry, *Government in America*, p. 313

6. All sounds are waves produced by the vibrations of material objects. In pianos and violins, the sound is produced by the vibrating strings; in a clarinet, by a vibrating reed. The human voice results from the vibration of the vocal cords. In each of these cases a vibrating source sends a disturbance through the surrounding medium, usually air, in the form of longitudinal waves. The *loudness* of sound depends on the amplitude of these waves, that is, on how much air is set into motion. The *pitch* of sound is directly related to the frequency of the sound waves, which is identical to the frequency of the vibrating source. The pitches produced by lower frequencies are heard as low bass tones, and higher pitches are produced by higher frequencies. (We will treat pitch and loudness further in the next chapter.) The human ear can normally hear sounds made by vibrating bodies of frequencies in the range between 16 and 20,000 hertz. Sound waves with frequencies below 16 hertz are called *infrasonic*, and those with frequencies above 20,000 hertz are called *ultrasonic*. We cannot hear infrasonic and ultrasonic sound waves.

–Hewitt, *Conceptual Physics*, p. 294

7. Union membership has traditionally come from the ranks of the blue-collar employees in manufacturing. However, the number of blue-collar employees has declined so that they account for only about 30 percent of the total labor force in the United States, and this trend is expected to continue. White-collar employees comprise almost 54 percent of the labor force, service employees about 14 percent, and agricultural employees just over 2 percent. Future union growth will depend upon the success of unions in organizing employees in occupations other than blue-collar, such as government employees, office-clerical employees, and educators. Even professional athletes are unionized.

—Pickle and Abrahamson, *Introduction to Business,* p. 189

8. Critics of advertising argue that most ads are tasteless and wasteful assaults on consumers' senses. Since products and services in monopolistically competitive markets are, by definition, close substitutes, product characteristics are difficult to differentiate with *actual* differences. Rather, critics point out that advertising creates only imagined differences. A large number of competitive firms have the incentive to advertise in this manner, creating a confusing array of messages to consumers. In this view, advertising allocates demand among competitors without increasing the total demand for the product. To increase the total demand for the product, such as fast-food hamburgers, cat food, or breakfast cereal, advertising must reduce either consumers' savings or their expenditures on other goods. If advertising is unsuccessful at this task, the critics allege, it is unproductive because it merely allocates demand among competing firms producing goods that are fundamentally alike.

—Ekelund and Tollison, *Economics,* p. 233

9. When robbery is studied as work it does not look very different from many legitimate business pursuits. The popular myth depicting robbery as a senseless, violent act of plunder perpetrated by equally senseless and violent individuals can be upheld on some occasions. But a robbery is more accurately pictured as having characteristics that lie on a number of continua, of which three of the more important are *planning, organizing,* and *skill at victim management.* Those who make robbery a regular pursuit are likely to be found in robberies at the high end of these continua; those who are opportunists, or who indulge in robbery in a repetitive but sporadic and unsystematic manner, will be involved in robberies at the low end. Thus robberies committed by professionals tend to exhibit high levels of planning, organization, and victim-management skills; those committed by opportunists out for a fast buck tend to exhibit little in the way of planning and organization, and it may be in robberies committed by such individuals that we find confusion, fear, and disorder when it comes to handling their own and the victims' stresses and tensions.

—Barlow, *Introduction to Criminology,* p. 196

10. In the photosynthesis of green plants, as the energy of sunlight falls on the green pigment in the leaves, carbon dioxide and water are used to make food, and water and oxygen are released. The release

of oxygen by those first photosynthesizers was a critical step in the direction of life's development. In a sense, the production of oxygen falls into the "good news–bad news" category. It's good news for us, of course, since we need oxygen, but as oxygen began to replace hydrogen as the most prevalent gas in the atmosphere, it sounded the death knell for many of the early heterotrophs. This is because oxygen is a disruptive gas, as we know from seeing the process of rusting. . . . So, in the early days of life on the planet, many life forms were destroyed by the deadly and accumulating gas.

–Wallace, *Biology: The World of Life*, p. 48

RECOGNIZING DETAILS

The details in a paragraph are those facts and ideas that prove, explain, support, or give examples of the main idea of the paragraph. Once the topic and main idea have been identified, recognizing the supporting details is a relatively simple matter. The more difficult job involved is the selection of the few key, or most important, details that clearly support the main idea.

All details in a paragraph relate to and in some way expand the paragraph's main idea, but not all these details are completely essential to the author's central thought. Some details are just meant to describe; others are meant to provide added, but not essential, information; still others are intended merely to repeat or restate the main idea.

On the other hand, the key supporting details within a paragraph are those statements that carry the primary supporting evidence needed to back up the main idea. To find the key supporting details in a paragraph, ask yourself, What are the main facts the author uses to back up or prove what he or she said about the topic?

In the following paragraph, the topic sentence is underlined twice; the key supporting details are underlined once. Notice how the underlined details differ, in the type and importance of the information they provide, from the remaining details in the paragraph.

Some analysts attribute this downturn in [employee satisfaction] to "blue-collar blues" or "white-collar woes" attendant on jobs that have become boring, routine, and mundane. Others suggest that the problem has less to do with the jobs than with changes in the employees themselves. Many managers, for example, have become less confident and loyal to their firms in the face of acquisitions, mergers, and cutbacks that have changed their companies and resulted in a loss of 500,000 managerial jobs since 1979. Many employees who devoted all their energies to their employer may now believe that their energies were misplaced. Young employees are more cynical than were their parents and have expectations about buying power and life-style that have been disappointed. Many of these employees place family life and other nonwork interests above their jobs and refuse promotions and transfers. Finally, highly trained professional employees may identify more with their professions than with their employers. The satisfaction of a professional employee often depends on the degree to which his or her professional skills are recognized and used by the employer.

> –Szilagyi and Wallace, *Organizational Behavior and Performance,*
> p. 75

All the underlined details give the primary reasons why employees are dissatisfied with their jobs. The details in the remainder of the paragraph offer examples or explain these reasons further.

EXERCISE 4 _____

Directions: *Each of the following statements could function as the topic sentence of a paragraph. After each statement are sentences containing details that may relate to the main idea statement. Read each sentence and make a check mark beside those with details that can be considered primary support for the main idea statement.*

1. *Topic sentence:*
    Licorice is used in tobacco products because it has specific characteristics that cannot be found in any other single ingredient.
    Details:
    _____ a. McAdams & Co. is the largest importer and processor of licorice root.
    _____ b. Licorice blends with tobacco and provides added mildness.
    _____ c. Licorice provides a unique flavor and sweetens many types of tobacco.
    _____ d. The extract of licorice is present in relatively small amounts in most types of pipe tobacco.
    _____ e. Licorice helps tobacco retain the correct amount of moisture during storage.

2. *Topic sentence:*
    Many dramatic physical changes occur during adolescence between the ages of 13 and 15.
    Details:
    _____ a. Voice changes in boys begin to occur at age 13 or 14.
    _____ b. Facial proportions may change during adolescence.
    _____ c. The forehead tends to become wider, and the mouth widens.
    _____ d. Many teen-agers do not know how to react to these changes.
    _____ e. Primary sex characteristics begin to develop for both boys and girls.

3. *Topic sentence:*
    The development of speech in infants follows a definite sequence or pattern of development.
    Details:
    _____ a. By the time an infant is six months old, he or she can make twelve different speech sounds.
    _____ b. Before the age of three months, most infants are unable to produce any recognizable syllables.
    _____ c. During the first year, the number of vowel sounds a child can produce is greater than the number of consonant sounds he can make.

_____ d. During the second year, the number of consonant sounds a child can produce increases.

_____ e. Parents often reward the first recognizable word a child produces by smiling or speaking to the child.

4. *Topic sentence:*

The two main motives for attending a play are the desire for recreation and the need for relaxation.

Details:

_____ a. By becoming involved with the actors and their problems members of the audience temporarily suspend their personal cares and concerns.

_____ b. In America today, the success of a play is judged by its ability to attract a large audience.

_____ c. Almost everyone who attends a play expects to be entertained.

_____ d. Plays allow the audience to release tension, which facilitates relaxation.

_____ e. There is a smaller audience that looks to theater for intellectual stimulation.

5. *Topic sentence:*

In some parts of the world, famine is a constant human condition and exists due to a variety of causes.

Details:

_____ a. In parts of Africa, people are dying of hunger by the tens of thousands.

_____ b. Famine is partly caused by increased population.

_____ c. Advances in medicine have increased life expectancies, keeping more people active for longer periods of time.

_____ d. Agricultural technology has not made substantial advances in increasing the food supply.

_____ e. Due to the growth of cities, populations have become more dense, and agricultural support for these population centers is not available.

6. *Topic sentence:*

The amount of alcohol a person consumes has been found to depend on a number of socioeconomic factors such as age, sex, ethnic background, and occupation.

Details:

_____ a. Some religions prohibit consumption altogether, and most encourage moderation.

_____ b. The lowest proportion of drinkers is found among people with an educational level of below sixth grade.

_____ c. People in a lower socioeconomic level drink more than people in a higher socioeconomic level.

_____ d. In some cultures drinking is common at meals, but these same cultures disapprove of drunkenness.

_____ e. Farm owners have the highest proportion of nondrinkers, while professionals and businessmen have the highest proportion of drinkers.

7. *Topic sentence:*

An individual deals with anxiety in a variety of ways and produces a wide range of responses.

Details:

_____ a. Anxiety may manifest itself by such physical symptoms as increased heart activity or labored breathing.

_____ b. Fear, unlike anxiety, is a response to real or threatened danger.

_____ c. Psychologically, anxiety often produces a feeling of powerlessness, or lack of direct control over the immediate environment.

_____ d. Temporary blindness, deafness, or the loss of the sensation of touch are examples of extreme physical responses to anxiety.

_____ e. Some people cannot cope with anxiety and are unable to control the neurotic behavior associated with anxiety.

8. *Topic sentence:*

An individual's status or importance within a group affects his or her behavior in that particular group.

Details:

_____ a. High-status individuals frequently arrive late at social functions.

_____ b. Once a person achieves high status, he or she attempts to maintain it.

_____ c. High-status individuals demand more privileges.

_____ d. Low-status individuals are less resistant to change within the group structure than persons of high status.

_____ e. There are always fewer high-status members than low-status members in any particular group.

9. *Topic sentence:*

An oligopoly is a market structure in which only a few companies sell a certain product.

Details:

_____ a. The automobile industry is a good example of an oligopoly, although it gives the appearance of being highly competitive.

_____ b. The breakfast cereal, soap, and cigarette industries, although basic to our economy, operate as oligopolies.

_____ c. Monopolies refer to market structures in which only one industry produces a particular product.

_____ d. Monopolies are able to exert more control and fixation of price than oligopolies.

_____ e. In the oil industry, because there are only a few producers, each producer has a fairly large share of the sales.

10. *Topic sentence:*

Advertising can be used to expand consumer choice as well as to limit it.

Details:

_____ a. Food stores that typically advertise their "specials" each Wednesday in the local paper are encouraging consumer choice.

_____ b. Department store advertising often makes the consumer aware of new products and styles, as well as of current prices of products.

_____ c. Misleading or excessive advertising is usually rejected by the consuming public.

_____ d. Exaggerated claims made by some advertisers serve to limit the consumer's actual knowledge and free choice of products.

_____ e. Advertising that provides little or no factual information, but attempts to make the brand name well known, actually restricts consumers' free choice.

EXERCISE 5 _____

Directions: Read each paragraph and identify the topic and location of the main idea. Write each in the space provided. Then underline the key supporting details.

1. Compared with vision and audition, taste is relatively poorly developed in humans. People often attribute the pleasure of eating good food to the sense of taste, but more often it is the smell that induces enjoyment. You have noticed, of course, that food resembles cardboard in flavor when a head cold congests your nasal passages. The tongue, which registers taste, is actually sensitive to a mere handful of properties, notably salty, sweet, sour, and bitter. These properties are detected by the 10,000 or so *taste buds* that line the tongue; taste buds live only a few days and then are replaced by new ones. Different taste buds are sensitive to different sensory properties, and they are not distributed uniformly on the tongue. . . . For example, the tip of the tongue is more responsive to sweetness, the base of the tongue to bitterness. However, most individual taste buds actually respond to more than one taste, so a substance's taste probably arises from the pattern of neural activity across many taste buds. . . . Of course, the tongue also senses the texture and temperatures of foods, which may add considerably to the enjoyment of eating.

   –Roediger et al., *Psychology*, p. 109

   Topic: _____

   Main idea: _____

2. In the economic sense, *utility* refers to the power that goods or services have to satisfy a human want. There are four types of utility: form, possession, place, and time. Form utility is produced when raw materials are extracted from nature and their structure or shape is changed so that they satisfy a human want. For example, wheat is ground into flour by the miller, and then the flour is converted into bread by a bakery. Form utility is a production utility. The other three types of utilities are included in the marketing process. If goods or services are to satisfy individuals, they must be in their possession (possession utility). For this to happen, goods and services must be moved from the place where they have limited usefulness to the location where they have maximum usefulness in fulfilling consumer wants (place utility). Furthermore, if goods (or services) are to be of value to the final consumers, they must be available when they are demanded (time utility). For example, an appliance dealer stocks more air-conditioning units during the spring and summer months, when demand is greatest.

   –Pickle and Abrahamson, *Introduction to Business*, pp. 201–202

   Topic: _____

   Main idea: _____

3. Perhaps we can best describe a theory by showing how one can be developed. Suppose someone comes up with an idea—one that

explains certain observed phenomena in nature. At first, it is regarded as just that, an idea. But after it has been carefully described and its premises precisely defined, it may then become a *hypothesis*—an idea that can be tested. In a sense, the hypothesis is the first part of an "if . . . then" statement. The "then" predicts the result of the hypothesis, so one can know by testing if the hypothesis is sound. A hypothesis can also stand as a provisional statement for which more data are needed. If rigorous, carefully controlled testing supports the hypothesis, more confidence will be placed in it, until it finally gains the status of a theory. The theory itself, however, may remain unproven and unprovable. A hypothesis, then, is a possible explanation to be tested, whereas a *theory* is a more-or-less verified explanation that accounts for observed phenomena in nature.

–Wallace, *Biology: The World of Life*, p. 28

Topic: _____

Main idea: _____

4. Freewriting is nothing more than putting down on paper all your thoughts exactly as they occur to you when you start thinking about writing a paper. And, as you know from having listened closely to your own thoughts, while your mind is working it jumps from idea to idea with little apparent order. Nor do the ideas come out as complete sentences. Nevertheless, there is value to committing this jumble of thoughts to paper despite their apparent randomness. Many writers, including professionals, use freewriting not only because they find it helps them to discover ideas about the topic that they did not know they had, or to make connections that had not previously occurred to them, but also because it helps clear out any minor annoyances that may be blocking their creativity. It is also useful because it provides a starting point on a project that seems, at first glance, too complex to organize coherently. In freewriting you begin with whatever is on the top of your mind and let your thoughts go where they choose. At this point, you forget about organizing, forget about correcting, forget about revising, since in this initial stage these concerns will only interrupt the free flow of your ideas.

–Anselmo et al., *Thinking and Writing in College*, p. 13

Topic: _____

Main idea: _____

5. The importance of formal organizations in modern complex societies can hardly be overestimated. Every day, we deal with some sort of formal organization in connection with work, food, travel, health care, police protection, or some other necessity of life. Organizations enable people who are often total strangers to work together toward common goals. They create levels of authority and channels of command that clarify who gives orders, who obeys them, and who does which tasks. They are also a source of continuity and permanence in a society's efforts to meet specific goals. Individual members may come and go, but the organization

continues to function. Thus formal organizations make it possible for highly complex industrialized societies to meet their most fundamental needs and pursue their collective aspirations.

–Eshleman and Cashion, *Sociology*, pp. 121–122

Topic: _____

Main idea: _____

6. Matter exists in four states: *solid*, *liquid*, *gaseous*, and *plasma*. In all states the atoms are perpetually moving. In solid state the atoms and molecules vibrate about fixed positions. If the rate of molecular vibration is increased sufficiently, molecules will shake apart and wander throughout the material, vibrating in nonfixed positions. The shape of the material is no longer fixed but takes the shape of its container. This is the liquid state. If more energy is put into the material and the molecules vibrate at even greater rates, they may break away from one another and assume the gaseous state. H_2O is a common example of this changing of states. When solid, it is ice. If we heat the ice, the increased molecular motion jiggles the molecules out of their fixed positions, and we have water. If we heat the water, we can reach a stage where continued molecular vibration results in a separation between water molecules, and we have steam. Continued heating causes the molecules to separate into atoms; if we heat the steam to temperatures exceeding 2000°C, the atoms themselves will be shaken apart, making a gas of free electrons and bare nuclei called plasma.

–Hewitt, *Conceptual Physics*, p. 160

Topic: _____

Main idea: _____

7. There are two kinds of government expenditures: direct purchases of goods and services and transfer payments. *Direct purchases* of newly produced goods and services include such items as missiles, highway construction, police and fire stations, consulting services, and the like. In other words, the government purchases real goods and services. *Transfer payments* are the transfers of income from some citizens (via taxation) to other citizens; these are sometimes called *income security transfers* or payments. Examples of transfer payments are Social Security contributions and payments, Aid to Families with Dependent Children, food stamp programs, and other welfare payments. These transfers do not represent direct purchase by the government of new goods and services, but they influence purchases of goods and services in the private sector. They are a growing part of government's role in the mixed economy.

–Ekelund and Tollison, *Economics*, p. 58

Topic: _____

Main idea: _____

8. Ordinary comparison shows similarities between two things *of the same class* (two computer keyboards, two technicians, two methods

of cleaning dioxin-contaminated sites). Analogy, on the other hand, shows some essential similarity between two things of *different classes* (report writing and computer programming, computer memory and post office boxes.) Analogies are good for emphasizing a point (e.g., Rain in our state is now as acidic as vinegar). Analogies are especially useful in translating something abstract, complex, or unfamiliar to laypersons—as long as the easier subject is broadly familiar to readers. For instance, an analogy between trite language and TV dinners (to make the point that both are effortless but unimpressive) would be lost on anyone who has never tasted a TV dinner. Analogy, therefore, calls for particularly careful analysis of audience.

–Dumont and Lannon, *Business Communications*, p. 83

Topic: _____

Main idea: _____

9. One hallmark of the postindustrial society is a revolution in communications. Information is processed and transmitted almost instantaneously, with a resultant explosion in both the amount of knowledge available and the speed with which it is communicated. Information doubles every five and one-half years. . . . Simultaneously, cultural change is more rapid today than ever before, and these two situations have made young people frequently better informed than their elders. . . . In times of slower cultural change, the older generation held the wisdom of the society, which they passed down to the younger generation as they saw fit. This is not so in a time of rapid change; young people are often exposed to more, sooner, than are their parents, and we are witnessing in postindustrial society the phenomenon of youth influencing societal standards. Mead . . . points to attitudes toward racism, sexuality, drug use, and popular music and art as areas in which this phenomenon is most obvious. And any parent who has tried to help an elementary school child with "computer literacy" homework is acutely aware that the child is gaining knowledge of which the parent never dreamed. In the last decades of the twentieth century, it may not be unlikely for a twenty-year-old to seem woefully old-fashioned to a fifteen-year-old!

–Fuhrmann, *Adolescence, Adolescents*, pp. 34–35

Topic: _____

Main idea: _____

10. Content theories of individual motivation focus on the question of what it is that energizes, arouses, or starts behavior. The answers to this question have been provided by various motivational theorists in their discussions of the needs or motives that drive people and the incentives that cause them to behave in a particular manner. A need or motive is considered an internal quality of the individual. Hunger (the need for food) and a steady job (the need for security) are seen as motives that arouse people and may cause them to choose a specific behavioral act or pattern of acts. Incentives, on the

other hand, are external factors associated with the goal or end result the person hopes to achieve through his or her actions. The income earned from a steady day of work (motivation by a need for security) is valued by the person. It is this value or attractiveness that is the incentive.

–Szilagyi and Wallace, *Organizational Behavior and Performance*, p. 94

Topic: _____

Main idea: _____

UNSTATED MAIN IDEAS

Occasionally, a writer does not directly state the main idea of a given paragraph in a topic sentence. Instead, he or she leaves it up to the reader to infer, or reason out, what the main idea of the paragraph is. This type of paragraph contains only details or specifics that relate to a given topic and substantiate an unstated main idea. To read this type of paragraph, start as you would for paragraphs with stated main ideas. Ask yourself the question for finding the topic: What is the one thing the author is discussing throughout the paragraph? Then try to think of a sentence about the topic that all the details included in the paragraph would support.

Read the paragraph in the following example. First, identify the topic. Then study the details and think of a general statement that all the details in the paragraph would support or prove.

Suppose a group of plumbers in a community decide to set standard prices for repair services and agree to quote the same price for the same job. Is this ethical? Suppose a group of automobile dealers agree to abide strictly by the used car blue book prices on trade-ins. Is this ethical? Two meat supply houses serving a large university submit identical bids each month for the meat contract. Is this ethical?

This paragraph describes three specific instances in which there was agreement to fix prices. Clearly, the main idea of the author is whether price collusion is ethical, but that main idea is not directly stated in a sentence anywhere within the passage.

EXERCISE 6 _____

Directions: *In each of these paragraphs, the main idea is not directly stated. Read the paragraph, identify the topic, and write it in the space provided. Then write a sentence that expresses the main idea of the passage.*

1. The first Congress consisted of 26 senators and 65 representatives. With each new state added to the union, the Senate has grown by two, so that it now has 100 members. As the nation's population grew, the size of the House of Representatives grew also. In 1922 the Congress passed a law setting the maximum size of the House at

435 members, where it remains today. . . . In the first House each member represented around 50,000 citizens. The average representative now serves some 550,000 constituents.

–Wasserman, *The Basics of American Politics*, p. 87

Topic: _____

Main idea: _____

_____

2. *Job analysis* involves the systematic collection of all information about a job to determine its requirements. This information should be obtained from a number of sources, such as the person performing the task, the immediate supervisor, observation by work-study specialists, and labor union representatives, in unionized companies. From the job analysis, a job description is prepared. The *job description* identifies the authority of the task, its location in the company, and the activities and major responsibilities of the job. Whereas the job description describes the task, the *job specification* focuses on people. It outlines the personal qualifications essential for completing the task, such as education, experience, mental and visual abilities; the supervisory responsibility for the position; the physical requirements of the task; accountability; the complexity of duties; working conditions; and work relations expected with others. This information is critical for human resource managers as they assist line managers in completing the staffing process.

–Pickle and Abrahamson, *Introduction to Business*, p. 152

Topic: _____

Main idea: _____

_____

3. In probability, each repetition of an experiment is called a *trial*. The possible results of each trial are *outcomes*. An example of a probability experiment is the tossing of a coin. Each trial of the experiment (each toss) has two possible outcomes, heads and tails, abbreviated *h* and *t,* respectively. If the two outcomes, *h* and *t,* are equally likely to occur, then the coin is not "loaded" to favor one side over the other. Such a coin is called *fair*. For a coin that is not loaded, this "equally likely" assumption is made for each trial.

–Miller and Heeren, *Mathematical Ideas*, p. 483

Topic: _____

Main idea: _____

_____

4. In 1914, for example, more than 70 percent of Russia's people still worked in agriculture. They had to compete against the efficient foreign farmers, who drove prices down. The tsarist minister of

finance, who oversaw a program of grain export to attract foreign loans, stated that "we may go hungry, but we will export." Export Russia did, but the famine of 1891 devastated the peasants in the European provinces of the country. Other farming classes also endured difficult times during the century, especially the Irish peasants, who in the 1840s suffered under the weight of the potato famine. The peasants of southern and eastern Europe had to struggle to maintain a tenuous existence.

–Wallbank et al., *Civilization Past and Present*, p. 556

Topic: _____

Main idea: _____

_____

5. Constructing a speech in a fashion that reveals the major conflicts between persons or groups is one way of gaining and holding attention. Another way of generating a sense of conflict is to use a narrative approach in retelling the story of a recent controversy. This is especially true if the audience senses they are getting inside information—incidents and events not generally known. In generating a sense of conflict, be certain that your representation of events is as accurate as possible. If you are detailing the sides of a controversy to audience members who belong to one or the other side, you can expect them to be critical of your depiction of their respective positions. Also be wary of using a "straw man" approach—setting up a sham conflict and then resolving it. The effectiveness of your message depends on the audience's perception of the sincerity and accuracy of your description.

–Ehninger et al., *Principles and Types of Speech Communications*, p. 46

Topic: _____

Main idea: _____

_____

6. As we noted earlier, when carbohydrates are taken into the body in excess of the body's energy requirements, they are stored temporarily as glycogen or, more permanently, as fats. Conversely, when the energy requirements of the body are not met by its immediate intake of food, glycogen and, subsequently, fat are broken down to fill these requirements. Whether or not the body uses up its own storage molecules has nothing to do with the molecular form in which the energy comes into the body. It is simply a matter of whether these molecules, as they are broken down, release sufficient numbers of calories.

–Curtis, *Biology*, p. 61

Topic: _____

Main idea: _____

_____

7. A sudden explosion at 200 decibels can cause massive damage in a fraction of a second; however, routine exposure to sounds less than 100 decibels can also cause significant hearing loss. Hearing loss from loud sounds is called *stimulation deafness*. Most people report such hearing loss for up to several hours after listening to a rock concert in an enclosed area. Not surprisingly, then, more permanent hearing loss is an occupational hazard for rock musicians, because they are exposed to such intense sound levels so frequently. It also occurs in many other occupations where people are exposed to loud noises for extended periods.

–Zimbardo, *Psychology and Life*, p. 169

Topic: _____

Main idea: _____

_____

8. No one has ever "seen" motivation, just as no one has ever "seen" learning. All we see are changes in behavior. To explain these observed changes, we make *inferences* about underlying psychological and physiological variables—"educated hunches" that are formalized in the concept of motivation. Among the words most commonly associated with motivation are *goals, needs, wants, intentions,* and *purposes;* all of which relate to factors that cause us to act. Two motivational terms that are frequently used by researchers in this area are *drive* and *motive.* Psychologists usually use the label *drive* to mean motivation for action that is assumed to be primarily biologically instigated, as in hunger. They often use *motive* to refer to psychologically and socially instigated motivation, which is generally assumed to be, at least in part, learned. A motive can be either conscious or nonconscious (in the ways we distinguished between them in chapter 7).

–Zimbardo, *Psychology and Life*, p. 376

Topic: _____

Main idea: _____

_____

9. For most of earth's history, the land was bare. A billion years ago, seaweeds clung to the shores at low tide and perhaps some gray-green lichens patched a few inland rocks. But, had anyone been there to observe it, the earth's surface would generally have appeared as barren and forbidding as the bleak Martian landscape. According to the fossil record, plants first began to invade the land a mere half billion years ago. Not until then did the earth's surface truly come to life. As a film of green spread from the edges of the waters, other forms of life—the heterotrophs—were able to follow. The shapes of these new forms and the ways in which they lived were determined by the plant life that preceded them. Plants supplied not only their food—their chemical energy—but also their nesting, hiding, stalking, and breeding places.

–Curtis, *Biology*, p. 573

Topic: _____

Main idea: _____

_____

10. A contract is not enforceable by law if it provides for actions that are not acceptable by law. Any contract that calls for criminal or civil wrongs is not a valid contract. For example, a contract in which one person agrees to beat up another person in exchange for money is not a valid and enforceable contract because it calls for a criminal act. In addition, a contract between two businesses that provides for price fixing is not a valid enforceable contract because it requires action that is a civil wrong under law.

–Pickle and Abrahamson, *Introduction to Business,* p. 417

Topic: _____

Main idea: _____

_____

EXERCISE 7 _____

Directions: *Turn to the sample textbook chapter included in Appendix B of this text. In the section "Homeotherms" on pages 418–424, read each paragraph and identify the topic and main idea. Then place brackets around the topic and underline the sentence that expresses the main idea.*

EXERCISE 8 _____

Directions: *Select a three-page section from a textbook that you have been assigned to read. After reading each paragraph, place brackets around the topic and then underline the sentence stating the main idea. If any of the paragraphs have an unstated main idea, write a sentence in the margin which summarizes the main idea. Continue reading and marking until you have completed the three pages.*

SUMMARY

A paragraph is a group of related sentences about a single topic. A paragraph has three essential elements:

1. Topic: the one thing the entire paragraph is about
2. Main idea: a direct statement or an implied idea about the topic
3. Details: the proof, reasons, or examples that explain or support the paragraph's main idea

A paragraph, then, provides explanation, support, or proof for a main idea (expressed or unexpressed) about a particular topic. A topic sentence expressing the main idea of the paragraph may be located anywhere within the paragraph, but the most common positions for this sentence are first, last, in the middle, or both first and last.

While most paragraphs contain a topic sentence that directly states the main idea of the paragraph, occasionally an author will write a paragraph in which the main idea is not stated in any single sentence. Instead, it is left up to you, the reader, to infer, or reason out, the main idea. To find the main idea when it is unstated, ask yourself the following question: What is the one thing (topic) this paragraph is about, and what is the author saying about this thing (main idea)?

9

Following Thought Patterns in Textbooks

> **Use this chapter to:**
> 1. *Increase your comprehension of passages and textbook selections.*
> 2. *Learn how to recognize patterns of thought in textbooks.*

Up to this point you have learned much about the structure and organization of sentences and paragraphs. You have learned how to identify a sentence's message, and you have seen how other parts of the sentence further explain that message. You have also learned how to identify the topic and main idea of a paragraph and how the remainder of the paragraph explains the main idea.

For you as a college student, however, the focus in reading will be neither individual sentences nor single paragraphs. Instead, you will be reading groups of paragraphs, or passages, organized into articles, essays, or sections of textbook chapters.

Although you will read a variety of materials, *most* of what you read will be textbooks, which are unique, highly organized information sources. If you become familiar with their organization and structure and learn to follow the writers' thought patterns, you will find that you can read them more easily. The skills you learn in reading textbooks can be applied to other types of reading, including articles and essays.

Reading a chapter can be compared to watching a football game. You watch the overall progression of the game from start to finish, but you also watch individual plays and notice how each is executed. Furthermore, you observe how several plays work together as part of a game strategy or pattern. Similarly, when reading a chapter, you are concerned with the progression of ideas. But you are also concerned with each separate idea and how it is developed and explained. Finally, you are concerned with how the ideas and details work together to form a pattern.

This chapter focuses on three important features of textbook chapters: (1) their overall structure or progression of ideas, (2) types of details used to explain each idea, and (3) organizational patterns (how ideas fit together).

RECOGNIZING THE STRUCTURE OF IDEAS

A textbook is divided into parts, each successively smaller and more limited in scope than the one before it. As a general rule, the whole text is divided into chapters; each chapter may be divided into sections; each section is subdivided by headings into subsections; and each subsection is divided into paragraphs. Each of these parts has a similar structure. Just as each paragraph has a main idea and supporting information, each subsection, section, or chapter has its own key idea and supporting information.

Locate the Controlling Idea and Supporting Information

The controlling idea in a textbook section is the broad, general idea the writer is discussing throughout the section. It is the central, most important thought that is explained, discussed, or supported throughout the section. It is similar to the main idea of the paragraph, but is a more general, more comprehensive idea that takes numerous paragraphs to explain.

The controlling idea, then, is developed or explained throughout the section. Subheadings are often used to divide a section into smaller units. Each subsection, or group of paragraphs, explains one idea or major concept, the central thought. Each paragraph within a subsection provides one main idea that supports or explains the central thought. As you read each paragraph, you should understand its function and connection to the other paragraphs in the section. The end of each section is an ideal checkpoint for monitoring your comprehension. Although the number of subheadings and paragraphs will vary, the structure of textbook sections is usually consistent (see Figure 9-1).

Read the section in Figure 9-2, "Sources of Stress," from a chapter in the book *Psychology* by Roediger et al. titled "Emotion and Stress." (*Note:* ellipses [. . .] indicate text omitted from the original.)

Notice that paragraph 1 of the section introduces the subject: stress. The paragraph then defines stress, states that it has a variety of causes, and gives some examples of stressful situations. The last sentence of the first paragraph states the controlling idea of the section: The most common sources of stress will be discussed. The subheadings divide the remaining text, and each identifies one source of stress. Each group of paragraphs under a subheading explains one source of stress (its central thought). Each paragraph beneath a subheading contributes one key piece of information (its main idea) that explains or supports the central thought. Then, within each paragraph, the main idea is supported with facts and details.

In the first subsection on life changes, the first sentence in paragraph 2 states the central thought of that section. Within that paragraph, life changes are discussed and a measurement scale is described. Each subsequent paragraph discusses one aspect of life change. Paragraph 3 is about how often changes occur; paragraph 4 compares the frequency of life changes in modern society with previous times; and paragraph 5 describes a measurement scale that rates life changes as positive or negative.

This example shows that the subheadings divided the section into four parts, or subsections. The section began with a general discussion of the subject and was divided into four smaller topics. This progression of ideas from large to small, general to particular, is typical of most text-

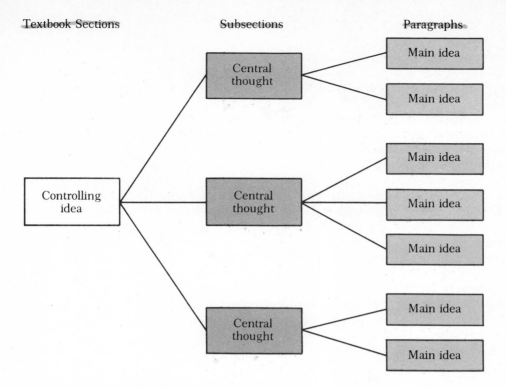

Textbook Sections	Subsections	Paragraphs

FIGURE 9-1   Organization of a Textbook Section

books. When you are familiar with and can follow this progression, your textbooks will seem more logical and systematic and easier to read.

EXERCISE 1

Directions: *Turn to the beginning of Chapter 4 on page 51 of this text and complete the following instructions.*

1. The controlling idea of the chapter is expressed in the first three introductory paragraphs. Underline it.
2. The dark-print headings divide the chapter into three parts, each of which is further divided by subheadings. How many main points are included under each?

EXERCISE 2

Directions: *Read the subsection "Health Care System and Health Policy Formation" beginning on page 388 of the psychology sample textbook chapter reprinted in Appendix A. Complete the following instructions.*

1. The controlling idea is presented in the first paragraph. Underline that idea.
2. The remaining paragraphs develop and explain this idea. For each paragraph, underline the main idea. Review your underlining. Notice how each paragraph provides further information about the delivery of health care.

SOURCES OF STRESS

When emotions are prolonged or excessive, the associated physiological changes can become detrimental to health. *Stress* is a general term that refers to physiological and psychological reactions to certain events in the environment. Generally, stress is created by a perceived threat to an individual's physical or psychological well-being, and the feeling that he or she is unable to deal with it. Prolonged or excessive emotion is only one source of stress. The list of things that bring on stress varies widely from individual to individual. Some events, such as the death of a loved one, cause stress for almost everyone; otherwise, the context of the event and the individual's appraisal of the event determine whether or not stress occurs. Retirement, for instance, threatens self-esteem and induces great stress in some people; it presents a welcome opportunity to do different things for others. Keeping the importance of the individual's perceptions in mind, we shall consider the most common sources of stress.

Life Changes

One general source of stress is life change. Any change in life that requires adaptation may cause some stress whether or not the change is beneficial. The greater the degree of change and necessary adaptation required, the greater the stress will be. To quantify life change, Holmes and Rahe and their colleagues developed the *Social Readjustment Scale (SRRS)*. They used people of many different ages and groups and obtained wide agreement on the seriousness of various events. . . .

Life changes take place at all ages but, naturally, how often each kind occurs differs at each age. Illness and death in the family, for example, become more frequent as one grows older. At some time most people will experience most of the stress-producing life changes. Studies using this scale have found that high life-change scores—totaling 300 or greater—are related to frequency of ailments, accidents, and athletic injuries.

Some theorists suggest that modern society produces more stress than did earlier periods of human life, in part because of the large number and rapidity of changes people now endure. . . .

Irwin G. Sarason and his colleagues recently modified the Holmes-Rahe scale by having subjects rate the severity of the perceived positive or negative impact of each relevant event. . . .

Minor Annoyances
....

Conflict
....

Chronic Discomfort
....

FIGURE 9-2   Excerpt from *Emotion and Stress*

EXERCISE 3 _____

Directions: *Choose a three- to four-page section from one of your textbooks which you have already read, then answer the following questions.*

1. What is the overall topic or subject discussed in this section?

_____

2. What is the controlling idea?

_____

_____

3. Is the section divided by subheadings? If so, underline the central thought in each subsection.

TYPES OF SUPPORTING INFORMATION

Authors use various types of supporting information to explain a controlling idea of a textbook section. Recognizing these types of supporting information is the key to understanding *how* the author develops and connects his or her ideas.

Examples

Usually a writer gives an example to make an idea practical and understandable. An example shows how a principle, concept, problem, or process works or can be applied in a real situation. In the following paragraph, notice how the writer explains how situations influence purchase behavior by giving the example of a tire blow out.

> The situations consumers find themselves in can also have direct influence on their purchase behavior. Consider, for example, the consumer behavior of a person who has a tire blow out one block away from a service station. The amount of information sought and the number of alternatives considered would vary substantially depending upon the status of the spare tire. Without a good spare, the consumer might purchase a new tire from the nearby gas station, particularly if it were the only seller of tires in the area. If, on the other hand, the spare was in good shape, the consumer might take considerable time in buying another tire, looking at which store had tires on sale and perhaps calling or visiting several stores to identify and evaluate the alternatives.

–Kinnear and Bernhardt, *Principles of Marketing*, p. 148

As you read examples, be sure to look for the connection between the example and the concept it illustrates. Remember, examples are important only for the ideas they illustrate.

Description

An author uses description to help you visualize the appearance, organization, or composition of an object, a place, or a process. Descriptions are usually detailed and are intended to help you create a mental picture of what is being described. Read the following description of the stylistic features of various artists' work.

> To turn now to our central topic, style in art, we can all instantly tell the difference between a picture by Van Gogh and one by Norman Rockwell or Walt Disney, even though the subject matter of all three pictures is the same, for instance, a seated woman. How can we tell? By the style, that is, by line, color, medium, and so forth—all of the things we talked about earlier in this chapter. Walt Disney's figures tend to be built up out of circles (think of Mickey Mouse), and the color shows no modeling or traces of brush strokes; Norman Rockwell's methods of depicting figures are different, and Van Gogh's are different in yet other ways. Similarly, a Chinese landscape, painted with ink on silk or on paper, simply cannot look like a Van Gogh landscape done with oil paint on canvas, partly because the materials prohibit such identity and partly because the Chinese painter's vision of landscape (usually lofty mountains) is not Van Gogh's vision. In short, we recognize certain *distinguishing characteristics* that mark an artist, or a period, or a culture, and these constitute the style.
>
> –Barnet, *A Short Guide to Writing About Art*, p. 40

You should be able to visualize, for example, what Walt Disney's figures look like or features of a Chinese landscape. Each detail contributes a bit of information which, when added to other bits, reveals its composition.

Facts and Statistics

Another way to support an idea is to include facts or statistics that provide information about the main or controlling idea. Read the following passage, and notice how facts and statistics are used to support the idea that age is a limiting factor in the war against poverty.

> Another limitation of the success of the War on Poverty involves age rather than residence or region. Most of the people who officially moved out of poverty, especially in the 1970s, were older. And even their relative gains began to be reversed in the early 1980s.
>
> Between 1970 and 1978, the number of poor people over 65 dropped by almost a million and a half. Most of this decline resulted from improved Social Security benefits. But this didn't mean that the low-income aged achieved genuine comfort and security. Many still lived uncomfortably close to the poverty line, and the poverty rate for the elderly remains higher than that of most other groups. (And the Social Security system itself, of course, has become ever more precarious in the face of economic stagnation and political criticism.)
>
> –Currie and Skolnick, *America's Problems*, p. 115

When reading factual support or explanations, remember these questions: *What? When? Where? How?* and *Why?* They will lead you to the most important facts and statistics contained in the passage.

Citation of Research Evidence

In many fields of study, authors support their ideas by citing research that has been done on the topic. Authors report the results of surveys, experiments, and research studies to substantiate theories or principles or to lend support to a particular viewpoint. The following excerpt from a social problems textbook reports the results of research conducted to describe the extent of family violence.

> One of the most extensive recent studies of family violence, conducted by the sociologists Murray Straus, Richard Gelles, and Suzanne Steinmetz, concluded that "violence between family members is probably as common as love." . . . On the basis of a sample survey of more than 2,000 families, the researchers estimated that in the course of a year, about one-sixth of married people have engaged in at least one act of violence against their spouse, ranging from pushing, shoving, or "throwing something" to "beating up spouse" and "using a knife or gun." And that over the course of their marriages, more than one-fourth of the spouses would be involved in an act of violence. The researchers argued that those figures probably *underestimated* the amount of serious violence between husbands and wives, partly because many failed to report or admit family violence and partly because the study didn't include divorced couples, who might be expected to have experienced even higher levels of violence while married. The informal estimate was that *50 to 60 percent of couples* had engaged in violence at some point over the course of their marriages.
>
> –Currie and Skolnick, *America's Problems*, pp. 266–267

When reading research reports, keep the following questions in mind. They will help you see the relationship between the research results and the author's controlling idea.

1. Why was the research done?
2. What did it show?
3. Why did the author include it?

EXERCISE 4 _____

Directions: *Read the following passages and identify the type of supporting information or detail that is used in each.*

1. Colors in your photographs will vary depending on the time of day that you made them. Photographing very early or late in the day can produce strikingly beautiful pictures simply because the light is not its usual "white" color.
   In the earliest hours of the day, before sunrise, the world is

essentially black and white. The light has a cool, shadowless quality. Colors are muted. They grow in intensity slowly, gradually differentiating themselves. But right up to the moment of sunrise, they remain pearly and flat.

As soon as the sun rises, the light warms up. Because of the great amount of atmosphere that the low-lying sun must penetrate, the light that gets through is much warmer in color than it will be later in the day—that is, more on the red or orange side because the colder blue hues are filtered out by the air. Shadows, by contrast, may look blue because they lack gold sunlight and also because they reflect blue from the sky.

The higher the sun climbs in the sky, the greater the contrast between colors. At noon, particularly in the summer, this contrast is at its peak. Film for use in daylight is balanced for midday sunlight, so colors appear accurately rendered. Each color stands out in its own true hue. Shadows at noon are more likely to be neutral black.

–Upton, *Photography*, p. 232

Type of detail: _Description_

2. In the early 1960s, for example, Thorsten Sellin and Marvin Wolfgang (1964) asked samples of judges, police, and university students to rate the seriousness of 141 offenses. They found much agreement. A later survey of adults in Baltimore (Rossi et al., 1974) again found much consensus on a similar list of illegal acts. But, this study did find a prominent difference among white and black respondents: blacks rated violence among family and friends lower in seriousness than did whites. Thus, although there may be general agreement on crime seriousness, subgroups of the population may not share the general attitude toward particular crimes.

The most recent, and by far the most extensive, study confirms these earlier findings (Wolfgang et al., 1985). A total of 204 crimes were rated by a national sample of sixty thousand respondents (though no one person rated more than 25 offenses). . . . Overall, there was broad consensus. Violent crimes were rated more serious than were property offenses, and drug dealing was taken seriously, as was virtually any offense that had the potential for harming or killing more than one person. The study showed also that people evaluate crimes according to their consequences for the victims, and not surprisingly, respondents who had been victims of crime intended to assign higher seriousness scores than did others. Whites tended generally to assign higher scores than did minority groups.

–Barlow, *Introduction to Criminology*, p. 9

Type of detail: _Citiation of Res_

3. The Earth's crust and the uppermost part of the mantle are known as the *lithosphere*. This is a fairly rigid zone that extends about 100 km below the Earth's surface. The crust extends some 60 km or so under continents, but only about 10 km below the ocean floor. The continental crust has a lower density than the oceanic crust. It is primarily a light granitic rock rich in the silicates of aluminum, iron, and magnesium. In a simplified view, the continental crust can be thought of as layered: On top of a layer of igneous rock

(molten rock that has hardened, such as granite) lies a thin layer of sedimentary rocks (rocks formed by sediment and fragments that water deposited, such as limestone and sandstone); there is also a soil layer deposited during past ages in the parts of continents that have had no recent volcanic activity or mountain building.

Sandwiched between the lithosphere and the lower mantle is the partially molten material known as the *asthenosphere*, about 150 km thick. It consists primarily of iron and magnesium silicates that readily deform and flow under pressure.

–Berman and Evans, *Exploring the Cosmos*, p. 145

Type of detail: _____

4.   Human beings, like all other animals, learn quickly to react to stimuli in their environments; we learn to sort out stimuli (experiences) into various categories of things or events in order to predict consequences. But, unlike most other animals, humans can go beyond sorting, even beyond understanding consequences—they can seek *coherence* in their environments. (1) We can *generalize* and *anticipate*. A baby who burns its hand on a hot stove, a match, and a metal sheet sitting in the sun quickly learns that "hot objects produce pain"; the baby can remember past instances of pain and anticipate future pain when it notices even previously unexperienced "hot objects" in its surroundings. (2) We search for *coherent structures* in our environments. Young children soon learn to seek relationships between and among items in their environment. They learn early that one set of furniture comprises a bedroom; another set, a kitchen; and another set, a playroom; they soon learn that living and dead objects are treated differently. By early elementary school, children can determine what is "foreground" or "figure" in a picture, and what is "background" or supporting detail. An important part of environmental control is understanding relationships between and among the environmental elements. (3) Structures become so important to us psychologically that we learn to *fill in or complete* missing elements. If someone says to you, "One, two, three, four," you almost automatically continue, "five, six, seven, eight." Cartoonists can draw a few features of a famous person, and most readers will be able to identify the person in question. This is because we all have what Gestalt psychologists term the "drive to complete," the need to complete missing elements and thus make sense out of some stimulus.

–Ehninger, *Principles and Types of Speech Communication*, pp. 151–52

Type of detail: _____Example_____

5.   As we'll see, infant death rates in this country are crucially affected by race. But it is important to realize that America's problem of infant mortality goes beyond race as well—even the *white* rate of infant death in the United States is higher than the rates in much of Western Europe and Japan.

Our high rates of infant mortality are a major reason why . . . Americans' life expectancy, especially for men, is somewhat lower than that of people in many other industrial societies. Life expectancy at birth is a tricky statistic; it represents an average of the chances of dying at any point in the life cycle. Thus, the fact that an American male at birth, at the end of the 1970s, could expect to live almost four years less than a Japanese and three years less than a Swede largely reflects the much higher chance that the American male might die during his first year. But these differences also persist through childhood and adolescence into young adulthood. In the mid-1970s, an American girl aged 1 to 4 had nearly twice the chance of dying as a Swedish girl those ages; a young American woman aged 15 to 24 had almost twice the chance of death faced by a young British woman. . . .

–Currie and Skolnick, *America's Problems*, pp. 266–267

Type of detail: _____

6. Sociologist Rosabeth Moss Kanter spent seven months studying a typical suburban nursery school located in the Midwest. According to Kanter, the teachers in this school believed that children who followed orders and exerted self-control were mentally healthy children. As a result, the teachers constantly urged the children to adapt to the planned classroom routine, and they set up a round of activities each day conducive to promoting, in Kanter's terms, the *organization child*—the child who is most comfortable when those in authority provide supervision, guidance, and roles to be fulfilled. In requiring children to adapt to such experiences, Kanter concludes, the schools both reflect and support the trend toward bureaucratization of life in American society.

   Similar conclusions have also been reached by Harry L. Gracey, a sociologist who studied classrooms in an eastern elementary school. One part of Gracey's research focused on kindergarten, which he came to call *academic boot camp*. Kindergarten works to teach the student role to children not previously conditioned to organized schooling. The content of the student role is "the repertoire of behavior and attitudes regarded by educators as appropriate to children in school." Such behaviors include willingness to conform to teacher demands and to perform the "work" at hand without resistance. Educators believe that children who have successfully learned the student role in kindergarten will function smoothly in the later grades.

–Neubeck, *Social Problems*, pp. 93–94

Type of detail: _____

7. There are really only two ways to gather information from human subjects about what they are currently doing, thinking, or feeling. One way is to watch what they do, the technique of observation; the other is to ask them, the technique of surveys. The many approaches included in each type of technique have several advantages and disadvantages. Firms frequently use both techniques to minimize disadvantages.

   There is a great variety of observational studies. A researcher stands near the entrance to a theater and observes the approximate age and sex of patrons entering the theater during certain times of the day and days of the week. Researchers comb through the garbage cans of Arizona residents (with permission) to identify what is being thrown away and, by inference from the packages, what is being bought. Toy manufacturers watch from behind one-way mirrors to see how children react to and play with prototypes of toys they are thinking of introducing. Observers in public places—airports, doctors' offices—watch to see how subjects read newspapers and magazines (front to back, right-hand or left-hand page). Researchers call on households and take a "pantry audit" to learn the quantity and brands of certain items on the kitchen or bathroom shelves.

—Russ and Kirkpatrick, *Marketing*, p. 92

Type of detail: _____

8. How many languages are spoken in the world today? Estimates range from three thousand to five thousand, but no one is really certain. . . . As many as three thousand different languages used by South American Indians alone have been named in the literature, but this high number is deceptive. Problems in identifying separate languages are many. In the South American studies, in many cases a single language has been identified by more than one name. Furthermore, many of the language studies that are available are of poor quality, making it difficult to tell whether the language described by one linguist is the same as that described by another. Some languages named are now extinct; other categories overlap or are inappropriate. Once such categories are eliminated, there appear to be only three hundred to four hundred Indian languages currently spoken in South America. Yet as Sorenson (1973: 312) has concluded, "the linguistic map of South America remains impressionistic at best," and similar problems exist elsewhere.

—Howard, *Contemporary Cultural Anthropology*, p. 80

Type of detail: _____

9. Otherwise known as the Landrum-Griffin Act, the Labor-Management Reporting and Disclosure Act of 1959 is aimed primarily at establishing guidelines for eliminating improper activities by either labor or management. One provision of the Act provides protection for the rights of union members. All union members may nominate candidates for union leadership, vote in union elections, attend union meetings, and vote on union matters. The Act also provides for filing reports that describe the organization, financial dealings, and business practices of the union and its officers and certain employees. Guidelines were established for handling union funds. The filing of the anticommunist affidavit required under the Taft-Hartley Act was repealed.

While the closed shop was declared illegal under the Taft-Hartley Act, the Landrum-Griffin Act exempted the construction industry by substituting a seven-day probationary period instead of the usual thirty-day period. As a practical matter, employers prefer to hire union members rather than nonunion members who would have to be replaced in seven days.

—Pickle and Abrahamson, *Introduction to Business*, p. 185

Type of detail: _____

10. The concept of *mafia* was also important in the Italian heritage. It refers not to the organization but, rather, to "a state of mind, a sense of pride, a philosophy of life, and a style of behavior which Sicilians recognize immediately." To describe someone as a *mafioso* does not necessarily mean that he is a member of the Mafia: it may simply mean that he is a man who is respected and held in awe. He is a man who seeks protection not through the law but by his own devices; he is a man who commands fear; he is a man who has dignity and bearing; he is a man who gets things done; he is a man to whom people come when in need; he is a man with "friends."

–Barlow, *Introduction to Criminology*, p. 297

Type of detail: _____

RECOGNIZING ORGANIZATIONAL PATTERNS

You have seen that passages and textbook sections are structured around a controlling idea and supporting information and details. The last step in reading these materials effectively is to become familiar with how information is organized.

Recognition of organizational patterns is a useful learning device. It is based on the principle of meaningfulness (see Chapter 3), which states that meaningful things are easier to learn and remember than those that are not. When you fit details into a pattern, you connect them so that each one helps you recall the rest. By identifying how the key details in a paragraph or passage form a pattern, you are making them more meaningful to you and, as a result, making them easier to remember.

Patterns are forms of schemata, or sets of familiar information. Once you recognize that a paragraph or passage follows a particular pattern, its organization becomes familiar and predictable.

Five organizational patterns are commonly used in textbook writing: definition, time sequence, comparison-contrast, cause-effect, and enumeration. These patterns may also appear together in various combinations, producing a mixed pattern. For each of these patterns, particular words and phrases are used to connect details and lead from one idea to another. These words are called *directional words* because they indicate the direction or pattern of thought.

Definition

One of the most obvious patterns is definition, which you will find in textbooks of most academic subjects. Each academic discipline has its own language or specialized terminology (see Chapter 19). One of the primary tasks of authors of introductory course textbooks, then, is to introduce their readers to this new language. Therefore, you will find many textbook sections in which new terms are defined.

Suppose you were asked to define the word *comedian* for someone unfamiliar with the term. First, you would probably say that a comedian is a person who entertains. Then you might distinguish a comedian from other types of entertainers by saying that a comedian is an entertainer who tells jokes and makes others laugh. Finally, you might mention as examples the names of several well-known comedians that have appeared on television. Although you may have presented it informally, your definition would have followed the standard, classic pattern. The first part of your definition tells what general class or group the term belongs to (entertainers). The second part tells what distinguishes the term from other items in the same class or category. The third part includes further explanation, characteristics, examples, or applications.

Read the following definition of *prejudice* taken from a sociology textbook.

> *Prejudice* is a rigid, emotional attitude often based on inadequate data, characterized by stereotyped thinking and involving a tendency to respond negatively toward certain identifiable groups or members of these groups. Prejudice does not involve any overt action or behavior, although it may serve as a stimulus to behavior. As it is an attitude, it is a hidden or covert characteristic, which people may or may not reveal to others.
>
> Prejudice is emotional, it involves feelings. These feelings are negative and are often revealed in the words used to describe a group. After the Japanese attacked Pearl Harbor, strong prejudice against them existed in this country. The Japanese were described as cunning, crafty, wily, slippery, shifty, treacherous, evasive, and underhanded, all obviously undesirable traits. Such negative connotations are also attached to the word *black*. For example, blacken, blackguard, Black Hand, blackleg, black magic, blackmail, and Black Mass. Of course, the word *white* can be used emotionally and negatively, as in white flag, white elephant, white feather, white-livered, and white plague.

–Wright and Weiss, *Social Problems*, p. 165

This definition has three parts: (1) The general class is stated first; (2) the distinguishing characteristics are then described; and (3) further explanation and examples are given. The first sentence states the general class–emotional attitude. The same sentence also gives distinguishing characteristics. The remainder of the passage further explains and gives examples of prejudice. When reading definitions, be sure to look for each of these parts. Passages that define often use directional words and phrases such as *refers to, defined as, consists of, is,* and *means.*

Time Sequence

One of the clearest ways to describe events, processes, procedures, and development of theories is to present them in the order in which they occurred. The event that happened first appears first in the passage; whatever occurred last is described last in the passage. Notice in the following example how the writer proceeds through time, describing the process of preparing a computer program.

> In the process of preparing a computer program to solve a particular problem the programmer performs a number of tasks. One thing that must be done is to code the program. As we have seen, this involves writing the instructions in the program. Before coding can begin, however, the programmer

must first understand the problem to be solved and then plan the solution procedure.

Understanding the problem involves determining the requirements of the problem and deciding how they can be met. The programmer must know what the program is required to do: what output must be produced and what computations must be performed. The programmer must also determine what resources (including input) are available to meet these requirements.

Once the problem is understood, the programmer can begin to design a program to solve it. The sequence of steps that is necessary to solve the problem must be carefully planned. This program-designing activity does *not* involve coding the program. Before coding can start, the programmer must think through the solution procedure completely because the sequence of steps must be carefully planned. The programmer sometimes writes down the solution procedure in rough notes using English or draws a diagram that represents the solution graphically.

After the solution to the problem has been planned, the program can be coded. The programmer uses his or her knowledge of the computer language, an understanding of the problem to be solved, and the program design determined previously. With this background, the programmer writes the program to solve the problem.

–Nickerson, *Fundamentals of Structured COBOL*, p. 24

Material using this pattern is relatively easy to read because you know what order the writer will follow. When reading sequential, organized material, pay attention to the order of and connection between events. When studying this material, remember that the order is often as important as the events themselves. To test your memory and to prepare information for study, list ideas in their correct order, or use a time line (see Chapter 13).

The time sequence pattern uses directional words to connect the events described or to lead you from one step to another. The most frequently used directional words are *first, second, later, next, before, then, finally, following, last, then,* and *finally.*

Comparison-Contrast

Many fields of study involve the comparison of one set of ideas, theories, concepts, or events with another. These comparisons usually examine similarities and differences. In anthropology, one kinship category might be compared with another; in literature, one poet might be compared with another; in biology, one theory of evolution might be compared with another. You will find that the comparison-contrast pattern is common in the textbooks used in these fields.

A comparison-contrast pattern can be organized three ways. A writer who is comparing two famous artists, X and Y, could use any of the following procedures:

1. Discuss the characteristics of artist X and artist Y and summarize their similarities and differences.

2. Consider their similarities first, then discuss their differences.
3. Consider both X and Y together for each of several characteristics. For instance, discuss the use of color by X and Y, then discuss the use of space by X and Y, then consider the use of proportion by X and Y.

Read the following paragraph, and try to determine which of the preceding patterns is used.

> In their original work both Darwin and that other great innovator who followed him, Gregor Mendel, used deductive reasoning to great effect. Both these giants of biology had been trained in theology. As a result, they were well acquainted with an intellectual tradition based on deduction. And since induction is difficult to apply in a field where so little can be directly observed, perhaps theology provided some of the essential intellectual tools both men needed to develop a viewpoint so different from prevailing theological thinking.
> Darwin and Mendel are linked in another fundamental way. Darwin could not explain how successful traits are passed on to successive generations, exposing his theory of natural selection to growing criticism. When Mendel was rediscovered, geneticists were paying a lot of attention to mutations. They still felt that natural selection of variants had a minor part in evolution. The major factor, they believed, was sudden change introduced by mutation. Not until the 1930s did biologists realize, at last, that Darwin's theory of natural selection and Mendel's laws of genetics were fully compatible. Together the two form the basis of population genetics, a major science of today.

–Laetsch, *Plants: Basic Concepts in Botany*, p. 393

The passage compares the characteristics of the work of Darwin and Mendel. The first paragraph presents their use of deductive reasoning. The second paragraph describes the compatibility of their theories.

In comparison-contrast passages, the way ideas are organized provides clues to what is important. In a passage that is organized by characteristics, the emphasis is placed on the characteristics. A passage that groups similarities and then differences emphasizes the similarities and differences themselves rather than the characteristics.

Directional words indicate whether the passage focuses on similarities, differences, or both: *in contrast, on the other hand, similarly, to compare, however, in comparison,* and *likewise.*

Cause-Effect

Understanding any academic discipline requires learning *how* and *why* things happen. In psychology it is not sufficient to know that people are often aggressive; you also need to know why and how people exhibit aggression. In physics it is not enough to know the laws of motion; you also must understand why they work and how they apply to everyday experiences.

The cause-effect pattern arranges ideas according to why and how they occur. This pattern is based on the relationship between or among events. Some passages discuss one cause and one effect—the omission of a command, for example, causing a computer program to fail. Most passages, however, describe multiple causes or effects. Some may describe the numerous effects of a single cause, such as unemployment producing an increase in crime, family disagreements, and diminished self-esteem. Others may describe the numerous causes of a single effect, such as increased unemployment and poverty along with decreased police protection causing a higher crime rate. Still others may present multiple causes and effects, such as unemployment and poverty producing an increase in crime and in family disputes.

Read the following passage, taken from a business marketing text, and determine which of the following patterns is used:

1. single cause–single effect
2. multiple causes–single effect
3. single cause–multiple effects
4. multiple causes–multiple effects

Many new products do not succeed—from 30 percent to 90 percent, in fact, depending on which estimate you choose. The reason may be inaccurate information about the market, bad estimates of how the market or the competition will react to the product, or just unfortunate timing. More often, the causes of failure are related to the four components of a seller's marketing mix. The product itself, for example, is sometimes defective, despite previous research and testing. The assortment of colors, or flavors, or package sizes might be wrong. Sometimes the product is not different enough for buyers to perceive any point of competitive superiority. Or perhaps it is too different and too complicated in operation to attract buyers. Its quality, performance, or some other characteristic may disappoint buyers who expected more.

The initial price may be too high or too low. Production and marketing costs may have been underestimated. Competitors may cut their prices, either in the test marketing step to distort the seller's findings, or in the commercialization step, or in both.

–Russ and Kirkpatrick, *Marketing,* p. 241

The passage offers numerous reasons why new products fail. Numerous causes, then, produce a single effect.

When you read and study ideas organized in a cause-effect pattern, focus on the connection between or among events. To make relationships clearer, determine which of the four cause-effect patterns is used. Directional words can help you determine the cause-effect relationship: *for, because, therefore, as a result, consequently, hence, due to,* and *thus.*

Enumeration

The primary function of textbooks is to present information. If there is a relationship or connection between or among ideas, this connection is usually emphasized and used to organize information. Many types of information, however, have no inherent order or connection. Lists of facts, characteristics, parts, or categories can appear in any order; thus writers use a pattern called enumeration. In this pattern, the information is often loosely connected with a topic sentence or controlling idea: "There are several categories of . . ." or "There are three types of . . ." and so forth. This listing pattern, sometimes called classification, divides a topic into subgroups or groups items according to a common characteristic.

Read the following paragraph, observing how the pattern proceeds from one type of neuron to another.

> Neurons come in many different shapes and sizes. Scientists usually classify them into three types: sensory neurons, motor neurons, and interneurons. . . . *Sensory neurons* receive and convey information about the environment. Their dendrites pick up signals directly from specialized *receptor cells* that respond to light, pressure, and other external stimuli. The retinas of each eye, for example, are made up of thousands of receptor cells. Sensory neurons pass information about the environment on to other neurons, and this process enables us to see, hear, touch, smell, and taste. . . . Whereas information is conveyed to the brain via sensory neurons, *motor neurons* carry signals from the brain and spinal cord to the muscles, organs, and glands of the body. The third and by far most common type of neuron in the human brain is the *interneuron*, which connects one neuron with another.
>
> –Roediger et al., *Psychology*, p. 39

One key to reading and studying this pattern is to be aware of how many items are enumerated so you can check your recall of them. It is also helpful to note whether the information is listed in order of importance, frequency, size, or any other characteristic. This will help you organize the information for easier recall.

Directional words are very useful in locating items in a list. As a writer moves from one item in a list to another, he or she may use such words as *first, second, finally, one, another,* and *primarily.*

Mixed Patterns

In many texts, sections and passages combine one or more patterns. In defining a concept or idea, a writer might explain a term by comparing it with something similar or familiar. In describing an event or process, a writer might include reasons for or causes of an event, or explain why the steps in a process must be followed in the prescribed order.

Read the following paragraph and determine what two patterns are used.

> Psychologists have long puzzled over how the perceptual systems generally achieve constancy. Why don't people appear to shrink as they walk away? The constancies can be understood by first examining the distinction between proximal and distal stimuli. *Proximal* (nearby) *stimuli* are the physical energy patterns that strike the sensory receptors. The retinal image is a proximal stimulus, as is the sound pattern that strikes our eardrums. *Distal* (distant) *stimuli* are the objects at a distance that give rise to the proximal stimuli. The existence of the perceptual constancies demonstrates that perceptual experience is tied more closely to distal stimuli than to proximal stimuli. Thus, if you pick up this book and move it closer to you and

then farther away, you will perceive the book's size and shape to remain the same; the distal stimulus, the book itself, does remain the same in size and shape, although the proximal stimulus, the retinal image of the book, fluctuates over a large range.

–Roediger et al., *Psychology*, p. 141

Two terms—*proximal* and *distal stimuli*—are defined, but for purposes of explanation, the terms are also compared. You can see, therefore, that the paragraph combines a definition pattern with a comparison-contrast pattern. Because the primary purpose of the paragraph is to define the terms, the predominant pattern is definition.

When reading mixed patterns, do not be overly concerned with identifying or labeling each pattern. Instead, look for the predominant pattern that carries the overall organization.

EXERCISE 5 _____

Directions: *Assume that each of the following sentences or group of sentences is the beginning of a textbook section. Based on the information contained in each, predict what organizational pattern is used throughout the passage. Look for directional words to help you identify the pattern.*

1. In large businesses, clerical jobs are usually very specialized in order to accomplish the work to be done in the most efficient manner. As a result, clerical work is very often routine and highly repetitive. _____

2. There are clear limitations to population growth and the use of natural resources. First, the food supply could be exhausted due to water, mineral, and soil depletion. _____

3. Unlike the statues of humans, the statues of animals found in Stone Age sites are quite lifelike. _____

4. When a patient enters a mental hospital, he is carefully tested and observed for twenty-four hours. Then a preliminary decision is made concerning medication and treatment. _____

5. One shortcoming of the clinical approach in treating mental illness is that definitions of normal behavior are subjective. Another shortcoming of the approach is that it assumes that when a patient has recovered he will be able to return to his previous environment. _____

EXERCISE 6 _____

Directions: *Read each of the following passages and identify the predominant organizational pattern used in each.*

1. **FAMILY STUDIES**

    Another method used to measure a genetic influence on behavior is to study families. Family members have similar genes. You share half your genes with your mother and half with your father. On average you also share half your genes with your brothers and sisters. However, most families also live together. So if families share a common trait it could be related to their common genes, to their common environment, or both.

One way to get around this problem is to study adopted children. Heston (1970) found subjects born to schizophrenic mothers who were permanently separated from them before they were one month old and were reared in foster or adoptive homes. Another group of children who also had been separated from their biological mothers before reaching one month of age and were reared in foster homes were used as controls. Their mothers had no record of psychiatric problems. As adults, the children of schizophrenic mothers showed significantly greater incidence of schizophrenia than the control subjects. These data, consistent with those from the twin studies, evidence a possible genetic factor in schizophrenia.

In another type of family study investigators measure a trait within a family over generations. The pattern of appearance of a trait in family members over generations can suggest specific hypotheses as to how genes are related to a trait. Not all genes are directly reflected in observable traits (phenotype is not the same as genotype). An example of this is a characteristic of genes termed *recessiveness*. Recessive genes will not be expressed in the phenotype unless both members of a pair of genes are the same. Blue eyes are produced by recessive genes. If one parent contributes genes for brown eyes and the other contributes genes for blue eyes, the child's eyes will be brown; the blue eye gene is recessive, the brown eye gene is dominant. Two brown-eyed parents could have a blue-eyed child if they both carried the recessive eye genes, and these recessive genes were contributed to the child by both parents.

–Roediger et al., *Psychology*, p. 78

Organizational pattern: ___Enumeration___

2. **COSMOLOGICAL SPECULATIONS AFTER GREEK COSMOLOGY**

Whether the universe "have his boundes or bee in deed infinite and without boundes" was the profound question English astronomer Thomas Digges (1546?–1595) asked himself. It appeared in Digges's 1576 book *Perfit Description of the Celestial Orbes*. A few decades later Galileo too wrote of an infinite and unbounded universe in his *Dialogues*, which was probably prompted by the fact he had seen with his telescope that the Milky Way consists of myriads of stars.

What is the Milky Way? Swedish philosopher Emanuel Swedenborg (1688–1772) speculated in 1734 that the stars formed one vast collection, of which the solar system was but one constituent. Thomas Wright (1711–1786) of England theorized in his 1750 work, *An Original Theory of the Universe*, that the Milky Way seems to be a bright band of stars because the sun lies inside a flattened slab of stars. He also suggested that there were other Milky Ways in the universe. Immanuel Kant (1724–1804), the noted philosopher, went beyond Wright's idea, suggesting in 1755 that the small oval nebulous objects seen with telescopes were other systems of stars or "island universes"; the phrase captured popular fancy a century and a half later. . . .

Besides these speculations observational evidence was also accumulating that could be used to reveal the structure of the Milky Way. In 1785 Herschel gave the first quantitative proof that the Milky Way was a stellar structure shaped like a flat disk, a grindstone. Since Herschel and others did not suspect that starlight might be dimmed by obscuring material between the stars, he deduced that the sun was near the center of the system.

–Berman and Evans, *Exploring the Cosmos*, pp. 333, 336.

Organizational pattern: _Time Seq   Date Seq._

3. **MINORITIES AND THE JOB MARKET**

Work, or the lack of work, crucially determines the way all of us live, so it isn't surprising that the distinctive pattern of significant gains for some groups in the minority population coupled with stagnation and even decline for others is intimately connected to the fortunes of minorities in the job market.

Untangling these issues is difficult because several different factors in the job market may contribute, simultaneously or in various combinations, to the inequality of minority and white income. One source of that inequality may be differences in the amount of work—or, put another way, the risks of not working—between the groups. Another may be differences in the earnings they receive when they do work. Both of these, in turn, are partly reflections of the kinds of jobs different groups typically hold, for this affects both the wages or salaries they receive when they work and the chances they face of being unemployed or intermittently employed. And all of these factors differ in their impact not only among the various minority groups but also among men and women within those groups.

–Currie and Skolnick, *America's Problems*, p. 161

Organizational pattern: _Cause - Effect_

4. **BIOGRAPHY OF KARL MARX**

Born in the ancient German Rhineland city of Trier, the son of middle-class Jewish parents who had converted to Protestantism, Karl Marx studied law. Significantly, for the development of his theories, he joined a circle of intellectuals who considered themselves to be young Hegelians. Despite his father's wishes, he switched to the study of philosophy, in which he received his Ph.D. at Jena in 1841. At that point his academic career came to an end, as he failed to receive a university teaching position.

Marx returned to the Rhineland where he began writing for a local liberal newspaper. He was struck by the inequities he saw around him, and as he read more deeply in the works of classical economists and French socialists, he became more aware of the economic factors in history. He moved to Paris, where he met Friedrich Engels (1820–95), whose father owned a a factory near

Manchester, England, and struck up a close, lifelong friendship with him. Marx' views and activities moved the Prussian authorities to request the French government to expel him, and he went on to Belgium. His studies, personal observations of the working classes, and discussions with Engels on the condition of the factory workers in Britain sharpened his distaste for capitalism.

–Wallbank et al., *Civilization Past and Present*, Vol. 2, p. 605

Organizational pattern: _Time Seq_

5. **PAIN**

Perception of pain is not well understood. We could not live without the capacity to experience pain because if we did not notice painful stimuli, we might well depart before the stimuli did. Some people feel no pain, that is, they lack sensitivity to it; while this might seem advantageous, they are in constant danger of serious yet undetected injury (Melzack, 1973). Pain does not always occur from damage to bodily tissues; amputees experience "phantom limb" pain in arms or legs long since severed. Psychiatric patients sometimes report severe pain for which no organic cause can be found (Veilleux & Melzack, 1976).

One explanation of pain is in terms of the *gate-control theory* of Melzack and Wall (1965). According to that theory, sensations of pain result from activation of certain nerve fibers that lead to specific centers of the brain responsible for pain perception. When these fibers are activated, say by an injury, the neural "gate" to the brain is opened for pain sensations. The theory also postulates another set of neural fibers that, when activated, reduce the effects of the pain fibers and "close the gate" on the pain sensations. The theory proposes that neural activity arising from other stimuli (e.g., those producing general excitement) may close the gate to pain signals. The important idea is that signals from the brain can be sent to other parts of the body to modify the incoming pain signals.

Gate-control theory may help explain some common phenomena of pain. For example, it has been reported that patients feel less pain when dentists working on them play music; the music may help close the gate for pain. Similarly, Melzack (1970) reports that amputees feel less phantom limb pain when the stump is massaged. The massaging may activate fibers that close the gate to pain.

–Roediger et al., *Psychology*, p. 111

Organizational pattern: _Enumeration Cause-Effect_

6. **INFORMAL AND FORMAL EDUCATION**

In nonindustrial societies most educational instruction is given by example; learning results from observation and imitation of relatives, peers, and neighbors. Children see how adults perform tasks and how they behave. At first, children's imitation is in the form of play—making toy bows and arrows and shooting at insects or making mud pies. Play slowly disappears as children begin to take a more substantial role in community work. From an early age children accompany their parents on their daily round of activities, watching and then assisting until eventually they are able to perform required adult tasks on their own. Some education in small-scale societies is more formalized. This is especially true of more esoteric subjects such as magic, curing, and playing a musical instrument. Sometimes formal education is also of a more universal nature, as when all Mardudjara male children are isolated for weeks and given instruction about religious and legal traditions in preparation for initiation.

In large-scale societies formal education tends to be more pervasive. Individuals are instructed formally in a wider range of topics and they spend more time in specialized institutional settings, or schools. This is not necessarily because there is more to learn; rather, it reflects a shift of emphasis in the way people are taught and who is responsible for their instruction. In most large-scale societies some governmental authority or large institution such as the church assumes a primary role in education, resulting in a loss of instructional autonomy at the family and community level. In such situations education functions not simply to provide instruction, but also to promote homogeneity and a sense of identification with the state that supersedes more local and personal loyalties. The aim is to promote a common national culture.

–Howard, *Contemporary Cultural Anthropology*, pp. 250–251

Organizational pattern: _Comparision_

7. **CAPITAL**

Capital is [a] produced means of production. Capital consists of goods we have produced but that we keep aside and use to produce other goods and services. *Capital goods* are thus distinguished from *consumer goods*, which we can use directly. Tools and machines, transportation and communication networks, buildings and irrigation facilities are capital goods. Farmers save a portion of their grain crop to use for seed in the next planting season. Their seed grain is a capital good which allows them to produce more in the future.

Education (including all types of training in useful skills) may be thought of as *human capital*. To build capital requires that we give up something today for something in the future. Like the farmers who give up grain, students give up jobs—and parents give up trips abroad—all for the opportunity to develop a stock of capital. Human capital is an important basis for the growing prosperity of U.S. workers.

The word "capital" is sometimes also used to mean a stock of money, as in *financial capital*, but this is not what we mean when we speak of capital as a factor of production. Financial capital is provided to business firms for construction of real capital goods. This is the way individuals help to save in the current period for the sake of greater production in the future.

–Chisholm and McCarty, *Principles of Economics*, p. 22

Organizational pattern: _definition_

8. INTERPERSONAL VERSUS MASS COMMUNICATION

Both interpersonal and mass communication are important in marketing. Personal selling requires interpersonal communication, while advertising, sales promotion, and publicity use mass communication techniques. . . .

A mass communication, such as an advertisement in a magazine, can more accurately deliver the same message to a larger audience than can an interpersonal communication, such as a salesperson's presentation to a customer. The latter changes with each attempt to communicate. The cost of reaching an individual through the mass media is substantially lower as well. However, mass communication is one-way; it has less likelihood of gaining the potential audience's selective attention, and it suffers from slow, and many times, inaccurate feedback.

Interpersonal communication has the benefits of being fast, and allowing two-way feedback. A buyer can respond instantly to a salesperson's presentation, and the salesperson can ask for clarification of the response. This greater flexibility in feedback allows the communicator to counter objections from the buyer and thus attain a greater change in attitude and behavior than is possible with mass communication. Interpersonal communication is much more efficient than mass communication. Unfortunately, interpersonal communication used for a large audience is slow and very expensive. One must thus compare the efficiency of using a particular type of communication with the cost involved. This comparison of communication efficiency with cost leads to what has been referred to as the *communication-promotion paradox*.

–Kinnear and Bernhardt, *Principles of Marketing*, pp. 438–439

Organizational pattern: ___Comparision___

9. SOCIETY

Culture is not created in a vacuum, nor by isolated individuals. It is the product of humans interacting in groups. From their parents and from others around them, humans learn how to act and how to think in ways that are shared by or comprehensible to people in their group. Humans are by nature social animals. From birth to death, humans are biologically conditioned to live not as separate individuals, but as members of groups. Since the beginning of human evolution, our survival has been a cooperative enterprise. Even hermits do not escape the rest of humanity, for everything they think, know, or believe has been conditioned by others. Culture is a group effort and is *socially shared*.

We sometimes speak of those who share the same cultural perceptions and modes of behavior as members of a society. A *society* is a collection of people who are linked to one another, either directly or indirectly, through social interaction. It is through their common experiences that members of a society evolve shared cultural attributes. Culture and society are complementary concepts; they are two sides of the same coin. Without culture, societies as we know them could not exist, for there would be no common basis for interpreting one another's behavior. Similarly, without a society there would be no culture, for there would be no interaction by which people could share their knowledge, values, and beliefs. The sharing of culture comes about through interaction, and predictable interaction is made possible through values and attitudes that people hold in common.

–Howard, *Contemporary Cultural Anthropology*, pp. 5–6.

Organizational pattern: ___definitin___

10. **THE PHYSICS OF LIGHT**

The two properties of light most important for the study of the psychology of vision are intensity and wavelength. The *intensity* of light affects the psychological experiences of *brightness* and *lightness* perception. In general, the more intense a light source, the brighter a light will appear. When light illuminates an object, part of it is absorbed and part reflected; the perceived lightness of an object depends on the proportion of light that is reflected. There is more to the perception of brightness and lightness, however, than intensity. A blacktop road will appear black whether it is seen in the evening, when there is relatively little light falling on it, or in broad daylight. In fact, a blacktop road in the noonday sun reflects more light to the eye than does a white shirt worn indoors in the evening. (You can verify that with any light meter, such as one built in many cameras.) Yet the road looks black and the shirt looks white. This is one of many bits of evidence that the eyes is much more complicated than a camera.

The second important property of light is *wavelength*, which affects the light's perceived color, or *hue*. Wavelength is the distance between adjacent wave crests, and it is measured in *nanometers*, or billionths of a meter. As the wavelength of light increases through the visible spectrum, which ranges roughly from 400 to 750 nanometers, humans perceive the color of the light as changing from violet through blue, green, yellow, and orange to red at the longest wavelengths. . . . Color perception, however, involves factors other than the registration of wavelength. For example, many colors such as brown, pink and even white are not in the spectrum. (Have you ever seen brown in a rainbow?) Such colors embody several different wavelengths, and the visual system in effect mixes the wavelengths to produce perception of a nearly infinite variety of colors.

–Roediger et al., *Psychology*, pp. 86–87

Organizational pattern: _____

EXERCISE 7 _____

Directions: *Refer to the biology sample textbook chapter reprinted in Appendix B. Using headings and first sentences of sections, predict and record the organizational patterns that are used in the chapter.*

Directions: *Refer to the first section of the psychology sample textbook chapter reprinted in Appendix A. Using subheadings and first sentences of paragraphs, predict and record the organizational patterns that are used in the section.*

SUMMARY

Textbooks are unique, highly organized sources of information. Becoming familiar with their organization and structure and learning to follow the writer's thought patterns are important textbook reading skills. A textbook is divided into parts: chapters, sections, subsections, and paragraphs. Although each is successively smaller in size and more limited in scope, each follows a similar organization and is built around a single idea with details that support and explain it. Textbook writers explain ideas by providing various types of supporting information: examples, description, facts and statistics, and citation of research evidence. These supporting details are often organized into one or more organizational patterns: definition, time sequence, comparison-contrast, cause-effect and enumeration.

PART FOUR

Textbook Reading Skills

Do you think of your textbooks as just something to read? If so, you may not be using them to full advantage. A textbook is much more than a book of chapters, parts of which are assigned by instructors at various times during the semester. Textbooks are actually learning tools or devices. A text is often one of your primary sources of information for a course, and it is a valuable teaching-learning tool when used effectively.

Textbooks are written for the purpose of presenting information about a subject that students need to know. Textbook authors, most of whom are college teachers, attempt to present the information in such a way that it can be learned easily by students. They use a variety of methods and include a variety of learning aids, all of them to help students learn the content of their texts. As a student, you want to be aware of these methods and learning aids and know how to use them to make reading and studying easier.

Since the textbook is most often your primary source of information in a college course, you will need to become familiar with techniques for effectively studying and learning textbook material. You will want to know how to learn as you read, and you will want to master the technique of marking a textbook as you read. Once you have identified and marked important information, you will want to organize it to make learning easier.

The textbook chapters reprinted in the appendixes of this book have been included for purposes of demonstration and practice. They are, however, only samples. While they have many similarities to other textbook chapters, do not expect to find every textbook chapter organized or presented exactly like these. The sample chapters have been included so that you can try out the techniques and suggestions given in this unit. You will notice, also, that the sample chapters are used many times throughout the unit to show how particular techniques are

continued

continued

applied or to illustrate particular aspects of effective textbook reading.

Chapter 10 describes features of textbooks designed to increase learning effectiveness. Chapter 11 presents techniques for underlining and marking textbooks, while Chapter 13 discusses the development of study-reading systems. Methods of organizing information are described in Chapter 14.

10

Textbook Aids to Learning

Use this chapter to:

1. *Find out how textbooks can make learning easier.*

2. *Learn how to take advantage of the various learning aids included in textbooks.*

Most college students think of their textbooks as merely chapters of information to be read and learned. What many students do not realize, however, is that textbooks contain not only facts and ideas to be learned but also a structure and guide to learning these facts and ideas.

Think about how your textbook differs from other books and references. What does your textbook contain that other information sources, such as encyclopedias, dictionaries, and library reference materials, do not? How does it differ from such familiar sources of factual information as newspapers, magazines, and nonfiction paperbacks?

In answering those questions, you probably thought of several unique features, such as recall or discussion questions, or vocabulary lists. Actually, a textbook has numerous learning aids that many students neglect to take advantage of. The purpose of this chapter, then, is to discuss those learning aids and to suggest how you can use them.

PREFATORY MATERIAL 6 parts

Most students think that their textbooks begin with the first chapter. Actually, much information is included in the material that comes before the first chapter.

Title and Subtitle

Try this test: Without looking, jot down the correct title and subtitle of each textbook you are using this semester. Then check the titles. How many did you get exactly right? Most students do not get more than one or two titles completely correct. Students are often in the habit of ignoring textbook titles, which are useful aids to learning.

The title and subtitle of a text are more than names or convenient labels. Titles are descriptive. They tell the reader much about the scope and purpose of the text and indicate the organization and level of difficulty. The title *An Introduction to Social Psychology* tells the reader that the text is basic and introductory and that the subject is limited to social psychology. The title *Early American History* and subtitle *Readings and Perspectives* indicate that the text is made up of articles (readings) written by different authors which are chosen to give the reader various points of view (perspectives) on early American history. From this title and subtitle, then, you learn something about the text's organization, its purposes, and the subject area it treats.

EXERCISE 1 _____

Directions: *List the titles of all the texts you are using this semester. After each title, identify what, if anything, it tells you about the text's organization and purpose.*

EXERCISE 2 _____

Directions: *Read each situation described below. Then underline the title of the text that would be most useful in the situation described.*

1. You are in the library trying to locate information for a term paper on drug use and abuse in the 1970s. In the card catalog you find the following texts are available. Which do you think would be most helpful?
   a. Experimental Research on Drug Therapy
   b. Drugs in Contemporary Society
   c. Drugs: A Clinical Evaluation

2. In your psychology class today, the instructor discussed instinct and learning in animals and mentioned that experiments are being done with a baby chimpanzee that is being raised by human parents. Researchers are interested to see what animal behaviors and what human behaviors the chimp develops. You decide that you would like to read more about this type of research. What text might contain further information on the subject?
   a. Physiological Bases of Human Behavior
   b. Animal Behavioral Research
   c. The Psychology Experiment: An Introduction

3. You just got a part-time job selling ad space in a local newspaper to area businesses. You realize that you need to learn how to approach potential customers and what to say to them. Which of the following texts might be useful?
   a. Executive Action in Marketing
   b. Salesmanship: Introductory Principles
   c. Business in Contemporary Society

Author(s)

On the title page, the first printed page of a professional text, you find the name of the author (or authors) and the professional title or the name of the college with which the author is affiliated. While you probably will not recognize the author's name, it is useful to be familiar with his or her credentials—that is, his or her qualifications to write the text.

Copyright Date

Located on the page after the title page, you will find the copyright notice. This contains the date when the book was first published. If you see more than one date, the earliest date indicates when the text was first published, while the others are dates when the text was revised or reprinted.

It is worthwhile to check the copyright to find out how up-to-date your text is. Of course, in some subject areas, a recent publication date is more important than it is in others. A book on Greek philosophy written ten years ago may still be complete and up-to-date, while a ten-year-old text on twentieth-century American history is incomplete and outdated.

When you are locating books in the library to complete an assignment or to write a paper, it is especially important to check the copyright date because in certain fields a current source of information is necessary. In the sciences, social sciences, and health-related fields, for example, new research, theories, and ideas are developed every year.

EXERCISE 3 _____

Directions: *The following is a list of textbook titles and their copyright dates. Place a check mark beside those you think are outdated.*

1. ____ *Principles of Behavior Modification* (1985)
2. ____ *Introduction to Data Processing* (1986)
3. ____ *Business Law* (1978)
4. ____ *Business Mathematics* (1980)
5. ____ *Speech Improvement: A Practical Program* (1974)
6. ____ *Logic and Philosophy* (1982)
7. ____ *The History of Music* (1984)
8. ____ *English for Business* (1975)
9. ____ *Economics in American Society* (1986)
10. ____ *Patterns in English History* (1974)

Preface

The preface is the author's introduction to the text. It contains basic information about the text that the author thinks you should be aware of before you begin reading.

The preface may contain the following information:

1. Why the author wrote the text (his or her purpose in writing)
2. For whom the book was written (audience)
3. The author's major points of emphasis
4. The author's particular slant or focus on the subject
5. How the author organized the book
6. Important references or authorities consulted when writing
7. Suggestions on how to use the text
8. Limitations or weaknesses of the text (subject areas the text does not cover, and so forth)

As you can see, each of the preceding items is important to know before you use a text. To get a better understanding of the values and importance of a preface, read the excerpt reproduced in Figure 10-1 from Helena Curtis's Preface to *Biology*.

EXERCISE 4 _____

Directions: *Now that you have read the sample preface, answer the following questions.*

1. How does the author think biology textbooks should approach the field of biology?

   _____

2. How has the field of biology changed in the past fifteen years?

   _____

3. In what area of biology is change occurring most rapidly?

   _____

4. What current controversial issue does Curtis address in her Preface?

   _____

5. How is the text organized?

   _____

After reading the sample preface, you can no doubt see how important it is to read the preface of any textbook to learn how the author presents information particularly vital in understanding the book's organization and content.

EXERCISE 5 _____

Directions *Select one of your textbooks and turn to the preface. Read the preface, and then answer the following questions. If the information is not included in the preface, leave the item blank.*

Title of text: _____

1. Why did the author write the textbook?

   _____

2. For whom was the book written?

   _____

3. What are the author's major points of emphasis?

   _____

Preface

This book is the result of an unusually broad cooperative venture. There were several essential factors in this venture. My own contribution was my long experience as a professional writer in the field of biology and a desire to communicate my interests and enthusiasms about the subject. Second, and more important, was the arrival on the publishing scene of a vigorous young company with fresh ideas and initiative. The third and by far the most important factor was the willingness of a large number of teachers and experts in all fields of biology to lend their assistance at every stage of the planning, writing, and innumerable revisions of the manuscript and illustrations.

The paragraph just quoted was written fifteen years ago in the preface to the first edition of *Biology*. There have been many changes since that time. For one thing, neither Worth Publishers nor I are quite so young, though we are, we hasten to add, just as vigorous. In retrospect, our youthful inexperience was one of our chief assets. Had we been less innocent, I do not think we would have dared as newcomers to undertake so vast a project as an introductory biology text. I still wonder how we did it.

Another change of slightly more importance has been in the general nature of biology textbooks. As a writer, I felt strongly that any book, textbook or not, had an obligation to be well written, interesting, and even, on occasion, entertaining. Biology, for me, is a source of pleasure and excitement, as it is for most of the men and women engaged in biological research. I did not understand why textbooks found it necessary to keep that information a trade secret. Robert Worth not only agreed with me but went one step further. He maintained that a book, even a textbook, should also be well crafted, handsomely illustrated, and even beautiful. Now there are many biology textbooks that are handsome and readable as well as serving their pedagogical functions. Bob and I are proud to have been part of this general trend.

The most important changes in these fifteen years have been, of course, in biology itself. There has been not only a flood of new information, but also of new ideas and unifying concepts. Moreover, the rate of change is itself increasing; the changes in the last four years have been enormous. In molecular genetics, in particular, there has been an absolutely unprecedented explosion of knowledge, made even more dramatic by the unexpected nature of much of what has been

FIGURE 10-1   Sample Preface

discovered. In such cases, where a subject is out-of-date before the printer's ink dries, the best one can hope to do is to establish a basis for the understanding not only of what is happening now, but what may happen a year from now.

Finally, there has been an extrabiological development that must affect all biology textbooks: the resurgence of creationism in a new but not very different form. The recent public debates were foreshadowed for me by letters from students who were using *Biology* and were obviously having difficulty reconciling these new (to them) ideas about evolution with their religious beliefs. While we may be impatient with those who attempt to impose creationist beliefs upon others, those students deserve our attention and respect. In the first edition of *Biology*, I simply tried to present current thinking about how evolution occurs, without taking enough time to explain the reasons why biologists so overwhelmingly accept—and have done so for considerably more than a hundred years—the fact that evolution has occurred. (" 'Shut up,' he explained," will always remain for me one of the greatest lines of modern literature.) This time I do present the evidence in what I hope is a quiet and nonbelligerent way. (Many young people do not like being told what to think, and I don't blame them.)

Despite these changes, this edition follows the same general pattern as the previous ones. The Introduction focuses on evolution, still the major theme of this text, as it must be of all modern biology texts. The chapter closes with a brief discussion of the controversies now going on. The purpose of this discussion is to make clear that there are two types of disagreement—one between scientists and nonscientists and the other between groups of scientists with opposing viewpoints. The former is not the business of science (though, of course, of concern to scientists), whereas the latter is not only the business of science but indeed its life's blood. Following this thread elsewhere in the book, I have identified areas of disagreement among scientists and instances where prevailing opinion has proved to be wrong. This tactic elicited criticism from some reviewers who feel it trivializes science and distracts the student from the more important business of learning the fundamentals of biology. As I look back over the changes in biological thought in just the last fifteen years, it seems to me that perhaps one of the most useful things a student should learn is a healthy skepticism about what he or she reads, even in textbooks. Scientific progress is a process that takes place only within the confines of the skull of human beings, which makes it both marvelous and fallible.

After the Introduction, this edition, as was the case with previous ones, follows the levels-of-organization approach. Part I deals with life at the subcellular and cellular level, Part II with organisms, and Part III with populations, ending with the evolution of the human species. Each part is divided into two or three sections. We have been tempted from time to time to reverse the order and begin with ecology, but the great majority of you who were surveyed were in favor of the present organization.

FIGURE 10-1   *(continued)*

4. Describe the author's particular slant or focus on the subject.

_____

5. How is the text organized?

_____

6. Did the author use important references or authorities in writing the text?

_____

7. What suggestions did the author give on how to use the book?

_____

8. What weaknesses or limitations does the author mention?

_____

To the Student

In some textbooks the author may include a section titled "To the Student" or "Introduction to the Text" instead of a preface. These sections tend to be more practical and informal than a preface. They usually offer advice, discuss learning strategies, or explain the various features of the text and how to use them. A sample "To the Student" excerpt taken from Zimbardo's _Psychology and Life_ is reproduced in Figure 10-2.

EXERCISE 6 _____

Directions: _Read the sample "To the Student" from Zimbardo's_ Psychology and Life _before answering the following questions._

1. Zimbardo presents seven general strategies for optimal learning. Which of these have you already learned in this book?

_____

2. Evaluate Zimbardo's suggestions for learning. Which ones will be useful in courses other than psychology?

_____

3. When does Zimbardo suggest you read the chapter outline and summary?

_____

4. How does Zimbardo define an educated person? Explain why you agree or disagree.

_____

To the Student

Tactics and Strategies for Getting the Most Out of This Book

Certainly your goal is to get a passing grade, or even a good grade, in this course and ultimately to get your college degree. Hopefully your goal extends further to becoming an educated person—someone who is interesting to others because that person is interested in the world of ideas. By analyzing, thinking, and theorizing not only to satisfy your pragmatic objectives but also to enjoy the discovery of learning, you come into contact with the most incredible phenomenon in the entire universe—the human mind. So before we begin to examine specific tactics for getting the best return for the time you invest in studying this text and in taking this introductory psychology course, it is well to mention some general strategies essential for optimal learning.

- ▶ Adopt the mentality of the athlete who wants to function at peak performance and is not satisfied being second best or one of the "also rans."
- ▶ Just as an athlete prepares for competition by effortful practice, you prepare for competitive examinations by careful reading, notetaking, and active rehearsal of what you have read in this text and heard in lectures.
- ▶ Performance improves with effective practice, and practice always takes time and effort, so be prepared to put in the time and to put out the effort to achieve your optimal academic performance.
- ▶ Sometimes good athletes "run against the clock" and not against the competition; they set personal best goals that extend what they have done in the past. Decide upon the personal goals you want to achieve in this course (and in others), over and above examination grades. Psychology is an inevitable part of your life and will continue to be long after this course is over, so an understanding of the principles of psychology as they apply to everyday life is a permanent gift you can give yourself.
- ▶ There are many demands on your attention and time, so it becomes critical not to waste either. You'll do best when you allocate your time wisely. You'll be able to resist distractions and temptations when you know there is a job to get done.

- ▶ To do the job requires planning ahead—writing down your goals, schedule, means to reach subgoals and end-goals, and allowing yourself to become task-oriented. You can achieve the balanced time perspective of a future focus for tasks to be accomplished and of a present focus so that when they are completed you can reward yourself with partying, or whatever hedonistic delight is appropriate—until it is time to move on to the next task.
- ▶ In the process of mastering *Psychology and Life,* you will extend your mental functioning in many significant dimensions that will reap the richest dividends throughout your life.

To help you realize the potential excitement of this unique journey through psychology and life you will have to put in sufficient time and effort to master a great many new terms, concepts, principles, implications, and extensions of ideas so that you can fully appreciate the process of psychological discovery and not be concerned solely with the destination marked by an end-term grade. We offer some suggestions for getting the best return on the time you invest in studying *Psychology and Life.* They are intended to promote comprehension and efficiency, and make you aware of the features that have been built into each chapter to help you.

- ▶ Set aside sufficient time to study for this course; there is much new technical information that will require careful reading and reflection, at least three hours per chapter.
- ▶ Find a study place with minimal distractions; reserve this spot for study and do nothing there other than reading, note-taking, and reviewing your course material.
- ▶ Keep a record or log of the number of hours (in half-hour intervals) that you put in studying for this course. Chart it on a cumulative graph (one that adds each new study time to the prior total).
- ▶ Begin each chapter by reviewing its *outline.* It shows you the topics that will be covered, their sequence, and the way they are related to one another.
- ▶ Next, skip to the end of the chapter and read the *Summary.* It will flesh out the outline by indicating the important themes, concepts, and conclusions, as well as the sequence in which they appear.

FIGURE 10-2   Sample "To the Student"

5. Is the author enthusiastic and excited about studying the field of psychology? If so, how do you know?

_____

Table of Contents

The table of contents of a textbook should be read before you begin to use the text. The table of contents is an outline of a book listing all the important topics and subtopics. The table of contents also shows the organization of the text and indicates the relationship of the major topics to one another. Various thought patterns that occur throughout the book are often evident. The relative importance of each topic can also be determined. By reading the table of contents, you are actually doing a very brief prereading of the entire text.

The table of contents is also useful to refer to before you begin reading any particular chapter. Although chapters are organized as separate parts of a textbook, it is important to recognize that they are parts of a whole—the text itself. Chapters relate and connect to one another. The material covered in any particular chapter is related to the information in the chapters that precede and follow it. Material in the preceding chapters may give background information or contain descriptions of earlier events, more basic theories, related problems, or early developments. Material in the following chapters may contain further developments, more complex theories, or effects or results.

Many current textbooks include a brief table of contents, listing only unit and chapter titles, followed by a complete table of contents that provides a detailed list of topics covered in each chapter. The brief table of contents is useful in understanding the overall organization and structure of the entire text. The complete table of contents is useful in working with individual chapters.

The brief table of contents shown in part in Figure 10-3 is taken from Helena Curtis's *Biology*. You can quickly see the main topics covered in the text. A portion of the complete table of contents for the same text is shown in Figure 10-4. Here you can see how each chapter is approached and what specific topics are covered.

EXERCISE 7 _____

Directions: *Now that you have read the sample tables of contents, answer the following questions in the space provided.*

1. Describe the overall organization of Part I.

_____

2. What is the purpose of the text's introduction? With what issues is it concerned?

_____

_____

Contents in Brief

FIGURE 10-3   **Sample Brief Contents**

Contents

viii CONTENTS

FIGURE 10-4 Sample Contents

3. What do you think is the purpose of including essays in each chapter?

_____

4. What characteristics of water do you expect will be covered in Chapter 2?

_____

IN-CHAPTER LEARNING AIDS

Textbook authors include important reading and study aids in each chapter. Some of the most useful aids are described in the following section.

Chapter Titles

Chapter titles are often mistakenly ignored. Many students, if interrupted while reading a text assignment, cannot recall the name of the chapter they are reading. Chapter titles serve the same function as textbook titles and subtitles. They tell the reader about the topics included in the chapters and provide clues about the organization, purpose, and point of view of the whole text. A chapter title tells you what to expect and starts you thinking about the topics discussed in the chapter before you begin reading. For example, if the title of a chapter is "The Nervous System: An Overview," you know the general topic—the nervous system—and you know that the purpose of the chapter is to provide a general picture, or overview, of the topic. You might expect that the chapter will be introductory and will probably discuss briefly the function, parts, and organization of the nervous system.

EXERCISE 8 _____

Directions: *Read the title of each text and the topic below it. Then underline the chapter of the text in which you would expect to find a discussion of the topic:*

1. Text: *Introduction to Anthropology*
   Topic: Development of male and female roles
   Chapters: a. "Discoveries of the First Humans"
   b. "Social Organization and Environment"
   c. "The Riddle of Heredity"

2. Text: *The American Family*
   Topic: Relationship between teenager and parents
   Chapters: a. "The Organization of the American Family"
   b. "The Adolescent Personality"
   c. "Teenagers and Dating"

3. Text: *Modern Economics*
   Topic: Leadership and control in large corporations

Chapters: a. "The Organization of the Modern Corporation"
   b. "Advantages and Disadvantages of the Corporate Form"
   c. "Ownership in the Large Corporation"

4. Text: *Life Insurance: An Introduction*
   Topic: Use of mortality tables (tables predicting the life span for various groups)
   Chapters: a. "The Measurement of Risk in Life Insurance"
      b. "Fundamental Principles of Policies"
      c. "Legal Concepts in Insurance"

5. Text: *Photography: A Guide to Basic Principles*
   Topic: How to achieve background and depth in a photograph
   Chapters: a. "Choosing Your Film"
      b. "First Steps for Beginning Photographers"
      c. "Composing a Photograph"

Chapter Preview

Research in educational psychology indicates that if readers have some knowledge of the content and organization of material *before* they begin to read it, their comprehension and recall increases. Consequently numerous textbooks begin each chapter with some kind of preview. There are several common forms.

Chapter Objectives: In some texts the objectives of each chapter are listed beneath its title, as is done in this book. The objectives are intended to focus your attention on important ideas and concepts. They are usually listed in the order in which the topics appear in the chapter, presenting an abbreviated outline of the main topics. This book introduces chapter objectives with "Use this chapter to," followed by a numbered list of chapter goals.

Chapter Outline: Other texts provide a brief outline of each chapter's contents. Formed from the headings and subheadings used in the chapter, the outline reflects both content and organization of the chapter. Refer to page 381 of the psychology sample textbook chapter reprinted in Appendix A. It presents an outline of key topics covered in the chapter. As you study a chapter outline, pay attention to the sequence and progression of topics and look for thought patterns.

Chapter Overview: Some textbook authors provide an overview or preview paragraph in which they state what the chapter is about, discuss why certain topics are important, focus the reader's attention on important issues, or indicate how the chapter relates to other chapters in the book.

Marginal Notations

Textbooks used to have wide empty margins, useful to students for jotting notes. Recently, some textbook authors have taken advantage of this available space to offer commentary on the text, pose questions based on the text, provide illustrations, examples, and drawings, or identify key vocabulary.

The best way to approach marginal notes is usually to refer to them once you have read the text to which they correspond. Often marginal notes can be used to review and check your recall. If the marginal notes are in the form of questions, go through the chapter section by section, answering each question. Test your ability to define each key term in your own words.

Headings

Interspersed throughout most textbook chapters are headings that are distinguished, usually by dark print (**boldface**) or *italics*. These headings have the same purpose as the label on a can of soup—they tell you what the contents are. Boldface and italic headings are labels for what is contained in the different sections of a chapter. They are two- or three-word summaries of what the section or passage is about.

Try to notice and think about the boldface heading before reading a section. Headings make reading easier; they tell you, in advance, what the section is about and what you are supposed to know when you finish. If you see the heading "Is memory chemical?" in a chapter on brain functions, you know you are supposed to have the answer to that question—along with the reason why memory is or is not chemical—when you finish the section. When you finish a section with the heading "Two complementary brains" you should know what the two brains are and how they complement each other, or work together.

Graphic Aids

Textbook chapters frequently include various types of graphic aids such as graphs, maps, pictures, and charts. It is tempting to skip over these aids because of the extra time involved in reading and interpreting them. You will find, however, that they are valuable learning aids. Pictures give you a vivid mental image of events. They are also useful memory tools. If you connect certain facts and events with a picture, when you recall the picture you will also recall the information associated with it.

Maps provide a visual description of the physical location of places. They are much more accurate than words in creating an understanding of position in space or in comparing the locations of two or more countries, cities, or other places. Like pictures, maps can serve as a visual memory aid and facilitate learning.

Graphs and charts are usually comparisons of two or more things and can be used to describe quickly a changing relationship over time. On a graph, for example, you can easily show how much inflation has increased yearly over the past ten years. If, however, you had to write in paragraph form a description of changing rates of inflation, the paragraph would be extremely long and complicated. In addition, the paragraph would not provide a quick overview of the trend or pattern of increase that you could see at a glance on a graph.

How to Read a Graph, Table, or Chart: To read a graph, table, or chart, use the following steps:

1. Read the title to determine what the overall purpose of the graph or chart is.

NUMBER OF BUSINESSES

Proprietorships 77% ▭ 12,702,000

Partnerships 8% ▭ 1,380,000

Corporations 15% ▭ 2,711,000

RECEIPTS OF BUSINESSES

Proprietorships 8% ▭ $506 billion

Partnerships 4% ▭ $292 billion

Corporations 88% ▭ $6,361 billion

PROFIT OF BUSINESSES

Proprietorships 18% ▭ $55 billion

Partnerships 5% ▭ $8 billion

Corporations 77% ▭ $239 billion

Exhibit 3-2

Number, receipts, and profit of proprietorships, partnerships, and corporations.
(SOURCE: *Statistical Abstract of the United States, 1984.*)

FIGURE 10-5   A Bar Graph

2. Read the headings on a chart or table or the legend on a graph. (The legend is made up of words or numbers written at the sides and bottom of the graph which tell you what units of measurement are used.)
3. Determine what two (or more) things are compared.
4. Study the graph or chart, noticing how the relationship between the two (or more) things changes.
5. Try to make a general statement explaining what the graph or chart shows or what trend or pattern is suggested.

In Figure 10-5 the title "Number, receipts, and profit of proprietorships, partnerships, and corporations" tells the purpose of the graph: to compare the number, amounts of money received, and profits of three different types of businesses. By studying this graph you can notice several trends or patterns. For example, corporations make the most profit and have the largest receipts, yet they are fewest in number. Partnerships, on the other hand, have the smallest profit and the lowest receipts and are fewest in number, while proprietorships, although large in number, have much lower receipts and profits than do corporations.

EXERCISE 9 ⎯⎯⎯⎯⎯⎯⎯⎯⎯⎯⎯⎯

Directions: *Study Figure 10-6 (a chart), Figure 10-7 (a line graph), and Figure 10-8 (a bar graph), using the five steps suggested for studying graphic aids. Then answer the questions for each figure.*

FIGURE 10-6

1. What is the overall purpose of this chart?

_____

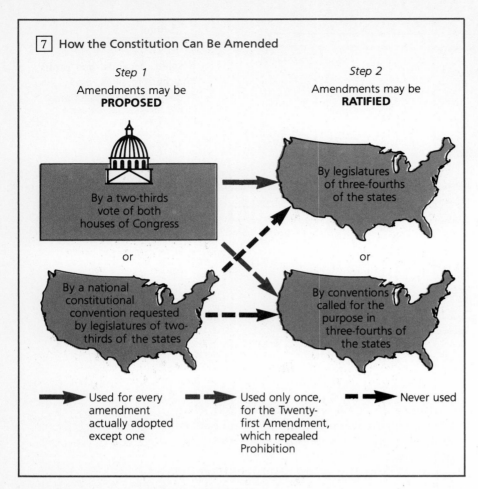

7 How the Constitution Can Be Amended

Step 1
Amendments may be
PROPOSED

By a two-thirds
vote of both
houses of Congress

or

By a national
constitutional
convention requested
by legislatures of two-
thirds of the states

Step 2
Amendments may be
RATIFIED

By legislatures
of three-fourths
of the states

or

By conventions
called for the
purpose in
three-fourths of
the states

→ Used for every amendment actually adopted except one

⇢ Used only once, for the Twenty-first Amendment, which repealed Prohibition

⇠ Never used

The Constitution set up two alternative routes for proposing amendments and two for ratifying them. Only one of the four possible combinations has really been used, but there are persistent calls for a constitutional convention to propose some new amendment or another. (Amendments to permit school prayers, to make abortion unconstitutional, and to require a balanced national budget are recent examples.)

FIGURE 10-6   A Chart Illustrating a Process

2. State the amendment process that is most commonly used.

   _____

3. Name the two processes that have never been used.

   _____

   _____

   FIGURE 10-7

1. What is the graph intended to show?

   _____

2. What are the stages in a product's life cycle?

   _____

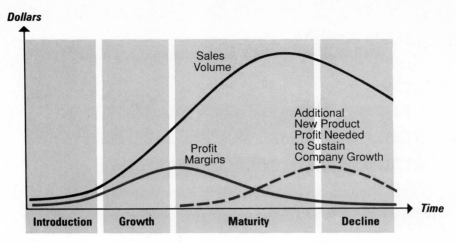

Figure 9-2
Basic Product
Life-cycle Model

FIGURE 10-7   A Line Graph

3. At what stage in its life cycle is a product most profitable?

   _____

4. At what point in the product life cycle is sales volume highest?

   _____

5. What relationship exists between sales volume and the need for additional profit?

   _____

   FIGURE 10-8

1. What was this graph constructed to show?

   _____

2. How is it organized?

   _____

   _____

3. What general trend or pattern do you notice about political expenditures?

   _____

4. Between what years did total expenditures increase most dramatically?

   _____

Figure 10.2   Political Expenditures in the United States, 1952–80*

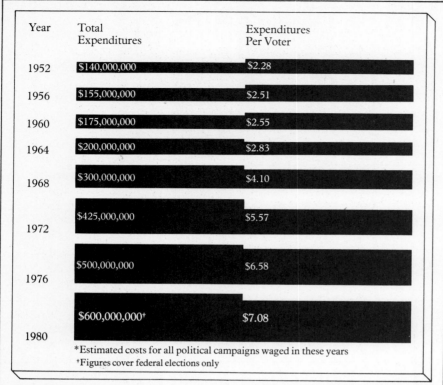

Year	Total Expenditures	Expenditures Per Voter
1952	$140,000,000	$2.28
1956	$155,000,000	$2.51
1960	$175,000,000	$2.55
1964	$200,000,000	$2.83
1968	$300,000,000	$4.10
1972	$425,000,000	$5.57
1976	$500,000,000	$6.58
1980	$600,000,000†	$7.08

*Estimated costs for all political campaigns waged in these years
†Figures cover federal elections only

Source: David W. Adamany, *Campaign Finance in America* (North Scituate, Mass.: Duxbury Press, 1972), p. 31; Herbert E. Alexander, *Money in Politics* (Washington, D.C.: Public Affairs Press, 1972); 1976 figures courtesy of Herbert E. Alexander; 1980 figures from David Adamany, "Political Finance in Transition," *Polity* (forthcoming), p. 7.

FIGURE 10-8   A Bar Graph

END-OF-CHAPTER AIDS ⑦

Chapter Summary

An end-of-chapter summary is useful to read both before and after you read a chapter. When read before the chapter, the summary will familiarize you with the chapter's basic organization and content. Be sure to reread the summary after you finish the chapter. It will provide a good review and help you tie together, or consolidate, the major points covered in the chapter. Read the summary of each of the sample textbook chapters reprinted in the appendixes (pages 409–410 and 424–425). Notice that each summary outlines the major points covered in the chapter.

Preview + Review

EXERCISE 10 _____

Directions: *Read each of the following chapter summaries and answer the questions that follow.*

1. Text: *Government in America*
    Chapter title: "The Global Connection"

Summary:

The world—its politics and its economics—intrudes on us more each year. In this chapter, we looked at America's global connection and the contours of our foreign policy.

The cold war began shortly after World War II, when the containment doctrine was made the basis of American foreign policy. Cold war gave way to hot wars in Korea and Vietnam, when the United States tried to contain communist advances. With containment came a massive buildup of our military apparatus, resulting in what some people called a "military-industrial complex." Gradually, containment has been balanced by détente, although we still maintain an enormous military apparatus.

For many years, the share of our national budget spent on defense declined. Advocates of a stronger military posture argued that the Soviet Union was becoming militarily superior to the United States. Ronald Reagan was one of those advocates of expanded defense spending, and his budget priorities reflected a greater commitment to the Department of Defense. Like presidents before him, Reagan grappled with the content as well as the amount of defense spending. The tangled decision making about the MX missile, for example, has extended over the administrations of three American presidents.

The American Gulliver has been strong in military power, but many of the world's issues today are not military ones. Interconnected issues of equality, economics, and energy and the environment have become important. As the inequalities between rich and poor nations widen, the North-South cleavage has become more important. The international economic system pulls the United States deeper and deeper into the world's problems as our own interdependence and vulnerability become more apparent. Also on the global policy agenda are issues of energy and the environment.

The world today is a world of new issues, where military power does not automatically bring success in foreign policy. In an era of a tight global connection, problems of equality, the economy, and energy and the environment do not merely parallel their domestic manifestations; the way foreign policy confronts the international face of these key issue areas shapes what we can do about them at home.

–Lineberry, p. 152

This chapter focuses on
a. national defense
b. world problems and issues
c. military issues
d. economic issues

2. Text: *The Economics of Money, Banking, and Financial Markets*
   Chapter title: "Multiple Deposit Creation"
   Summary:
   1. There are four players in the money supply process: (1) the central bank, (2) banks (depository institutions), (3) depositors, and (4) borrowers from banks.

2. The central bank in the United States is the Federal Reserve System, also called "The Fed." It conducts monetary policy, clears checks, and performs a regulatory function. The Fed has monetary liabilities (currency in circulation and reserves), which make up the bulk of the monetary base; it has assets of government securities and the discount loans it grants to banks.

3. The Fed provides reserves to the banking system by purchasing bonds or by making loans to the banks. A single bank can make loans up to the amount of its excess reserves, thereby creating an equal amount of deposits. The banking system can create a multiple expansion of deposits, because as each bank makes a loan and creates deposits, the reserves find their way to another bank, which uses them to make loans and create additional deposits. In the simple model of multiple deposit creation in which banks do not hold on to excess reserves, the multiple increase in checkable deposits (simple deposit multiplier) equals the reciprocal of the required reserve ratio.

4. The simple model of multiple deposit creation has serious deficiencies. Decisions by depositors to increase their holdings of currency or of banks to hold excess reserves will, for example, result in a smaller expansion of deposits than the simple model predicts. All four players—the Fed, banks, depositors, and borrowers from banks—are important in the determination of the money supply.

–Mishkin, p. 251

The chapter is primarily concerned with
a. the relationship among banks
b. the process of deposits and loans in banking
c. management and organizational structure of banks
d. the functions of the Fed

Chapter Questions

Many texts include discussion or review questions at the end of each chapter. Try to quickly read through these questions *before* you begin the chapter. The questions serve as a guide to what is important in the chapter and what you should know when you finish the chapter. Turn to page 425 of the sample textbook chapter reprinted in Appendix B for examples of review questions.

After reading the chapter, use these questions to test yourself on what you understood and can remember. Review them again when preparing for an exam covering the chapter.

Vocabulary List—New Terminology

Some textbook authors include a list of new terms introduced in the chapter. This list may appear either at the beginning or end of the chapter and is a useful study aid in preparing for exams. Many instructors include on their exams items that test student mastery of the new terms introduced in their courses, especially in introductory courses. The vocabulary list is a fast way of reviewing. For suggestions on how to learn new terminology, see Chapter 19.

References

Some texts include a list of references at the end of each chapter. Other texts may have one complete list of references at the end of the entire text. In this case it may be labeled "Bibliography." References are books or articles to which you can refer to get further information on the topics discussed in the chapter. This reference list is particularly useful when you have completed an assignment or do a term paper that requires you to locate other information sources. The reference list frequently contains some of the most useful or most authoritative books and articles on a given subject. In some instances, using the reference list can save you hours of time trying to locate adequate sources in the library.

Appendix

The appendix, located at the end of a text, is made up of extra information and materials that the author wanted to include in the text. Frequently, these are things that help students learn more about the subject matter, or items that must be referred to regularly. In an American history text, appendixes might include a copy of the Constitution, of the Declaration of Independence, a map of the United States, and a list of the terms of office of American presidents. Appendixes to a chemistry book might contain an equivalency table of weights and measures, a table of periodic elements, and an answer key to problems at the end of the chapters.

As soon as you buy a text, check to see if it has an appendix, and if so, find out what it contains. Many students waste time and energy searching for information contained right in the text.

Glossary

A glossary is an alphabetical listing of new vocabulary words that are used in the text. The meaning of each word is also included. Located in the back of the text, the glossary serves as a minidictionary. To make it even more convenient to use, attach some paper clips to the first page of the glossary in each of your texts. The paper clips will enable you to turn directly to the glossary without hunting and fumbling.

The glossary is easier to use than a regular dictionary. As you know, words have several meanings, and regular dictionaries list all of the most common meanings. To find the meaning of a word in a dictionary, you have to sort through all the meanings until you find one that suits the way the word is used in the text. A glossary, on the other hand, lists only one meaning—and it is the meaning intended by the author of your text. The glossary can save you time and eliminates the chance of selecting a meaning not consistent with the meaning used in the text.

Listed below are both a regular dictionary definition and a glossary definition for a common term used in psychology, *displacement*. Compare the definitions. You can readily see how much easier and faster it is to locate the meaning in the glossary than in the dictionary entry.

Glossary entry

displacement. The psychoanalytic defense mechanism by which feelings toward one object are refocused on a substitute object.[1]

Dictionary entry

dis·place·ment (dis-plās′mənt) *n.* **1. a.** The act of displacing. **b.** The condition of being displaced. **2.** *Chemistry.* A reaction in which one kind of atom, molecule, or radical is removed from combination and replaced by another. **3.** *Physics.* **a.** The weight or volume of a fluid displaced by a floating body, used especially as a measurement of the weight or bulk of ships. **b.** A vector, or the magnitude of a vector, from the initial position to a subsequent position assumed by a body. **4.** *Psychoanalysis.* The shifting of an emotional affect, as of anger, from an appropriate to an inappropriate object.[2]

In the dictionary, you have to sort through six different meanings, and even then you do not get a specific definition of the term as used in the field of psychology. The glossary entry, on the other hand, gives a clear and concise definition of the term as it is used by the author.

The glossary can serve as a useful study aid, particularly at the end of a course when you have completed the text. The glossary is actually a list of words for which you should have learned the meanings. The easiest way to check whether you have learned these new terms is to go through each column of the glossary, covering up the meanings with an index card or folded sheet of paper. Read each word and try to give a definition for it. You might write the definition or just make up the definition mentally. Then uncover the meaning and see if you were correct. Keep track of those you miss and study them later.

Index

At the end of the text you will find an index—an alphabetical listing of topics covered in the book. When you purchase a text, take a quick look at the index to see how it's organized. Some indexes contain both main and subtopics arranged together in a single, alphabetical sequence. Other indexes may have the main topics arranged alphabetically with the subtopics that relate to a particular topic arranged in alphabetical sequence under each. These are indexes with multiple alphabetical sequences. The following are examples of each type.

Single alphabetical sequence (topics only):

Model bank, 310
Modified rebuy system, 202
Money income, 186
Monopolistic competition, 598–602

Multiple alphabetical sequences (topics and subtopics):

Schader-Singer experiment, 252–254, 510
Schedules, reinforcement, 136–140

In some texts you may find a name index as well as a subject index. This index provides an alphabetical listing of individuals mentioned in the text.

EXERCISE 11 _____

Directions: *Evaluate the front and end matter of one of your textbooks. Place a check mark in the appropriate box in the following list if the particular feature is present.*

CHECKLIST   Textbook Features

Preface

☐ The purpose of the text is stated.
☐ The intended audience is indicated.
☐ The preface explains how the book is organized.
☐ The author's credentials are included.
☐ Distinctive features are described.
☐ Major points of emphasis are discussed.
☐ Aids to learning are described.

Table of Contents

☐ Brief table of contents is included.
☐ The chapters are grouped into parts or sections.
☐ Thought pattern(s) throughout the text are evident.

Appendix

☐ Useful tables and charts are included.
☐ Supplementary documents are included.
☐ Background or reference material is included.

Glossary

☐ The text contains a glossary.
☐ Word pronunciation as well as meaning is provided.

Index

☐ A subject index is included.
☐ A name index is included.

EXERCISE 12 _____

Directions: *Evaluate one of your textbooks to see what learning/study aids it contains. Use the following chart.*

Chapter preview

What preview format is used?
What is its primary purpose?
What thought pattern(s) is evident?
How could it be used for review?

Marginal notes

What format is used?
How can they be used for study and review?

Graphic aids

What graphic aids are included?
What concepts are they intended to emphasize?

Review questions

Do the questions provide an outline of chapter content (compare them with chapter headings)?
What type(s) of thinking do they require? Are they primarily factual, or do they require critical thinking?

Key terminology

How many, if any, words are already familiar?
How difficult do you predict the chapter to be?

Chapter summary

Does it list the main topics the chapter will cover?
Is a thought pattern evident?

Suggested readings

What types of sources are listed?
To which topics do they refer?

SUMMARY

While textbooks are important sources of information, they are also valuable learning aids. Textbooks contain many features that are included for the sole purpose of helping you read, study, and learn the content of the text. At the beginning of the text, the title, subtitle, author's name and credentials, and copyright date all provide a perspective on the nature and type of text. The preface, "to the student" section, introduction, and table of contents provide more specific information about the scope and focus of the text. The preface and introduction describe the text and include specific information about the intended audience as well as the purposes and limitations of the text. The table of contents serves as an outline of the text, showing the relationship and relative importance of topics covered in the text.

Within each chapter there are also particular aids to understanding and retention. The chapter title and chapter introduction both provide an overall perspective on the chapter content. Chapter previews focus your attention on important topics and ideas. Marginal notations are used to provide commentary, ask questions, or identify key terms. Boldface headings serve as labels or titles that summarize the content of each section. Within each chapter, graphic aids such as maps, graphs, charts, and pictures assist the reader by visually emphasizing important concepts and ideas. At the end of each chapter, the chapter summary, chapter questions, and vocabulary list provide an outline of important information and terminology presented in the chapter.

At the end of the text, the index, glossary, list of references, and appendix aid the reader by organizing what has been presented in the text or by introducing valuable additional information. The index provides for rapid location of specific information; the glossary functions as a minidictionary, listing all important terminology used in the text. The references recommend sources of further information for many of the topics discussed in the text. The appendix contains additional information or supplementary information, which is frequently useful to the reader proceeding through the text.

11

Textbook Underlining and Marking

Use this chapter to:

1. *Learn to underline textbooks effectively.*
2. *Develop a system of textbook marking.*

As you have already discovered, most college courses have lengthy and time-consuming reading assignments. Just completing reading assignments is a big job. Have you begun to wonder how you will ever go back over all those textbook chapters when it is time for an exam?

THE PROBLEM OF TEXTBOOK REVIEW

Let's suppose that it takes you at least four hours to read carefully a forty-page chapter for one of your courses. Assume that your text has ten chapters of approximately forty pages each. It would take a total of forty hours, then, to read completely through the text once. Suppose that your instructor is giving a final exam that will cover the entire text. If the only thing you did to prepare for the final was to reread the whole text, it would take close to another forty hours to study for the exam; but one additional reading is no guarantee that you will pass the exam.

There is a technique you could have used to review and study the chapters of your text adequately at exam time. You could have underlined and marked important ideas and facts as you were first reading the chapters. Then, when you were ready to review, you would have had to read and study only what you marked. If you had marked or underlined 15 to 20 percent of the chapter material, you would have cut down your rereading time by 80 to 85 percent, or thirty-two hours! Of course, to prepare effectively for the exam, it would have been necessary to review in other ways besides rereading, but you would have had time left in which to use these other ways.

HOW TO UNDERLINE TEXTBOOKS

To learn how to underline textbooks effectively, start with the following guidelines:

1. Read first; then underline. As you are reading to develop skill in underlining, it is better, at first, to read a paragraph or section first, and then go back and underline what is important to remember and review. Later, when you've had more practice underlining, you may be able to underline while you read.
2. Read the boldface headings. Headings are labels, or overall topics, for what is contained in that section. Use the headings to form questions that you expect to be answered in the section.
3. After you have read the section, go back and underline the parts that answer your questions. These will be parts of sentences that express the main ideas, or most important thoughts, in the section. In reading and underlining the following section, you could form questions like those suggested and then underline as shown:

Questions to ask: What is the propositional form?
What is the narrative form?

PROPOSITIONAL VS. NARRATIVE FORM

Finally, speaking styles can differ greatly in another important way: Some styles are highly *propositional*—that is, they are dominated by an argumentative method of composition; while other styles are highly *narrative*—that is, they are dominated by storytelling. When using a propositional form of speaking, the speaker offers a series of claims or assertions and supports each one with evidence the audience should consider important. When using a narrative form, the speaker offers a story which contains a message or "moral" the audience should consider compelling.

–Ehninger, *Principles and Types of Speech Communication*, p. 230

4. As you identify and underline main ideas, look for important facts that explain or support the main idea and underline them too.
5. When underlining main ideas and details, do not underline complete sentences. Underline only enough so that you can see what is important and so that your underlining makes sense when you reread. Notice how only key words and phrases are underlined in the following:

DEFINING FROM ORIGINAL SOURCES

Sometimes you can reinforce a series of feelings or attitudes you wish an audience to have about a concept by telling them where the word came from: "*Sincere* comes from two Latin words: *sine*, meaning 'without,' and *ceres*, meaning 'wax.' In early Rome, a superior statue was one in which the artisan did not have to cover his mistakes by putting wax into flaws. That statue was said to be *sine ceres*—'without wax.' Today, the term *a sincere person* carries some of that same meaning. . . . " This is called an *etymological definition* when you <u>trace a word's meaning back</u> into its <u>original language</u>. It's termed a *genetic definition* when you explain <u>where the idea</u> rather than the word <u>comes from</u>. You could, for instance, explain the American concept of freedom of speech by looking at important discussions of that idea in eighteenth-century England, and then showing how the American doctrine took its shape from our ancestors' British experiences. <u>Defining from original sources</u>, either of the word or of the idea, <u>gives</u> an <u>audience</u> a <u>sense of continuity</u> and at times <u>explains certain nuances of meaning</u> we cannot explain in any other way.

–Ehninger, *Principles and Types of Speech Communication*, p. 232

ASPECTS OF EFFECTIVE UNDERLINING

For your underlining to be effective and useful to you as you study and review, it must follow four specific guidelines: (1) the right amount of information must be underlined; (2) the underlining must be regular and consistent; (3) it must be accurate; and (4) it must clearly reflect the content of the passage. Suggestions for and examples of each of these guidelines are given in the following paragraphs.

Underline the Right Amount

Students frequently make the mistake of underlining either too much or too little. If you underline too much, the passages you have marked will take you too long to reread when studying. If you underline too little, you won't be able to get any meaning from your underlining as you review it. To get an idea of each mistake, study the passages below.

TOO MUCH UNDERLINING

<u>The Shah attempted rapid modernization of his country</u> [Iran]. He sent thousands of young Iranians <u>abroad for an education, subsidized new industries</u>, and introduced some <u>land reforms</u>. He <u>purchased</u> huge quantities of <u>arms</u>. Some $14 billion worth was bought from the United States alone. This crash <u>program of modernization</u>, however, <u>was his undoing</u>. It caused many <u>areas of friction and discontent</u>. <u>Inflation rose</u> rapidly to <u>50 percent</u> annually. Bad planning placed too much emphasis on industry and the cities, <u>neglecting agriculture and the villages</u>. Thousands of peasants flocked to the cities, especially Teheran, where <u>areas of slums and blight sprang up</u>. But worst of all, the <u>rapid modernization threatened the integrity of the Iranian cultural fabric</u>.

–Wallbank et al., *Civilization Past and Present*, p. 953

TOO LITTLE UNDERLINING

The <u>Shah attempted rapid modernization</u> of his country [Iran]. He sent thousands of young Iranians abroad for an education, subsidized new industries, and introduced some land reforms. He purchased huge quantities of arms. Some $14 billion worth was bought from the United States alone. This crash <u>program of modernization</u>, however, <u>was his undoing</u>. It caused many areas of friction and discontent. <u>Inflation</u> rose rapidly to <u>50 percent</u> annually. Bad planning placed too much emphasis on industry and the cities, neglecting agriculture and the villages. Thousands of peasants flocked to the cities, especially Teheran, where areas of slums and blight sprang up. But worst of all, the rapid <u>modernization threatened</u> the integrity of the <u>Iranian cultural fabric</u>.

EFFECTIVE UNDERLINING

The <u>Shah</u> attempted <u>rapid modernization</u> of his country [<u>Iran</u>]. He sent thousands of young Iranians abroad for an education, subsidized new industries, and introduced some land reforms. He purchased huge quantities of arms. Some $14 billion worth was bought from the United States alone. This <u>crash program of modernization</u>, however, <u>was his undoing</u>. It caused many areas of friction and discontent. <u>Inflation rose rapidly</u> to <u>50 percent</u> annually. Bad planning placed too much emphasis on industry and the cities, neglecting agriculture and the villages. Thousands of <u>peasants flocked</u> to the <u>cities</u>, especially Teheran, where areas of <u>slums and blight sprang up</u>. But worst of all, the rapid modernization <u>threatened</u> the integrity of the <u>Iranian cultural fabric</u>.

Almost all of the first passage is underlined. To underline nearly all of the passage is as ineffective as not underlining at all because it does not sort out or distinguish important from unimportant information. In the second passage, only the main point of the paragraph is underlined, but very sketchily—not enough detail is included. The underlining in the third passage is effective; it identifies the main idea of the paragraph and includes sufficient detail to make the main idea clear and understandable.

As a rule of thumb, try to underline no more than one-quarter to one-third of each page. This figure will vary, of course, depending on the type of material you are reading. Here is another example of effective underlining. Notice that approximately one-third of each paragraph is underlined.

"HIGH-TECH" CRIME: THE CRIMINAL AND THE COMPUTER

<u>Technological change advances criminal opportunities</u> as well as noncriminal ones. Nowhere is this more in evidence than in the realm of electronics. We live in an era of high technology, one in which electronic brains and silicon chips rule much of the behavior of people and machines. The more computers we have and the more things we can get them to do, the more opportunities there are for computer crime. Estimates of the <u>annual losses</u> from <u>computer-related crimes</u> go as high as <u>$5 billion</u>, and in all likelihood the figure will go much higher (Kolata, 1982).

The <u>range of computer crimes</u> is <u>vast</u> and <u>growing</u>. . . .

Embezzlement, industrial espionage, theft of services (for example, using a computer that belongs to someone else for one's private business), invasion of privacy, copyright violations, destruction of information or programs, falsification of data, and a host of fraudulent transactions are just a few of the computer-related abuses that have come to light.

The potential for computer crime is staggering, and that fact is now recognized in legislative and enforcement circles. But most of the preventive work so far initiated is privately organized and paid for. Hundreds of companies have sprung up in recent years peddling advice and technology to counteract the new breed of high-tech criminal. The 1980s will be a profitable decade for both computer criminals and those in the business of prevention.

–Barlow, *Introduction to Criminology*, p. 252

Develop a Regular and Consistent System of Underlining

As you develop your textbook underlining skills, you should focus on this second guideline: Develop a system for deciding what type of information you will underline and how you will mark it. First, decide what type of information you want to mark. Before marking anything, decide whether you will mark only main ideas or whether you will mark main ideas and details. You should also decide whether you will underline or mark definitions of new terminology and, if so, how will you distinguish them from other information marked in the paragraph. Second, it is important to use whatever system and type of underlining you decide on consistently so that you will know what your underlining means when you review it. If you sometimes mark details and main ideas and other times underline only main ideas, you will find that, at review time, you are unsure of what passages are marked in what way, and you will be forced to reread a great deal of material.

You may decide to develop a system for separating main ideas from details, major points from supporting information. When you review underlining done this way, you will immediately know what is the most important point of the paragraph or section, and you will not get bogged down in the details—unless you need to. One such system uses double underlining for main points and single underlining for details. Another system might be use asterisks to distinguish the main points. A third choice might be to use two colors of ink to distinguish main ideas and details.

Each of the following paragraphs has been underlined using one of the suggested systems. You will notice that the paragraphs vary in the type of information marked in each.

VERSION 1

MODELING VIOLENCE

Many scholars believe that aggression is learned, just like any other behavior. One prominent theory is that we learn it by imitation or modeling the behavior of people we "look up to." Albert Bandura (1973) showed that the behavior of aggressive models is readily imitated by experimental subjects, whether observed in the flesh or via film. In one <u>well-known</u> <u>experiment</u>, Bandura played a film of a <u>woman</u> sitting on, <u>beat-</u><u>ing, kicking,</u> and hacking an inflatable <u>doll</u>. After witnessing the film, nursery <u>school children</u>, when placed in a room with a similar doll, <u>duplicated the woman's behavior</u> and also engaged in other aggressive acts.

–Barlow, *Criminology,* p. 140

VERSION 2

MODELING VIOLENCE

Many scholars believe that <u>aggression is learned</u>, just like any other behavior. One <u>prominent theory</u> is that <u>we learn it</u> <u>by imitation or modeling</u> the <u>behavior</u> of <u>people we "look up</u> <u>to."</u> Albert Bandura (1973) showed that the behavior of aggres-sive models is readily imitated by expermental subjects, whether observed in the flesh or via film. In one <u>well-known</u> <u>experiment</u>, Bandura played a film of a <u>woman</u> sitting on, <u>beat-</u><u>ing, kicking,</u> and hacking an inflatable <u>doll</u>. After witnessing the film, nursery <u>school children</u>, when placed in a room with a similar doll, <u>duplicated the woman's behavior</u> and also engaged in other aggressive acts.

VERSION 3

MODELING VIOLENCE

Many scholars believe that <u>aggression is learned</u>, just like any other behavior. One <u>prominent theory</u> is that we <u>learn it</u> <u>by imitation or modeling</u> the <u>behavior</u> of <u>people we "look up</u> <u>to."</u> Albert Bandura (1973) showed that the behavior of aggres-sive models is readily imitated by experimental subjects, whether observed in the flesh or via film. In one <u>well-known</u> <u>experiment</u>, Bandura played a film of a <u>woman</u> sitting on, <u>beat-</u><u>ing, kicking,</u> and hacking an inflatable <u>doll</u>. After witnessing the film, nursery school <u>children</u>, when placed in a room with a similar doll, <u>duplicated the woman's behavior</u> and also engaged in other aggressive acts.

EXERCISE 1 ─────────────────

Directions: *Read the following passage. Then evaluate the effectiveness of the underlining, making suggestions for improvement.*

SCARCITY OF HUMAN FOSSILS

Humans are a maddeningly poor source of fossils. In 1956, the paleontologist <u>G. H. R. von Koenigswald</u> calculated that if all the then-<u>known fragments of human beings</u> older than the Neandertal people were gathered together they could be comfortably <u>displayed on a</u> <u>medium-sized table</u>. Although many more fossils of early hominids have been found since then, discoveries are still rare.

Why are human fossils so scarce? <u>Why can one go to good fossil sites almost anywhere in the world and find millions of shell remains</u> or thousands of bones of extinct reptiles and mammals, while peoples earlier than Neandertal are known from only a handful of sites at which investigators, working through tons of deposits, pile up other finds by the bushel basket before recovering a single human tooth?

There are many reasons. First, the <u>commonness of marine fossils</u> is a direct reflection of the <u>abundance of these creatures</u> when they were alive. It also reflects the tremendous span of time during which they abounded. Many of them swarmed through the waters of the earth for hundreds of millions of years. When they died, they sank and were covered by sediments. <u>Their way of life</u>—their life in the water—<u>preserved them</u>, as did their extremely durable shells, the only parts of them that now remain. <u>Humans,</u> by contrast, have never been as numerous as oysters and clams. They <u>existed in small numbers,</u> reproduced slowly and in small numbers, and lived a relatively long time. They were more intelligent than, for example, dinosaurs and were perhaps less apt to get mired in bogs, marshes, or quicksands. Most important, their way of life was different. They were <u>not sea creatures</u> or riverside browsers but <u>lively, wide-ranging food-gatherers and hunters.</u> They often lived and died in the open, where their bones could be gnawed by scavengers and bleached and decomposed in the sun and rain. In hot climates, particularly in tropical forests and woodlands, the soil is likely to be markedly acid. Bones dissolve in such soils, and early humans who lived and died in such an environment would have had a very poor chance of leaving remains that would last until today. Finally, <u>human ancestors</u> have been on <u>earth only a few million years.</u> There simply has not been as much time for them to scatter their bones about as there has been for some of the more ancient species of animals.

–Campbell, *Humankind Emerging*, pp. 22–23

EXERCISE 2 _____

Directions: *Read each paragraph or passage and then underline the* main idea *and* important details *in each. You may want to try various systems of underlining as you work through this exercise.*

1. **GENERAL BUYING POWER INDEXES**

    It is possible to estimate the market potential in specific regions for many products by using indexes of relative buying power. The index may be either a *single-* or *multiple-factor* index. For example, a single-factor index might use summary Internal Revenue Service income data, by state, as a measure of market potential. If total American market potential for a product is estimated to be $100 million, and all potential buyers have incomes over $50,000, and California has 20 percent of all people with incomes above $50,000, then the estimated potential in California would be $20 million ($100 million $\times$ .2).

    In industrial markets, a widely accepted single-factor index is the *Sales & Marketing Management Survey of Industrial Purchasing Power*. This annual index uses data on the value of shipments of industrial goods. The index is organized according to categories of the Standard Industrial Classification industry groups and uses geographic area as its measure of potential. For example, it would report the value of paper products shipped into the New England area.

It is usually more accurate to use *multiple factors* to construct an index. One very well-known consumer market index is the *Sales & Marketing Management Survey of Buying Power*. It is constructed by weighting population by two, effective buying income by five, and total retail sales by three. Data in this index are provided at the state, county, and city level. For example, if Texas is rated as having 10 percent of buying power, then 10 percent of the total American market potential would be allocated to Texas.

–Kinnear and Bernhardt, *Prinicples of Marketing,* p. 223

2. TYPES OF INTERVIEW QUESTIONS

Because the communicative basis of interviews is made up of questions and answers, a skilled interviewer must be practiced in phrasing and organizing useful questions. Six types of questions are often asked. *Primary questions* introduce some topic or area of inquiry, while *follow-up questions* probe more deeply or ask for elaboration or clarification. Thus, if you are interviewing a local newspaper editor for a feature article, you might begin with "What background did you have before becoming editor?" and follow up with "Would you elaborate on your experience as a copy editor— what did you do in that position?" You also will develop *direct questions* ("How long have you been the editor?") and *indirect questions* ("What is your goal for the paper five years from now?"). Direct questions allow you to gather information quickly, while indirect probes let you see interviewees "thinking on their feet," structuring materials and responses and exploring their own minds. Interviewers also employ both *open* and *closed* questions. A closed question specifies the direction of the response—"Do your editorials serve to create public concern about local issues?" An open question allows the interviewee to control the categories of response—"How do you perceive your role in the community?" Closed questions require little effort from the interviewee and are easy to "code" or record; open questions allow interviewers to observe the interviewee's habits, to let them feel in control of the interaction. Of course, these various types of questions overlap: You can use a direct or indirect question as your primary question; a closed question can be direct ("Do you function most as editor, reporter, or lay-out specialist?") or indirect ("Of the various jobs you perform—editor, reporter, lay-out specialist—which do you enjoy the most?"). Overall, primary, direct, and closed questions tend to produce a lot of "hard" information quickly; follow-up, indirect, and open questions produce more thought and interpretation—grounds for understanding and analyzing interviewees and their motivations, capacities, and expectations. As you plan interviews, learn to blend questions of all six types—to build an *interview schedule*.

An interview schedule is your effort to organize specific questions so as to elicit systematically the materials and opinions you are seeking. Like any other organizational pattern, an interview schedule should have a rationale, one which *(1)* permits you to acquire systematic information or opinion, and *(2)* seems reasonable to the interviewee, avoiding confusing detours and repetitions. Interview schedules normally are built in one of two forms: the *traditional schedule* and the *branching schedule.*

–Ehninger, *Principles and Types of Speech Communication*, pp. 142–143

3. **ANALYZING THE PROBLEM OF UNEMPLOYMENT**

The Employment Act of 1946 set forth the goal of maintaining maximum employment. The law made it the clear responsibility of the federal government to establish policies for achieving this goal.

An effective policy for full employment depends first on correct analysis of the sources of unemployment. Identifying these sources will enable policymakers to design effective programs to correct each type. Economists have classified unemployment into three categories, depending on the cause: frictional, cyclical, and structural.

FRICTIONAL UNEMPLOYMENT

Economists define normal full employment as the condition that exists when approximately 97 to 98 percent of the civilian labor force is employed. The remaining 2 or 3 percent are unemployed because of *frictional unemployment*—unemployment caused by difficulties in the movement of workers from job to job or among workers entering the labor force for the first time.

Frictional unemployment is necessary and even desirable in a dynamic economy. It is a reflection of the healthy growth or decline of different sectors of the economy. Markets and production techniques are constantly changing to reflect changes in consumer demand. Workers must move out of declining industries and into expanding industries. If there were no frictional unemployment, expanding industries would have to bid up the wages of employed workers, aggravating tendencies toward inflation.

In recent years, frictional unemployment has come to constitute a larger portion of total employment. This is primarily because of the growing numbers of married women and teenagers in the job market, with typically higher rates of entry and re-entry into the labor force than adult male workers.

Frictional unemployment is, by definition, temporary. Its effects may be relieved by better job information and aids to worker mobility. For example, workers can be provided job counseling, or they can be paid grants to finance a move to a new location where jobs are more plentiful.

CYCLICAL UNEMPLOYMENT

The term "mass unemployment" brings to mind the more awesome evil of *cyclical unemployment*—unemployment associated with cycles of economic activity. The Great Depression provides the best example of this type of unemployment. During the Great Depression, the unemployment rate reached as high as 25 percent of the labor force.

Typically, economic activity grows in spurts. Periods of great optimism and growth are followed by slower growth or decline. Once homes are equipped with video recorders, microwave ovens, and personal computers, demand for consumer goods diminishes. Retailers cut back on inventories and cancel orders to wholesalers.

The whole economic system seems to pause before the next round of innovations brings on a new outpouring of gadgets, and the cycle begins again.

Cyclical swings in employment are most severe in industries producing durable goods. The purchase of an auto, refrigerator, or sewing machine can be postponed if family heads are worried about their jobs. Cyclical swings are less severe in the production of nondurable goods and services. Purchases of food, clothing, and health services, for instance, cannot generally be postponed.

When consumer demand declines, blue-collar production workers are more likely to suffer unemployment than professional or supervisory workers. One reason is the specialized functions of the latter workers, which the firm cannot afford to lose to other firms. Another is the fact that many professional workers are covered by contracts that protect their jobs.

Federal economic policy to stimulate consumer demand was developed following the Depression as a means of controlling cyclical unemployment. Expansionary fiscal and monetary policies make cyclical unemployment less a threat to our economic system today than in former years.

STRUCTURAL UNEMPLOYMENT

More threatening to our prosperity and social health is the growing problem of structural unemployment. *Structural unemployment* is caused by an imbalance between the structure of the labor force, on the one hand, and the requirements of modern industry, on the other. When available labor skills fail to correspond to the needs of industry, there is unemployment. Substantial unemployment may persist even though there are job vacancies. Structural unemployment is worsened by the entry of untrained workers (such as teenagers) into the labor force.

The greatest needs in business today are for skilled workers and for workers in the growing service sector. For example, there are extreme shortages of workers in machine trades, engineering, nursing, transport, and finance. Federal and state programs to train workers in new skills, better job information and counseling, and private on-the-job training can help relieve structural unemployment.

–McCarty, *Dollars and Sense: An Introduction to Economics*, pp. 213–214

Underline Accurately

A third guideline for marking textbooks is to be sure that the information that you underline accurately conveys the thought of the paragraph or passage. In a rush, students often overlook the second half of the main idea expressed in a paragraph, miss a crucial qualifying statement, or mistake an example or contrasting idea for the main idea. Read the paragraph in the following example and evaluate the accuracy of the underlining.

It has long been established that the <u>American legal court system</u> is an <u>open and fair system</u>. Those suspected to be guilty of a criminal offense are given a <u>jury trial</u> in which a <u>group of impartially selected citizens</u> are asked to <u>determine</u>, based upon <u>evidence presented</u>, the <u>guilt</u> or <u>innocence</u> of the person on trial. In actuality, however, this system of jury trial is fair to everyone except the jurors involved. Citizens are <u>expected</u> and, in many instances, <u>required</u> to <u>sit on a jury</u>. They have little or no choice as to the time, place, or any other circumstances surrounding their participation. Additionally, they are expected to leave their job and accept jury duty pay for each day spent in court in place of their regular on-the-job salary. The <u>jury</u> must <u>remain on duty until</u> the <u>case is decided</u>.

In the preceding paragraph, the underlining indicates the main idea of the paragraph: The legal system that operates in American courts is open and fair. The paragraph starts out by saying that the legal system has long been established as fair but then goes on to say (in the third sentence) that the system is actually unfair to one particular group—the jury. In this case, the student who did the underlining missed the real main statement of the paragraph by mistaking the introductory contrasting statement with the main idea.

Make Your Underlining Understandable for Review

As you underline, keep the fourth guideline in mind: Be certain that your underlining clearly reflects the content of the passage so that you will be able to reread and review it easily. Try to underline enough information in each passage so that the passage reads smoothly when you review it.

Read these two versions of underlining of the same passage. Which underlining is easier to reread?

VERSION 1

Capital may be thought of as <u>manufactured resources</u>. Capital includes the tools and equipment that strengthen, extend, or <u>replace human hands</u> in the production of goods and services: hammers, sewing machines, turbines, bookkeeping machines, and components of finished goods. Capital resources <u>permit "roundabout" production</u>: through capital, goods are produced indirectly by a kind of <u>tool</u>, rather than directly by <u>physical labor</u>. To construct a capital resource requires that we <u>postpone production</u> of consumer goods today so that we may produce <u>more in the future</u>. (Economists do not think of money as capital, since money by itself cannot produce anything at all. However, money is a convenient means of exchanging resources used in production.)

VERSION 2

Capital may be thought of as <u>manufactured resources</u>. Capital <u>includes</u> the <u>tools and equipment</u> that strengthen, extend, or replace human hands in the production of goods and services: hammers, sewing machines, turbines, bookkeeping machines, and components of finished goods. <u>Capital resources permit "roundabout" production</u>: through capital, goods are produced indirectly by a kind of tool, rather than directly by physical labor. To <u>construct a capital resource</u> requires that we <u>postpone production</u> of consumer goods <u>today</u> so that we may

<u>produce more in the future.</u> (Economists do not think of money as capital, since money by itself cannot produce anything at all. However, <u>money</u> is a convenient <u>means</u> of <u>exchanging resources</u> used in production.)

–McCarty, *Dollars and Sense,* pp. 213–214

A good way to check to see if your underlining is understandable for review is to reread only your underlining. If parts are unclear right after you read it, you can be sure it will be more confusing when you reread it a week or a month later. Be sure to fix ineffectual underlining in one paragraph before you continue to the next paragraph. You may find it useful, at first, to use a pencil for underlining. Then, when the underlining in a passage needs revising, you can accomplish this easily by erasing.

TESTING YOUR UNDERLINING

As you are learning underlining techniques, it is important to check to be certain that your underlining is effective and will be useful for review purposes. To test the effectiveness of your underlining, take any passage that you have underlined in Exercise 2 and reread only the underlining. Then ask yourself the following questions:

1. Have I underlined the right amount or do I have too much or too little information underlined?
2. Have I used a regular and consistent system for underlining?
3. Does my underlining accurately reflect the meaning of the passage?
4. As I reread my underlining, is it easy to follow the train of thought or does the passage seem like a list of unconnected words?

EXERCISE 3 _____

Directions: *Turn to the section of psychology sample chapter in Appendix A of this text titled "Psychological Stress Reactions" (page 396–399). Now read this section and underline the main ideas and important details. When you have finished, test your underlining. Use the four preceding questions for testing your underlining. Make any changes that will make your underlining more consistent, accurate, or understandable.*

EXERCISE 4 _____

Directions: *Choose a three- to four-page passage from one of your textbooks. Read the selection and underline main ideas, the important details, and key terms that are introduced. When you have finished, test your underlining using the four questions above, and make any changes that will improve your underlining.*

MARKING A TEXTBOOK

As you were underlining paragraphs and passages in the earlier part of this chapter, you may have realized that underlining alone is not sufficient, in many cases, to separate main ideas from details and both of these from new terminology. You may have seen that underlining does not easily show the relative importance of ideas or indicate the relationship of facts and ideas. Therefore, it is often necessary to mark, as well as underline, selections that you are reading. Suggestions for marking are shown in Table 11-1.

Two versions of the same paragraph, excerpted from *Conceptual Human Physiology* by Davis, Holtz, and Davis, follow. The first version contains only underlining, while in the second both underlining and marking are used. Which version more easily conveys the meaning of the passage?

TABLE 11-1   Textbook Marking

Type of Marking	Example
Circling unknown words	*def* . . . redressing the apparent (asymmetry) of their relationship . . .
Marking definitions	*def* To say that the balance of power favors one party over another is to introduce a disequilibrium.
Marking examples	*ex* . . . concessions may include negative sanctions, trade agreements . . .
Numbering lists of ideas, causes, reasons, or events	. . . components of power include ①self-image, ②population, ③natural resources, and ④geography
Placing asterisks next to important passages	* Power comes from three primary sources . . .
Putting question marks next to confusing passages	?→ . . . war prevention occurs through institutionalization of mediation . . .
Making notes to yourself	*check def in soc text* . . . power is the ability of an actor on the international stage to . . .
Marking possible test items	T There are several key features in the relationship . . .
Drawing arrows to show relationships	. . . natural resources . . . control of industrial manufacture capacity
Writing comments, noting disagreements and similarities	*Can terrorism be prevented through similar balance?* . . . war prevention through balance of power is . . .
Marking summary statements	*sum* . . . the greater the degree of conflict, the more intricate will be . . .

VERSION 1

EPILEPSY

Epilepsy is a disorder that affects the excitable cells, or neu-rons, of the nervous system; neurons of the brain, usually those of the cerebral cortex, become hyperactive, or hyperex-citable. This neuronal hyperactivity leads to the development of *seizures* (convulsions) that tend to recur on a chronic basis. Seizures include brief episodes of uncontrollable motor, sen-sory, or psychic disturbances that interrupt the individual's normal activities.

Epilepsy may be idiopathic (essential), in which no brain pathology can be identified, or it may be symptomatic, or sec-ondary, to a previous brain disease or injury. Conditions that may produce epilepsy are head injuries, including birth inju-ries; brain tumors; inflammatory conditions of the brain; hypo-glycemia, or low blood sugar; toxic conditions, such as uric acid buildup or alcohol withdrawal; or lack of oxygen to the brain cells. The development of epilepsy seems to depend on a combination of genetic and environmental factors, in which persons with a genetic predisposition have greater chances of developing epilepsy when environmental conditions favor it.

VERSION 2

EPILEPSY

def (*Epilepsy*) is a disorder that affects the excitable cells, or neu-rons, of the nervous system; neurons of the brain, usually those of the cerebral cortex, become hyperactive, or hyperex-citable. This neuronal hyperactivity leads to the development

Symptoms of *seizures* (convulsions) that tend to recur on a chronic basis. Seizures include brief episodes of uncontrollable motor, sen-sory, or psychic disturbances that interrupt the individual's normal activities. ①

2 types Epilepsy may be idiopathic (essential), ① in which no brain pathology can be identified, or it may be ②symptomatic, or sec-ondary, to a previous brain disease or injury. Conditions that may produce epilepsy are head injuries, including birth inju-ries; brain tumors; inflammatory conditions of the brain; hypo-

Causes glycemia, or low blood sugar; toxic conditions, such as uric acid buildup or alcohol withdrawal; or lack of oxygen to the brain cells. The development of epilepsy seems to depend on a combination of genetic and environmental factors, in which persons with a genetic predisposition have greater chances of developing epilepsy when environmental conditions favor it.

As you can see, in Version 2 the two types of epilepsy are easy to iden-tify. Numbering the types makes them immediately noticeable and distin-guishes them from the remainder of the passage.

Summary Words

Writing summary words or phrases in the margin is one of the most valuable types of textbook marking. It involves pulling together ideas and summarizing them in your own words. This summarizing process forces you to think and evaluate as you read and makes remembering easier. Writing summary phrases is also a good test of your understanding. If you cannot state the main idea of a section in your own words, you probably do not understand it clearly. This realization can serve as an early warning signal that you may not be able to handle a test question on that section.

To illustrate effective marking of summary phrases, the following sample passage has been included. First, read through the passage. Then look at the marginal summary clues.

DATA

Computers process data. A computer gets data from input devices and sends data to output devices. It stores data in internal storage and in auxiliary storage. It performs computations and makes logical decisions using data. The instructions in a program tell the computer how to process the data.

Data must be arranged or organized in a way that makes it easier to process. In this subsection we explain the main concepts of data organization. We also discuss data input and output.

DATA ORGANIZATION

Data is composed of symbols or *characters*. There are three basic types of characters: *numeric characters* or *digits* (0, 1, . . . , 9), *alphabetic characters* or *letters* (A, B, . . . , Z), and *special characters* (comma, decimal point, equal sign, and so forth). A *blank* or *space* is considered a special character; it is often very important in computer data processing.

3 types of characters

Although a single character can represent data, more often groups of characters convey information. A related group of characters, representing some unit of information, is called a *field*. For example, a person's name is a field; it is a group of characters that conveys specific information. A social security number is also a field. Similarly, a person's address, pay rate, age, and marital status are fields. A field usually contains several characters but can consist of a single character (such as a code field for marital status).

field

If a field contains only numeric characters, it is called a *numeric field* and we say that it contains *numeric data*. For example, a person's pay rate is a numeric field. A field that can contain any type of characters is called an *alphanumeric field*; that is, it contains *alphanumeric data*. For example, a street address (such as 123 MAIN ST.) consists of digits (123), letters (MAIN ST), and special characters (blank spaces and a period). Hence it is alphanumeric data and forms an alphanumeric field. Sometimes we refer to a field that contains all numbers as alphanumeric. For example, a social security number, which consists of nine digits, is a numeric field; but it may also be called an *alphanumeric field*. *Alphanumeric* means that the field can contain *any type of characters*; *numeric* means that the field can contain *only numeric characters*.

numeric data

alphanumeric data

Fields are grouped together to provide information about a single entity such as a person or event. Such a related group of fields is called a *record*. For example, all of the fields containing information about a single employee (such as employee name, social security number, address, pay rate, and so on) form an employee information record.

record

Finally, all of the records that are used together for one purpose are called a *file*. For example, all of the employee information records for a business make up the employee information file. The file consists of as many records as there are employees in the business.

file

To summarize, data is composed of numeric, alphabetic, and special characters. A group of related characters is called a field. A field can be numeric or alphanumeric. A record is a group of related fields and a file is a group of related records.

–Nickerson, *Fundamentals of Structured COBOL,* pp. 8–9

Summary notes are most effectively used in passages that contain long and complicated ideas. In these cases it is simpler to write a summary phrase in the margin than to underline a long or complicated statement of the main idea and supporting details.

To write a summary clue, try to think of a word or phrase that accurately states in brief form a particular idea presented in the passage. Summary words should "trigger" your memory of the content of the passage.

EXERCISE 5 _____

Directions: *Read the following textbook selection. Then mark as well as underline important information contained in the passage.*

BASIS OF SOCIAL ORGANIZATION

Although monkeys and apes differ from each other in important ways, they share many characteristics. Of these, certainly the most interesting is that they are all social species (except perhaps the orangutan) and their societies are highly organized. We first need to ask ourselves several questions. What are the advantages of social life? Why are so many mammal and bird species social and why have the Hominoidea developed this characteristic to such lengths? Four kinds of advantage are usually proposed by zoologists:

1. Several pairs of eyes are better than one in the detection of predators and in their avoidance. Defense by a group is also far more effective. Three or four male baboons constitute an impressive display and can frighten any predator, even a lion. A single baboon is a dead baboon.
2. Food finding and food exploitation and handling, as well as defense (of a carcass, for example) are more efficient at times when food is in fairly ample supply. We shall see that in some monkeys social groups subdivide when food is sparse and widely scattered.
3. Reproductive advantages accrue from social groups because regular access to the opposite sex is ensured.
4. Social groups permit extensive socialization with peers and elders and the opportunity for learning from them. Among animals such as the higher primates, this is a factor of the greatest importance.

These factors are probably the most important in bringing about the selection of social life in animals such as primates. Although considerable variation may occur within a species, especially under different environmental conditions, only a few Old World primate species (including the gibbons and siamang, a large gibbon) normally live in groups consisting only of an adult male, female, and young. The remaining seventy-odd species of Old World primates all live in social groups that number as high as five hundred individuals but most commonly number between ten and fifty.

But how are these societies organized? Far from being a structureless collection of rushing, squalling animals, primate societies are remarkably stable and usually serene and quiet. Order is maintained in primate societies through a complex interrelationship of several factors. One factor is the animals' prolonged period of dependence: infant apes and monkeys, like human infants, are far from self-sufficient, and maintain a close relationship with their mothers longer than most other animals.

—Campbell, *Humankind Emerging,* pp. 131–132

IS UNDERLINING AN EFFECTIVE MEANS OF PREPARATION FOR STUDY?

In a study conducted by Willmore,* a group of college students were each taught four study techniques: underlining, outlining, SQ3R (discussed in Chapter 12), and reading. The students then applied each of the four techniques to four different chapters in a college text. Tests were given on each chapter. Students scored significantly higher on the test when they used underlining as a study technique than when using any of the other three methods.

WHY UNDERLINING AND MARKING WORK

Underlining and marking are effective ways to prepare for study for several very important reasons. First, the process of underlining forces you to sift through what you have read to identify important information. This sifting or sorting helps you keep your mind on what you are doing. Second, underlining and marking keep you physically active while you are reading. The physical activity helps to direct or focus your concentration on what you are reading. Third, when you are underlining you are forced to weigh and evaluate what you read. In other words, you must think about and react to what you are reading in order to decide whether to underline it. Fourth, underlining helps you to see the organization of facts and ideas as well as their connections and relationships to one another because you are forced to look for these things in order to mark and underline effectively. Finally, underlining demonstrates to you whether you have understood a passage you have just read. If you have difficulty underlining, or

*D. J. Willmore, "A Comparison of Four Methods of Studying a College Textbook." Ph.D. diss., University of Minnesota, 1966.

your underlining is not helpful or meaningful after you have finished reading, you will know that you did not understand the passage.

EXERCISE 6 ―――――――――――――――

Directions: *Turn to the section of the psychology sample textbook chapter, pp. 396–399, that you underlined to complete Exercise 3. Review the section and add marking and summary words that would make the section easier to study and review.*

EXERCISE 7 ―――――――――――――――

Directions: *Select a three- to four-page selection from one of your textbooks. Underline and mark main ideas, important details, and key terms. Include summary words, if possible.*

SUMMARY

Reading textbook chapters is a long and time-consuming process. As you read, you encounter a considerable amount of information that you know you will need to study and review for your next exam or quiz. To be able to locate this information quickly when you study, it is necessary to underline and mark important information as you read. Without a system of underlining and marking, it would be necessary to reread an entire chapter in order to review it effectively. This chapter offers step-by-step instructions for underlining and marking textbooks.

After offering some general suggestions to follow in underlining, four specific guidelines for effective underlining are given: (1) underline the right amount, (2) develop a regular and consistent system of underlining, (3) underline accurately, and (4) make your underlining understandable for review. A system for marking as well as underlining is discussed. Marking involves the use of marginal notes, summary words, and symbols that can make a passage easier to review.

12

Study-Reading for Academic Disciplines

Use this chapter to:

1. *Organize into a system for study-reading the various reading and study techniques you have learned.*

2. *Learn to adapt your system for different courses.*

Does reading textbook assignments take a long time? Do you have to spend much time studying and reviewing what you have read in order to remember it? Then, when you spend considerable time and effort reviewing and studying, are you still dissatisfied with the amount of information you remember or how well you score on exams covering the material you studied? If so, you may need to learn a new way to read and study textbook assignments. One very efficient way is to develop a system that will enable you to study as you read.

THE DISTINCTION BETWEEN READING AND STUDY

Some students think that reading and studying are the same thing. They consider the time spent reading as time spent studying. Other students completely separate the two skills. They will read something one evening and plan to study it later. Actually reading and studying are different mental processes that should be combined and done together. Reading is a way of taking in new ideas and identifying information to be learned. Studying is learning the information by organizing and storing it in your memory. This chapter will show you how to combine reading and studying into an effective system that will increase your understanding, help you to concentrate, and increase the amount of material you are able to remember. As the first step, it will be helpful to look at a system that has been carefully researched and used by many college students for nearly fifty years.

A CLASSIC SYSTEM: SQ3R

In 1941, a psychologist named Francis P. Robinson developed a study-reading system called SQ3R. The SQ3R system, based on principles of learning theory, was carefully researched and tested. Continuing experimentation has confirmed its effectiveness. Since that time SQ3R has been taught to thousands of college students and has become widely recognized as the classic study-reading system.

As a step toward developing your own personalized system, look at SQ3R as a model. Once you see how and why SQ3R works, you can modify or adapt it to suit your own academic needs.

Steps in the SQ3R System

The SQ3R system involves five basic steps that integrate reading and study techniques. As you read the following steps, some of them will seem similar to the skills you have already learned.

S—Survey: Try to become familiar with the organization and general content of the material you are to read.

1. Read the title.
2. Read the lead-in or introduction. (If it is extremely long, read just the first paragraph.)
3. Read each boldface heading and the first sentence following each.
4. Read titles of maps, charts, or graphs; read the last paragraph or summary.
5. Read the end-of-chapter questions.
6. After you have surveyed the material, you should know generally what it is about and how it is organized.

See Chapter 5 for a more detailed explanation of how to survey.

Q—Question: Try to form questions that you can answer as you read. The easiest way to do this is to turn each boldface heading into a question. (The section of Chapter 6 titled "Formulating Purposes for Reading" discusses this step in depth.)

R—Read: Read the material section by section. As you read, look for the answer to the question you formed from the heading of that section.

R—Recite: After you finish each section, stop. Check to see if you can answer your question for the section. If you can't, look back to find the answer. Then check your recall again. Be sure to complete this step after you read each section.

R—Review: When you have finished the whole reading assignment, go back to each heading; recall your question and try to answer it. If you can't recall the answer, be sure to look back and find the answer. Then test yourself again.

The SQ3R method ties together much of what you have already learned about active reading. The first two steps activate your background knowledge and establish questions to guide your reading. The last two steps provide a means of monitoring your comprehension and recall.

Why SQ3R Works

Results of research studies overwhelmingly suggest that students who are taught to use a study-reading system understand and remember what they read much better than students who have not been taught to use such a system.

In one research study designed to test the effectiveness of the SQ3R system,* the reading rate and comprehension level of a group of college students were measured before and after learning and using the SQ3R system. After students learned the SQ3R method, the average reading rate increased by 22 percent; the comprehension level increased by 10 percent.

If you consider for a moment how people learn, it becomes clear why study-reading systems are effective. One major way to learn is through repetition. Consider the way you learned the multiplication tables. Through repeated practice and drills, you learned $2 \times 2 = 4, 5 \times 6 = 30, 8 \times 9 = 72$, and so forth. The key was repetition. Study-reading systems provide some of the repetition necessary to ensure learning. Compared with the usual once-through approach to reading textbook assignments that provide one chance to learn, SQ3R provides numerous repetitions and increases the amount learned.

SQ3R has many psychological advantages over ordinary reading. First, surveying (prereading) gives you a mental organization or structure—you know what to expect. Second, you always feel that you are looking for something specific rather than wandering aimlessly through a printed page. Third, when you find the information you're looking for, it is rewarding; you feel you have accomplished something. And if you can remember the information in the immediate and long-term recall checks, it is even more rewarding.

4 psyc advantages

EXERCISE 1 _____

Directions: *Turn to the sample textbook chapter included in Appendix A of this text. Read the section of the chapter titled "The Concept of Stress," beginning on page 390, using the SQ3R method. The following SQ3R worksheet will help you get started. Fill in the required information as you go through each step.*

SQ3R WORKSHEET

   S—SURVEY:

Read the title of the chapter, the introduction, each boldface heading, and the summary, and look at any pictures or graphs included.

1. What is the chapter about?

_____

*F. P. Robinson, *Effective Study* (New York: Harper & Row, 1941), p. 30.

2. What major topics are included?

_____

Q—QUESTION 1:

Turn the first heading into a question.

_____

R—READ:

Read the material following the first heading, looking for the answer to your question.

R—RECITE:

Reread the heading and recall the question you asked. Briefly answer this question in your own words without looking at the section. Check to see if you are correct.

_____

_____

Q—QUESTION 2:

Turn the second heading into a question.

_____

R—READ:

Read the material following the second heading, looking for the answer to your question.

R—RECITE:

Briefly answer the question.

_____

_____

Q—QUESTION 3:

Turn the third heading into a question.

_____

R—READ:

Read the material following the third heading, looking for the answer to your question.

R—RECITE:

Briefly answer the question.

_____

_____

_____

Continue using the question, read, and recite steps until you have finished each part of the chapter. Then complete the review step.

R—REVIEW:

Look over the total chapter by rereading the headings. Try to answer the question you made from each heading.

Answer to Question 1:

_____

_____

Answer to Question 2:

_____

_____

Answer to Question 3:

_____

_____

Check to see that your answers are correct.

DEVELOPING YOUR OWN STUDY-READING SYSTEM

Using SQ3R as a base or model, you can adapt it to work more effectively for you. Before you start, you should know that although SQ3R was the first system to be developed and is still regarded as the classic one, many other systems have been developed. Each uses the steps in SQ3R as a base, with additions or modifications. For example, a system called SQ4R has been developed which is similar to SQ3R except for an added "Rite" step that involves writing notes. Other recognized systems have included additional steps such as "Summarize," "Evaluate," "Annotate," "Reflect," or "Test."

To develop your own system you will need to (1) analyze your learning style to determine what techniques work best for you, and (2) adapt, add, or modify the steps in SQ3R to suit your style.

Analyzing Your Learning Style

Throughout this text you have probably found that some techniques work better than others. This is perfectly natural and consistent with learning theory. You may also have noted that you learn somewhat differently from others. Both findings are due to variations in *learning style*. Each person has his or her own set of cognitive (mental) factors that make some learning methods easier than others. Just as everyone's personality is unique, so is everyone's learning style. Some students, for example, learn best visually. Seeing charts, diagrams, drawings, or pictures—rather than reading or listening—appeals to them. Other students are auditory learners —they learn best by listening. Such a student, for instance, would learn more quickly from an instructor's lecture than from a textbook chapter on the same topic.

As part of developing your own study-reading system, try to analyze your learning style. Table 12-1 presents a list of questions that may be helpful in analyzing your learning style.

Adapting a Study-Reading System to Suit Your Learning Style

When you have discovered some features of your learning style, you can adapt the SQ3R system to suit it. For instance, if writing outlines helps you recall idea structures, then replace the recite step with an "Outline" step and make the review step a "Review of Outline" step. Or, if you have discovered that you learn well by listening, replace the recite and review steps with the "Tape Record" and "Listen" steps, in which you dictate and

TABLE 12-1   Analyzing Your Learning Style

Do You Prefer to (circle one):

study alone	or	study with groups?
study facts	or	study concepts and ideas?
listen to lectures	or	read textbooks?
learn from hands-on experience	or	learn by reading or listening?
follow step-by-step directions to perform a task	or	discover or figure out how to complete a task?
use visual means of processing information (diagrams, charts)	or	use verbal means of processing information (reading, writing, listening)?
learn in a structured environment (formal lecture class)	or	learn in a less structured environment (group discussion, class participation, activities)?
focus on details and specifics	or	focus on broad ideas, trends, and concepts?

record information to be learned and then review it by listening to the tape.

As you are no doubt beginning to see, there are numerous possibilities for developing your own study-reading system. The best approach is to test variations until you find the most effective system.

EXERCISE 2 _____

Directions: *As a step toward analyzing your own learning style, make a list of what you know about how you learn. Indicate both strengths and weaknesses. Look for patterns.*

_____

_____

_____

_____

_____

EXERCISE 3 _____

Directions: *Taking into account the characteristics of your learning style, decide how to change the SQ3R system. Then, describe each step of your modified study-reading system.*

_____

_____

_____

_____

_____

ADAPTING YOUR SYSTEM FOR VARIOUS ACADEMIC DISCIPLINES

Various academic disciplines require different kinds of learning. In an English composition and literature class, for example, you learn skills of critical interpretation, while in a chemistry course you learn facts, principles, and processes. A history course focuses on events, their causes, their significance, and long-term trends.

Because different courses require different types of learning, they also require different types of reading and study; therefore, you should develop a specialized study-reading approach for each subject. The following subjects are some of the most common academic disciplines studied by beginning college students, for which changes in a study-reading system are most important. For each, possible modifications in a study-reading system are suggested.

Mathematics

Sample problems are an important part of most math courses; therefore, you would add a "Study the Problems" step, in which you would try to see how the problems illustrate the theory or process explained in the chapter. This step might also include working through or reviewing additional practice problems.

Literature

When reading novels, essays, short stories, or poetry in a composition and literature class, you are usually asked to interpret, react, and write about what you read. For reading literature, then, you might drop the recite step, use the review step for the literal content (who did what, when, and where?), and add two new steps: "Interpret" and "React." In the interpret step, you would analyze the characters, their actions, and the writer's style and point of view to determine the writer's theme or message. In the react step, you might ask questions such as, What meaning does this have for me? How effectively did the writer communicate his or her message? Do I agree with this writer's view of life? You should make notes about your reactions, which could be a source of ideas if a paper is assigned.

Sciences

When reading and studying biology, chemistry, physics, or any other science, prereading is particularly important because most of the material is new. You might quickly read each end-of-chapter problem to discover what principles and formulas are emphasized in that chapter. The sciences emphasize facts, principles, formulas, and processes; therefore, build a "Rite" or "Record" step in which you underline, outline, or write study sheets.

Social Sciences

Introductory courses in the social sciences (psychology, sociology, anthropology, economics, political science) often focus on a particular discipline's basic problems or topics. These courses introduce specialized vocabulary and the basic principles and theories on which the discipline operates.

For social science courses, then, build a "Vocabulary Review" step into your study-reading system. A "Rite" or "Underline" step is also needed to provide an efficient method for review and study.

Other Academic Disciplines

This brief chapter does not permit discussion of modifications for every academic discipline. Most likely, you are taking one or more courses not previously mentioned. **To adapt your study-reading system to these courses, ask yourself the following questions:**

1. What type of learning is required? What is the main focus of the course? Often the preface or the first chapter of your text will answer these questions. The instructor's course outline or objectives may be helpful.
2. What must I do to learn this type of material?

Learn to "read" the instructor of each course. Find out what each expects, what topics and types of information each feels are important, and how your grades are determined. Talk with other students in the course or with students who have already taken the course to get ideas for useful ways of studying.

EXERCISE 4 _____

Directions: *The sample textbook chapters reprinted in the appendixes represent two very different academic disciplines—psychology and biology. How would you modify the SQ3R system to study-read each chapter? Consider chapter features as well as content.*

Psychology and Life

_____

_____

Biology

_____

_____

EXERCISE 5 _____

Directions: *List each of the courses for which you are currently registered. Then briefly indicate what changes in your study-reading system you intend to make for each course.*

_____

_____

_____

_____

_____

_____

SUMMARY

To learn the information presented in a college textbook, you must do more than simply read the assigned material. The information must be reviewed and studied, then transferred to your long-term memory. This chapter described a classic study-reading system for learning and reviewing as you read. This system, called SQ3R, provides a step-by-step procedure for reading a textbook chapter. SQ3R is presented as a model or base for developing your own personalized system. The steps in the SQ3R system are

Survey: Quickly become familiar with the overall organization and content of the material before beginning to read.

Question: Use the boldface headings to develop specific questions that you will attempt to answer as you read.

Read: Read in an active, searching manner, looking for answers to the questions you asked.

Recite: Test yourself regularly by stopping and trying to recall the content of the section that you just read. Check to see if you can answer the questions you developed in the question step. Go back and reread information you forgot.

Review: After reading the entire chapter, try to recall the content of each section by answering the question you developed for that section.

As a first step in developing your own study-reading system, you were shown how to analyze your learning style. Once you discovered how to learn most effectively, you were then shown how to adapt the SQ3R system to your own learning style.

Because many academic disciplines require different types of learning, you must make your study-reading system suit these differences. This chapter suggested adaptations for mathematics, literature, sciences, and social sciences. Guidelines were offered for making adaptations in other academic disciplines.

13

Methods of Organizing Information

Use this chapter to:

1. *Learn how to organize information for easier learning.*
2. *Learn how to condense information and pull ideas together.*
3. *Learn how to develop visual study aids.*

Do you feel overwhelmed by the volume of facts, dates, events, ideas, definitions, formulas, principles, and theories you must learn in each course? Do you wonder if you will be able to learn all of them?

The key to learning large amounts of information is to organize and condense it. Basically, this involves looking for patterns, differences, similarities, or shared characteristics and then grouping, rearranging, and reducing the information into manageable pieces. To do this, you will have to think about the information and look for the relationships and connections. This in itself is a form of review and rehearsal that will facilitate learning. Three methods of organizing information—outlining, summarizing, and using visual and organizational charts and diagrams—will be discussed in this chapter. As you learn these methods, you will see that they are based on many of the learning principles outlined in Chapter 3, especially meaningfulness and categorization. You will also see that the methods are unique; each uses a different format and varies in the way information is treated. The method you select for a particular course will depend on the type of material, the type of learning required, and the characteristics of your learning style.

The first step in using any of these methods is to sort the information and to identify what is to be learned. If you have underlined and marked your reading assignments and have taken notes on important ideas in class lectures, you have completed this first step.

ORGANIZING BY OUTLINING

Outlining is an effective way of organizing the relationship among ideas. From past experiences, many students think of an outline as an exact, detailed, organized listing of all information in a passage; they consider outlining as routine copying of information from page to page and, therefore, avoid doing it.

Actually, an outline should *not* be a recopying of ideas. Think of it, instead, as a means of pulling together important information and recording it to show how ideas interconnect. It is a form of note-taking that provides a visual picture of the structure of ideas within a textbook chapter.

Outlining has many advantages, one being that you learn while you write it. Outlining forces you to think about the material you read and to sort out the important ideas from those that are less important. Because it requires you to express ideas in your own words and to group them together, you are able to test whether you have understood what you read. Finally, thinking about, sorting, and expressing ideas in your own words is a form of repetition, or rehearsal, and helps you to remember the material.

How to Develop an Outline

To be effective, an outline must show (1) the relative importance of ideas, and (2) the relationship between ideas. The easiest way to achieve this is to use the following format:

I.   Major topic
   A. First major idea
      1. First important detail
      2. Second important detail
   B. Second major idea
      1. First important detail
         a. Minor detail or example
      2. Second important detail
II. Second major topic
   A. First major idea

Notice that the more important ideas are closer to the left margin, while less important details are indented toward the middle of the page. A quick glance at an outline indicates what is most important, and how ideas support or explain one another.

Here are a few suggestions for developing an effective outline:

1. Don't get caught up in the numbering and lettering system. Instead, concentrate on showing the relative importance of ideas. How you number or letter an idea is not as important as showing what other ideas it supports or explains. Don't be concerned if some items don't fit exactly into outline format.
2. Be brief; use words and phrases, never complete sentences. Abbreviate words and phrases where possible.
3. Use your own words rather than "lifting" most of the material from the text. It is acceptable to use the author's key words and specialized terminology.
4. Be sure that all information underneath a heading supports or explains it.
5. All headings that are aligned vertically should be of equal importance.

Now study the sample outline in Figure 13-1, which is based on the sample textbook section "Sources of Stress." To refer to this section, turn to page 399 in Appendix A.

I. Sources of Stress

    A. Major Life Stressors (changes in life events)
       1. Social Readjustment Rating Scale (SRRS)
          a. measures intensity of change in LCUs (Life Change Units)
          b. LCU rises before major illness ∴ increased susceptibility
          c. LCU high during illness
       2. Life Experiences Survey (LES)
          a. measures increase and decrease in change
          b. measures personal significance of change
       3. Measurement problems — above done in retrospect; recent studies prospective (look ahead)
       4. Conclusion: stressful events are bad for your health

    B. Little Hassles — daily frustrations affect your health

    C. Catastrophic Events
       1. Five stages in response to disaster
          a. shock
          b. automatic reaction
          c. shared purpose
          d. letdown
          e. recovery

    D. Societal and Environmental Problems
       1. Children
          a. fear of nuclear war
          b. uneasiness about future — helplessness, anger toward adults
       2. Adults
          a. employment and economic security
          b. health problems increase in economic downswings
       3. Environmental Pollution
          a. example: chemical contamination; nuclear disasters
          b. cause both immediate stress to those directly involved and world-wide stress
          c. U. S. Court of Appeals gave psych. stress legal status

FIGURE 13-1   Sample Outline

How Much Information to Include

Before you begin to outline, decide how much information to include. An outline can be very brief and cover only major topics, or at the other extreme, it can be very detailed, providing an extensive review of information.

How much detail you include in an outline should be determined by your purpose for making it. For example, if you are outlining a collateral reading assignment for which your instructor asked that you be familiar with the author's viewpoint and general approach to a problem, then little detail is needed. On the other hand, if you are outlining a section of an anatomy and physiology text for an upcoming objective exam, a much more detailed outline is needed. To determine the right amount of detail, ask yourself, What do I need to know? What type of test situation, if any, am I preparing for?

When to Use Outlining

Outlining is useful in a variety of situations.

1. When using reference books or reading books you do not own, outlining is an effective way of taking notes.
2. When reading material that seems difficult or confusing, outlining forces you to sort ideas, see connections, and express them in your own words.
3. When you are asked to write an evaluation or critical interpretation of an article or essay, it is helpful to briefly outline the factual content. The outline will reflect development and progression of thought and help you analyze the writer's ideas.
4. In courses where order or process is important, an outline is particularly useful. In a data processing course, for example, in which various sets of programming commands must be performed in a specified sequence, an outline would be a good way to organize the information.
5. In the natural sciences, in which classifications are important, outlines help you record and sort information. In botany, for example, one important focus is the classification and description of various plant groups. An outline would enable you to list subgroups within each category and to keep track of similar characteristics.

EXERCISE 1 ⎯⎯⎯⎯⎯⎯⎯⎯⎯⎯

Directions: *Write a brief outline of the textbook excerpt entitled "Society" on page 163, passage 9.*

EXERCISE 2 ⎯⎯⎯⎯⎯⎯⎯⎯⎯⎯

Directions: *Write a brief outline of Chapter 12, "Study-Reading for Academic Disciplines," beginning with page 212 of this text. Assume you are preparing for an essay exam on the chapter.*

EXERCISE 3 _____

Directions: *Write a brief outline for the section "Altering Bodily Reactions" (page 404) of the sample textbook chapter reprinted in Appendix A. Assume you are preparing for a multiple-choice exam on the chapter.*

EXERCISE 4 _____

Directions: *Choose a section from one of your textbooks, and write a brief outline reflecting the organization and content of that section.*

SUMMARIZING

A summary is a brief statement or list of ideas that identifies the major concepts in a textbook section. Its main purpose is to record the most important ideas in an abbreviated and condensed form. A summary is briefer and less detailed than an outline. It goes one step beyond an outline by pulling together the writer's thoughts and making general statements about them. In writing a summary or making summary notes, you may indicate how the writer makes his or her point or note the types of supporting information the writer provides.

Writing a summary forces you to go beyond separate facts and ideas and consider what they signify as a whole. Summarizing encourages you to consider questions such as, What is the writer's main point? and How does the writer prove or explain his or her ideas? It is also a valuable study technique that will clarify the material.

How to Summarize

While most students think of a summary as a correctly written paragraph, when written for your own study and review purposes it may be in either paragraph or note format. If you choose a note format, however, be sure that you record ideas and not just facts. Here are a few suggestions for writing useful summaries:

1. Start by identifying the author's main point; write a statement that expresses it.
2. Next, identify the most important information the writer includes to support or explain his or her main point. Include these main supporting ideas in your summary.
3. Include any definitions of key terms or important new principles, theories, or procedures that are introduced.
4. The amount of detail you include, if any, will depend on your purpose for writing the summary and on the type and amount of recall that you need.
5. Although examples are usually not included in a summary, include several representative examples if you feel the material is complex and cannot be understood easily without them.
6. Depending on the type of material you are summarizing, it may be appropriate to indicate the author's attitude and approach toward the subject and to suggest his or her purpose for writing.

7. Try to keep your summary objective and factual. Think of it as a brief report that should reflect the writer's ideas, not your evaluation of them.
8. Let your purpose guide and determine the amount and type of information you include in your summary.

Now read the summary in Figure 13-2, based on the section "Sources of Stress," beginning on page 399 of the sample textbook chapter reprinted in Appendix A. After you have studied the sample summary, compare it with the outline of the same material shown in Figure 13-1.

When to Use Summaries

Summaries are particularly useful in learning situations in which factual, detailed recall is not needed.

Preparing for Essay Exams: Summarizing ideas to be learned for possible exam topics is an excellent way to study for an exam. Because essay exam questions often require you to summarize information you have learned on a particular topic, writing summaries is a way to practice taking the exam, simulating real conditions.

Reading Literature: When reading literature, you are most often required to interpret and react to the ideas presented. To do so, you must be familiar with the basic plot (in fiction) or literal presentation of ideas (in nonfiction). Seldom, however, are you required to learn and recall specific actions, events, or facts. Writing a plot summary (describing who did what, when, and where) for fiction and a content summary for nonfiction are useful means of review.

> There are numerous sources of stress. Major life stressors and changes in life events, affect health. Two instruments measure these changes: (1) the SRRS rates intensity of changes, and (2) the LES measures increases and decreases in changes and their personal significance. Small hassles and frustrations also create stress and affect health. Other sources of stress that affect health are catastrophic events and environmental problems.

FIGURE 13-2   Sample Summary

Collateral Reading Assignments: In many undergraduate courses, instructors give additional reading assignments in sources other than your own text. These assignments may be given to supplement information in the text, to present a different or opposing viewpoint, to illustrate a concept, or to show practical applications. Usually, in-depth recall of particular facts and information is not expected. Your instructor probably wants you to understand the main points and their relation to topics covered in the text or in class; therefore, a fairly detailed summary would be a useful study aid for collateral readings.

Laboratory Experiments/Demonstrations: A summary is a useful means of recording the results of a laboratory experiment or class demonstration in a natural science course. While laboratory reports usually specify a format that includes careful reporting of procedures and listing of observations, a summary is often included. Reviewing summaries is an efficient way of recalling the purpose, procedure, and outcome of lab and classroom experiments conducted throughout the semester.

EXERCISE 5 _____

Directions: *Write a brief summary of the textbook excerpt subtitled "Capital," page 162 of this text (item 7).*

EXERCISE 6 _____

Directions: *Write a summary of the section "Adaptations to Extreme Temperatures," beginning on page 420, of the sample textbook chapter reprinted in Appendix B.*

EXERCISE 7 _____

Directions: *Refer to the section from one of your textbooks that you used to complete Exercise 4 on page 226. Write a summary of the information presented in this section.*

CONCEPT MAPPING: A VISUAL MEANS OF ORGANIZING IDEAS

Concept mapping is a visual method of organizing information. It involves drawing diagrams to show how ideas or concepts in an article or chapter are related. Mapping provides a picture or visual representation of how ideas are developed and connected. Maps group and consolidate information and make it easier to learn. The extent to which you make use of mapping will depend on your learning style. Some students, especially those with a visual learning style, prefer mapping to outlining. Other students find mapping to be freer and less tightly structured than outlining. The degree to which you use mapping will also depend on the types of courses you are taking. Some types of information are more easily learned by using mapping than are others.

Maps can take numerous forms. You can draw them in any way that shows the relationships of ideas. Figure 13-3 shows two sample maps.

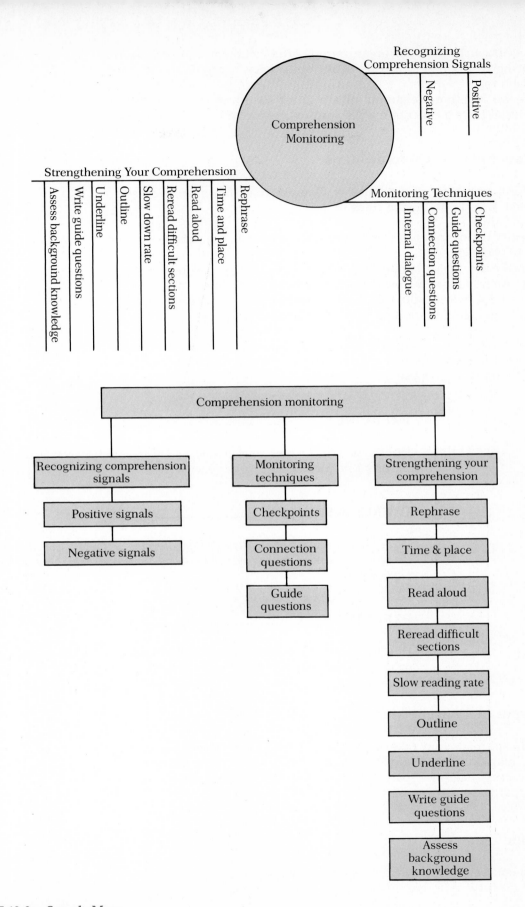

FIGURE 13-3   Sample Maps

Each was drawn to show the organization of the section on comprehension monitoring in Chapter 6 in this book. Refer back to pages 85–91, then study each map.

For an additional example of a concept map, refer to page 391 in Appendix A. Here a concept map is used to present a model of stress.

How to Draw Concept Maps

Think of a map as a picture or diagram that shows how ideas are connected. Use the following steps in drawing a map.

1. Identify the overall topic or subject and write it in the center or at the top of the page.
2. Identify the major supporting information that relates to the topic. State each fact or idea on a line connected to the central topic.
3. As you discover details that further explain an idea already mapped, draw a new line branching from the idea it explains.

How you arrange your map will depend on the subject matter and how it is organized. Like an outline, it can be either quite detailed or very brief, depending on your purpose.

EXERCISE 8 _____

Directions: *Draw a concept map showing the organization of any section of Chapter 1 in this text.*

EXERCISE 9 _____

Directions: *Draw a concept map showing how the section "Psychological Stress Reactions" reprinted in the psychology sample textbook chapter (page 396) is organized.*

EXERCISE 10 _____

Directions: *Select a section from one of your textbooks. Draw a concept map that reflects its organization.*

Types of Concept Maps

Concept maps may take numerous forms. This section presents five types of maps useful for organizing specific types of information: time lines, process diagrams, part/function diagrams, organizational charts, and comparison-contrast charts.

Time Lines

In a course in which chronology of events is the central focus, a time line is a useful way to organize information. To visualize a sequence of events, draw a single horizontal line and mark it off in yearly intervals, just as a ruler is marked off in inches, then write events next to the appropriate year. The time line in Figure 13-4, for example, was developed for an American history course in which the Vietnam War was being studied. It shows the sequence of events and helps you to visualize them.

EXERCISE 11 _____

Directions: *The following passage reviews the ancient history of maps. Read the selection and then draw a time line that helps you visualize these historical events. (Remember that* B.C. *refers to time before Christ and numbers increase as time moves back in history.)*

In Babylonia, in approximately 2300 B.C., the oldest known map was drawn on a clay tablet. The map showed a man's property located in a valley surrounded by tall mountains. Later, around 1300 B.C., the Egyptians drew maps that detailed the location of Ethiopian gold mines and that showed a route from the Nile Valley. The ancient Greeks were early mapmakers as well, although no maps remain for us to examine. It is estimated that in 300 B.C. they drew maps showing the earth to be round. The Romans drew the first road maps, a few of which have been preserved for study today. Claudius Ptolemy, an Egyptian scholar who lived around 150 A.D., drew one of the most famous ancient maps. He drew maps of the world as it was known as that time, including 26 regional maps of Europe, Africa, and Asia.

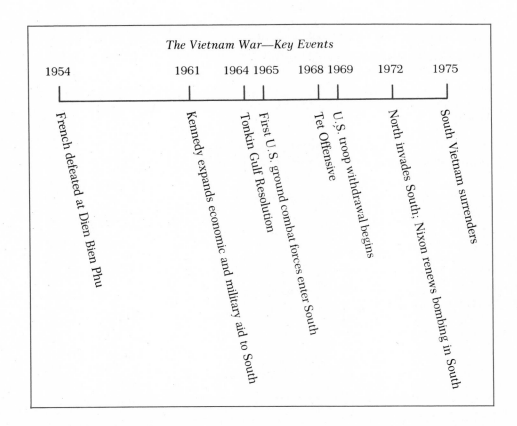

Figure 13-4　A Time Line

Process Diagrams

In the natural sciences as well as other courses such as economics and data processing, processes are an important part of course content. A diagram that describes visually the steps, variables, or parts of a process will aid learning. A biology student, for example, might use Figure 13-5, which describes the food chain and shows how energy is transferred through food consumption from lowest to highest organisms. Notice that this student included an example, as well as the steps in the process, to make the diagram clearer.

Another example of a process diagram is found on page 413 of the biology sample textbook chapter in Appendix B. It explains how heat is exchanged between a mammal and its environment.

EXERCISE 12 _____

Directions: *The following paragraph describes the process through which malaria is spread by mosquitoes. Read the paragraph and then draw a process diagram that shows how this process occurs.*

Malaria, a serious tropical disease, is caused by parasites, or one-celled animals, called protozoa. These parasites live in the red blood cells of humans as well as in the female anopheles mosquitoes. These mosquitoes serve as hosts to the parasites and carry and spread malaria. When an anopheles mosquito bites a person who already has malaria, it ingests the red blood cells that contain the malaria parasites. In the host mosquito's body, these parasites multiply rapidly and move to its salivary glands and mouth. When the host mosquito bites another person, the malaria parasites are injected into the victim and enter his or her blood stream. The parasites again multiply and burst the victim's blood cells, causing anemia.

Part/Function Diagrams

In courses that deal with the use and description of physical objects, labeled drawings are an important learning tool. In a human anatomy and

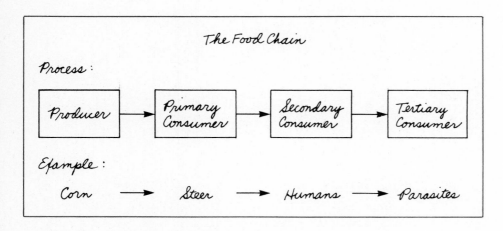

FIGURE 13-5   A Process Diagram

physiology course, for example, the easiest way to study the parts and functions of the inner, middle, and outer ear is to use a drawing of the ear. Study it and sketch a drawing of the ear; then test your recall of ear parts and their function.

An example of a part/function diagram appears on page 417 of the biology sample textbook chapter in Appendix B. It shows how the human skin is involved in temperature regulation.

EXERCISE 13 ————————————————

Directions: *The following paragraph describes the earth's structure. Read the paragraph and then draw a diagram that will help you visualize how the earth's interior is structured.*

At the center is a hot, highly compressed *inner core,* presumably solid and composed mainly of iron and nickel. Surrounding the inner core is an *outer core,* a molten shell primarily of liquid iron and nickel with lighter liquid material on the top. The outer envelope beyond the core is the *mantle,* of which the upper portion is mostly solid rock in the form of olivine, an iron-magnesium silicate, and the lower portion chiefly iron and magnesium oxides. A thin coat of metal silicates and oxides (granite), called the *crust,* forms the outermost skin.

–Berman and Evans, *Exploring the Cosmos,* p. 145

Organizational Charts

When reviewing material that is composed of relationships and structures, organizational charts are useful study aids. In a business management course, suppose you are studying the organization of a small temporary clerical employment agency. If you drew and studied the organizational chart shown in Figure 13-6, the structure would become apparent and easy to remember.

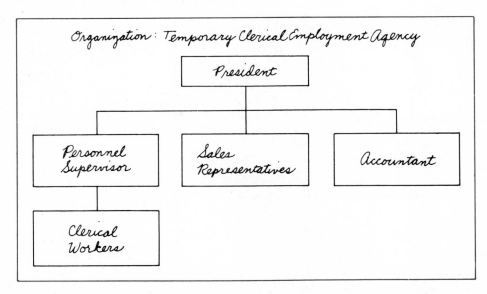

FIGURE 13-6   An Organizational Chart

Directions: *The following paragraph describes one business organizational structure that is studied in business management courses. Read the paragraph and then draw a diagram that will help you visualize this type of organization.*

It is common for some large businesses to be organized by *place*, with a department for each major geographic area in which the business is active. Businesses that market products for which customer preference differs from one part of the country to another often use this management structure. Departmentalization allows each region to focus on its own special needs and problems. Often the president of such a company appoints several regional vice-presidents, one for each part of the country. Then each regional office is divided into sales districts, each supervised by a district director.

Comparison-Contrast Charts

A final type of visual aid that is useful for organizing factual information is the comparison-contrast chart. Based on the categorization principle of learning, this method of visual organization divides and groups information according to similarities or common characteristics. Suppose in a marketing and advertising course you are studying three types of market survey techniques: mail, telephone, and personal interview surveys. You are concerned with factors such as cost, level of response, time, and accuracy. In your text this information is discussed in paragraph form. To learn and compare this information in an efficient manner, you could draw a chart such as the one shown in Figure 13-7.

Market Survey Techniques

Type	Cost	Response	Accuracy
Mail	usually the cheapest	higher than phone or personal interview	problems with misunderstanding directions
Phone	depends on availability of WATS line	same as personal interview	problems with unlisted phones and homes w/out phones
Personal interview	most expensive	same as phone	problems with honesty when asking personal or embarrassing questions

FIGURE 13-7   A Comparison-Contrast Chart

Now turn to page 403 in Appendix A. A comparison-contrast chart is used there to compare the two types of coping strategies.

EXERCISE 15 _____

Directions: *The following passage describes the major physical differences between humans and apes. Read the selection and then arrange the information into a chart that would make the information easy to learn.*

    Numerous physical characteristics distinguish humans from apes. While apes' bodies are covered with hair, the human body has relatively little hair. While apes often use both their hands and feet to walk, humans walk erect. Apes' arms are longer than their legs, while just the reverse is true for humans. Apes have large teeth, necessary for devouring coarse, uncooked food, and long canine teeth for self-defense and fighting. By comparison, human teeth are small and short. The ape's brain is not as well developed as that of the human being. Humans are capable of speech, thinking, and higher-level reasoning skills. These skills enable humans to establish culture, thereby placing the quality and level of human life far above that of apes.

    Humans are also set apart from apes by features of the head and face. The human facial profile is vertical, while the ape's profile is *prognathous*, with jaw jutting outward. Humans have a chin; apes have a strong lower jaw, but no chin. Human nostrils are smaller and less flaring than those of the ape. Apes also have thinner, more flexible lips than human beings.

    Man's upright walk also distinguishes him from apes. The human spine has a double curve to support his weight, while an ape's spine has a single curve. The human foot is arched both vertically and horizontally, but, unlike the apes, is unable to grasp objects. The human torso is shorter than that of apes. It is important to note that many of these physical traits, while quite distinct, differ in degree rather than in kind.

EXERCISE 16 _____

Directions: *Refer to the sections "Poikilotherms" and "Homeotherms" in the biology sample textbook chapter, pages 416–421. Draw a comparison-contrast chart that analyzes traits of these two types of animals.*

EXERCISE 17 _____

Directions: *Draw a process diagram that shows how temperature regulation occurs in mammals. Refer to the section of the biology sample textbook chapter titled "The Mammalian Thermostat," pages 419–420.*

EXERCISE 18 _____

Directions: *Draw a concept map that describes the principles of heat balance. Refer to the section in the biology sample textbook chapter titled "Principles of Heat Balance," pages 413–416.*

EXERCISE 19 _____

Directions: *Draw a part/function diagram or process map that describes the heat conserving mechanisms in the legs of an Arctic animal. Refer to pages 422–424 in the biology sample textbook chapter in Appendix B.*

SUMMARY

This chapter explained how to organize and condense information so that it is easy to learn and remember. Three methods of organizing information were presented: outlining, summarizing, and mapping.

Outlining is a form of organizing information that provides a visual picture of the ideas. An outline indicates the relative importance of ideas and shows the relationship between these ideas. Summarizing is the process of recording the most important ideas of a passage in a condensed, abbreviated form. Mapping presents a visual representation of the information while showing relationships. The five types discussed are time lines, process diagrams, part/function diagrams, organizational charts, and comparison-contrast charts.

PART FIVE

Classroom Performance Skills

The average college student spends between fifteen and eighteen hours in class each week. Attending class, then, represents a significant portion of a student's weekly schedule. Since such a large amount of time is spent in class each week, it is important to use this time effectively. While attending class, you can actually be doing things to help you learn, make studying easier, and earn better grades. Among the most important classroom skills are note-taking, test-taking, and participating in class discussions.

Taking notes on class lectures is extremely valuable. Class lecture notes are an important source of information and are excellent study aids. Chapter 14 ("Note-taking Techniques") will show you how to take good notes and suggest how you can use them effectively in study.

Participation in classroom discussions is expected by many college instructors. While you may be reluctant at first to become involved, you will find taking part in discussions an excellent way of keeping yourself interested, learning while in class, and showing the instructor that you are interested and involved. Chapter 15 ("Participating in Class Activities and Projects") will present information on how to prepare for discussions, how to get involved, and how to study for or learn from discussion classes.

Besides the time spent in class each week, students are expected to spend time outside class. One important out-of-class activity is preparation for exams. And, of course, how thoroughly you prepare and study largely determines how well you perform on quizzes and exams. Chapter 16 ("Preparing for Exams") will discuss how to study for exams. Chapter 17 ("Taking Exams") will discuss how to do well on an exam while you are taking it.

continued

continued

Another activity that requires considerable time and effort outside class is writing papers. Some instructors require brief essays, reports, or reaction papers, while others require a research paper. Chapter 18 (''Preparing Written Assignments and Research Papers'') offers suggestions for writing all types of papers, and outlines a step-by-step procedure for researching and writing research papers.

14

Note-taking Techniques

Use this chapter to:

1. *Find out what information to write down and what to skip during a lecture.*
2. *Learn how to take notes so that they are easy to study later.*

WHY NOTE-TAKING IS IMPORTANT

As you sit in a class in which the instructor lectures, it is easy to just sit back and listen, especially if the instructor and the subject are interesting or exciting. At the time information is presented, it may seem that you will always be able to remember it. Unfortunately, memory fades quickly, and a lecture that is vivid in your memory today will be only vaguely familiar several weeks later. Because instructors expect you to remember and apply facts and ideas presented in each lecture throughout the semester, it is necessary to take notes as lectures are given. A set of good lecture notes is a valuable study aid that will help you get good grades in a course.

SHARPENING YOUR LISTENING SKILLS

The first step in taking good lecture notes is to sharpen your listening skills. The average adult spends 31 percent of his or her waking hours listening. By comparison, 7 percent is spent on writing, 11 percent on reading, and 21 percent on speaking. Listening, then, is an essential communication skill. During college lectures listening is especially important; it is your primary means of acquiring information.

Have you ever found yourself not listening to a professor who was lecturing? Her voice was loud and clear, so you certainly could hear her, but you weren't paying attention—you "tuned her out." This situation illustrates the distinction between hearing and listening. Hearing is a passive, biological process in which sound waves are received by the ear. Listening, however, is an intellectual activity involving the processing and interpretation of incoming information. Listening must be intentional, purposeful, and deliberate. You must plan to listen, have a reason for listening, and carefully focus your attention. Use the following suggestions to sharpen your listening skills.

1. *Approach listening as a process similar to reading.* When you read, you not only recognize words, you understand, connect, and evaluate ideas. Similarly, listening is not simply a process of hearing words. It is a comprehension process in which you grasp ideas, assess their importance, and connect them to other ideas. All of the reading comprehension skills you developed in Part Three of this text are useful for listening as well. Focus on identifying main ideas, evaluating the importance and connection of details in relation to the main idea. Be alert for transitions—speakers tend to use them more frequently than writers. Also try to identify patterns of thought to improve both comprehension and recall.

2. *Focus on content, not delivery.* It is easy to become so annoyed, upset, charmed, or engaged with the lecturer as an individual that you fail to comprehend the message he or she is conveying. Force yourself to focus on the content of the lecture and disregard the personal style and characteristics of the lecturer.

3. *Focus on ideas, not facts.* If you concentrate on recording and remembering separate, unconnected facts, you are doomed to failure. Remember, your short-term memory is extremely limited in span and capacity, so while you are focusing on certain facts, it is inevitable that you will ignore some and forget others. Instead, listen for ideas, trends, and patterns.

4. *Listen carefully to the speaker's opening comments.* As your mind refocuses from prior tasks and problems, it is easy to miss the speaker's opening remarks. However, these are among the most important. Here the speaker may establish connections with prior lectures, identify his or her purpose, or describe the lecture's content or organization.

5. *Attempt to understand the lecturer's purpose.* If not stated explicitly, try to reason it out. Is the purpose to present facts, raise and discuss questions, demonstrate a trend or pattern, or present a technique or procedure?

6. *Fill the gap between rate of speech and rate of thinking.* Has your mind ever wandered back and forth during a lecture? Although you may be interested in what the speaker is saying, do you seem to "have time" to think about other things while listening? This is natural, since the rate of speech is much slower than the speed of thought. The average rate of speech is around 125 words per minute, whereas the rate at which you can process ideas is over 500 words per minute. To listen most effectively, use this gap to think about lecture content. Anticipate what is to follow, think of situations in which the information might be applied, pose questions, or make the information "fit" your prior knowledge and experience.

7. *Approach listening as a challenging mental task.* We all know concentration and attention are necessary for reading, yet many of us treat listening as something that should occur without effort. Perhaps due to the constant barrage of spoken words we are bombarded with through radio, television, and conversation, we assume that listening occurs automatically. Lectures, however, are a concentrated form of oral communication that require you to put higher-level attention and thinking skills into gear.

PREPARING FOR A LECTURE CLASS

Before you attend a lecture class, you should become familiar with the main topic of the lecture and be aware of important subtopics and related subjects.

Understanding the lecture and taking notes will be easier if you have some idea of what the lecture is about. If your instructor assigns a textbook chapter that is related to the lecture, try to read the assignment before attending. If you are unable to read the entire chapter before class, at least preread the chapter to become familiar with the topics it covers. If no reading assignment is given in advance, check your course outline to determine the topic of the lecture. Then preread the sections of your text that pertain to the topic.

Once you arrive at a lecture class, get organized before it begins. Take your coat off and have your notebook, pen, and textbook chapter, if needed, ready to use. While waiting for class to begin, try to recall the content of the previous lecture: Think of three or four key points that were presented. Check your notes, if necessary. This process will activate your thought processes, focus your attention on course content, and make it easier for you to begin taking notes right away.

HOW TO TAKE LECTURE NOTES

A good set of lecture notes must accomplish three things. First, and most important, your notes must serve as a record or summary of the lecture's main points. Second, they must include enough details and examples so that you can recall the information several weeks later. Third, your notes must in some way show the relative importance of ideas presented and reflect the organization of the lecture.

Record Main Ideas

The main ideas of a lecture are the points the instructor emphasizes and elaborates. They are the major ideas that the details, explanations, examples, and general discussion support. Instructors frequently give many clues to what is important in a lecture. Here are a few ways speakers show what is important.

Change in Voice: Some lecturers change the tone or pitch of their voices in order to emphasize major points. A speaker's voice may get louder or softer or higher or lower as he or she presents important ideas.

Change in Rate of Speech: Speakers may slow down as they discuss important concepts. Sometimes a speaker goes so slowly that he or she seems to be dictating information. If a speaker giving a definition pauses slightly after each word or phrase, it is a way of telling you that the definition is important and you should write it down.

Listing and Numbering Points: A lecturer may directly state that there are "three important causes" or "four significant effects" or "five possible situations" as he or she begins discussing a particular topic. These expressions are clues to the material's importance. Frequently, a speaker further identifies or emphasizes the separate, particular facts or ideas that make up the "three causes" or "four effects" with words such as *first, second*, and *finally*, or *one effect, a second effect, another effect*, and *a final effect*.

Writing on the Chalkboard: Some lecturers write key words or outlines of major ideas on the chalkboard as they speak. While not all important ideas are recorded on the chalkboard, you can be sure that if an instructor does take the time to write a word or phrase on the chalkboard, it is important.

Use of Audiovisuals: Some instructors emphasize important ideas, clarify relationships, or diagram processes or procedures by using audiovisual aids. Commonly used are overhead projectors that project on a screen previously prepared material or information the instructor draws or writes. Also, an instructor may use movies, filmstrips, videotapes, or photographs to emphasize or describe important ideas and concepts.

Direct Announcement: Occasionally, an instructor will announce straightforwardly that a concept or idea is especially important. He or she may begin by saying, "Particularly important to remember as you study is . . . ," or "One important fact that you must keep in mind is. . . . " The instructor may even hint that such information would make a good exam question. Be sure to mark hints like these in your notes. Emphasize these items with an asterisk or write *exam?* in the margin.

Nonverbal Clues: Many speakers give as many nonverbal as verbal clues to what is important. Often lecturers provide clues to what they feel is important through their movements and actions as well as their words. Some lecturers walk toward their audience as they make a major point. Others may use hand gestures, pound the table, or pace back and forth as they present key ideas. While each speaker is different, most speakers use some nonverbal means of emphasizing important points.

EXERCISE 1 _____

Directions: *Select one of your instructors and analyze his or her lecture style. Attend one lecture, and, as you take notes, try to be particularly aware of how he or she lets you know what is important. After the lecture, try to analyze your instructor, using the following questions:*

1. Did the instructor change his or her voice? When? How?

    _____

2. Did his or her rate of speech vary? When?

    _____

3. Did the instructor list or number important points?

    _____

4. Did the instructor use the chalkboard?

    _____

5. Did he or she directly state what was important?

    _____

6. What nonverbal clues did the instructor give?

Record Details and Examples

A difficult part of taking notes is deciding how much detail to include with the main ideas. Obviously you cannot write down everything, since lecturers speak at the rate of about 125 words per minute. Even if you could take shorthand, it would be nearly impossible to record everything the lecturer says. As a result, you have to be selective and record only particularly important details. As a rule of thumb, record a brief phrase that summarizes each major supporting detail. Try to write down a phrase for each detail that directly explains or clarifies a major point.

If an instructor gives you several examples of a particular law, situation, or problem, be sure to write down in summary form at least one example. Record more than one if you have time. While at the time of the lecture it may seem that you completely understand what is being discussed, you will find that a few weeks later you really do need the example to help you recall the lecture.

Record the Organization of the Lecture

As you write down the main ideas and important details of a lecture, try to organize or arrange your notes so that you can easily see how the lecture is organized. By recording the organization of the lecture, you will be able to determine the relative importance of ideas, and you will know what to pay most attention to as you study and review for an exam.

A simple way to show a lecture's organization is to use indentation. Retain a regular margin on your paper. Start your notes on the most important of the topics at the left margin. For less important main ideas, indent your notes slightly. For major details, indent slightly more. Indent even more for examples and other details. The rule of thumb to follow is this: The less important the idea, the more it should be indented. Your notes might be organized like this:

Major topic
  Main idea
    detail
    detail
      example
  Main idea
    detail
    detail
    detail
Major topic
  Main idea
    detail
      example

Notice that the sample looks like an outline but is missing the Roman numerals (I, II, III), capital letters (A, B, C), and Arabic numerals (1, 2, 3) that are usually contained in an outline. Also notice, however, that this system of note-taking does accomplish the same major goal as an outline—it separates important information from less important information. This indentation system, like an outline, shows at a glance how important a particular fact or idea is. If the organization of a lecture is obvious, you may wish to use a number or letter system in addition to indenting.

The notes in Figures 14-1 and 14-2 show that effective lecture notes should record main ideas, important details, and examples, and that they should reflect the lecture's organization. Both sets of notes were taken on the same lecture. One set of notes is thorough and effective; the other is lengthy and does not focus on key ideas. Read and evaluate each set of notes.

Make Note-taking Easier

If you record main ideas, details, and examples, using the indentation system to show the lecture's organization, you will take adequate notes. However, there are some tips you can follow to make note-taking easier, to make your notes more complete, and to make study and review easier.

Use Ink: Pencil tends to smear and is harder to read.

I. Social Stratification   Soc. 106
   Def's   9/16
        Soc. Strat.- hierarchy of ranks that exist in
                    society
        Status - criteria to find position in soc.
               - depends partly on roles
        2 types
            1. ascribed status - handed down, inherited
                ex.: titles, race, wealth, ethnic background
            2. achieved status - things you control
                ex.: education, jobs

II. Social Mobility
    Def. - how indiv. moves in hierarchy
         - amt. of movement depends on society

    2 Types
        1. caste - ex.: India - no mobility -
                you inherit class + status
        2. open - large amt. of achieved status -
                great mobility - ex.: U.S.A.

FIGURE 14-1   Notes Showing Lecture Organization

Social Stratification

Social stratification — defined as the ranks that exist in society - the position that any person has - ascribed status - it is handed down - example: titles. A second kind is achieved - it is the kind you decide for yourself.

Social stratification is important in understanding societies.

How a person moves up and down + changes his social status is called mobility. Some societies have a lot of mobility. Others don't have any - example is India.

There are 2 kinds of movement.
1. Caste system is when everybody is assigned a class and they must stay there without any chance to change.
2. Open - people can move from one to another. This is true in the United States.

FIGURE 14-2   Less Effective, Unfocused Lecture Notes

Use a Standard-sized Notebook and Paper: Paper smaller than 8½″ × 11″ doesn't allow you to write as much on a page, and it is more difficult to see the overall organization of a lecture if you have to flip through a lot of pages.

Keep a Separate Notebook or Section for Each Course: You need to have notes for each course together so that you can review them easily.

Date Your Notes: For easy reference later, be sure to date your notes. Your instructor might announce that an exam will cover everything presented after, for example, October 5. If your notes are not dated, you will not know where to begin to study.

Leave Blank Spaces: To make your notes more readable and make it easier to see the organization of ideas, leave plenty of blank space. If you know you missed a detail or definition, leave additional blank space. You can fill it in later by checking with a friend or referring to your text.

Mark Assignments: Occasionally an instructor will announce an assignment or test date in the middle of a lecture. Of course you will jot it down, but be sure to mark "Assignment" or "Test Date" in the margin so that you can find it easily and transfer it to your assignment notebook.

Mark Ideas That Are Unclear: If an instructor presents a fact or idea that is unclear, put a question mark in the margin. Later, ask your instructor or another student about this idea.

Sit in the Front of the Classroom: Especially in large lecture hall, it is to your advantage to sit near the front. In the front you will be able to see and hear the instructor easily—you can maintain eye contact and observe his or her facial expressions and nonverbal clues. If you sit in the back, you may become bored, and it is easy to be distracted by all the people in front of you. Because of the people seated between you and the instructor, a feeling of distance is created. You may feel that the instructor is not really talking to you.

Don't Plan to Recopy Your Notes: Some students take each day's notes in a hasty, careless way and then recopy them in the evening. These students feel that recopying helps them review the information and think it is a good way to study. Actually, recopying often becomes a mechanical process that takes a lot of time but very little thought. Time spent recopying can be better spent reviewing the notes in a manner that will be suggested later in this chapter.

Avoid Tape-recording Lectures: As a maximum effort to get complete and accurate notes, some students resort to tape-recording each lecture. After the lecture, they play back the tape and take notes on it, starting and stopping the tape as needed. This is a tremendously time-consuming technique and very inefficient in terms of the time spent relative to the amount of learning that occurs. In using the tape system, a student has to spend at least an additional hour in playback for every hour spent in class just to complete his or her notes.

Use Abbreviations: To save time, try to use abbreviations instead of writing out long or frequently used words. If you are taking a course in psychology, you would not want to write out *p-s-y-c-h-o-l-o-g-y* each time the word is used. It would be much faster to use the abbreviation *psy*. Try to develop abbreviations that are appropriate for the subject areas you are studying. The abbreviations shown in Figure 14-3, devised by a student in business management, give you an idea of the possibilities. Notice that both common and specialized words are abbreviated.

Common words	*Abbreviation*	*Specialized words*	*Abbreviation*
and	+	organization	org.
with	w/	management	man.
compare		data bank	D.B.
comparison	comp.	structure	str.
importance	imp't	evaluation	eval.
advantage	adv.	management	
introduction	intro.	by objective	MBO
continued	cont'd.	management	
		information	MIS
		system	
		organizational	
		development	OD
		communication	
		simulations	comm/sim.

FIGURE 14-3   Abbreviations for Use in Note-taking

As you develop your own set of abbreviations, be sure to begin gradually. It is easy to overuse abbreviations and end up with a set of notes that are almost meaningless.

EXERCISE 2 _____

Directions: *Select one set of lecture notes from a class you recently attended. Reread your notes and look for words or phrases you could have abbreviated. Write some of these words in the space provided.*

Word   *Abbreviation*

_____   _____

_____   _____

_____   _____

_____   _____

_____   _____

_____   _____

_____   _____

_____   _____

_____   _____

Overcoming Common Note-taking Problems

Instructors present lectures differently, use various lecture styles, and organize their subjects in different ways. It is therefore common to experience difficulty taking notes in one or more courses. Table 14-1 identifies common problems associated with lecture note-taking and offers possible solutions.

HOW TO EDIT YOUR NOTES

After you have taken a set of lecture notes, do not assume that they are accurate and complete. Most students find that they missed some information and were unable to record as many details or examples as they would have liked. Even very experienced note-takers are faced with these problems. Fortunately, the solution is simple. Do not plan on taking a final and complete set of notes during the lecture. Instead, record just enough

TABLE 14-1 Common Note-taking Problems

Problem	Solution
"My mind wanders and I get bored."	Sit in the front of the room. Be certain to preview assignments. Pose questions you expect to be answered in the lecture.
"The instructor talks too fast."	Develop a shorthand system; use abbreviations. Leave blanks and fill them in later.
"The lecturer rambles."	Preview correlating text assignments to determine organizing principles. Reorganize your notes after the lecture.
"Some ideas don't seem to fit anywhere."	Record them in the margin or in parentheses within your notes for reassessment later during editing.
"Everything seems important." *or* "Nothing seems important."	You have not identified key concepts and may lack necessary background knowledge (see Chapter 6)—you do not understand the topic. Preview related text assignments.
"I can't spell all the new technical terms."	Record them phonetically, the way they sound; fill in correct spellings during editing.
"The instructor uses terms without defining them."	Record terms as used; leave space to record definitions later; consult text glossary or dictionary.
"The instructor reads directly from text."	Mark passages in text; write instructor's comments in the margin. Record page references in your notes.

during the lecture to help you remember a main idea, detail, or example. Leave plenty of blank space; then, if possible, sit down immediately after the lecture and review your notes. Fill in the missing information. Expand, or make more complete, any details or examples that are not fully explained. This process is called *editing*. It is essentially a process of correcting, revising, and adding to your notes to make them more complete and accurate. Editing notes for a one-hour lecture should take no more than five or ten minutes.

If your are unable to edit your notes immediately after a lecture, it is critical that you edit them that evening. The longer the time lapse between note-taking and editing, the less effective editing becomes. Also, the greater the time lapse, the more facts and examples you will be unable to recall and fill in.

The sample set of lecture notes in Figure 14-4 has been edited. The notes taken during the lecture are in black; the additions and changes made during editing are in color. Read the notes, noticing the types of information added during editing.

Anxiety + Defense Mechanisms   Psyc. 602
                                                  10/12

I. Anxiety
        def generalized
             gen fear or worry
     Levels
        1. moderate - productive
             athletes - higher level of phys. functioning
             test-taking - certain amt helps - keeps you alert
        2. Extreme - uncomfortable ex: nauseous,
                        extremely nervous, hands shaking
                     - can be reduced by defense mechanism

II. Defense Mech
        def - unconscious devices to protect self and /or keep self
                under control
             ex: student who is hostile toward teacher
                  explains it to himself by saying that "the
                                                   teacher hates me"
     Types of Def. Mechanism
        1. Repression - to drive out of consciousness
             ex: student - math instructor   student forgets
                  to keep app't with math instructor because
                  he's afraid he will be told he is failing the
                  course.
        2. Regression - reaction to anxiety by going back to less
             mature behavior
             ex: college student applying for job but
                  doesn't get it - pouts + says the
                  interviewer cheated + hired son of
                  his best friend.

FIGURE 14-4   Edited Lecture Notes

HOW TO STUDY YOUR NOTES

Taking and editing lecture notes is only part of what must be done to learn from your instructor's lectures. You also have to learn and review the notes in order to do well on an exam. To study lecture notes, try to apply the same principles that you use in learning material in your textbooks. (1) Do not try to learn your notes by reading them over and over. Rereading is not an efficient review technique because it takes too much time relative to the amount you learn. (2) As in reading textbook assignments, identify what is important. You must sort out what you will learn and study from all the rest of the information that you have written in your notes. (3) Have a way of checking yourself—of deciding if you have learned the necessary information. In studying textbooks, you use the "Recite" step of the SQ3R method to check your recall of what you have read; you can use fact cards or summary sheets to test your recall further. For studying lecture notes, there is a system that uses similar techniques of study: the *recall clue system*.

The Recall Clue System

The recall clue system helps make the review and study of lecture notes easier and more effective. You will notice that it is very similar to the summary word technique suggested in Chapter 11. To use the recall clue system, follow these steps:

1. Leave a two-inch margin at the left side of each page of notes.
2. This margin stays blank while you are taking notes.
3. After you have edited your notes, fill in the left margin with words and phrases that briefly summarize the notes.

The recall clues should be words that will trigger your memory and help you recall the complete information in your notes. These clues function as memory tags. They help you pull out, or retrieve, from your memory any information that is labeled with these tags. Figure 14-5 shows a sample of notes in which the recall clue system has been used. When you

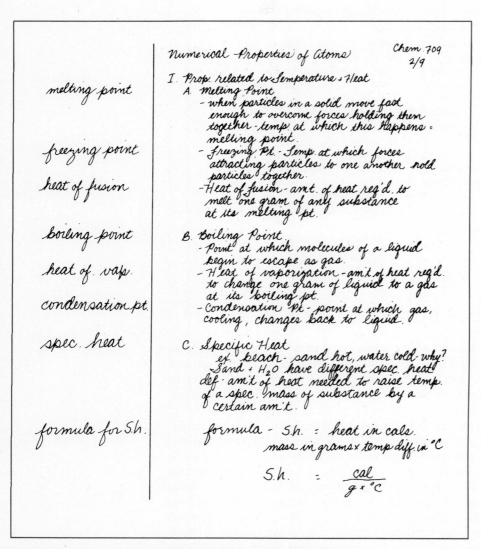

FIGURE 14-5   Lecture Notes with Recall Clues Added

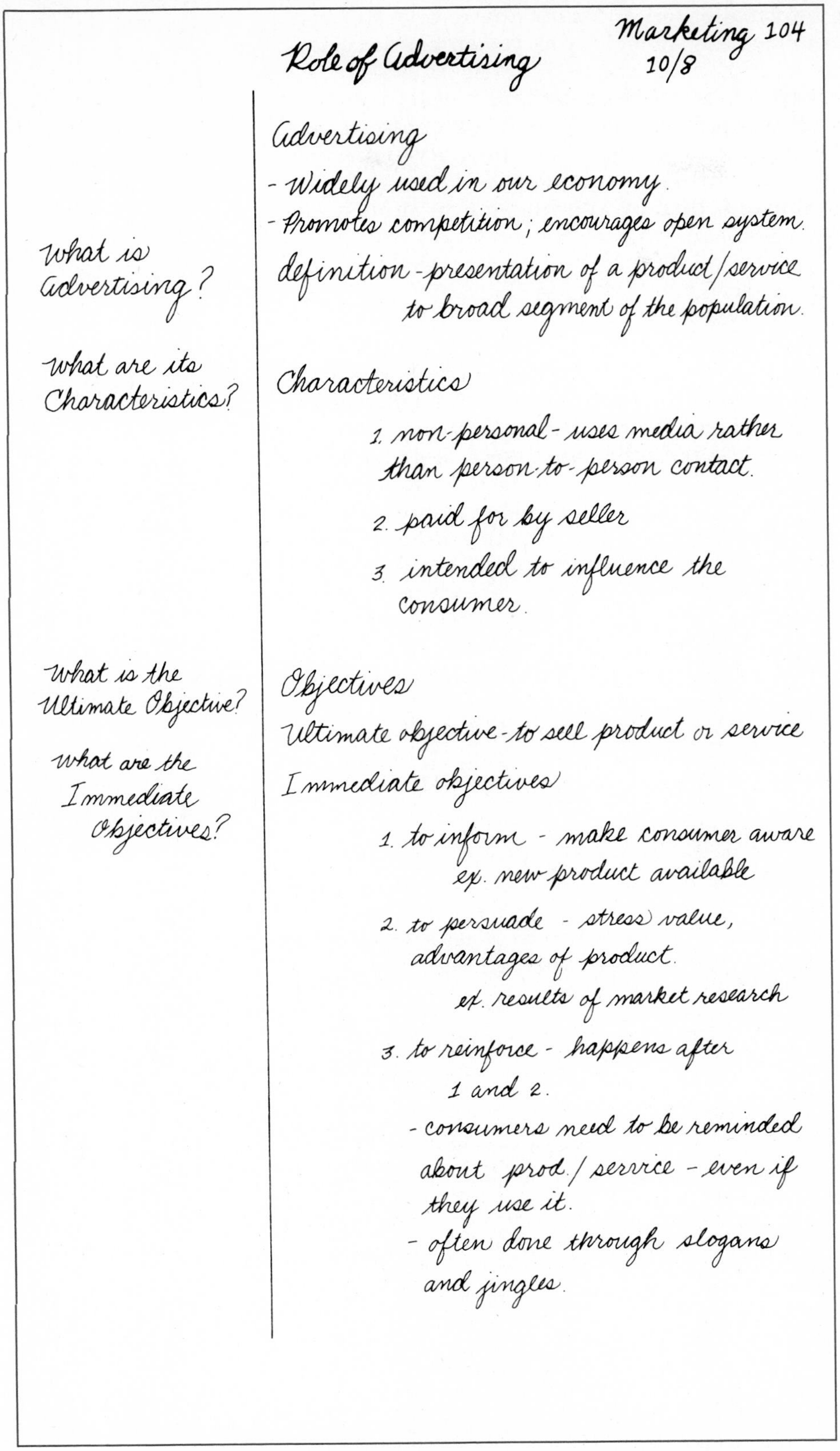

Role of Advertising   Marketing 104
                                              10/8

Advertising
- Widely used in our economy.
- Promotes competition; encourages open system.
- definition - presentation of a product/service
                 to broad segment of the population.

what is
Advertising?

Characteristics

what are its
Characteristics?

1. non-personal - uses media rather
   than person-to-person contact.

2. paid for by seller

3. intended to influence the
   consumer.

what is the
Ultimate Objective?

Objectives
Ultimate objective - to sell product or service

what are the
Immediate
Objectives?

Immediate objectives

1. to inform - make consumer aware
              ex. new product available

2. to persuade - stress value,
   advantages of product.
        ex. results of market research

3. to reinforce - happens after
       1 and 2.
     - consumers need to be reminded
       about prod./service - even if
       they use it.
     - often done through slogans
       and jingles.

FIGURE 14-6   Lecture Notes with Recall Questions Added

are trying to remember information on an exam, the recall clue from your notes will work automatically to help you remember necessary information.

A variation on the recall clue system that students have found effective is to write questions rather than summary words and phrases in the margin (see Figure 14-6). The questions trigger your memory and enable you to recall the information that answers your question. The use of questions enables you to test yourself, thereby allowing you to simulate an exam situation.

Using the Recall Clue System

To study your notes using the recall clue system, cover up the notes with a sheet of paper, exposing only the recall clues in the left margin. Then read the first recall clue and try to remember the information in the portion of the notes beside it. Then slide the paper down and check that portion to see if you remembered all the important facts. If you remembered only part of the information, cover up that portion of your notes and again check your recall. Continue checking until you are satisfied that you can remember all the important facts. Then move on to the next recall clue on the page, following the same testing-checking procedure.

To get into the habit of using the recall clue system, mark off with a ruler a two-inch column on the next several blank pages in each of your notebooks. Then when you open your notebook at the beginning of the class, you will be reminded to use the system.

This chapter has offered numerous techniques and suggestions for taking effective lecture notes. Use the checklist shown in Figure 14-7 to refresh your memory on them and evaluate your own note-taking.

EXERCISE 3 _____

Directions: *Read the sample set of notes in Figure 14-8. Fill in the recall clues or formulate questions that would help you study and learn the notes.*

	Yes	No
1. Notes are titled and dated.		
2. A separate line is used for each key idea.		
3. Less important ideas are indented.		
4. Abbreviations and symbols are used.		
5. The organization of the lecture is apparent.		
6. Words and phrases (not entire sentences) are recorded.		
7. Examples and illustrations are included.		
8. Sufficient explanation and detail are included.		
9. Adequate space is left for editing.		
10. Marginal space is available for recall clues.		

FIGURE 14-7   Note-taking Checklist

I Psychoanalytic theory - created by Sigmund Freud

A. free association - major diagnostic techniques in psychoanalysis; patient reports whatever comes to mind / holds nothing back.

B. repression - psych. process of driving ideas out of consciousness

C. suppression - conscious of an idea, but won't tell anyone about it.

D. trauma - particularly disturbing event; most psych. disturbances traceable to a trauma.

E. interp. of dreams - dreams - fantasies which person believes to be true / have profound influence on personality devlpmt.

F. Id - power system of personality providing energy.
   1. pleasure principle - all unpleasant events should be avoided.
    • a. primary process - normal logic does not operate.
      ex. bizarre dreams, hallucinations

G. Ego - strategist of personality / concerned w/ what a person CAN do.
   1. reality principle - distinction between real + unreal rather than dist. between pleasure + pain. Satisfies id in a realistic manner.
    a. secondary process - rational, logical, critical.

H. Superego - "good versus bad", rewards and punishments.
   1. conscience - critical, punitive aspect of superego.

FIGURE 14-8 Sample Lecture Notes

Directions: *For each course that you are taking this semester, use the recall clue system for at least one week. Use the recall clues to review your notes several times. At the end of the week, evaluate how well the system works for you.*

1. What advantages does it have?

    _____

2. Did it help you remember facts and ideas?

    _____

3. Are there any disadvantages?

    _____

SUMMARY

Because many college instructors expect you to remember and apply facts and ideas in their class lectures, it is necessary to take good lecture notes, edit them properly, and develop a system for studying them effectively.

Effective lecture notes should accomplish three things. First, good notes should summarize the main points of the lecture. Well-taken lecture notes are a valuable aid to study. Second, lecture notes should include enough details and examples so that you can completely understand and recall the information several weeks later. Third, the notes should show the relative importance of ideas and reflect the organization of the lecture. The chapter provided specific suggestions on how to accomplish each of these goals and offered numerous tips on making note-taking easier.

After taking a set of lecture notes, it is necessary to correct, revise, fill in missing or additional information, and expand your notes to make them more complete. This process of editing your notes results in clearer, more accurate notes form which to study.

Effective study of lecture notes follows many of the same principles and procedures that are used for studying textbook chapters. The recall clue system is a way of making study and review easier and more effective. A two-inch margin at the left of each page of notes is left blank during note-taking. Later, as you reread your notes, you then write in the margin words and phrases that briefly summarize the notes. These phrases, or recall clues, trigger your memory and help you recall information in the notes.

15

Participating in Class Activities and Projects

Use this chapter to:

1. *Learn to ask and answer questions in class.*
2. *Prepare for class discussions.*
3. *Work effectively on group projects.*
4. *Prepare and make oral presentations.*

While the lecture is still the most common method of teaching in college classes, many instructors have recently begun to incorporate more discussion and group activities into their course organization. Considerable research on teaching effectiveness indicates that students learn from each other as well as from the instructor. Consequently, some of your classes will likely involve group projects or assignments, small group or panel discussions, or oral presentations. Also, once you begin to take specialized courses in your major, you will be enrolled in smaller classes or seminars in which group participation is essential.

ASKING AND ANSWERING QUESTIONS

Asking and answering questions in class is an important aspect of many college courses; even in lecture courses, instructors may invite questions at the end of class. For some large lecture courses, you might be required to register for a weekly recitation class. Its purpose is to provide a forum for students to ask and answer questions, as well as to discuss lecture content. Furthermore, in some courses a portion of your grade is determined by your class participation.

Many students are hesitant to ask or answer questions; often because they are concerned about how their classmates and instructor will respond. They fear that their question may seem "dumb" or that their answer may be incorrect. This fear is one that must be conquered early in your college career. Asking questions is often essential to complete and thorough understanding, and you will find that once you've asked a question, other students will be glad you asked because they had the same question in mind. Answering questions posed by your instructor gives you an opportunity to evaluate how well you have learned or understood course content as well as to demonstrate your knowledge. Use the following suggestions to build the habit of asking and answering questions:

1. To get started, as you read an assignment jot down several questions that might clarify or explain it better. Bring your list to class. Refer to your list as you speak, if necessary.
2. When you ask a question, state it clearly and concisely. Don't ramble or make excuses for asking.
3. Remember, most instructors invite and respond favorably to questions; if your question is a serious one, it will be received positively. Don't pose questions for the sake of asking a question. Class time is limited and valuable.
4. In answering questions, formulate your responses mentally before you volunteer them.
5. Think of answering questions as a means of identifying yourself to the instructor as a serious, committed student, as well as a means of learning.

PARTICIPATING IN CLASS DISCUSSIONS

In courses designed to encourage students to think, react to, and evaluate ideas and issues, class discussions are a common form of instruction. Class discussion courses differ from lecture classes in three ways. First, the amount of advance preparation differs greatly. Second, your responsibility and involvement are of a different level and type. Finally, the manner in which you study, review, and are evaluated for group activities is different from techniques used in lecture classes. You may find, for example, that you are graded, in part, on the quality and effectiveness of your participation, rather than solely by tests and exams.

Preparing for Class Discussions

Preparing for a class discussion demands more time and effort than does getting ready for a lecture class. In a lecture class, most of your work comes *after* the class, editing your notes and using the recall clue system to review them. The opposite is true for discussion courses. Most of your work is done *before* you go to class. You must spend considerable time reading, evaluating, and making notes. The following suggestions will help you get ready for a discussion class.

Read the Assignment: Usually a class discussion is about a particular topic (issue, problem). Frequently, instructors give textbook or library reading assignments that are intended to give you some background information. The reading assignments are also meant to start you thinking about a topic, show you different points of a view about an issue, or indicate some aspects of a problem. Read carefully the material assigned. Do not just skim through it as you might for a lecture class. Instead, read the assignment with the purpose of learning all the material. Use a variation of the SQ3R method to help you learn, and mark and underline important ideas as you read.

Review: Make Notes for Discussion: After you have read the assignment, review it with the purpose of identifying and jotting down the following:

1. Ideas, concepts, or points of view you do not understand. Keep a list of these; you can use the list as a guide to form questions during class.
2. Ideas and points with which you disagree or strongly agree. By jotting these down you will have some ideas to start with if your instructor asks you to react to the topic.
3. Good and poor examples. Note examples that are particularly good or particularly poor. These will help you to react to the topic.
4. Strong arguments and weak arguments. As you read, try to follow the line of reasoning, and evaluate any arguments presented. Make notes on your evaluations; the notes will remind you of points you may want to make during the discussion.

Getting Involved in Class Discussions

Discussion classes require greater, more active involvement and participation than do lecture classes. In lecture classes, your main concern is to listen carefully and to record notes accurately and completely. In discussion classes, your responsibility is much greater. Not only do you have to take notes, but you also have to participate in the discussion. The problem many students experience in getting involved in discussions is that they do not know what to say or when to say it. Here are a few instances when it might be appropriate to speak. Say something when:

1. You can ask a serious, thoughtful question.
2. Someone asks a question that you can answer.
3. You have a comment or suggestion to make on what has already been said.
4. You can supply additional information that will clarify the topic under discussion.
5. You can correct an error or clarify a misunderstanding.

To get further involved in the discussion, try the following suggestions:

1. Even if you are reluctant to speak before a group, try to say something early in the discussion; the longer you wait, the more difficult it becomes. Also, the longer you wait, the greater the chance someone else will say what you were planning to say.
2. Make your comments brief and to the point. It is probably a mistake to say too much rather than too little. If your instructor feels you should say more, he or she will probably ask you to explain or elaborate further.
3. Try to avoid getting involved in direct exchanges or disagreements with other class members. Always speak to the group, not individuals, and be sure that your comments relate to and involve the entire class.
4. When you feel it is appropriate to introduce a new idea, clue your listeners that you are changing topics or introducing a new idea. You might say something like "Another related question . . . ," or "Another point to consider is. . . ."
5. When you think of comments or ideas that you want to make as the discussion is going on, jot them down. Then when you get a chance to

speak, you will have your notes to refer to. Notes help you organize and present your ideas in a clear and organized fashion.

6. Try to keep an open mind throughout the discussion. Leave personal dislikes, attitudes toward other members of the group, and your own biases and prejudices aside.

7. Organize your remarks. First, connect what you plan to say with what has already been said. Then state your ideas as clearly as possible. Next, develop or explain your idea.

8. Watch the group as you speak. When making a point or offering a comment, watch both your instructor and others in the class. Their responses will show whether they understand you or need further information, whether they agree or disagree, whether they are interested or uninterested. You can then decide, based on their responses, whether you made your point effectively or whether you need to explain or defend your argument more carefully.

Note-taking During Class Discussions

While most of your energy in a class discussion is consumed by following and participating in the discussion, it is important to take summary notes while the discussion is going on. Your notes should not be as detailed as they would be for a lecture class; record only the key topics discussed and the important concepts and ideas brought into the discussion.

Editing the notes you take in discussion classes is essential. Because you have so little time and mental energy to devote to note-taking during the discussion, it is very important to fill in and complete your notes later.

Reviewing and Studying for Discussion Classes

Just as preparing for and participating in discussion classes differ from preparing for and participating in lecture classes, so does the review-study process for discussion classes require slightly different techniques from those used for lecture classes. Fortunately, since more work is done prior to attending a discussion class, less is required after it. To review and study for a discussion class, be sure to:

1. Review your notes; use the recall clue system to check your recall of important information.

2. Review any reading assignment given prior to the class discussion. You may want to reread the assignment. Given the new ideas and perspectives introduced in class, you will probably find new ways of approaching and viewing the information presented in the assignment. As you review, be sure to mark and underline any information that you now realize is particularly important or has direct bearing on the discussion.

3. Anticipate possible test or exam questions based on your notes, the reading assignment, and your recall of the discussion. Most likely, your instructor will give you either essay or short-answer questions on exams. Objective questions (true/false, multiple choice, or matching) would be rather difficult to construct if there is little or no clear base of factual information. Essay or short-answer questions lend themselves more readily to the concerns, purposes, and goals your instructor most likely has for a discussion course. (For specific techniques of

preparing for and taking essay and short-answer exams refer to the next chapter.) Pay particular attention to topics for which your instructor allowed the most discussion time and those with which your instructor seemed to get most involved.

EXERCISE 1 ━━━━━━━━━━━━━━━━

Directions: *Review the section "Sources of Stress," beginning on page 399 in the sample textbook chapter reprinted in Appendix A. Assume that you have been assigned this section of the chapter as preparation for a discussion class. What notes would you make and what questions would you be ready to ask as you prepared for the discussion? Record your notes and questions on a separate sheet.*

WORKING EFFECTIVELY ON GROUP PROJECTS

Many assignments and class activities involve working with a small group of classmates. For example, a sociology instructor might divide the class into groups and ask each group to brainstorm solutions to economic or social problems of the elderly. Your political science professor might create a panel to discuss the private and collective consequences of voting. Group presentations may be required in a business course, or groups in your American history class might be asked to research a topic.

Group projects are intended to enable students to learn from one another by viewing each other's thinking processes and by evaluating each other's ideas and approaches. Group activities also develop valuable skills in interpersonal communication that are essential in career and work-related situations. Some students are reluctant to work in groups because they feel that they are not in control of the situation; they dislike having their grade depend on the performance of others as well as themselves. Use the following suggestions to make your group function effectively:

1. Select alert, energetic classmates if you are permitted to choose with whom you work.
2. Be an active, responsible participant. Accept your share of the work and expect others to do the same. Approach the activity with a serious attitude, rather than joking or complaining about the assignment. This will establish a serious tone and cut down on wasted time.
3. Because organization and direction are essential for productivity, every group needs a leader. Unless some other competent group member immediately assumes leadership, take a leadership role. While leadership may require more work, you will be in control. (Remember, too, that leadership roles are valuable experiences for your career.) As the group's leader, you will need to direct the group in analyzing the assignment, organizing a plan of action, distributing work assignments, planning, and if the project is long-term, establishing deadlines.
4. Take advantage of individual strengths and weaknesses. For instance, a person who seems indifferent or is easily distracted should not be assigned the task of recording the group's findings. The most organized, outgoing member might be assigned the task of making an oral report to the class.

5. Be assertive. If a group member fails to do his or her share of the work, clearly express your concern. Be direct and nonthreatening; don't hint about deadlines or angrily accuse the person of ruining your grade.

EXERCISE 2 _____

Directions: *Suppose you are part of a five-member group that is preparing for a panel discussion on gun control for a sociology class. One group member is very vocal and opinionated. You fear she is likely to dominate the discussion. Another group member is painfully shy and has volunteered to do double research if he doesn't have to speak much during the discussion. A third member appears uninterested and tends to sit back and watch as the group works and plans. How should the group respond to each of these individuals? List several possible solutions to each problem.*

PREPARING AND MAKING ORAL PRESENTATIONS

Oral presentations may be group or individual. Groups may be asked to report their findings, summarize their research, or describe a process of procedure. Individual presentations are often summaries of research papers, reviews or critiques, or interpretations of literary or artistic works. Use the following suggestions to make effective oral presentations:

1. Understand the purpose of the assignment. Analyze it carefully before beginning to work. Is the presentation intended to be informative? Are you to summarize, evaluate, or criticize?
2. Collect and organize your information. Refer to Chapter 18 for specific techniques.
3. Prepare outline notes. Use index cards (either 3″ × 5″ or 5″ × 8″) to record only key words and phrases.
4. Consider the use of visual aids. Depending on the type of assignment as well as your topic, diagrams, photographs, or demonstrations may be appropriate and effective in maintaining audience interest.
5. Anticipate questions your audience may ask. Review and revise your notes to include answers.
6. Practice delivery. This will build your confidence and help overcome nervousness. First, practice your presentation aloud several times by yourself. Time yourself to be sure you are within any limits. Then practice in front of friends and ask for criticism. Finally, tape-record your presentation. Play it back, looking for ways to improve it.
7. Deliver your presentation as effectively as possible. Engage your audience's interest by maintaining eye contact; look directly at other students as you speak, and make a deliberate effort to speak slowly; when you are nervous, your speech tends to speed up. Be enthusiastic and energetic.

If you need additional information or help with making oral presentations, consult your college's learning lab or obtain a guidebook on public speaking from your campus library.

As a variation on oral presentations, some instructors might ask each student (or group) to lead one class discussion, or they might organize panel discussions. As in oral presentations, organization is the essential ingredient for these activities. Plan ahead, outlining topics to be discussed, questions to be asked, or issues to confront.

EXERCISE 3 _____

Directions: *You are to make a three-minute oral presentation on learning and study methods you have found effective in a particular course you are taking this semester. Prepare a set of outline notes for your presentation, and practice delivery of your presentation. Then, answer the following questions.*

1. How did you organize your presentation?

   _____

2. Did prepearation of your presentation force you to analyze how you learn in the course you chose?

   _____

3. How did you improve your presentation through practice?

   _____

SUMMARY

Although some instructors prefer the lecture method as a means of conducting their classes, others use class activities, discussions, group projects, or oral presentations to direct students' learning. Asking and answering questions is an essential part of some college courses. Asking questions enables you to clarify course content: answering them allows you to evaluate the level and quality of your learning.

Class discussions allow students to learn from each other by assessing and evaluating each other's ideas. A substantial amount of advance preparation is required before you attend discussion classes. Preparation often includes carefully reading any assignments and taking notes for discussion. Your notes might include specific comments, ideas, and questions you could contribute to the discussion. During the class, you are expected to get involved, to participate in the discussion. As the discussion is going on, it is important to take summary notes that can be expanded during a later editing process.

As you review and study after the class discussion, first review your notes and check your recall of the information by using the recall clue system suggested for taking lecture notes. Then review and mark any reading assignment you completed prior to the discussion. Finally, try to anticipate test or exam questions that could be based on your notes, the reading assignment, and your recall of the discussion.

Group projects require you to work closely with other students to complete an assignment. Organization and active participation by each group member are essential to group productivity. Oral presentations, either group or individual, require careful preparation, practice, and effective delivery.

16

Preparing for Exams

Use this chapter to:

1. *Get organized for study and review.*
2. *Find out how to learn the material to be covered in an exam.*

Tests, quizzes, and examinations are important parts of most college courses because they help to determine grades. Tests are also important as learning experiences. Daily or weekly quizzes force you to keep up with reading assignments and attend class regularly. Also, it is through preparing for and taking exams that a student consolidates, or ties together, concepts and facts learned in a course. Finally, it is through the review and study involved in preparing for an exam that information is learned or stored in your memory.

Studying is the most important thing you can do to increase your chance of passing an exam. When exam papers are returned, you may hear comments like "I spent at least ten hours studying. I went over everything, and I still failed the exam!" Students frequently complain that they spend large amounts of time studying and do not get the grades they think they deserve. Usually the problem is that although they did study, they did not study the best way.

A second mistake students make is to begin studying only when the date of an exam is announced. These students may read textbook assignments as they are given, but they hurry through them, planning to study them carefully later. Some students do the same with their lecture notes— they take them but do not edit or review them until an exam is announced. These delay tactics result in last-minute study, or cramming. Research indicates that cramming is *not* an effective learning method and confirms that continuous review, the alternative to cramming, is superior.

The most important steps in preparing for exams are (1) organizing your study and review, (2) identifying what to learn, (3) connecting and synthesizing ideas, and (4) learning and memorizing the material.

ORGANIZING YOUR STUDY AND REVIEW

The timing of your review sessions is crucial to achieving good test results. Organize your review sessions, using the suggestions discussed in the following sections.

Organize Your Time

1. Schedule several review sessions at least one week in advance of an exam. Set aside specific times for daily review, and incorporate them into your weekly schedule. If you are having difficulty with a particular subject, set up extra study times.
2. Spend time organizing your review. Make a list of all chapters, notes, and handouts that need to be reviewed. Divide the material, planning what you will review during each session.
3. Reserve time the night before the exam for final, complete review. Do not study new material during the session. Instead, review the most difficult material, checking your recall of important facts or information for possible essay questions.

When studying for an exam or test, find out whether it will be objective, essay, or a combination of both. If your instructor does not specify the type of exam when he or she announces the date, ask during or after class. Most instructors are willing to tell students what type of exam will be given—sometimes they simply forget to mention it when announcing the exam. If an instructor chooses not to tell you, do not be concerned; at least you have shown that you are interested and are thinking ahead.

Be sure you know what material the exam will cover. Usually your instructor will either announce the exam topics or give the time span that the exam will cover. Also, find out what your instructor expects of you and how he or she will evaluate your exam. Some instructors expect you to recall text and lecture material; others expect you to agree with their views on a particular subject; still others encourage you to recall, discuss, analyze, or disagree with the ideas and information they have presented. You can usually tell what to expect by the way quizzes have been graded or classes have been conducted.

Attend the Class Before the Exam

Be sure to attend the class prior to the exam. Cutting class to spend the time studying, although tempting, is a mistake. During this class the instructor may give a brief review of the material to be covered or offer last-minute review suggestions. Have you ever heard an instructor say "Be sure to look over . . . " prior to an exam? Listen carefully to how the instructor answers students' questions; these answers will provide clues about what the exam will emphasize.

Consider Studying with Others

Consider whether it would help you to study with another person or with a small group of students from your class. Be sure to weigh the following advantages and disadvantages of group study, then decide whether group study suits your learning style.

Group study can be advantageous for the following reasons.

1. Group study forces you to become actively involved with the course content. Talking about, reacting to, and discussing the material aids learning. If you have trouble concentrating or "staying with it" when studying alone, group study may be useful.

2. One of the best ways to learn something is to explain it to someone else. By using your own words and thinking of the best way to explain an idea, you are analyzing it and testing your own understanding. The repetition of explaining something you already understand also strengthens your learning.

Group study can, however, have disadvantages.

1. Unless everyone is serious, group study sessions can turn into social events in which very little study occurs.
2. Studying with the wrong people can produce negative attitudes that will work against you. For example, the "None of us understands this and we can't all fail" attitude is common.
3. By studying with someone who has not read the material carefully or attended classes regularly, you will waste time reviewing basic definitions and facts that you already know, instead of focusing on more difficult topics.

EXERCISE 1 _____

Directions: *Plan a review schedule for an upcoming exam. Include material you will study and when you will study it.*

IDENTIFYING WHAT TO STUDY

In preparing for an exam, review every source of information—textbook chapters and lecture notes—as well as sources sometimes overlooked, such as old exams and quizzes, the instructor's handouts, course outlines, and outside assignments. Talking with other students about the exam can also be helpful.

Textbook Chapters

All chapters assigned during the period covered by the exam or relating to the topics covered in the exam must be reviewed. Review of textbook chapters should be fairly easy if you have kept up with weekly assignments, used your own variation of a study-reading system, and marked and underlined each assignment.

Lecture Notes

In addition to textbook chapters, all relevant notes must be reviewed. This too is easy if you have used the note-taking and editing system presented in Chapter 14.

Previous Exams and Quizzes

Be sure to keep all old tests and quizzes, which are valuable sources of review for longer, more comprehensive exams. While most instructors do not repeat the same test questions, old quizzes list important facts, terms, and ideas. The comprehensive exam will probably test your recall of the same information through different types of questions. Pay particular attention to items that you got wrong; try to see a pattern of error. Are you missing certain types of questions? If so, spend extra time on these questions.

Instructor's Handouts

Instructors frequently distribute duplicated sheets of information, such as summary outlines, lists of terms, sample problems, maps and charts, or explanations of difficult concepts. Any material that an instructor prepares for distribution is bound to be important. As you review these sheets throughout the course, date them and label the lecture topic to which they correspond. Keep them together in a folder or in the front of your notebook so that you can refer to them easily.

Outside Assignments

Out-of-class assignments might include problems to solve, library research, written reactions or evaluations, or lectures or movies to attend. If an instructor gives an assignment outside of class, the topic is important. Because of the limited number of assignments that can be given in a course, instructors choose only those that are most valuable. You should, therefore, keep your notes on assignments together for easy review.

Talk with Other Students

Talking with classmates can help you identify the right material to learn. By talking with others, you may discover a topic that you have overlooked or recognize a new focus or direction.

CONNECTING AND SYNTHESIZING INFORMATION

Once you have identified what material must be learned, the next step is to make learning easier by drawing together, or synthesizing, the information. In your close study of chapters and lecture notes, do not get lost in details and lose sight of major themes or processes. When concentrating on details, you can miss significant points and fail to see relationships. Exams often measure your awareness of concepts and trends as well as your recall of facts, dates, and definitions. The following suggestions will help you learn to synthesize information.

Get a Perspective on the Course

To avoid overconcentration on detail and to obtain perspective on the course material, step back and view the course from a distance. Imagine that all your notes, textbook chapters, outlines, and study sheets are arranged on a table and that you are looking down on them from a peephole in the ceiling. Then ask yourself, What does all that mean? When put together, what does it all show? Why is it important?

Look for Relationships

Study and review consist of more than just learning facts. Try to see how facts relate and interconnect. In learning the periodic table of chemical elements, for example, you should do more than just learn names and symbols. You should understand how elements are grouped, what similar properties they share, and how the groups are arranged.

Look for Patterns and the Progression of Thought

Try to see how or why the material was covered in the order it was presented. How does one class lecture relate to the next? To what larger topic or theme are they connected? For class lectures, check the course outline or syllabus that was distributed at the beginning of the course. Since it lists major topics and suggests the order in which they will be covered, your syllabus will be useful in discovering patterns.

Similarly, for textbook chapters, try to focus on the progression of ideas. Study the table of contents to see the connection between chapters you have read. Often chapters are grouped into sections based on similar content.

Watch for the progression or development of thought. Ask yourself, What is the information presented in this chapter leading up to? What does it have to do with the chapter that follows? Suppose in psychology you had covered a chapter on personality traits; next you were assigned a chapter on abnormal and deviant behavior. You would ask yourself, What do the two chapters have to do with each other? In this case, the first chapter on personality establishes the standard or norm by which abnormal and deviant behavior is determined.

Interpret and Evaluate

Do not let facts and details camouflage important questions. Remember to ask yourself, What does this mean? How is this information useful? How can this be applied to various situations? Once you have identified the literal content, stop, react, and evaluate its use, value, and application.

Prepare Study Sheets

The study sheet system is a way of organizing and summarizing complex information by preparing a mini-outline. It is most useful for reviewing material that is interrelated, or connected, and needs to be learned as a whole rather than as separate facts. Types of information that should be reviewed on a study sheet include:

1. Theories and principles
2. Complex events with multiple causes and effects
3. Controversial issues—pros and cons
4. Summaries of philosophical issues

	Problem-focused Approach	Emotion-focused Approach
Purpose	Deal directly w/cause of stress	Change feelings or thoughts about threat
Example	Study martial arts to prevent physical attack	Watch TV to "forget" a problem
How it is Accomplished	**Steps** 1. Appraise situation 2. Identify available resources 3. Make response to remove or lessen threat	**Alternatives** Use of drugs — ex: alcohol Consciously planned distractions Ego defense mechanisms
Limitations	Resources may not be available	May perpetuate depression Indecisive coping style may result

FIGURE 16-1   Sample Study Sheet

5. Trends in ideas, or data
6. Groups of related facts

Look at the sample study sheet in Figure 16-1, which was made by a student preparing for an exam on the sample textbook chapter included in Appendix A. You will notice that the study sheet organizes information on two approaches to coping with stress and presents them in a form that permits easy comparison.

To prepare a study sheet, first select the information to be learned. Then outline the information, using as few words as possible. Group together important points, facts, and ideas that relate to each topic.

EXERCISE 2 _____

Directions: *Prepare a study sheet for the selection "Sources of Stress," beginning on page 399 of the psychology sample chapter reprinted in Appendix A.*

EXERCISE 3 _____

Directions: *Prepare a study sheet for a topic you are studying in one of your courses. Include all the information you need to learn in order to prepare for an exam.*

LEARNING AND MEMORIZING

The methods and procedures you use to learn and to remember depend on the type of exam for which you are preparing. You would study and learn information differently for a multiple-choice test than you would for an essay exam.

Exams can be divided into two basic types: objective and essay. Objective tests are short-answer tests in which you choose one or more answers from several that are given, or supply a word or phrase to complete a statement. Multiple-choice, true/false, matching, and fill-in-the-blank questions are types of objective tests. In each of these, the questions are constructed so that the answers you choose are either right or wrong; scoring is completely objective, or free from judgment.

Essay tests require you to write answers to questions in your own words. You have to recall information, organize it, and present it in an acceptable written form. This is different from recognizing the correct answer among given choices, or from recalling a word or phrase. Because essay exams differ from objective tests, you must use different methods in preparing and reviewing for each.

Review for Objective Tests

Objective tests usually require you to recognize the right answer. On a multiple-choice test, for example, you have to pick the correct answer from the choices given. In true/false tests, you have to recognize the true and false statements. In matching tests, you have to recognize which two items go together. One goal in reviewing for objective tests, then, is to become so familiar with the course material that you can recognize and select the right answers.

Use Underlining and Marking

Your underlining of reading assignments can be used in several ways for review. First, reread your underlining in each chapter. Second, read the chapter's boldface headings and form a question for each, as you did in the "Question" step in the SQ3R system. Try to answer your question; then check your underlining to see if you were correct. Finally, review special marks you may have included. If, for example, you marked new or important definitions with a particular symbol, go through the chapter once and note these terms, checking your recall of their meanings.

Use the Recall Clues in Your Lecture Notes

Go back through each set of lecture notes and check your recall by using the marginal recall clue system. Test yourself by asking questions and trying to recall answers. Mark in red ink the things you have trouble remembering. Then use a different color of ink the second time you go through your notes, marking information you can't recall.

Use Study Aids

Use all study sheets, outlines, summaries, and organizational charts and diagrams that you have prepared to review and learn course content. To learn the information on a study sheet or outline, first read through it several times. Then take the first topic, write it on a sheet of paper, and see if you can fill in the information under the topic on your study sheet or outline. If you can't recall all the information, test yourself until you have learned it. Continue in this way with each topic.

Use the Index Card System

The index card system is an effective way of reviewing for objective tests. Using 3″ × 5″ index cards (or just small sheets of paper), write part of the information on the front, the remainder on the back. To review the dates of important events, write the date on the front, the event on the back; to review vocabulary, put each term on the front of one card, with its definition on the back. See the sample index cards shown in Figure 16-2, which were made by a student preparing for an objective exam on the biology chapter reprinted in Appendix B.

To study these cards, look at the front of each and try to remember what is written on the back. Then turn the card over to see if you are correct. As you go through your pack of cards, sort them into two stacks—those you know and those you do not remember. Then go back through the stack that you don't know, study each, and retest yourself, again sorting the cards into two stacks. Continue this procedure until you are satisfied that you have learned all the information. Go through your cards in this manner two or three times a day for three or four days before the exam. On the day of your exam, do a final, once-through review so that the information is fresh in your mind.

The index card system has several advantages. First, it is time-efficient; by sorting the cards, you spend time learning what you do not know and do not waste time reviewing what you have already learned. Second, by having each item of information on a separate card rather than in a list on a single sheet of paper, you avoid the danger of learning the items in a certain order. If you study a list of items, you run the risk of being able to remember them only in the order in which they are written on the list. When a single item appears out of order on an exam, you may not remember it. By sorting and occasionally shuffling your index cards, you avoid learning information in a fixed order. A third advantage of the index card system is that these cards are easy to carry in a pocket or purse. It is therefore easier for you to space your review of the material. If carried with you, the cards can be studied in spare moments—even when you don't have textbooks or notebooks with you. Moments usually wasted waiting in supermarket lines, doctors' offices, gas stations, or traffic jams can be used for study.

The index card system is more appropriate for learning brief facts than for reviewing concepts, ideas, and principles or for understanding sequences of events, theories, and cause-effect relationships. For this reason it works best when studying for objective tests that include short-answer questions such as "fill in the blanks." This type of question requires you to recall brief facts rather than simply to recognize them.

EXERCISE 4 _____

Directions: *Prepare a set of index cards (at least twenty) for a chapter or section of a chapter that you are studying in one of your courses. Then learn the information on the cards, using the sorting technique described previously.*

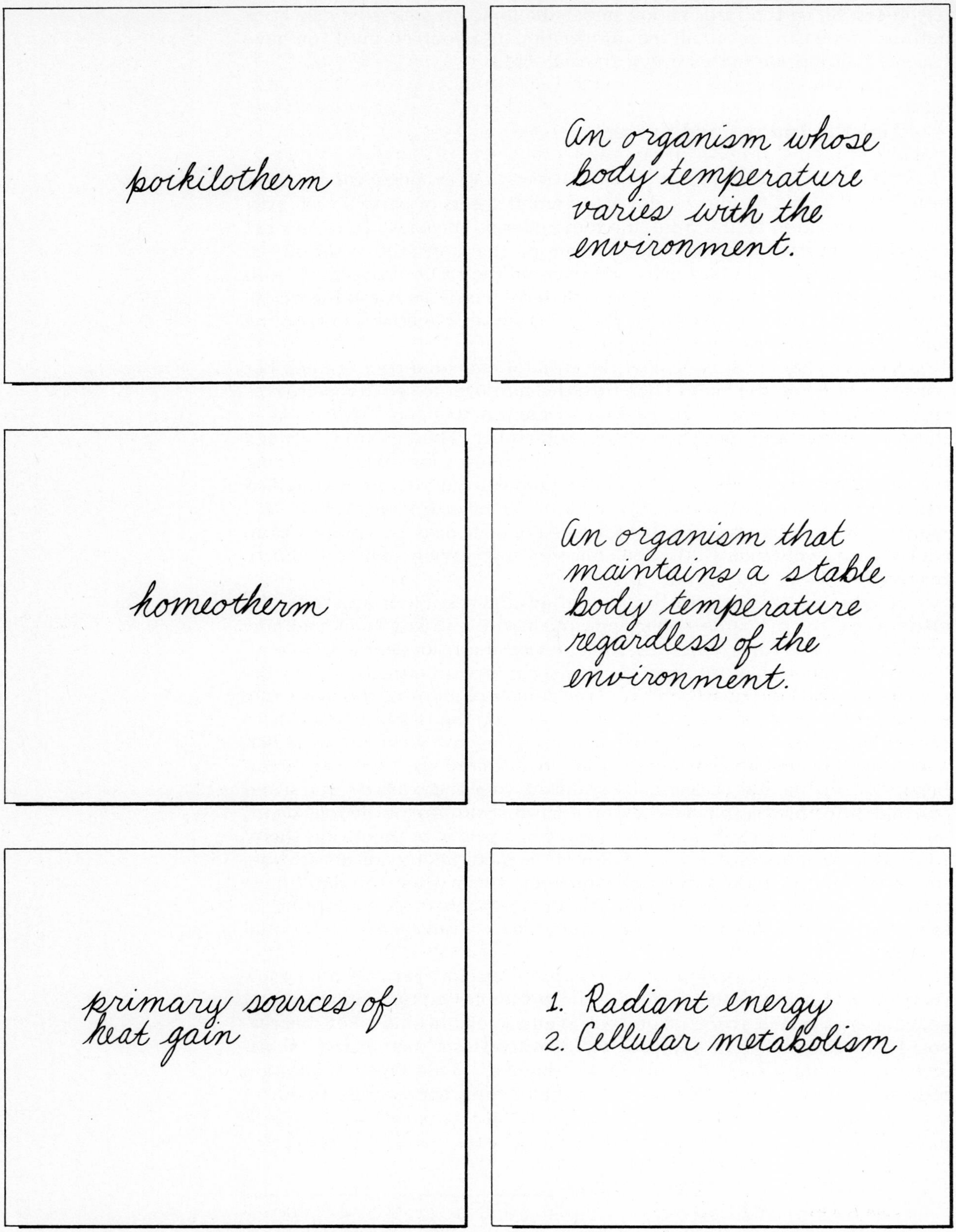

poikilotherm

An organism whose body temperature varies with the environment.

homeotherm

An organism that maintains a stable body temperature regardless of the environment.

primary sources of heat gain

1. Radiant energy
2. Cellular metabolism

FIGURE 16-2 Sample Study Cards

Test Yourself

Check to be sure you have learned all the necessary facts and ideas. By testing yourself before the instructor tests you, you are preparing in a realistic way for the exam. If you were entering a marathon race, you would prepare for the race by running—not by playing golf. The same is true of test-taking; preparation requires practice tests that you give yourself—not simply rereading chapters or staring at pages of notes.

Review for Essay Exams

Essay exams demand complete recall. Starting with a blank sheet of paper, you are required to retrieve from your memory all the information that answers the question. Then you must organize that information and express your ideas about it in acceptable written form.

To review for an essay exam, first identify topics that may be included in the exam. Then learn and organize enough information so that you can write about each topic.

Predict Essay Questions: In choosing topics to study, you attempt to predict what questions will be included on the exam. There are several sources from which you can choose topics. First, you can use boldface textbook headings to identify important topics or subtopics. End-of-chapter discussion questions and recall clues written in the margins of your lecture notes may also suggest topics. Remember to check the course outline distributed by your instructor at the beginning of the course. This outline frequently contains a list of major topics covered in the course.

Study the Topics Selected: Once you have made your choices, identify what aspects of the topics you should review. Perhaps the best source of information is your instructor, who probably has been consciously or unconsciously giving clues all semester about what the most important topics are. Train yourself to watch and listen for these clues. Specifically, look for your instructor's approach, focus, and emphasis with respect to the subject matter. Does your history instructor emphasize causes and dates of events? Is he or she more concerned with historical importance and lasting effects of events? Is your ecology instructor concerned with specific changes that a pollutant produces or its more general environmental effects?

After you have identified the aspects of each topic, prepare a study sheet on each. Include all the information you would want to remember if you were going to write an essay on each topic. As you prepare these study sheets, organize the information so that you could write a clear, concise essay on every topic. You might organize the causes of a particular historical event in order of importance or in chronological order. By organizing the information, you will be able to remember it more easily when you take the exam. After your study sheets are prepared, study each one, trying to recall the major subtopics you included. Also, test yourself to see if you can recall the specific facts under each topic.

Use a Key-Word Outline: To improve your memory, and to ensure that you will write an organized essay answer, try the key-word system, which helps you remember information by summarizing each idea with a single word or phrase. You can memorize each key word or phrase in a particular order. Together, these words and phrases form a mini-outline of the ideas or topics you want to include in your essay. You might test the effectiveness of your key-word outline and your ability to recall it by formulating your own exam questions and then writing complete or outline-form answers to the questions. When you are taking the exam, write the key-word mini-outline for each question on a scrap of paper or on the back of the exam paper before you start to write your answer. The outline will be an easy-to-follow guide to all the major points to include in your essay.

Refer again to the sample study sheet in Figure 16-1. The study sheet was made by a student preparing for an essay exam that was to be based in part on the psychology textbook chapter reprinted in Appendix A. Among the topics this student chose to review was stress. She predicted that her instructor might include a question on the approaches to coping with stress. From her study sheet, the student made the key-word list shown in Figure 16-3, which briefly outlines various aspects of the two major approaches to stress. By learning this list, the student will be well prepared to discuss the advantages and disadvantages of the two approaches.

EXERCISE 5 _____

Directions: *Predict several questions that an instructor might ask on an essay exam covering the psychology textbook chapter included in Appendix A (pages 381–410). Write them in the space provided.*

_____

_____

_____

_____

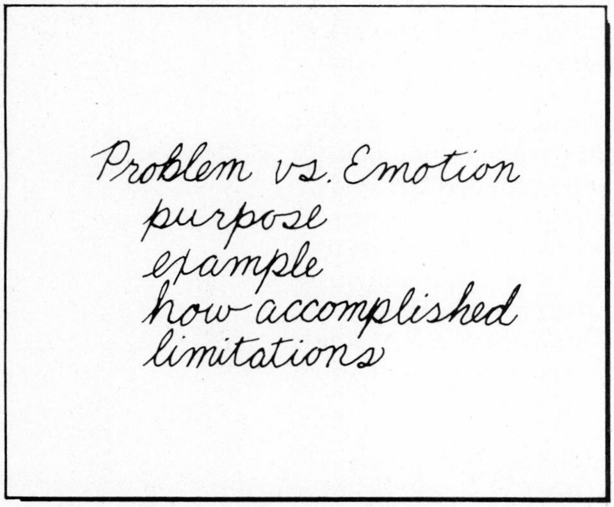

Problem vs. Emotion
purpose
example
how accomplished
limitations

FIGURE 16-3 **Sample Key-Word Outline**

EXERCISE 6 _____

Directions: *Assume you are preparing for an essay exam in one of your courses. Predict several questions that might be asked for one textbook chapter and write them in the space provided.*

_____

_____

_____

EXERCISE 7 _____

Directions: *Choose one of the essay exam questions that you wrote in Exercise 5. Prepare a study sheet that summarizes the information on the topic. Then reduce that information on your study sheet to a key-word outline.*

SUMMARY

Tests, exams, and quizzes are an important part of most college courses because they determine grades and serve as learning experiences. Preparing for an exam involves four steps. The first, organizing for study and review, requires planning and scheduling your time so that all the material is reviewed carefully and thoroughly. In the second step, identifying what to study, suggestions are given for reviewing all sources of information to determine what material is to be learned. Once the material is identified, the next step is to organize and connect the facts and ideas into a meaningful body of information. Learning and memorizing, the final step, require learning the material in a manner that is most appropriate for the type of exam to be taken. For objective exams, study sheets and the index card system should be used. For essay exams, study sheets and key-word outlines are suggested.

17

Taking Exams

Use this chapter to:

1. *Learn how to approach exams in an organized, systematic manner.*

2. *Become test-wise by learning test-taking tips for each type of exam.*

Thorough, careful study and review are the two most important things you can do to ensure that you will get a good exam grade. Test-taking skills and techniques, however, if used to full advantage, can influence your grade by as much as 10 or 15 points. The manner in which you approach the exam, how you read and answer objective tests, and how carefully you read, organize, and write your answer to an essay exam can influence your grade. This chapter will discuss each of these aspects of becoming test-wise and will also discuss a problem that interferes with many students' ability to do well on exams: test anxiety.

GENERAL SUGGESTIONS FOR TAKING EXAMS

The following suggestions will help you approach any exam in an organized, systematic way.

Take Necessary Materials

When going to any exam, be sure to take along any materials you might be asked or allowed to use. Be sure you have an extra pen, and take a pencil in case you must make a drawing or diagram. Take paper—you may need it for computing figures or writing essay answers. Take along anything you have been allowed to use throughout the semester, such as a pocket calculator, conversion chart, or dictionary. If you are not sure whether you may use them, ask the instructor.

Get There on Time

It is important to arrive at the exam room on time, or a few minutes early, to get a seat and get organized before the instructor arrives. If you are late, you may miss instructions and feel rushed as you begin the exam.

If you arrive too early (fifteen minutes ahead), you risk anxiety induced by panic-stricken students questioning each other, trading last-minute memory tricks, and worrying about how difficult the exam will be.

Sit in the Front of the Room

If you have a choice, the most practical place to sit in an exam room is at the front. There you often receive the test first and get a head start. There, also, you are sure to hear directions and corrections and can easily read any changes written on the chalkboard. Finally, it is easier to concentrate and avoid distractions at the front of the room. At the back, you are exposed to distractions such as a student dropping papers or cheating, or the person in front who is already two pages ahead of you.

Preread the Exam

Before you start to answer any of the questions, quickly page through the exam, noticing the directions, the length, the type of questions, and the general topics covered. Prereading provides an overview and perspective of the whole exam. Prereading also helps eliminate the panic you may feel if you go right to the first few questions and find that you are unsure of the answers.

Plan Your Time

After prereading the exam, you will know the numbers and types of questions included. You should then estimate how much time you will spend on each part of the exam. The number of points each section is worth (the point distribution) should be your guide. If, for example, one part of an exam has twenty multiple-choice questions worth one point each and another part has two essays worth forty points each, you should spend much more time answering the essay questions than working through the multiple-choice items. If the point distribution is not indicated on the test booklet, you may want to ask the instructor what it is.

As you plan your time, be sure to allow a minute or two to preread the exam. Also allow three to four minutes at the end of the exam to review what you have done, answering questions you skipped and making any necessary corrections or changes.

To keep track of time, wear a watch. Many classrooms do not have wall clocks, or you may be sitting in a position where the clock is difficult to see.

If you were taking an exam with the following question and point distribution, how would you divide your time? Assume the total exam time is sixty minutes.

Type of Question	Number of Questions	Total Points
Multiple choice	25 questions	25 points
True/false	20 questions	20 points
Essay	2 questions	55 points

You should probably divide your time as indicated:

Prereading	1–2 minutes
Multiple choice	15 minutes
True/false	10 minutes
Essay	30 minutes
Review	3–4 minutes

Because the essays are worth twice as many points as either of the other two parts of the exam, it is necessary to spend twice as much time on the essay portion.

Read the Questions Carefully

Most instructors word their questions so that what is expected is clear. A common mistake students make is to read more into the question than is asked for. To avoid this error, read the question several times, paying attention to how it is worded. If you are uncertain of what is asked for, try to relate the question to the course content. Don't anticipate hidden meanings or trick questions.

EXERCISE 1 _____

Directions: *For each of the exams described below, estimate how you would divide your time.*

1. Time limit: 75 minutes

Type of Question	Number of Questions	Total Points
Multiple choice	20 questions	40 points
Matching	10 questions	10 points
Essay	2 questions	50 points

How would you divide your time?

Prereading	_____ minutes
Multiple choice	_____ minutes
Matching	_____ minutes
Essay	_____ minutes
Review	_____ minutes

2. Time limit: 40 minutes

Type of Question	Number of Questions	Total Points
True/false	15 questions	30 points
Fill-in-the-blank	10 questions	30 points
Short answer	10 questions	40 points

How would you divide your time?

Prereading	_____ minutes
True/false	_____ minutes
Fill-in-the-blank	_____ minutes

HINTS FOR TAKING OBJECTIVE EXAMS

When taking objective exams—usually multiple choice, true/false, or matching—remember the following hints, which may give you a few more points.

Read the Directions

Before answering any questions, read the directions. Often an instructor may want the correct answer marked in a particular way (underlined rather than circled). The directions may contain crucial information that you must know in order to answer the questions correctly. If you were to ignore directions such as the following and assume the test questions were of the usual type, you could lose a considerable number of points.

True/False Directions

Read each statement. If the statement is true, mark a T in the blank to the left of the item. If the statement is false, add and/or subtract words that will make the statement correct.

Multiple-Choice Directions

Circle all the choices that correctly complete the statement.

Without reading the true/false directions, you would not know that you should correct incorrect statements. Without reading the multiple-choice directions, you would not know that you are to choose more than one answer.

Leave Nothing Blank

Before turning in your exam, be sure you have answered every question. If you have no idea about the correct answer to a question, guess— you might be right. On a true/false test, your chances of being correct are 50 percent; on a four-choice multiple-choice question, your odds are 25 percent.

Students frequently turn in tests with some items unanswered because they leave difficult questions blank, planning to return to them later. Then, in the rush to finish everything, they forget to go back to them. The best way to avoid this problem is to choose what look like the best answers and mark the question numbers with an X or a check mark; then, if you have time at the end of the exam, you can give them more thought. If you run out of time, at least you will have attempted to answer them.

Look for Clues

If you encounter a difficult question, choose what seems to be the best answer, mark the question so that you can return to it, and keep the item in mind as you go through the rest of the exam. Sometimes you will see some piece of information later in the exam that reminds you of a fact or idea. At other times you may notice information that, if true, contradicts an answer you had already chosen.

Don't Change Answers Without Good Reason

When reviewing your exam answers, don't make a change unless you have a specific reason for doing so. If a later test item made you remember information for a previous item, by all means make a change. If, however, you are just having second thoughts about an answer, leave it alone. Your first guess is usually the best one.

Hints for Taking True/False Tests

When taking true/false tests, watch for words that qualify or change the meaning of a statement; often, just one word makes it true or false. Consider the following oversimplified example:

All dogs are white.

Some dogs are white.

The first statement is obviously false, whereas the second is true. In each statement, only one word determined whether the statement was true or false. While the words and statements are much more complicated on college true/false exams, you will find that one word often determines whether a statement is true or false. Read the following examples:

All paragraphs must have a stated main idea.

Spelling, punctuation, and handwriting *always* affect the grade given to an essay answer.

When taking notes on a lecture, try to write down *everything* the speaker says.

In each of these examples, the italicized words modify—or limit—the truth of each statement. When reading a true/false statement, look carefully for any limiting words, such as *all, some, none, never, always, usually, frequently, most of the time.* To overlook these words may cost you several points on an exam.

Read Two-Part Statements Carefully: Occasionally you may find a statement with two or more parts. In answering these items, remember that both or all parts of the statement must be true in order for it to be correctly marked true. If part of the statement is true and another part is false, then mark the statement false, such as in the following example:

The World Health Organization (WHO) has been successful in its campaign to eliminate smallpox and malaria.

While it is true that WHO has been successful in eliminating smallpox, malaria is still a world health problem and has not been eliminated. Because only part of this statement is true, it should be marked false.

Look for Negative and Double-Negative Statements: Test items that use negative words or word parts can be confusing. Words such as *no, none, never, not, cannot* and beginnings of words such as *in-, dis-, un-, it-,* or *ir-* are easy to miss and always alter the meaning of the statement. For items containing negative statements, make it a habit to underline or circle them as you read.

Statements that contain two negatives such as the following are even more confusing.

It is not unreasonable to expect that Vietnam veterans continue to be angry about their exposure to Agent Orange.

In reading these statements, remember that two negatives balance or cancel out each other. "Not unreasonable," then, can be interpreted to mean "reasonable."

Make Your Best Guess: When all else fails and you are unable to reason out the answer to an item, use these three last-resort rules of thumb:

1. Absolute statements tend to be false. Because there are very few things that are always true and for which there are no exceptions, your best guess is to mark statements that contain words such as *always, all, never,* or *none* as false.
2. Mark any item that contains unfamiliar terminology or facts as false. If you've studied the material thoroughly, trust that you would recognize as true anything that was a part of the course content.
3. When all else fails, it is better to guess true than false. It is more difficult for instructors to write false statements than true statements. As a result, many exams have more true items than false.

EXERCISE 2 ────────────

Directions: The following true/false test is based on content presented in the sample chapter in Appendix B of this text. Read each item. Then find and underline the single word that, if changed or deleted, could change the truth or falsity of the statement. In the space provided at the right, indicate whether the statement is true or false by marking T for true and F for false.

1. Less energy is consumed by a hibernating animal than by an active one. _____

2. All mammals have a layer of subcutaneous fat that functions as a thermostat control. _____

3. Constancy of body temperature is characteristic only of humans. _____

4. An increase in metabolic rate always lowers fuel consumptions. _____

5. Skin receptors for hot and cold are the most important source of information about temperature change. _____

6. The elevation of body temperature known as a fever is due not to a malfunction of the hypothalamic thermostat but to its resetting.

    _____

7. All terrestrial reptiles are poikilotherms.

    _____

8. All poikilotherms vary their temperature with the environment and lose body heat primarily through convection.

    _____

9. A camel would be better adapted to its environment if it had all-over fat distribution rather than localized fat deposits in its hump.

    _____

10. Most small desert animals are nocturnal.

    _____

Hints for Taking Matching Tests

Matching tests require you to select items in one list that can be paired with items in a second list. Use the following tips to answer matching tests.

1. Glance through both lists before answering any items to get an overview of the subjects and topics the test covers. Next, try to discover a pattern. Are you asked to match dates with events, terms with meanings, people with accomplishments?
2. Answer the items you are sure of first, lightly crossing off items as they are used.
3. Don't choose the first answer you see that seems correct; items later in the list may be better choices.
4. If the first column consists of short words or phrases and the second is lengthy definitions or descriptions, save time by reverse matching; that is, look for the word or phrase in column 1 that fits each item in column 2.

Hints for Taking Short-Answer Tests

Short-answer tests require you to write a brief answer, usually in list or sentence form, such as asked by the following example.

List three events that increased U.S. involvement in the Vietnam War.

In answering short-answer questions, be sure to:

1. Use point distribution as a clue to how many pieces of information to include. For a nine-point item asking you to describe the characteristics of a totalitarian government, give three ideas.
2. Plan what you will say before starting to write.
3. Use the amount of space provided, especially if it varies for different items, as a clue to how much should be written.

Hints for Taking Fill-in-the-Blank Tests

Items that ask you to fill in a missing word or phrase within a sentence require recall of information rather than recognition of the correct answer. It is important, therefore, to look for clues that will trigger your recall.

1. Look for key words in the sentence and use them to decide what subject matter and topic are covered in the item.
2. Decide what type of information is required. Is it a date, name, place, new term?
3. Use the grammatical structure of the sentence to determine the type of word called for. Is it a noun, verb, or qualifier?

Hints for Taking Multiple-Choice Tests

Multiple-choice exams are among the most frequently used types of exams and are often the most difficult to answer. The following suggestions should improve your success in taking multiple-choice tests.

1. Read all choices first, considering each. Do not stop with the second or third choice, even if you are sure that you have found the correct answer. Remember, on most multiple-choice tests your job is to pick the *best* answer, and the last choice may be better than the preceding answers.
2. Some multiple-choice tests include combinations of previously listed choices, as in the following test item.

> Among the causes of slow reading is (are)
> a. lack of comprehension
> b. reading word-by-word rather than in phrases
> c. poorly developed vocabulary
> d. making too few fixations per line
> e. a and b
> f. a, b, and c
> g. a, b, c, and d

The addition of choices that are combinations of previous choices tends to be confusing. Treat each choice, when combined with the stem, as a true or false statement. As you consider each choice, mark it true or false. If you find more than one true statement, select the choice that contains the letters of all the true statements you identified.

3. Use logic and common sense. Even if you are unfamiliar with the subject matter, it is sometimes possible to reason out the correct answer. The following item is taken from a history exam on Japanese-American relations after World War II.

> Prejudice and discrimination are
> a. harmful to our society because they waste our economic, political, and social resources
> b. helpful because they ensure us against attack from within

   c. harmful because they create negative images of the
      United States in foreign countries
   d. helpful because they keep the majority pure and
      united against minorities

Through logic and common sense, it is possible to eliminate choices b and d. Prejudice and discrimination are seldom, if ever, regarded as positive, desirable, or "helpful," since they are inconsistent with democratic ideals. Having narrowed your answer to two choices, a or c, you can see that choice a offers a stronger, more substantial reason why prejudice and discrimination are harmful. What other countries think of the United States is not as serious as the waste of economic, political, and social resources.

4. Study items that are very similar. When two choices seem very close and you cannot decide between them, stop and examine each. First, try to express each in your own words. Then analyze how they differ. Often this process will lead you to recognize the correct answer.

5. Look for qualifying words. As in true/false tests, the presence of qualifying words is important. Because many statements, ideas, principles, and rules have exceptions, you should be careful in selecting items that contain such words as *best, always, all, no, entirely,* and *completely,* all of which suggest that something is always true, without exception. Also be careful of statements containing such words as *none, never,* and *worst,* which suggest things that are never true without exception. Items containing words that provide for some level of exception, or qualification, are more likely to be correct; a few examples are *often, usually, less, seldom, few, more,* and *most.*

    In the following example, notice the use of italicized qualifying words:

    In most societies
      a. values are *highly* consistent
      b. people *often* believe and act on values that are
         contradictory
      c. *all* legitimate organizations support the values of the
         majority
      d. values of equality *never* exist alongside prejudice
         and discrimination

In this question, items c and d contain the words *all* and *never,* suggesting that those statements are true without exception. Thus if you did not know the answer to this question based on content, you could eliminate items c and d on the basis of the level of qualifiers.

6. Some multiple-choice questions require application of knowledge or information. You may be asked to analyze a hypothetical situation or to use what you have learned to solve a problem. Here is an example taken from a psychology text.

    Carrie is comfortable in her new home in New Orleans. When she gets dressed up and leaves her home and goes to the supermarket to buy the week's groceries, she gets nervous and upset and thinks that something is going to happen to her. She feels the same way when walking her four-year-old son Jason in the park or playground.

Carrie is suffering from
   a. shyness
   b. a phobia
   c. a personality disorder
   d. hypertension

In answering questions of this type, start by crossing out unnecessary information that can distract you. In the preceding example, distracting information includes the woman's name, her son's name, where she lives, why she goes to the store, and so forth.

7. If a question concerns steps in a process or order of events or any other information that is likely to confuse you, ignore the choices and use the margin or scrap paper to jot down the information as you can recall it. Then select the choice that matches what you wrote.

8. Avoid selecting answers that are unfamiliar or that you do not understand. A choice that looks complicated or uses difficult words is not necessarily correct. If you have studied carefully, a choice that is unfamiliar to you is probably incorrect.

9. As a last resort, when you do not know the answer and are unable to eliminate any of the choices as wrong, guess by picking the one that seems most complete and contains the most information. This is a good choice because instructors are always careful to make the best answer completely correct and recognizable. In doing so, the choice often becomes long or detailed.

10. Make educated guesses. In most instances you can eliminate one or more of the choices as obviously wrong. Even if you can eliminate only one choice, you have reduced the odds on a four-choice item from one in four to one in three. If you can eliminate two choices, you have reduced your odds to one in two, or 50 percent. Don't hesitate to play the odds and make a guess—you may gain points.

HINTS FOR TAKING STANDARDIZED TESTS

At various times in college you may be required to take a standardized test, which is a commercially prepared, timed test used nationally or statewide to measure skills and abilities. Your score compares your performance to large numbers of other students throughout the country or state. The SAT and ACT are examples of standardized tests; many graduate schools require a standardized test as part of their admission process. Here are a few suggestions for taking this type of test.

1. Most standardized tests are timed, so the pace at which you work is a critical factor. You need to work at a fairly rapid rate, but not so fast as to make careless errors.

2. Don't plan on finishing the test. Many of the tests are designed so that no one finishes.

3. Don't expect to get everything right. Unlike classroom tests or exams, you are not expected to get most of the answers correct.

4. Find out if there is a penalty for guessing. If there is none, then use the last twenty or thirty seconds to randomly fill in an answer for each item that you have not had time to do. For every four items that you guess, the odds are that you will get one item correct.

5. Get organized before the timing begins. Line up your answer sheet and test booklet so you can move between them rapidly without losing your place.

HINTS FOR TAKING ESSAY EXAMS

Essay questions are usually graded on two factors: what you say and how you say it. It is not enough, then, simply to include the correct information. The information must be presented in a logical, organized way that demonstrates your understanding of the subject you are writing about. There can be as much as one whole letter grade difference between a well-written and poorly written essay, although both contain the same basic information. This section offers suggestions for getting as many points as possible on essay exams.

Read the Question

For essay exams, reading the question carefully is the key to writing a correct, complete, and organized answer.

Read the Directions First: The directions may tell you how many essays to answer and how to structure your answer, or specify a minimum or maximum length for your answer.

Study the Question for Clues: The question usually includes three valuable pieces of information. First, the question tells you the topic you are to write about. Second, it contains a limiting word that restricts and directs your answer. Finally, the question contains a key word or phrase that tells you how to organize and present answers. Read the essay question in this example:

(key word)　(limiting word)　　　(topic)　　　　(limiting word)
Compare the causes of the Vietnam War with the causes of the

　(topic)
Korean War.

In this example you have two topics—the Vietnam War and the Korean War. The question also contains a limiting word that restricts your discussion to these topics and tells you what to include in your answer. In this sample question, the limiting word is *causes*. It tells you to limit your answer to a discussion of events that started, or caused, each war. Do not include information about events of the war or its effects. The key word in the sample question is *compare*. It means you should consider the similarities, and possibly the differences, in the causes of the two wars. When directed to compare, you already have some clues as to how your answer should be written. One possibility is to discuss the causes of one war and then the causes of the other and finally to make an overall statement about their similarities. Another choice is to discuss one type of cause for each of the wars, and then go on to discuss another type of cause for each. For instance, you could discuss the economic causes of each, then the political causes of each.

There are several common key words and phrases used in essay questions. They are listed in Table 17-1.

TABLE 17-1   Key Words Used in Essay Questions

Key Words	Example	Information to Include
Discuss	Discuss Laetrile as a treatment for cancer.	Consider important characteristics and main points.
Enumerate	Enumerate the reasons for U.S. withdrawal from Vietnam.	List or discuss one by one.
Illustrate	State Boyle's law and illustrate its use.	Explain, using examples that demonstrate or clarify a point or idea.
Compare	Compare the causes of air pollution with those of water pollution.	Show how items are similar as well as different; include details or examples.
Contrast	Contrast the health care systems in the United States with those in England.	Show how the items are different; include details or examples.
Define	Define thermal pollution and include several examples.	Give an accurate meaning of the term with enough detail to show that you really understand it.
Explain	Explain why black Americans are primarily city dwellers.	Give facts and details that make the idea or concept clear and understandable.
Trace	Trace the history of legalized prostitution in Nevada.	Describe the development or progress of a particular trend, event, or process in chronological order.
Evaluate	Evaluate the strategies our society has used to treat mental illness.	React to the topic in a logical way. Discuss the merits, strengths, weaknesses, advantages, or limitations of the topic.
Summarize	Summarize the arguments for and against offering sex education courses in public schools.	Cover the major points in brief form; use a sentence and paragraph form.
Describe	Describe the experimentation that tests whether plants are sensitive to music.	Tell how something looks or happened, including how, who, where, why.
Justify	Justify former President Carter's attempt to rescue the hostages in Iran.	Give reasons that support an action, event, or policy.

TABLE 17-1 (Continued)

Key Words	Example	Information to Include
Criticize	Criticize the current environmental controls to combat air pollution.	Make judgments about quality or worth; include both positive and negative aspects.
Prove	Prove that ice is a better cooling agent than water when both are at the same temperature.	Demonstrate or establish that a concept or theory is correct, logical, or valid.

Watch for Questions with Several Parts

A common mistake that students often make is to fail to answer all parts of an essay question. Most likely, they get involved with answering the first part and forget about the remaining parts. Questions with several parts come in two forms. The most obvious form is as follows.

For the U.S. invasion of Granada, discuss the
  a. causes
  b. immediate effects
  c. long-range political implications

A less obvious form that does not stand out as a several-part question includes the following.

Discuss *how* the Equal Rights Amendment was developed and *why* its passage has aroused controversy.

When you find a question of this type, underline or circle the limiting words to serve as a reminder.

Make Notes As You Read

As you read a question the first time, you may begin to formulate an answer. When this occurs, jot down a few key words that will bring these thoughts back when you are ready to organize your answer.

EXERCISE 3 _____

Directions: *Read each of the following essay questions. For each question, underline the topic, circle the limiting word, and place a box around the key word.*

1. Discuss the long-term effects of the trend toward a smaller, more self-contained family structure.
2. Trace the development of monopolies in the late nineteenth and early twentieth centuries in America.

3. Explain one effect of the Industrial Revolution on each of three of the following:
   a. transportation
   b. capitalism
   c. socialism
   d. population growth
   e. scientific research
4. Discuss the reason why, although tropical plants have very large leaves and most desert plants have very small leaves, cactus grows equally well in both habitats.
5. Describe the events leading up to the War of 1812.
6. Compare and contrast the purpose and procedures in textbook marking and lecture note-taking.
7. Briefly describe a complete approach to reading and studying a textbook chapter that will enable you to handle a test on that material successfully.
8. List four factors that influence memory or recall ability, and explain how each can be used to make study more efficient.
9. Summarize the techniques a speaker or lecturer may use to emphasize the important concepts and ideas in a lecture.
10. Explain the value and purpose of the prereading technique, and list the steps involved in prereading a textbook chapter.

Organize Your Answer

As mentioned before, a well-written, organized essay often gets a higher grade than a carelessly constructed one. Read each of these examples and notice how they differ. Each essay was written in response to this instruction on a psychology final exam: Describe the stages involved in the memory process.

EXAMPLE 1

Memory is important to everybody's life. Memory has special ways to help you get a better recollection of things and ideas. Psychologists believe that memory has three stages: encoding, storage, and retrieval.

In the encoding stage, you are putting facts and ideas into a code, usually words, and filing them away in your memory. Encoding involves preparing information for storage in memory.

The second stage of memory is storage. It is the stage that most people call memory. It involves keeping information so that it is accessible for use later in time. How well information is stored can be affected by old information already stored and newer information that is added later.

The third step in memory is retrieval, which means the ability to get back information that is in storage. There are two types of retrieval—recognition and recall. In recognition, you have to be able to identify the correct information from several choices. In recall, you have to pull information directly from your memory without using the recognition type of retrieval.

EXAMPLE 2

Memory is very complicated in how it works. It involves remembering things that are stored in your mind and being able to pull them out when you want to remember them. When you pull information out of your memory it is called retrieval. How well you can remember something is affected by how you keep the information in your mind and how you put it in. When keeping, or storing, information you have to realize that this information will be affected by old information already in your memory. Putting information in your memory is called encoding, and it means that you store facts and ideas in word form in your memory. Information stored in your memory can also be influenced by information that you add to your memory later.

There are two ways you can retrieve information. You can either recognize it or recall it. When you recognize information you are able to spot the correct information among other information. When you recall information you have to pull information out of your head. Recall is what you have to do when you write an essay exam.

While these two essays contain practically the same information, the first will probably receive a higher grade. In this essay, it is easy to see that the writer knows that there are three stages in the memory process and knows how to explain each. The writer opens the essay by stating that there are three stages and then devotes one paragraph to each of the three stages.

In the second essay it is not easy to find out what the stages of memory are. The paragraphs are not organized according to stages in the memory process. The writer does not write about one stage at a time in a logical order. Retrieval is mentioned first; then storage and retrieval are discussed further. At the end, the writer returns to the topic of retrieval and gives further information.

Here are a few suggestions to help you organize your answer.

1. Think before you start to write. Decide what information is called for and what you will include.
2. Make a brief word or phrase outline of the ideas you want to include in your answer.
3. Study your word outline and rearrange its order. You may want to put major topics and important ideas first and less important points toward the end; or you may decide to organize your answer chronologically, discussing events early in time near the beginning and mentioning more recent events near the end. The topic you are discussing will largely determine the order of presentation.
4. If the point value of the essay is given, use that information as a clue to how many separate points or ideas may be expected. For an essay worth 25 points, for example, discussion of five major ideas may be expected.

Use Correct Paragraph Form

Be sure to write your answers in complete, correct sentences and to include only one major point in each paragraph. Each paragraph should have a main idea, usually expressed in one sentence. The remainder of the paragraph should explain, prove, or support the main idea you state. Also, use correct spelling and punctuation.

Begin Your Answer with a Topic Sentence

Your first sentence should state what the entire essay is about and suggest how you intend to approach it. If a question asks you to discuss the practical applications of Newton's three laws of motion, you might begin by writing, "There are many practical applications of Newton's laws of motion." Then you should proceed to name the three laws and their practical applications, devoting one paragraph to each law. If you have time, your final paragraph may be a summary or review of the major points you covered in the essay.

Make Your Main Points Easy to Find

Because many essay exam readers have a large number of papers to read in a short period of time, they tend to skim (look for key ideas) rather than read everything; therefore, state each main point at the beginning of a new paragraph. For lengthy answers or multipart questions, you might use headings or the same numbering used in the question. Use space (two lines) to divide your answers into different parts.

Include Sufficient Explanation

A frequent criticism instructors make of student essay answers is the failure to explain or to support ideas fully. By following the rule of thumb of only one major idea per paragraph, you avoid this danger and force yourself to explain major points. If you think of answering an essay question as a process of convincing your instructor that you have learned the material, then you are likely to include enough explanation. Another rule of thumb is also useful: Too much information is better than too little.

Avoid Opinions and Judgments

Unless the question specifically asks you to do so, do not include your personal reaction to the topic. When you are asked to state your reactions and opinions, include reasons to support them.

Make Your Answer Readable

Because there is a certain amount of judgment and personal reaction involved as an instructor reads your answer, it is to your advantage to make your paper as easy to read as possible. It is annoying to an instructor to try to read poor handwriting and carelessly written answers.

1. Use ink—it is easier to read and does not smear.
2. Use clean, unwrinkled 8½″ × 11″ paper. Reading a handful of small sheets is difficult and confusing.

3. Number your pages and put your name on each sheet.
4. Do not scratch out sentences you want to omit. Draw a single line through each and write *omit* in the margin.
5. If the paper is thin or ink runs, write on only one side.
6. Leave plenty of space between questions. Leave a 1″–2″ margin at each side. The instructor will need space to write comments.

Proofread Your Answer

After you have written an essay, read it twice. Before reading your essay the first time, read the question again. Then check to see that you have included all necessary facts and information and that you have adequately explained each fact. Add anything you feel improves your answer. Then read the essay a second time, checking and correcting all the mechanical aspects of your writing. Check for hard-to-read words and errors in spelling and punctuation. Again, make all necessary corrections.

If You Run Out of Time

Despite careful planning of exam time, you may run out of time before you finish writing one of the essays. If this happens, try to jot down the major ideas that you would discuss fully if you had time. Often, your instructor will give you partial credit for this type of response, especially if you mention that you ran out of time.

If You Don't Know the Answer

Despite careful preparation, you may forget an answer. If this should happen, do not leave a blank page; write something. Attempt to answer the question—you may hit upon some partially correct information. The main reason for writing something is to give the instructor a chance to give you a few points for trying. If you leave a blank page, your instructor has no choice but to give you zero points. Usually when you lose full credit on one essay, you automatically eliminate your chance to get a high passing grade.

EXERCISE 4 _____

Directions: *Organize and write a response to one of the following essay questions.*

1. Five organizational patterns are commonly used in textbook writing: comparison-contrast, definition, time sequence, cause-effect, and enumeration. Discuss the usefulness of these patterns in predicting and answering essay exam questions.
2. Describe three strategies that have improved your reading skills. Explain why each is effective.
3. Describe your approach to time management. Include specific techniques and organizational strategies that you have found effective.

CONTROLLING TEST ANXIETY

Do you get nervous and anxious just before an exam begins? If so, your response is normal; most students feel some level of anxiety before an exam. In fact, research indicates that some anxiety is beneficial and improves your performance by sharpening your attention and keeping you alert.

Research also shows that very high levels of anxiety can interfere with test performance. Some students become highly nervous and emotional and lose their concentration. Their minds seem to go blank and they are unable to recall material they have learned. They also report physical symptoms: Their hearts pound, it is difficult to swallow, or they break out in a cold sweat.

Test anxiety is a complicated psychological response to a threatening situation, and it may be related to other problems and past experiences. The following suggestions are intended to help you ease text anxiety. If these suggestions do not help, the next step is to discuss the problem with a counselor.

Be Sure Test Anxiety Is Not an Excuse

Many students say they have test anxiety when actually they have not studied and reviewed carefully or thoroughly. The first question, then, that you must answer honestly is this: Are you in fact *unprepared* for the exam and, therefore, should have every reason to be anxious?

Get Used to Test Situations

Psychologists who have studied anxiety use processes called "systematic desensitization" and "simulation" to reduce test anxiety. Basically, these are ways of becoming less sensitive or disturbed by tests by putting yourself in testlike conditions. Although these are complicated processes often used by trained therapists, here are a few ways you can use these processes to reduce test anxiety.

1. Become familiar with the building and room in which the test is given. Visit the room when it is empty and take a seat. Visualize yourself taking a test there.
2. Develop practice or review tests. Treat them as real tests and do them in situations as similar as possible to real test conditions.
3. Practice working with time limits. Set an alarm clock and work only until it rings.
4. Take as many tests as possible, even though you dislike them. Always take advantage of practice tests and make-up exams. Buy a review book for the course you are taking, or a workbook that accompanies your text. Treat each section as an exam and have someone else correct your work.

Control Negative Thinking

Major factors that contribute to text anxiety are self-doubt and negative thinking. Just before and during an exam, test-anxious students often think, "I won't do well," "I'm going to fail," "What will my friends think of me when I get a failing grade?" This type of thinking predisposes you to failure; you are telling yourself that you expect to fail. By thinking in this way you prevent or block your chances for success.

One solution to this problem is to send yourself positive rather than negative messages. Say to yourself, "I have studied hard and I deserve to pass," "I know that I know the material," or "I know I can do it!" Remember, being well prepared is one of the best ways to reduce test anxiety.

Compose Yourself Before the Test Begins

Don't take an exam on an empty stomach; you will feel queasy. Have something light or bland to eat. Some students find that a brisk walk outside before going to an exam helps to reduce tension.

Before you begin the test take thirty seconds or so to calm yourself, to slow down, and to focus your attention. Take several deep breaths, close your eyes, and visualize yourself calmly working through the test. Remind yourself that you have prepared carefully and have every reason to do well.

Answer Easy Questions First

To give yourself an initial boost of confidence, begin with a section of the test that seems easy. This will help you to work calmly and you will prove to yourself that you can handle the test.

SUMMARY

This chapter offered suggestions on how to improve exam grades by approaching tests in a systematic, organized manner. This involves taking the necessary materials, arriving on time, deliberately choosing a seat in a nondistracting section of the room, prereading the exam, and planning the time you will devote to various sections of the exam. Techniques for taking objective and essay exams were discussed. In taking any type of objective exam, read the directions carefully, leave nothing blank, and look for clues that will help you recall the information. Specific suggestions were given for taking true/false, matching, short-answer, fill-in-the-blank, and multiple-choice exams. When taking an essay exam, it is important to read the question carefully to determine exactly what type of response your instructor wants. Essay answers should be carefully organized and written in an easy-to-read form. The problem of test anxiety was defined, and several methods for overcoming it were presented.

18

Preparing Written Assignments and Research Papers

Use this chapter to:

1. *Learn how to prepare common types of written assignments.*
2. *Develop a step-by-step procedure for writing research papers.*

Do you have difficulty getting started on writing assignments? When you start writing do you feel as though you have nothing to say? Have you ever worked hard on a paper and still not received a grade that was worth all the time and effort you put in? If you answered yes to any of these questions, your response is typical of many college students. Many students find writing to be a difficult, often frustrating, task. In fact, many professional writers experience the same difficulty generating ideas and getting started. One purpose of this chapter is to offer some practical suggestions for getting started on and successfully completing the most common types of college writing assignments. Another is to provide specific step-by-step procedures for organizing and writing a research paper.

WHY WRITTEN ASSIGNMENTS ARE GIVEN

If you are going to put in all the effort that is required to complete a writing assignment, it often helps to understand why instructors assign them. You know that instructors use papers as a means of evaluating your learning and awarding grades. More important, however, writing assignments are a means of helping you learn. Putting your ideas on paper forces you to think them through, draw them together, and examine how they relate to one another. If you can put important concepts and ideas from the course into your own words, you will retain them longer and begin to put them to use more readily. Often, once you have recorded your ideas, you will find that you need additional information or that you need to read what others have written about the topic. Instructors thus may assign a paper for the purpose of encouraging you to learn more about a particular topic.

How to Take Advantage of Written Assignments

Most students, if given their choice, would rather take an exam than write a paper. Actually, written assignments have several advantages over exams. In fact, you might think of a paper as a golden opportunity to demonstrate what you know. An exam is usually a one-time-only, you-know-it-or-you-don't pressured situation. A written assignment allows you unlimited time, unlimited references, and the opportunity to ask for help from friends or from your instructor. When a paper is assigned, then, think of it as an opportunity to work in an open-ended, nonpressured way. Relax, take your time, and prove what you know.

TYPES OF WRITTEN ASSIGNMENTS

There are several types of writing that an instructor may assign to you. The most common types are listed here along with a brief description of what is usually expected in each.

Essay Exams

Although essay exams are not papers, they do constitute a major portion of assigned writing in some courses. The most important thing to remember in writing essay exams is to answer each question *clearly* and *specifically*. Take time to figure out what the instructor is asking for, then write your essay in direct response to the question (see Chapters 16 and 17 for more information on studying for and taking essay exams).

Essays or Compositions

Many instructors give assignments that require you to present or discuss your own ideas on a particular topic. Often this type of assignment is simply called a paper. A philosophy instructor might ask you, for instance, to write a paper explaining your views on abortion. Usually the instructor specifies the topic or the general subject area to write about. An exception may occur in English composition classes, when you are allowed to select a topic but the instructor specifies *how* you are to write or organize your paper. Often, too, the instructor suggests a particular length, either in number of words or pages.

When a paper of this type is given, listen carefully as the instructor announces and discusses the assignment. At that time, the instructor will often indicate what is expected. Jot down the instructor's exact wording of the assignment so that you can refer to it before you begin writing. Also jot down any examples he or she may give. You might find them useful as a starting point for generating ideas.

If the assignment is unclear or you feel you do not understand what is expected, do not hesitate to check with others in the class or to ask the instructor after class. It is your responsibility to let your instructor know if you do not understand what you are to do. If you decide to speak with your instructor, try to ask specific questions rather than simply saying you do not understand the assignment. By asking specific questions, you are more likely to get information that will help you to complete the assignment.

If you are required to write about a topic that you know little or nothing about, it is worthwhile to spend an hour or so in the library reading about the topic. Once you have learned a little about the topic, you will feel more confident writing about it.

Factual Reports

Another type of writing assignment commonly used in college courses is the report. When you write a report you are expected to present factual information on a particular topic. In a chemistry course, a summary or description of a laboratory experiment might be considered a report. In a psychology class, you might be asked to observe the behavior of a particular group of people and report your observations. In sociology, you might be asked to do a survey and report your findings. Most often your instructor will suggest, or perhaps require, that you follow a particular format. The length will often be dictated by the nature of the assignment. Here are a few specific guidelines for writing reports:

1. Be thorough. Include all important details.
2. Be concise. Express your ideas clearly and in the briefest possible way.
3. Be accurate. Because you are reporting facts or observations, be certain that the information you include is correct.
4. Avoid flowery language, creative or humorous touches.
5. If you do not have sufficient information, be sure to check reference books to acquire what you need. Do not hesitate to use the library if your text does not contain the information you need.
6. If no format is suggested by your instructor, devise a logical format with headings or subheadings before you begin writing.
7. Do not include reactions, opinions, or interpretation of your topic unless your instructor has indicated that you should do so.

Reaction Papers

Unlike a report, a reaction paper should present your opinion on or reaction to a particular topic. You may be asked to react to something you've read, such as a poem or short story, or to describe your feelings about a film, lecture, play, recording, or demonstration. The length of a reaction paper may vary, but it is usually a one- or two-page paper. To write reaction papers effectively, use the following suggestions:

1. Think before you write. Decide what your reactions really are: You may need to review or reread the material (if you are reacting to something you have read) or any notes that you may have.
2. Be sure to state and briefly describe what your reaction paper is about.
3. Organize or group your reactions in some way. Don't just write reactions as they occur to you.
4. As a means of getting started and of collecting ideas, discuss the topic with a friend.

Research Papers

The research paper is the longest and most time-consuming type of writing assignment. Because of the amount of work it requires, the research paper is usually weighted heavily in determining your final course grade. A research paper or "term paper" involves locating information and ideas about a particular topic and organizing them in written form. The first step is to research the topic in the library, locating and reading appropriate books, periodicals, and reference sources. As you read, you should record, in note form, information you may want to include in your paper. Then, once you've collected sufficient information, organize your information and write the paper. (Specific suggestions for writing and researching this type of paper will be presented later in the chapter)

GENERAL SUGGESTIONS FOR WRITING PAPERS

When they begin working on a paper, many students just pick up a pen and start writing the paper. This is usually not the best way to begin. In writing, as in reading, there are certain things you can do before you begin writing a paper as well as after you have written it that can help ensure that you have produced an acceptable, well-constructed work. The steps, or stages, that most good writers go through in writing a paper are prewriting, organizing, writing, revising, and proofreading.

Prewriting

You might think of prewriting as a process similar to prereading. When prereading (see Chapter 5) you are in a sense getting ready to read, focusing your attention on the material and anticipating the content and organization. When you write, you also need to get ready by making decisions about the purposes, overall organization, and content of what you will write. Here are a few suggestions for how to get off to a good start:

Get Organized: As is true for reading and study, when and where you write is important. Choose a time of day when you can concentrate and a place free of distractions. Have plenty of paper, pens, pencils, and a dictionary available. Begin by reviewing what your assignment is. Reread either your instructor's statement of the assignment, if presented in writing, or your notes on the assignment if it was given orally. As you review, look for clues about what specifically is expected.

Once you are familiar with the nature and scope of the assignment, try to establish a time schedule for its completion. Never try to complete a paper in one evening. You need time to let the paper rest; this allows you to come back to it later to reconsider what you've written in a different perspective and with a critical eye.

Choose a Manageable Topic: In many cases, except for research papers, the topic is defined by your instructor or by the nature of the assignment. In the event that you do have a choice, use the following guidelines:

1. Choose a topic that interests you. You will find that it is much easier to maintain a high level of concentration and motivation if the topic is genuinely interesting. Also, ideas will flow more easily if you are involved with your topic.
2. Choose a topic you know something about. If you do not know much

about a topic, it is very difficult—in some cases almost impossible—to write about it. So, unless you are prepared to learn about a topic before writing about it, avoid topics that you know little about.

3. Choose a topic that can be handled effectively in the length of paper you are writing. For example, you could not do a good job of discussing the general topic "Religions of the World" in a three-page paper. There are many religions in the world, and each has its own set of beliefs, rituals, and codes for living. It would be impossible to discuss each in the length of paper assigned. A much better, more manageable topic would be something like "Changing Trends in Catholicism in the Twentieth Century." This topic is more specific than "Religions of the World" and is a manageable part of that broader topic. Techniques for narrowing a subject to a workable topic will be discussed later in this chapter.

Develop Ideas About the Topic: Once you have chosen a topic, the next step is to generate or develop ideas about your topic. If you have trouble, as many students do, in finding something to say, you might try a technique called free writing. Figure 18-1 shows a portion of free writing on the topic of the changing American family. It works like this: Take a piece of paper and just start writing anything that comes into your mind about the topic. Do not be concerned about whether you are writing in complete sentences or whether the ideas make sense or connect to one another. You might think of free writing as a type of "brainstorming," or thinking of a variety of ideas on a topic. Keep writing continuously for a set period of time, four to five minutes or so. If you cannot think of an idea about the topic, write whatever else comes to mind.

When you've finished, reread what you have written. You will be surprised at the number of different ideas that you have thought of. Then, underline or rewrite those ideas that seem worth including in your paper.

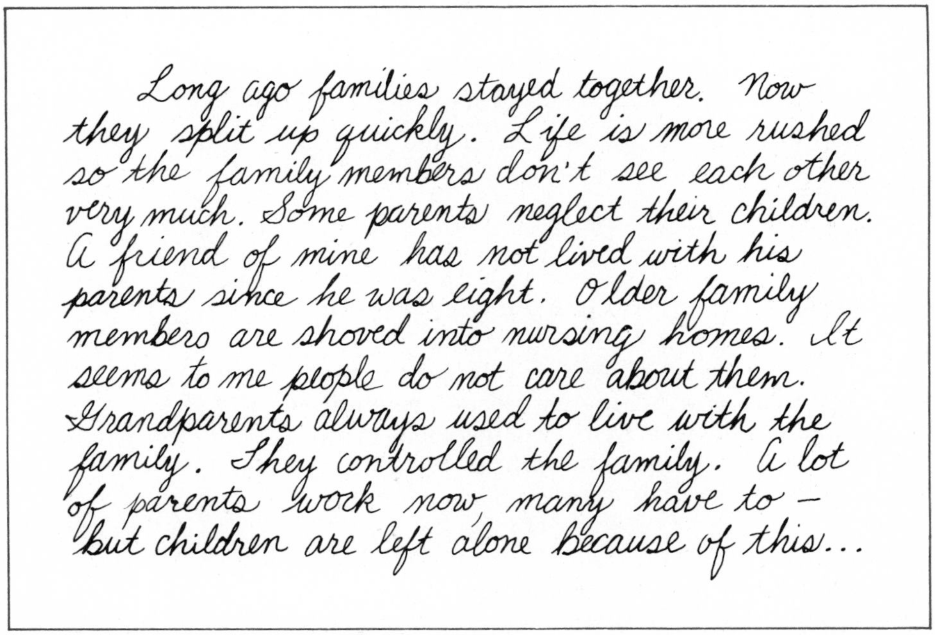

Long ago families stayed together. Now they split up quickly. Life is more rushed so the family members don't see each other very much. Some parents neglect their children. A friend of mine has not lived with his parents since he was eight. Older family members are shoved into nursing homes. It seems to me people do not care about them. Grandparents always used to live with the family. They controlled the family. A lot of parents work now, many have to — but children are left alone because of this...

FIGURE 18-1   An Example of Free Writing

An alternative technique to generate ideas is to take five minutes or so and write down all the questions you can think of on your topic. For instance, you might write the following questions about the topic of the role of computers in our daily lives:

How do computers affect our lives?
Have computers changed our way of life?
Who allows computers to influence us?
Do computers invade our right to privacy?
Are computers economically important?
Is computer skill a marketable job skill?
Can computers replace men and women in the work force?

When you've finished, reread the questions, and as you did in free writing, try to identify those that, when answered, would be worth including in your paper.

EXERCISE 1 _____

Directions: *Choose one of the topics listed below. Free-write about that topic for five minutes.*

Topics
1. Television watching
2. Sports in America
3. Protecting the environment

EXERCISE 2 _____

Directions: *Choose one of the topics given below. Write as many questions as you can think of about the topic. Limit your time to five minutes.*

Topics
1. Unemployment and how it affects our lives
2. The value of college education
3. Soap operas

Organizing and Outlining

Once you have identified some ideas to include in your paper, the next step is to organize them. This involves arranging the ideas in an order that will result in an understandable and well-written paper. The most effective way of organizing your ideas is to make an outline. An outline will help you see the relationship of ideas to one another. To accomplish this, use the following steps:

1. Quickly list the ideas in the order in which you wrote them.
2. Read through the list, looking for ideas that are similar or those that should follow one another.
3. Rewrite your outline, trying to group ideas together so that they are

listed in a logical order (an order that would be a sensible approach to discussing your topic).

Writing a Draft

After you have organized your ideas, you are ready to begin writing the first draft of your paper. Here are a few suggestions:

1. Always plan on revising and recopying your paper. Your first draft should never be your final copy.
2. As you begin, be concerned only with getting your ideas down on paper. Do not be concerned with exact word choice or with correct punctuation. You can check and correct those details later.
3. Use your outline as a guide. Discuss the ideas in the order in which they appear in the outline.
4. Be sure to explain each idea completely. A common fault instructors find with student papers is that they do not include enough detail. Try to include, where appropriate, examples, reasons, descriptions, or other supporting information.
5. Do not hesitate to make changes as you think of them.

Revising

Revision is the step that can make a good paper a better one or an unacceptable paper acceptable. Revision involves rereading, rewriting, and making changes to improve both the content and organization of your paper. Here are a few suggestions to follow:

1. Do not revise as soon as you have finished writing. Instead, try to allow a lapse of time between writing and revision. This lapse gives you the distance and objectivity that you do not have immediately on completing your draft.
2. If you have trouble finding anything wrong with your paper, ask a friend to read and criticize it. Also, ask him or her to summarize what your paper said. This will allow you to see if you have expressed your ideas clearly and accurately.
3. To evaluate your own paper, try asking yourself the following questions:
   a. Are the ideas clearly expressed?
   b. Do the ideas tie together to form a unified piece of writing?
   c. Is each major idea supported with facts and details?

Proofreading

Once you have prepared the final copy of your paper, be sure to read it to detect errors in spelling, punctuation, grammar, and usage. At this point, try to ignore the idea flow and simply check each sentence to be sure that it does not contain errors. To locate spelling errors, try reading the paper backward, word by word. To locate sentence structure errors, read the paper backward sentence by sentence. If your paper is typewritten, also check for typographical errors such as omitted words or sentences and transposed letters.

Although you may not think it is fair, your paper's physical appearance and grammatical correctness will actually influence its grade. It pays to make sure your work is error free. After all, it would be unfortunate to spend a great deal of time and effort on a research paper only to have it downgraded because you did not take a few minutes to proofread and make final corrections.

WRITING RESEARCH PAPERS

In assigning a research paper, your instructor is asking you to learn about a topic and then to organize and to summarize what you have learned. You are expected to learn on your own, using whatever resources and references are available. Completing a research paper, then, involves much more than just writing. It involves topic selection, locating appropriate sources of information, reading, taking notes, and organizing the information. In fact, writing is actually the final step in the process of acquiring and organizing information on a particular topic.

The purpose of this portion of the chapter is to offer general guidelines for completing a successful research paper. After providing some general tips for getting started, the section will present a step-by-step procedure for collecting information and writing the paper.

Tips for Getting Started

The first college research paper you do is always the most difficult. The reason for this is that you are learning *how* to do the paper while doing it. Once you have mastered the techniques for writing research papers, later ones will be much easier and less time consuming. Here are a few tips to help you get started:

1. Find out how important the research paper is by finding out how heavily the paper counts in your final course grade. This information will help you to determine how much time and effort you should put into the paper.

2. Get an early start. Even if the paper is not due until the end of the semester, start working on the paper as soon as possible. Starting early may enable you to produce a good rather than barely acceptable paper. Also, if you have not done a research paper before, you will need time to become familiar with the process.

   There are several other advantages to starting early. You will find books and references readily available in the library, while if you wait until everyone is working on papers, popular sources will be in use or checked out by other students. Also, starting early gives you time to acquire information you may need from other libraries through interlibrary loan services. Finally, an early start allows you time to think, to organize, and even to make mistakes and be able to correct them.

3. Ask your instructor for advice. If you experience difficulty, ask your instructor for help with a particular problem. Through their experience with the subject matter, instructors are often able to suggest alternate approaches to the topic, recommend a particular reference, or suggest a different organization. However, do not go to see your

instructor until you have wrestled with the problem and find yourself at a standstill. When you do see your instructor, take your notes, outlines, and rough drafts.

STEPS IN WRITING A RESEARCH PAPER

In paging through the remainder of this chapter, you might think that writing a research paper is a very complicated process. You will see that eleven steps are shown and that they appear to be fairly detailed. If you follow each step, however, you will discover that you are carefully led through a fairly routine process of focusing your paper, collecting information, and writing the paper. The steps are:

1. Narrow your topic.
2. Determine the purpose of the paper.
3. Locate appropriate sources of information.
4. Refine the topic through further reading.
5. Write a tentative thesis statement.
6. Collect information.
7. Form an outline.
8. Write a first draft.
9. Revise the draft.
10. Prepare the final copy.
11. Prepare the bibliography.

Step 1: Narrow Your Topic

Choosing and narrowing your topic is critical to producing a good paper. If you begin with an unmanageable topic, regardless of how hard you work, you will be unable to produce an acceptable paper. Also, your task is much easier if you choose a manageable topic—one for which information is readily accessible and understandable. Some instructors might require that you select a topic within a specific subject area; others may accept any topic that pertains to the course. In either case choice is involved.

The most important consideration in selecting a topic is to choose one that is neither too broad nor too narrow. If you choose a topic that is too broad, it will be impossible for you to cover all its aspects adequately. On the other hand, if it is too specific, you may have difficulty finding enough to write about. For most students, the tendency is to select a topic that is too general.

Suppose you are taking a course in ecology and the environment and you have been assigned a fifteen-page research paper. Your instructor will allow you to choose any topic related to the course of study. You have always been interested in environmental pollution and decide to do your research paper on this subject. Because there are many causes of pollution, many types of pollution, and many effects of pollution, both immediate and long-term, you realize that the general topic of environmental pollution is much too broad. To narrow or limit this topic, you might choose one type of pollution—such as water pollution—and then decide to research its causes or effects. Or you might decide to limit your topic to a study of the different types of chemicals that pollute the air.

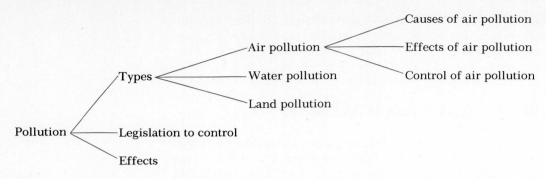

FIGURE 18-2   Narrowing a Topic

It is often necessary to narrow your topic two or three times. The process of narrowing a topic might be diagrammed as shown in Figure 18-2.

Once you have a subject area or a broad topic in mind, try to think of ways your topic could be subdivided. Often you will first have to acquire some general background about the subject. For ideas to start with, check the card catalog in the library under your subject and read the subject headings that immediately follow it to see how the subject is divided. Also, check an encyclopedia to see how the subject is divided, then skim quickly through to learn a little about the topic. Depending on your subject, you may also wish to consult other texts in the subject area to get a brief overview of the field. Make a list of possible topics. As an alternate approach, make a list of questions that might be asked about the subject. Each of your questions suggests a possible division of your subject. You may find it necessary to further limit these divisions as you gather information.

EXERCISE 3 _____

Directions: *Assume that one of your instructors has assigned a research paper on one of the following subjects. Choose a subject and narrow it to a topic that is manageable in a ten- to twenty-page paper. If necessary, check the card catalog, an encyclopedia entry, or various texts in the field. Use an outline like the one shown below.*

Subjects

1. Clothing styles and fashion
2. Test-tube babies
3. Sports
4. Death
5. Pornography

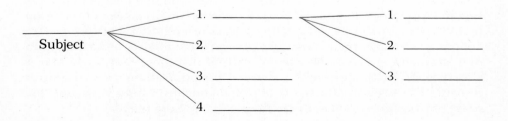

Step 2: Determine the Purpose of the Paper

Once you have narrowed your topic, the next step is to determine the purpose of your paper. You should decide whether you want to prove something about your topic, inform others about it, or explain or analyze it. In some cases, your purpose may have already been defined by your instructor when he or she assigned the research paper. Most of the time, however, you will need to decide how you will approach your topic. To determine your approach, ask yourself, What do I want to accomplish by writing this paper? Whatever approach you select will directly affect how you proceed from this point. The type of sources you consult, the amount of reading you do, and the thesis that you state and develop are each shaped by your purpose.

Step 3: Locate Appropriate Sources of Information

Your campus library, its librarians, and its reference materials are the keys to locating appropriate sources of information on your topic. If you have not used the library on your campus, take a half hour or so to visit the library just to become acquainted with its organization and the services it offers. Do not try to begin researching your topic until you know what is available in the library and how to use it. Be sure to find out:

1. how the card catalog is organized
2. how the books are arranged on the shelves
3. where the reference section is located
4. whether a reference librarian is available
5. whether there is a photocopy machine
6. where periodicals (journals and magazines) are located
7. the procedure for checking out books and periodicals
8. whether your library participates in an interlibrary loan system
9. if a floor plan of the library is available

If you feel lost in the library or find that you are unfamiliar with many of the reference materials, check to see what assistance the library has to offer. Some libraries offer one- to two-hour workshops on library usage and research skills; others have pamphlets, brochures, or videotapes that provide basic information on using the campus library. If none of these services is available, ask the reference librarian for assistance. After all, a reference librarian's primary responsibility is to assist students in using the library.

Rules of Thumb for Locating Sources: When you are generally familiar with the library, you are ready to begin locating sources of information. There are several rules of thumb to follow:

1. Proceed from general to specific. Locate general sources of information first; then, once you have an overview of the topic, locate more detailed references on particular aspects of the topic.
2. Locate as many sources as possible. Your research paper is expected to cover your topic thoroughly. In collecting information, therefore, you must be sure that you do not overlook important aspects of the topic. By locating and checking as many references as possible, you can be

certain that you have covered the topic completely. Once you have read several sources, it is possible to skim additional sources, checking to see what new information is provided.

3. Record all sources used. Many students waste valuable time by failing to keep a complete record of all references used. An important part of any research paper is the bibliography, or list of all the references you use to write the paper (see Step 11, page 309). To prepare this bibliography in the easiest way possible, just write down each source as you use it. If you forget to do this, you will have to spend additional time later, checking back and trying to locate each source you used.

The easiest way to record bibliographical information is to use a separate 3″ × 5″ index card for each source. Later you will see that the cards enable you to alphabetize your references easily. To avoid wasting time recopying or rewriting information, record it in the exact form in which it should appear in the bibliography.

4. Ask for assistance. If you have difficulty locating information or if you are not certain that you have exhausted all possible sources, ask the reference librarian for assistance. Most librarians are ready and willing to guide serious students in their research.

Using the Card Catalog: The key to every library is the card catalog. It is an easy-to-use record of all the books and periodicals that the library owns. Two, three, or more separate cards are filed for each book in the library. Each book may be listed by author, by title, and by subject(s) covered. The card briefly describes what the book includes and contains a call number that you can use to locate the book on the shelf. The card catalog, then, is one of the first places to start in researching a topic.

Using Reference Materials: In addition to its holdings of books and periodicals, libraries have a reference section that contains general references, sources that cannot be checked out. Among the most common reference materials are encyclopedias, dictionaries, periodical indexes, almanacs, biographical dictionaries, atlases, and statistical handbooks. Also, many libraries contain a reserve section in which instructors "reserve," or place on restricted use, important, useful sources that many students wish to use. The reference librarian is available to assist you in using these sources.

Step 4: Refine the Topic Through Further Reading

To become familiar with the range and scope of your topic and to acquire background information, it is useful to read or skim several general sources of information. Your purpose at this point is to learn enough about your topic to be able to refine the direction, or focus, of your paper. Again, a good starting point is the encyclopedia. The entry will provide you with an overview of your topic and may suggest directions for further limiting your topic. Other useful sources include textbooks on the general subject of which your topic is part, or books written on the subject.

Since your purpose is to get an overview of the topic, do not try to read everything. You might read parts of the material and skip others. Do not try to take notes on your reading yet. Instead, just jot down on index cards references that would be useful for later, more thorough reading. Also, jot down any ideas that might come to mind about how to approach, to further limit, or to organize your topic. Continue sampling general sources until you find that most of what you are reading is no longer new and that you have already read it in another source.

Step 5: Write a Tentative Thesis Statement

A thesis statement is a one-sentence statement of what your paper is about. It states the idea you will develop throughout the paper. You might think of a thesis statement as similar to the topic sentence of a paragraph or the central thought of a passage. Each states, in a general way, what the paragraph or passage is about. Similarly, the thesis statement indicates to your reader what your paper will be about.

Here are a few examples of thesis statements that could be written for the topic of effects of air pollution:

Air pollution has had a dramatic effect on the lives of twentieth-century Amreicans.

Air pollution has been the primary cause of numerous health-related problems for Americans.

Public concern over the long-range effects of air pollution has forced industrial reform.

Notice that each specifically states what the writer intends to show about air pollution and its effects.

Since you have so far done only preliminary reading and research, your thesis statement is only tentative. You should plan on changing, revising, or narrowing this statement as you proceed through the remaining steps. Right now your thesis statement should express the idea you *think* your paper will explain or discuss. In a sense, the thesis statement further narrows your topic by limiting your paper to a specific focus or approach.

EXERCISE 4

Directions: *Assume that each of the following is the topic of a research paper. For each, write a thesis statement that suggests a direction of development or focus for the topic.*

1. *Topic:* Cigarette Smoking and Health

   Thesis statement: _____

   _____

2. *Topic:* The Progress of the Women's Movement

   Thesis statement: _____

   _____

3. *Topic:* The Draft for Women

   Thesis statement: _____

   _____

4. *Topic:* Choosing a Career

    Thesis statement: _____

    _____

5. *Topic:* Gay Rights

    Thesis statement: _____

    _____

Step 6: Collect Information: Reading and Note-taking

Now that you have written a tentative thesis statement, the next step is to collect and record the information that supports your thesis.

Reading Reference Material: In reading reference material, you clearly define your purpose for reading; you are looking for facts and ideas that will help you prove, explain, or support your thesis statement. However, reading reference sources is very different from reading textbooks. In textbooks you are reading for retention and recall of most of the information presented. When reading reference material, on the other hand, not all information is useful or important. Also, you are not trying to remember everything you read; instead, when you find a useful piece of information, you can write it down for later reference.

Prereading is a valuable skill in identifying sources that may contain information on your topic. Once you have located a book in the card catalog and then found it on the library shelves, take a few minutes to preview it to determine if it contains useful information before you check it out. You can save yourself valuable time and avoid carrying home armloads of books by prereading to select only appropriate, usable sources.

Because high retention is not required when reading reference material you can afford to skim, scan, or skip large portions of material (see Chapter 22 for skimming and scanning techniques). In fact, trying to read everything, regardless of whether you use it in your paper, would be an extremely inefficient use of time.

Taking Notes: The manner and form in which you take notes largely determines whether writing your paper will be a relatively simple or extremely difficult, time-consuming task. The next two steps, developing an outline and writing the paper, require that the information you collect be in a form that can be rearranged or placed in a specific order.

One effective way to take notes is to use index cards; 5″ × 8″ and 4″ × 6″ sizes are best. Some students prefer to use separate full sheets of paper. Use a separate card or sheet of paper for each different subtopic, or different aspect of your topic. Record the author's last name and the pages you used in the upper right corner. In the upper left corner, write the subtopic that the notes are concerned with. Be sure to write on only one side of the cards. A sample note card or sheet might look like the one shown in Figure 18-3.

Here are a few suggestions for taking good research notes:

1. Record the information in your own words, instead of copying the author's words. By recording the author's wording, you run the risk of

go back to the research stage to check new sources. Do not be discouraged by these additional steps; remember, the first few times you write a research paper, you are learning *how* to do the assignment. Therefore some extra time and effort may be required initially.

Step 10: Prepare the Final Copy

Once you are satisfied that you have made sufficient revision to produce a good research paper, you are ready to prepare the final copy for submission. It is generally agreed that a typewritten copy is strongly desirable. Some instructors require typewritten copy; most prefer it to handwritten papers. If you have poor, illegible handwriting, your instructor may become annoyed while reading the paper and may unconsciously react to your paper negatively or critically. A typewritten copy, on the other hand, presents a neat appearance and suggests that you care enough about your work to present it in the best possible form.

An important part of preparing a final copy, regardless of whether it is handwritten or typed, is proofreading. Once you have prepared the final copy, be sure to take the time to read it through and correct spelling, punctuation, and grammar. If you are weak in one or more of these areas and cannot easily recognize your own errors, ask a friend to proofread your paper and point out or mark the errors.

Step 11: Prepare the Bibliography

The final steps to completing a research paper are to prepare a list, or bibliography, of all the sources that you used to write the paper, and to prepare any endnotes necessary. Endnotes list in consecutive order the sources from which you have taken quotations or which contained unique or specialized information particular to a certain source. Endnotes are called footnotes if placed at the bottom of each page rather than in a consecutive list at the end of the paper. You will need to consult a handbook to determine the specialized format endnotes require.

As mentioned earlier, if you kept careful records as you collected your information, preparing a bibliography is a relatively simple task. In the bibliography you simply list alphabetically all the sources you consulted. Also, you must use a consistent form for listing the information. Depending on your instructor, as well as the subject area with which you are working, different formats may be expected. Although each format requires basically the same information, arrangement of information as well as punctuation may vary. Some instructors may specify a particular format, while others may accept any standard, consistent format. If your instructor prefers a particular format, by all means use it.

It is well worth the initial cost to purchase a handbook or style guide that explains a particular format. Among the most commonly used handbooks that explain how to do a bibliography as well as how to handle many of the other stylistic features of research papers are

> *The MLA Handbook for Writers of Research Papers, Theses, and Dissertations*, 2nd ed. (New York: Modern Language Association, 1984).
>
> Turabian, Kate L. *A Manual for Writers*, 5th ed. (Chicago: University of Chicago Press, 1987).

SUMMARY

Written assignments and research papers are an important part of many college courses. There are several types of writing that instructors assign: essay exams, essays or compositions, factual reports, reaction papers, and research papers. Writing a good paper involves much more than picking up a pen and starting to write. The steps involved in writing any type of paper are prewriting, organizing, writing, revising, and proof-reading. Writing a research paper is a process of acquiring and organizing information on a particular topic. It involves selecting an appropriate topic, locating useful sources of information, reading, taking notes, and organizing information. This chapter presented some tips for getting started and then outlined a step-by-step approach for completing a research paper. The steps are as follows:

1. Narrow your topic.
2. Determine the purpose of the paper.
3. Locate appropriate sources of information.
4. Refine the topic through further reading.
5. Write a tentative thesis statement.
6. Collect information.
7. Form an outline.
8. Write a first draft.
9. Revise the draft.
10. Prepare the final copy.
11. Prepare the bibliography.

PART SIX

Vocabulary Development

Vocabulary development is crucial to the development of effective and efficient reading. *Vocabulary* means the ability to recognize individual words and to associate meaning with the particular combination of letters that form a word.

Words are symbols; they are groups of letters that stand for, or represent, either a physical object or an idea. The word *table* can call to our minds a physical reality—an object with a flat, plane surface, usually supported by four perpendicular legs, and used for holding objects or for eating dinner. The word *love*, on the other hand, does not represent a physical object; it symbolizes the feeling of one person toward another. The combination of the letters *t-a-b-l-e* or *l-o-v-e* has no real meaning in itself; it is only when the combination of letters is associated with a particular object or idea that it becomes meaningful. Take, for example, *hoglag;* you can read it, you can pronounce it, but it has no meaning for you (it is a non-sense word). You have not built up any associations between this combination of letters and a physical object or idea. The major task involved in building vocabulary, then, is to increase the number of associations you can make between words (combinations of letters) and the physical objects or ideas they stand for.

The number of word-meaning associations you have acquired defines your vocabulary level. Adult vocabulary levels vary greatly—some adults are functionally illiterate, whereas others have attained an amazing mastery of words. The average adult knows the meanings of thousands of words. Since you, as a college student, are above the educational level of most adults, you should strive to develop your vocabulary beyond an average adult level.

There are a number of methods you can use to develop your vocabulary. Those presented in this part of the text are limited to those that are the most practical and immediately beneficial.

continued

continued

Chapter 19 is concerned with expanding both general and specialized (discipline-related) vocabulary. Suggestions are given for developing a sense of word awareness, and useful reference sources are discussed. A vocabulary card system for learning and remembering new words is also presented.

Chapter 20 presents a practical method of figuring out the meaning of an unknown word in a sentence, paragraph, or passage. By using the words around an unknown word, or its *context*, it is often possible to determine the meaning of the word. The chapter will focus on specific techniques for effectively using clues in the context to derive word meanings. It also discusses analyzing word parts—prefixes, roots, and suffixes—as a means of unlocking word meaning and of building vocabulary. Tables of common prefixes, roots, and suffixes are included.

19

Expanding Your Vocabulary

Use this chapter to:

1. *Learn how to expand your vocabulary.*
2. *Learn the best way to pick up new terminology introduced in a course.*

A strong vocabulary can be a valuable asset, both in college and later in your career. Considerable research evidence suggests that students who are the most successful in school are those with the largest vocabularies. Other research ties job advancement to vocabulary level. In one study, successful business executives were found to have the highest vocabulary of any occupational group.

Your vocabulary is also an important personal characteristic upon which people form first but lasting impressions of you. Your vocabulary reveals a lot about you and is particularly important in job interviews, oral class presentations, discussion group classes, and papers and exams that you write.

How would you rate your vocabulary? Many students answer either "good" or "terrible," but vocabulary knowledge is not an either/or, two-choice situation. Try the following quiz, which will help you realize that vocabulary ability is much more than "Either I know the word or I don't." Do not be concerned with how you score on the quiz; its purpose is to make a point, not to measure your vocabulary level.

VOCABULARY QUIZ _____

1. Read through the following list of words. If you can define the word, mark *D* in the space provided. If you've heard or seen the word before and have a general idea of what it means, mark *G* in the space. If the word is completely unfamiliar, mark *U*.

acrid	_____	interlude	_____
peripheral	_____	peregrine	_____
liquidate	_____	juror	_____
jaded	_____	litigation	_____
interior	_____	kumquat	_____
interject	_____		

2. How many different meanings can you think of for the word *run*?

_____

3. What does the word *cones* mean when used in a human anatomy and physiology course?

_____

4. Could a fugue be played at a concert?

_____

5. Does a cake baking in an oven have a fetid odor?

_____

6. You have probably heard the French expression *faux pas*. Can you define it?

_____

7. Use the word *credit* in a sentence in which it does not refer to college course work or a credit card.

_____

8. All of the following words mean "unable to do something." How do they differ in meaning? When would you use each?

     incapable   powerless   incompetent

_____

_____

Now check your answers in the answer key.

From this quiz, you should see that expanding your vocabulary involves much more than just looking up words you don't know. It involves learning new meanings and uses for words you already know. It involves taking vaguely familiar words that have an unclear or fuzzy meaning and sharpening their focus so you can put them to use. It involves learning specialized or technical meanings of everyday words for particular academic disciplines. Finally, it involves learning new words, both general and technical, that you have never heard or seen before.

GENERAL APPROACHES TO VOCABULARY EXPANSION

Expanding your vocabulary requires motivation, positive attitudes, and skills, the first of which is most important. To improve your vocabulary, you must be willing to work at it, spending both time and effort to notice and learn new words and meanings. Keep in mind that intent to remember is one of the principles of learning (see Chapter 3). Unless you intend to remember new words you hear or read, you will probably forget them. Your attitude toward reading will also influence the extent to which your vocabulary develops. If you enjoy reading and you read a broad range of subjects, you will frequently encounter new words. On the other hand, if you read only when required to do so, your exposure to words will be limited. Finally, your skills in using reference sources, in handling specialized terminology, and in organizing a system for learning new words will influence your vocabulary development.

The remainder of this chapter will focus on the skills you need to build your vocabulary. Before you continue, however, read the following suggestions for expanding your vocabulary.

Read Widely: One of the best ways to improve your vocabulary is by reading widely and diversely, sampling many different subjects and styles of writing. Through reading you encounter new words and new uses for familiar words. You also see words used in contexts that you had not previously considered.

College is one of the best places to begin reading widely. As you take elective and required courses, you are exposed to new ideas, as well as the words that express them clearly and succinctly. While you are a student, use the range of required and elective reading to expand your vocabulary.

Look for Five-Dollar Words to Replace One-Dollar Words: Some words in your vocabulary are general and vague. While they convey meaning, they are not precise, exact, or expressive. Try to replace these one-dollar words with five-dollar words that convey your meaning more directly. The word *good* is an example of a word that has a general, unclear meaning in the following sentence:

> The movie was so good, it was worth the high admission
> price.

Try substituting the following words in the preceding sentence: exciting, moving, thrilling, scary, heart-tugging. Notice how each of these gives more information than the word *good*. These are the types of words you should strive to use in your speech and writing.

Build a Sense of Word Awareness: Get in the habit of noticing new or unusual words when reading and listening. Learn to pay attention to words and notice those that seem useful. One of the first steps in expanding your vocabulary is to develop a sense of word awareness. At the college level, many new words you learn do not represent new concepts or ideas. Instead, they are more accurate or more descriptive replacements for simpler words and expressions that you already know and use. Once you begin to notice words, you will find that many of them automatically become part of your vocabulary.

Your instructors are a good resource for new words. Both in formal classroom lectures and in more casual discussions and conversations, many instructors use words that students understand but seldom use. You will hear new words and technical terms that are particular to a specific academic discipline.

Other good sources are textbooks, collateral reading assignments, and reference materials. If you are like most students, you understand many more words than you use in your own speech and writing. As you read, you will encounter many words with which you are vaguely familiar but which you cannot define. When you begin to notice these words, you will find that many of them become part of your vocabulary.

Consider Working with a Vocabulary Improvement Program: If you feel motivated to make improvements in a concentrated program of study, consider setting aside a block of time each week to work with a vocabulary improvement program. A variety of paperbacks on the market are designed to help you improve your vocabulary. The average bookstore should have several to choose from. Also, microcomputer programs, some in game formats, are available to strengthen general vocabulary. Check with your college's learning lab or library to see what is available.

USING REFERENCE SOURCES

Once you have developed a sense of word awareness and have begun to identify useful words to add to your vocabulary, the next step is to become familiar with the references you can use to expand your vocabulary.

Dictionaries: Which One to Buy

A common question students ask is, Which dictionary should I buy? There are several types of dictionaries, each with its own purpose and use. A pocket or paperback dictionary is an inexpensive, shortened version of a standard desk dictionary. It is small enough to carry with you to your classes and costs around five dollars.

A desk dictionary is a more complete, thorough dictionary. Although a pocket dictionary is convenient, it is also limited. A pocket edition lists about 55,000 words, whereas a standard desk edition lists up to 150,000 words. Also, the desk edition provides much more complete information about each word. Desk dictionaries are usually hardbound and cost over twenty dollars.

Several standard dictionaries are available in both desk and paperback editions. These include the *Random House Dictionary of the English Language, Webster's Collegiate Dictionary,* and the *American Heritage Dictionary of the English Language.*

Another type is the unabridged dictionary, which can be found in the reference section of any library. The unabridged edition provides the most complete information on each word in the English language.

Deciding whether to purchase a desk or pocket dictionary will depend on your needs as well as what you can afford. It would be ideal to have both. A pocket dictionary is sufficient for checking spelling and for looking up common meanings of unfamiliar words. To expand your vocabulary by learning additional meanings of words or to do any serious word study, you need a desk dictionary.

Uses of the Dictionary

Most students are familiar with the common uses of a dictionary: (1) to look up the meaning of words you don't know, and (2) to check the spelling of words. A dictionary can be useful in many other ways because it contains much more than just word meanings. For most entries you will find a pronunciation key, word origin, part(s) of speech, variant spellings, and synonyms. At the beginning or end of many desk dictionaries you will find information on language history and manuscript form, lists of symbols, and tables of weights and measures.

A dictionary is the basic tool for expanding your vocabulary. Get in the habit of consulting your dictionary whenever you see or hear a somewhat familiar word that you don't use and can't define precisely. Locate the word, read each meaning, and find the one that fits the way the word was used when you read or heard it. Use the vocabulary card system suggested later in this chapter to record and learn these words.

EXERCISE 1

Directions: *Use a desk dictionary to answer the following questions.*

1. What does the abbreviation *obs.* mean?

   _____

2. What does the symbol *c.* stand for?

   _____

3. How many meanings are listed for the word *fall?*

   _____

4. How is the word *phylloxera* pronounced? (Record its phonetic spelling.)

   _____

5. What is the plural spelling of *addendum?*

   _____

6. Can the word *protest* be used other than as a verb? If so, how?

   _____

7. The word *prime* can mean first or original. List some of its other meanings.

   _____

8. What does the French expression *savoir faire* mean?

   _____ Savoir - To know   faire - make _____

9. List three synonyms for the word *fault.*

   _____

10. List several words that are formed using the word *dream*.

Thesauruses

A thesaurus, or dictionary of synonyms, is a valuable reference for locating a precise, accurate, or descriptive word to fit a particular situation. Suppose you are searching for a more precise term for the expression *looked over*, as used in the following sentence:

My instructor looked over my essay exam.

The thesaurus lists the synonyms seen in Figure 19–1. Right away you can identify a number of words that are more specific than the phrase *looked over*. The next step, then, is to choose a word from the entry that most closely suggests the meaning you want to convey. The easiest way to do this is to "test out" or substitute various choices in your sentence to see which one is most appropriate; check the dictionary if you are not sure of a word's exact meaning.

Many students misuse the thesaurus by choosing words that do not fit the context. *Be sure to use words only when you are familiar with all their shades of meaning.* Remember, a misused word is often a more serious error than a wordy or imprecise expression.

The most widely used thesaurus was originally compiled by the English scholar Peter Roget and is known today as *Roget's Thesaurus;* it is readily available in an inexpensive paperback edition.

VERBS **12. see, behold, observe, view, witness, perceive, discern, spy,** espy, descry, **sight,** have in sight, make out, spot [coll.], twig [coll.], discover, notice, distinguish, recognize, ken [dial.], **catch sight of,** get a load of [slang, U.S.], take in, look on *or* upon, cast the eyes on *or* upon, **set** *or* **lay eyes on, clap eyes on** [coll.]; pipe, lamp, nail, peg [all slang]; **glimpse,** get *or* catch a glimpse of; see at a glance, see with half an eye; see with one's own eyes.

13. look, peer, direct the eyes, turn *or* bend the eyes, lift up the eyes; **peek, peep,** pry, take a peep *or* peek; play at peekaboo *or* bopeep; get an eyeful [coll., U.S.].

14. look at, take a look at, take a gander at [slang, U.S.], have a looksee [slang, U.S.], look on *or* upon, gaze at *or* upon; **watch, observe,** pipe [slang], **view, regard;** keep in sight *or* view, hold in view; look after, follow; spy upon.

15. scrutinize, survey, eye, ogle, contemplate, look over, give the eye [slang], give the once-over *or* double-O [slang, U.S.]; examine, **inspect** 484.31; size up [coll.], take one's measure [slang].

16. gaze, gloat, fix ~, fasten *or* rivet the eyes upon, keep the eyes upon; eye, ogle; **stare,** look [coll.], goggle, **gape, gawk** [coll.], gaup *or* gawp [dial.], gaze open-mouthed; crane, crane the neck; rubber, **rubberneck,** gander [all slang, U.S.]; look straight in the eye, look full in the face, hold one's eye *or* gaze, stare down; strain the eyes.

17. glare, glower, look daggers.

18. glance, glimpse, glint, cast a glance, glance at *or* upon, take a glance at, take a slant *or* squint at [slang].

19. look askance *or* **askant,** give a sidelong look, cut one's eye [slang], glime [dial.]; squint, look asquint; cock the eye; **look down one's nose** [coll.].

20. leer, leer the eye, look leeringly, give a leering look.

21. look away, avert the eyes; look another way, break one's eyes away, stop looking, turn away from, turn the back upon; drop one's eyes *or* gaze, cast one's eyes down; avoid one's gaze, cut eyes [coll.].

FIGURE 19-1 Sample Thesaurus Entry

EXERCISE 2

Directions: *Replace the underlined word or phrase in each sentence with a more descriptive word or phrase. Use a thesaurus to locate your replacement.*

1. When Sara learned that her sister had committed a crime, she was <u>sad</u>.
2. Compared to earlier chapters, the last two chapters in my chemistry text are <u>hard</u>.
3. The instructor spent the entire class <u>talking about</u> the causes of inflation and deflation.
4. The main character in the film was a <u>thin</u>, talkative British soldier.
5. We went to see the film that won the Academy Award for the best picture; it was <u>great</u>!

Subject Area Dictionaries

Many academic disciplines have specialized dictionaries that list important terminology used in that field. They give specialized meanings and suggest how and when to use a word. For the field of music there is *The New Grove Dictionary of Music and Musicians*, which lists and defines the specialized vocabulary of music. Other subject area dictionaries include *Taber's Cyclopedic Medical Dictionary*, *A Dictionary of Anthropology*, and *A Dictionary of Economics*.

Be sure to check if there is a subject area dictionary for your courses and area of specialization. Most of these dictionaries are available only in hardbound copies and are likely to be expensive. Many students, however, find them to be worth the initial investment. You will find that most libraries have copies of specialized dictionaries in their reference section.

EXERCISE 3

Directions: *List below each course you are taking this term. Using your campus library, find out if a subject area dictionary is available for each discipline. If so, list their titles below.*

Course   *Subject Area Dictionary*

_____   _____

_____   _____

_____   _____

_____   _____

LEARNING SPECIALIZED TERMINOLOGY

Each subject area can be said to have a language of its own—its own set of specialized words that makes it possible to describe and discuss accurately topics, principles and concepts, problems, and occurrences related to the subject area.

One of the first tasks facing both college instructors and textbook authors is the necessity of introducing and teaching the specialized language of an academic field. This task is especially important in introductory, first-semester courses in which a student studies or encounters the subject area for the first time. In an introduction to psychology course, for instance, you often start by learning the meaning of *psychology* itself—what the study is devoted to, what it encompasses, how it approaches situations, events, and problems. From that point you move on to learn related terms: *behavior, observations, hypothesis, experiment, variables, subjects,* and so forth.

Often the first few class lectures in a course are introductory. They are devoted to acquainting students with the nature and scope of the subject area and to introducing students to the specialized language.

The first few chapters within a textbook are introductory too. They are written to familiarize students with the subject of study and acquaint them with its specialized language. In one economics textbook, thirty-four new terms were introduced in the first two chapters (forty pages). In the first two chapters (twenty-eight pages) of a chemistry book, fifty-six specialized words were introduced. A sample of the words introduced in each text is given below. From these lists you can see that some of the words are words of common, everyday usage that take on a specialized meaning; others are technical terms used only in the subject area.

New Terms:
Economics Text

capital
ownership
opportunity cost
distribution
productive contribution
durable goods
economic system
barter
commodity money

New Terms:
Chemistry Text

matter
element
halogen
isotope
allotropic form
nonmetal
group (family)
burning
toxicity

EXERCISE 4 _____

Directions: *Turn to the biology sample textbook chapter in Appendix B, pages 412–425. Identify as many new terms as you can and record them in the space provided below.*

Total Specialized Words: _____

Examples of Specialized Vocabulary.

_____

_____

_____

_____

EXERCISE 5 _____

Directions: *Select any two textbooks you are currently using. In each, turn to the first chapter and check to see how many specialized terms are introduced. List the total number of terms. Then list several examples.*

Textbook 1: _____   *Textbook 2:* _____
                (title)   *(title)*

Total specialized words: _____   *Total specialized words:* _____

Examples of Specialized Words: *Examples of Specialized Words:*

1. _____   1. _____

2. _____   2. _____

3. _____   3. _____

4. _____   4. _____

5. _____   5. _____

Recognition of specialized terminology is only the first step in learning the language of a course. More important is the development of a systematic way of identifying, marking, recording, and learning the specialized terms. Since new terminology is introduced in both class lectures and course textbooks, it is necessary to develop a procedure for handling the specialized terms in each.

Specialized Terminology in Class Lectures

As a part of your note-taking system, develop a consistent way of separating new terms and definitions from other facts and ideas. You might circle or draw a box around each new term; or as you edit your notes (make revisions, changes, or additions to your notes after taking them), underline each new term in red; or mark "def." in the margin each time a definition is included. The mark or symbol you use is a matter of preference; the important thing is to find some way to identify definitions for further study. In addition, as part of your editing process, check each definition to be sure that it is complete and readable. Also, if you were not able to record any explanation or examples of new terms, add them as you edit. If the definitions you recorded are unclear, check with a friend or with your instructor. The last step in handling new terminology presented in class lectures is to organize the terms into a system for efficient study. One such system will be suggested later in this chapter.

Specialized Terminology in Textbooks

Textbook authors use various means to emphasize new terminology as they introduce it. In some texts, new vocabulary is printed in italics, boldface type, or colored print. Other texts indicate new terms in the margin of each page. Still the most common means of emphasis, however, is a "new terms" or "vocabulary list" at the beginning or end of each chapter.

While you are reading and underlining important facts and ideas, you should also mark new terminology. Be sure to mark and to separate definitions from other chapter content. (The mark or symbol you use is your choice.)

Occasionally in textbooks you may meet a new term that is not defined or for which the definition is unclear. In this case, check the glossary at the back of the book for the meaning of the word. Make a note of the meaning in the margin of the page.

The glossary, a comprehensive list of terms introduced throughout the text, is an aid that can help you learn new terminology. At the end of the course, when you have covered all or most of the chapters, the glossary can be used to review terminology. Use the glossary to test yourself; read an entry, cover up the meaning and try to remember it, then check to see if you were correct. As you progress through a course, however, the glossary is not an adequate study aid. A more organized, systematic approach to learning unfamiliar new terms is needed.

THE VOCABULARY CARD SYSTEM

Once you have identified and marked new terminology, both in your lecture notes and in your textbook, the next step is to organize the words for study and review. One of the most efficient and practical ways to accomplish this is the vocabulary card system. Use a $3'' \times 5''$ index card for each new term. Record the word on the front and the meaning on the back. If the word is particularly difficult, you might also include a guide to its pronunciation. Underneath the correct spelling of the word, indicate in syllables how the word sounds. For the word *eutrophication* (a term used in chemistry meaning "overnourishment"), you could indicate its pronunciation as "you-tro-fi-kay'-shun." On the back of the card, along with the meaning, you might want to include an example to help you remember the term more easily. A sample vocabulary card, front and back, is shown in Figure 19-2.

Front of Card

Back of Card

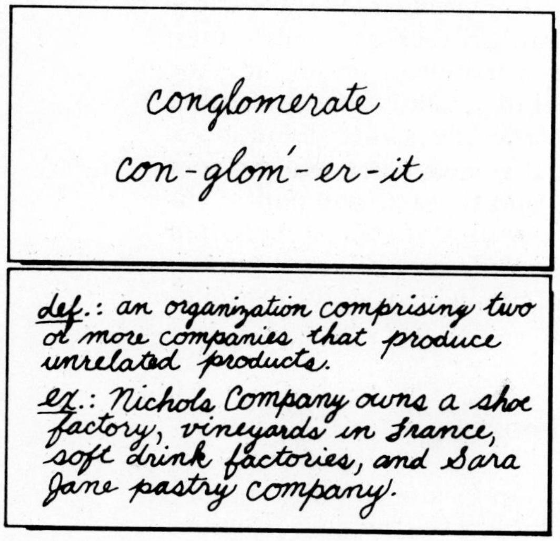

FIGURE 19-2   Sample Vocabulary Card

Use these cards for study, for review, and for testing yourself. Go through your pack of cards once, looking at the front and trying to recall the meaning on the back. Then reverse the procedure; look at the meanings and see if you can recall the terms. As you go through the pack in this way, sort the cards into two piles: words you know and words you don't know. The next time you review the cards, use only cards in the "don't know" pile for review. This sorting procedure will help you avoid wasting time reviewing words you have already learned. Continue to review the cards until you are satisfied that you have learned each new term. To prevent forgetting, it will be necessary to review the entire pack of cards periodically.

EXERCISE 6 ————————————————

Directions: *Select two or three sets of notes on a particular topic from any course you are taking. Prepare a set of vocabulary cards for the new terms introduced. Review and study the cards.*

EXERCISE 7 ————————————————

Directions: *Select one chapter from any of the textbooks you are currently using. Prepare a vocabulary card for each new term introduced in the chapter. Review and study the cards.*

SUMMARY

Vocabulary is an important personal asset that can directly contribute to your success in college and later in your career. Expanding your vocabulary is a relatively simple process and does not require large investments of time or money. All that is needed is a sense of word awareness, familiarity with information sources, and a system for learning new words.

Developing a sense of word awareness means paying attention to and noticing words. Good sources of new words, both general and specialized, include your instructors and textbooks, as well as collateral readings and reference sources. References that are useful in expanding your vocabulary include the dictionary, the thesaurus, and subject-area dictionaries. Specialized terminology, those words used within an academic discipline, are especially important to learn. While taking notes and reading textbooks, pay special attention to these words. Once general and specialized vocabulary have been identified, the vocabulary card system provides an easy and efficient way to learn each.

20

Using Context and Word Parts

Use this chapter to:

1. *Learn techniques to figure out the meaning of a word from the words around it.*

2. *Learn the types of clues that can suggest the meaning of a particular word in a sentence, paragraph, or passage.*

3. *Learn how to figure out word meanings using prefixes, roots, and suffixes.*

What should you do when you are reading a passage and you come to a word you don't know? If your instructor asked this question, you might reply, "I'd look the word up in the dictionary." And as you said this, you would know that in fact you don't often take the time to check the dictionary and were only giving an answer you thought your instructor wanted to hear and would agree with.

Actually, looking up a word in a dictionary is not the first thing to do when you meet a word you don't know. In fact, a dictionary is your last resort, something to turn to when all else fails. Instead, it is best to try to figure out the meaning of the word from the words around it in a sentence, paragraph, or passage that you are reading. Very often, among these surrounding words are various types of clues that make it possible to reason out the meaning of the unknown word. The words around an unknown word that contain clues to its meaning are referred to as the *context*. The clues themselves are called *context clues*. There are four basic types of context clues that you can use in determining word meanings in textbook material: *definition, example/illustration, contrast,* and *logic of the passage*.

If a word's context does not provide clues to its meaning, you might try breaking it into parts. Analyzing a word's parts, known as its *prefix, root,* and *suffix,* also provides clues to its meaning.

USING CONTEXT CLUES

Definition Context Clues

The most obvious type of context clue is a direct statement of the meaning of a new term by an author. Usually this occurs in textbook writing when the author is aware that the word is new to the reader and takes the time to give an accurate definition of the term. In the first chapter of a chemistry book, the term *chemical reaction* is defined:

A chemical reaction is an interaction involving different atoms, in which chemical bonds are formed, or broken, or both.[1]

Some writers signal you directly that they are presenting a definition with expressions such as "Mass is . . . " or "Anthropology can be defined as. . . . " Other writers, however, are less direct and obvious when they include a definition. Parentheses may be used to give a definition, partial definition, or synonym of a word, as in the following sentence:

Scientists measure temperature with two scales: the Celsius (or centigrade) scale (C), and the Kelvin (or thermodynamic) scale (K).[2]

Or an author may employ the parenthetical use of commas or dashes to include a brief definition or synonym within the sentence:

To begin with, he (Mendel) needed true-breeding plants, plants that showed little variation from generation to generation.[3]

or

The importance of bipedalism—two-leggedness—cannot be overestimated.[4]

Finally, an author may simply insert a synonym directly within the sentence:

Another central issue, that of the right of a state to withdraw or secede from the Union, was simply avoided.[5]

EXERCISE 1 ───────────────

Directions: *In each sentence, locate the part of the sentence that gives a definition or synonym of the underlined word. Underline this portion of the sentence.*

1. A democracy is a form of government in which the people effectively participate.[6]
2. The amount of heat that it takes to melt one gram of any substance at its melting point is called the heat of fusion.[7]
3. Linoleic acid is an essentially fatty acid necessary for growth and skin integrity in infants.[8]
4. When a gas is cooled, it condenses (changes to a liquid) at its condensation point.[9]
5. But neither a monkey nor an ape has thumbs long enough or flexible enough to be completely opposable, able to reach comfortably to the tips of all the other fingers, as is required for our delicate yet strong precision grip.[10]

Example/Illustration Context Clues

Authors frequently explain their ideas and concepts by giving specific, concrete examples or illustrations. Many times, when an example is given that illustrates, or explains, a new term, you can figure out the meaning of the term from the example. Suppose, for instance, that you frequently confuse the terms *fiction* and *nonfiction* and you are given the following assignment by your instructor: *Select any nonfiction book and write a critical review; you can choose from a wide range of books such as an autobiography, sports, "how-to" manuals, commentaries on historical periods, or current consumer-awareness paperbacks.* From the examples given, you can easily see that *nonfiction* refers to books that are factual, or true.

Writers sometimes give you an advance warning or signal that they are going to present an example or illustration. Phrases that signal an example or illustration to follow include *for example, for instance, to illustrate, such as, included are*, and so on. Read the following examples:

Some everyday, common <u>solutions</u> include gasoline, antifreeze, soda water, seawater, vodka, and ammonia.

Specifically, management of a New York bank developed a strategic plan to increase its customers by making them see banks as offering a large variety of services rather than just a few <u>specialized services</u> (cashing checks, putting money into savings accounts, and making loans).[11]

EXERCISE 2 _____

Directions: *Read each sentence and write a definition or synonym for each underlined word. Use the illustration/example context clue to help you determine word meanings.*

1. Since then a near <u>symbiotic</u> relationship has developed between the player and the fan in the stands watching him—that phrase "I just die when the Chiefs (or the Rams, or the Mets, or whatever)" . . . the fan's forefinger raised to denote that his team (and he) are Number One, the "we did it, we did it," and the self-satisfied smiles on the faces of the people coming down the stadium ramps after their teams have won.[12]

   Easy understood symbol

2. The play contained a variety of <u>morbid</u> events: the death of a young child, the suicide of her mother, and the murder of an older sister.

   Sicking horrifying, decusting death

3. Psychological disturbances are sometimes traceable to a particular <u>trauma</u> in childhood. For example, the death of a parent may produce long-range <u>psychological effects</u>.

   traumatic experience, unexepected

4. To <u>substantiate</u> his theory, Watson offered experimental evidence,

case study reports, testimony of patients, and a log of observational notes.

To back-up, enforce

5. There are many <u>phobias</u> that can seriously influence human behavior; the two most common are claustrophobia (fear of confined spaces) and acrophobia (fear of heights).

fears in general

6. <u>Homogeneous</u> groups, such as classes of all boys, or social organizations of high-IQ people, or country clubs of wealthy families, have particular roles and functions.

specific group of ~~humans~~ , classes

Contrast Context Clues

It is sometimes possible to figure out the meaning of an unknown word from a word or phrase in the context that has an opposite meaning. To use a simple example, in the sentence "Sam was thin, but George was obese," a contrasting or opposite description is set up between George and Sam. The word *but* signals that an opposite or contrasting idea is to follow. By knowing the meaning of *thin* and knowing that George is the opposite of thin, you figure out that *obese* means "not thin," or *fat*.

Most often when an opposite or contrasting meaning is given, there is a signal word or phrase in the sentence which indicates a change in the direction of the thought. Most commonly used are these signal words or phrases: *on the other hand, however, while, but, nevertheless, on the contrary*. Note the following example.

The Federalists, from their <u>pessimistic</u> viewpoint, believed the Constitution could protect them by its procedures, while the more positive Anti-Federalists thought of the Constitution as the natural rights due to all people.

In the preceding example, if you did not know the meaning of the word *pessimistic*, you could figure it out because a word appears later in the sentence that gives you a clue. The sentence is about the beliefs of two groups, the Federalists and the Anti-Federalists. The prefix *anti-* tells you that they hold opposite or differing views. If the Federalists are described as "pessimistic" and their views are opposite those of the Anti-Federalists, who are described as "more positive," you realize that *pessimistic* means the opposite of positive, or *negative*.

Here is another example:

Most members of Western society marry only one person at a time, but in other cultures <u>polygamy</u> is common and acceptable.

In this sentence, by the contrast established between Western society and other cultures, you can infer that *polygamy* refers to the practice of marriage to more than one person at a time.

EXERCISE 3 _____

Directions: *Read each sentence and write a definition or synonym for each underlined word. Use the contrast context clue to help you determine the meaning of the word.*

1. The philosopher was <u>vehement</u> in his objections to the new grading system, while the more practical historian, on the other hand, expressed his views calmly and quietly.

   _____ forceful loud _____

2. The mayor was very <u>dogmatic</u> about government policy, while the assistant mayor was more lenient and flexible in his interpretations.

   _____ strict, ridiget _____

3. Instead of evaluating each possible solution when it was first proposed, the committee decided it would <u>defer</u> judgment until all possible solutions had been proposed.

   _____ delayed _____

4. The <u>tenacious</u> islanders responded reluctantly to the government compromise on land settlement, whereas the immigrants agreed immediately to the government offer.

   _____ hold on _____

5. Cultures vary in the types of behavior that are considered socially acceptable. In one culture, a man may be <u>ostracized</u> for having more than one wife, while in other cultures, a man with many wives is an admired and respected part of the group.

   _____ not admired + not respected, shout-out _____

Context Clues in the Logic of a Passage

One of the most common ways in which context provides clues about the meaning of an unknown word is through logic or general reasoning about the content of a sentence, or about the relationship of ideas within a sentence. Suppose that before you read the following sentence you did not know the meaning of the word *empirical*.

Some of the questions now before us are <u>empirical</u> issues that require evidence directly bearing on the question.[13]

From the way *empirical* is used in the sentence, you know that an empirical issue is one that requires direct evidence, and from that information you can infer or reason that *empirical* has something to do with proof or supporting facts.

Now suppose that you did not know the meaning of the term *cul-de-sac* before reading the following sentence:

A group of animals hunting together can sometimes maneuver

the hunted animal into a <u>cul-de-sac</u>: out onto a peak of high
land, into a swamp or river, or into a gully from which it cannot escape.[14]

From the mention of the places into which a hunted animal can be
maneuvered—a gully, a peak, or a swamp—you realize that the hunters
have cornered the animal and that *cul-de-sac* means a blind alley or a situation from which there is no escape.

EXERCISE 4

Directions: *Read each of the following sentences and write a synonym or
definition for each underlined word or term. Look for logic of the passage context
clues to help you figure out the meaning of each.*

1. The lecturer stumbled frequently and misquoted his sources;
   however, he <u>redeemed</u> himself by injecting humor and sarcasm into
   the lecture.

   _____

2. The two philosophical theories were <u>incompatible</u>: one
   acknowledged the existence of free will; the other denied it.

   _____

3. When the judge pronounced the sentence, the convicted criminal
   shouted <u>execrations</u> at the jury.

   _____

4. The police officer was <u>exonerated</u> by a police review panel of any
   possible misconduct or involvement in a case of police bribery.

   _____

5. The editor would not allow the paper to go to press until certain
   passages were <u>expunged</u> from an article naming individuals involved
   in a political scandal.

   _____

EXERCISE 5

Directions: *Each of the following sentences contains an underlined word or
phrase whose meaning can be determined from the context. Underline the part of
the sentence that contains the clue to the meaning of the underlined words. Then,
in the blank below, identify what type of context clue you used.*

1. <u>Separation of powers</u> is the principle that the powers of government
   should be separated and put in the care of different parts of the
   government.[15]

   _____

2. Samples of moon rock have been analyzed by <u>uranium dating</u> and found to be about 4.6 billion years old, or about the same age as the earth.[16]

_____

3. Like horses, human beings have a variety of <u>gaits</u>; they amble, stride, jog, and sprint.[17]

_____

4. In the past, <u>malapportionment</u> (large differences in the populations of congressional districts) was common in many areas of the country.[18]

_____

5. Tremendous <u>variability</u> characterizes the treatment of the mentally retarded during the medieval era, ranging from treatment as innocents to being tolerated as fools to persecution as witches.[19]

_____

EXERCISE 6 _____

Directions: _Read each of the following paragraphs. For each underlined word, use context to determine its meaning. Write a synonym or brief definition in the space provided._

1. Popular writings on mental disorders are being continually <u>supplemented</u> by dramatic presentations in the theaters, in the movies, and on television. In addition, the daily press regularly carries accounts of the behavior of seemingly demented persons and often seeks to lend <u>legitimacy</u> to its accounts by <u>citing</u> commentary by mental health professionals, who more often than not have never examined the offender. Such "armchair" diagnoses are probably useless, or worse, in the majority of cases. We seem to have an <u>insatiable</u> curiosity about bizarre behavior, and most of us <u>avidly</u> seek and devour the newspaper, radio, and TV accounts available on the subject. Though we surely learn some things from these accounts, we also may be narrowing our perspective: such accounts are written for the popular media; they are typically simplified and can appear to give answers when, in fact, they barely succeed in posing the correct questions.

   –Coleman, _Abnormal Psychology and Modern Life_, p. 10.

   a. supplemented _____

   b. legitimacy _____

   c. citing _____

   d. insatiable _____

   e. avidly _____

2. **EVOLUTIONISM**

A central topic in many areas of psychology is the contributions of *nature*, or hereditary influences, and *nurture*, or environmental influences to behavioral development. This issue has its origins in the evolutionary theory developed by Charles Darwin. His theory maintains three principles: (a) all species evolved over millions of years; (b) differences between species are because of hereditary differences; and (c) differences within a species are related to differences among its members in terms of their individual differences in fitness. Those most fit to adapt to environmental changes and challenges passed on their genes and reproduced more of their kind. These ideas were based on Darwin's careful observations of species throughout the world during his five-year journey on the ship *Beagle* and were presented in *Origin of Species* (1859) and *Descent of Man* (1871).

Evolutionary theory challenged the doctrine of *creationism*, which asserted that all species were created by an act of God, with humans being a special case of direct divine creation. Just as Copernicus' theory of the universe moved the earth out of the center of the solar system, Darwin's theory pushed man and woman out of the center arena of existence by giving them a common ancestry with animals. Darwin's doctrine further shook notions of homo sapien supremacy by dragging human origin down from the heavens into the muck of evolutionary slime.

–Zimbardo, *Psychology and Life*, p. 13.

a. nature _____

b. nurture _____

c. maintains _____

d. evolved _____

e. adapt _____

f. creationism _____

g. divine _____

h. arena _____

3. Scarcity is not the same as poverty. Even the rich have to reckon with scarcity. The wealthy individual who can afford to give millions of dollars to a favorite charity or to endow a university with a building that will bear his or her name must still choose among benefactions. For most of us the problem of choice is far more urgent. We schedule our limited time so that each activity yields the greatest possible reward—hours for economics and chemistry and minutes for errands. We allocate our limited funds so that our expenditures yield the greatest possible usefulness—gym shoes and bus fare this week, but the laundry will have to wait.

–Chisholm, *Principles of Economics*, p. 20.

a. endow _____

b. benefactions _____

c. allocate _____

d. expenditures _____

4. That Darwin was the founder of the modern theory of evolution is well known. In order to understand the meaning of his theory, however, it is useful to look briefly at the intellectual climate in which it was <u>formulated</u>. Aristotle (384–322 B.C.), the first great biologist, believed that all living things could be arranged in a hierarchy. This hierarchy became known as the <u>Scala Naturae</u>, or ladder of nature, in which the simplest creatures had a humble position on the bottommost rung, mankind occupied the top, and all other organisms had their proper places between. Until the end of the last century, many biologists believed in such a natural <u>hierarchy</u>. But whereas to Aristotle living organisms had always existed, the later biologists (at least those of the Occidental world) believed, in <u>harmony</u> with the teachings of the Old Testament, that all living things were the products of a <u>divine</u> creation. They believed, moreover, that most were created for the service or pleasure of mankind. Indeed, it was pointed out, even the lengths of day and night were planned to <u>coincide</u> with the human need for sleep.

–Curtis, *Biology*, p. 1.

a. formulated _____

b. *Scala Naturae* _____

c. hierarchy _____

d. harmony _____

e. divine _____

f. coincide _____

ANALYZING WORD PARTS

Mark and Elaine were taking a course in biology. While walking to class one day, Mark complained to Elaine, "I'll never be able to learn all this vocabulary!" Does this complaint sound familiar? They agreed that they needed some system, since learning each new word separately would be nearly impossible. Have you felt the same way in some of your courses?

The purpose of this section is to present a system of vocabulary learning. This system works for specific courses in which a great deal of new terminology is presented as well as for building your overall, general vocabulary. The approach is based on analyzing word parts. Many words in the English language are made up of word parts called *prefixes*, *roots*, and *suffixes*. Think of these as beginnings, middles, and endings of words. These word parts have specific meanings and when added together can help you figure out the meaning of the word as a whole. Let's begin with a few words from biology:

poikilotherm   homeotherm   endotherm   ectotherm

Each of these terms appeared in the biology sample textbook chapter in Appendix B on temperature regulation in various life forms. You could learn the definition of each term separately, but learning would be easier and more meaningful if you could see the relationship between the terms.

Each of the four words has as its root *-therm*, which means heat. The meaning of the prefix, or beginning, of each word is given below:

poikilo- = changeable
homeo- = same or constant
endo- = within
ecto- = outside

Knowing these meanings can help you determine the meaning of each word:

poikilotherm = organism with variable body temperature (i.e., cold-blooded)
homeotherm = organism with stable body temperature (i.e., warm-blooded)
ectotherm = organism that regulates its temperature by taking in heat from the environment or giving off heat to the environment
endotherm = organism that regulates its temperature internally

When you first start using this method you may not feel as if you're making progress; in this case you had to learn four prefixes and one root to figure out four words. However, what may not be obvious as yet is that these prefixes will help unlock the meaning of numerous other words, not only in the field of biology but also in related fields and in general vocabulary usage. Here are a few examples of words using each of the above word parts:

therm-	*poikilo-*	*homeo- (homo-)*	*ecto-*	*endo-*
thermal	poikilocyte	homeostasis	ectoparasite	endocytosis
thermodynamics	poikilocytosis	homogeneous	ectoderm	endoderm

The remainder of this section will focus on commonly used prefixes, roots, and suffixes that are used in a variety of academic disciplines. In various combinations, these will unlock the meanings of thousands of words. For example, more than ten thousand words begin with the prefix *non-*.

Once you have mastered the prefixes, roots, and suffixes given in this chapter, you should begin to identify word parts that are commonly used in each of your courses. For example, a partial list made by one student for his psychology course is shown in Figure 20-1. Keep these lists in your course notebooks or use index cards, as described later in this chapter.

Psychology

neuro- nerves, nervous
system
phob- fear
auto- self

path- feeling,
suffering
homo- same
hetero- different

FIGURE 20-1   Sample List of Prefixes

Before learning specific prefixes, roots, and suffixes, it is useful to be aware of the following:

1. In most cases, a word is built upon at least one root.
2. Words can have more than one prefix, root, or suffix.
    a. Words can be made up of two or more roots (*geo / logy*).
    b. Some words have two prefixes (*in / sub / ordination*).
    c. Some words have two suffixes (beauti / *ful / ly*).
3. Words do not always have a prefix and a suffix.
    a. Some words have neither a prefix nor a suffix (read).
    b. Others have a suffix but no prefix (read / *ing*).
    c. Others have a prefix but no suffix (*pre* / read).
4. Roots may change in spelling as they are combined with suffixes. Some common variations are noted on page 337.
5. Sometimes you may identify a group of letters as a prefix or root but find that it does not carry the meaning of the prefix or root. For example, in the word *internal*, the letters *inter* should not be confused with the prefix *inter-*, meaning "between." Similarly, the letters *mis* in the word *missile* are part of the root and are not the prefix *mis-*, which means "wrong" or "bad."

Prefixes

Prefixes, appearing at the beginning of many English words, alter or modify the meaning of the root to which they are connected. Table 20-1 lists common prefixes grouped according to meaning.

EXERCISE 7 _____

Directions: *Use the prefixes listed in Table 20-1 to help determine the meaning of each of the underlined words in the following sentences. Write a brief definition or synonym for each. If you are unfamiliar with the root, you may need to check a dictionary.*

1. The instances of <u>abnormal</u> behavior reported in the mass media are likely to be extreme.

    _____

    _____

TABLE 20-1 Common Prefixes

Prefix	Meaning	Sample Word
Prefixes indicating direction, location, or placement		
circum-	around	circumference
com-, col-, con-	with, together	compile
de-	away, from	depart
ex-/extra-	from, out of, former	ex-wife
hyper-	over, excessive	hyperactive
inter-	between	interpersonal
intro-/intra-	within, into, in	introduction
mid-	middle	midterm
post-	after	post-test
pre-	before	premarital
re-	back, again	review
retro-	backward	retrospect
sub-	under, below	submarine
super-	above, extra	supercharge
tele-	far	telescope
trans-	across, over	transcontinental
Prefixes referring to amount or number		
bi-	two	bimonthly
equi-	equal	equidistant
micro-	small	microscope
mono-	one	monocle
multi-	many	multipurpose
poly-	many	polygon
semi-	half	semicircle
tri-	three	triangle
uni-	one	unicycle
Prefixes meaning "not" (negative)		
a-, an-, ab-	not	asymmetrical
anti-	against	antiwar
contra-	against, opposite	contradict
dis-	apart, away, not	disagree
mis-	wrong, bad	misunderstand
non-	not	nonfiction
pseudo-	false	pseudoscientific
un-	not	unpopular

2. The two theories of language development are not fundamentally incompatible, as originally thought.

   _____

3. When threatened, the ego resorts to irrational protective measures, which are called defense mechanisms.

   _____

4. Freud viewed the interplay among the id, ego, and superego as of critical importance in determining behavioral patterns.

   _____

5. The long-term effects of continuous drug use are irreversible.

   _____

EXERCISE 8 _____

Directions: *Write a synonym or brief definition for each of the following underlined words. Check a dictionary if the root is unfamiliar.*

1. a substandard performance _____

2. to transcend everyday differences _____

3. telecommunications equipment _____

4. a hypercritical person _____

5. a retroactive policy _____

6. superconductive metal _____

7. extracurricular activities _____

8. postoperative nursing care _____

9. a blood transfusion _____

10. antisocial behavior _____

11. to misappropriate funds _____

12. a microscopic organism _____

13. a monotonous speech _____

14. a pseudointellectual essay _____

15. a polysyllabic word _____

Roots

Roots carry the basic or core meaning of a word. Hundreds of root words are used to build words in the English language. Thirty of the most common and most useful are listed in Table 20-2. Knowing the meanings of these roots will assist you in unlocking the meanings of many words. For example, if you know that the root *dic-* or *dict-* means "tell" "say," then you would have a clue to the meanings of such words as *predict* (to tell what will happen in the future), *contradiction* (a statement that is contrary or opposite), and *diction* (wording or manner of speaking).

TABLE 20-2   Common Roots

Root	Meaning	Sample Word
aster, astro	star	astronaut
aud, audit	hear	audible
bio	life	biology
cap	take, seize	captive
chron(o)	time	chronology
corp	body	corpse
cred	believe	incredible
dict, dic	tell, say	predict
duc, duct	lead	introduce
fact, fac	make, do	factory
geo	earth	geophysics
graph	write	telegraph
log, logo, logy	study, thought	psychology
mit, miss	send	dismiss
mort, mor	die, death	immortal
path	feeling, disease	sympathy
phono	sound, voice	telephone
photo	light	photosensitive
port	carry	transport
scop	seeing	microscope
scrib, script	write	inscription
sen, sent	feel	insensitive
spec, spic, spect	look, see	retrospect
tend, tent, tens	stretch, strain	tension
terr, terre	land, earth	territory
theo	god	theology
ven, vent	come	convention
vert, vers	turn	invert
vis, vid	see	invisible
voc	call	vocation

Directions: *Write a synonym or brief definition for each of the underlined words. Consult Tables 20-1 and 20-2 as necessary.*

1. a <u>monotheistic</u> religion _____

2. a <u>subterranean</u> tunnel _____

3. a <u>chronicle</u> of events _____

4. a <u>conversion</u> chart _____

5. <u>exportation</u> policies _____

6. leading an <u>introspective</u> life _____

7. to <u>speculate</u> on the results _____

8. <u>sensuous</u> music _____

9. a <u>versatile</u> performance _____

10. an <u>incredible</u> explanation _____

11. infant <u>mortality</u> rates _____

12. <u>tensile</u> strength of a cable _____

13. a <u>vociferous</u> crowd _____

14. a logical <u>deduction</u> _____

15. a <u>corporate</u> earnings report _____

Suffixes

Suffixes are word endings that often change the part of speech of a word. For example, adding the suffix -*y* to a word changes it from a noun to an adjective and shifts the meaning—for example, *cloud, cloudy*. Often several different words can be formed from a single root word with the addition of different suffixes. Here are a few examples:

Root: *Class*
      classify
      classification
      classic

Common suffixes grouped according to meaning are listed in Table 20-3.

EXERCISE 10 _____

Directions: *Write a synonym or brief definition of each of the underlined words. Consult a dictionary if necessary.*

1. terrorist activities _____

2. a graphic description _____

3. a materialistic philosophy _____

4. immunity to disease _____

5. impassable road conditions _____

6. a speech impediment _____

7. intangible property _____

8. instinctive behavior _____

9. interrogation techniques _____

10. the communist sector _____

11. obvious frustration _____

12. global conflicts _____

13. in deference to _____

14. piteous physical ailments _____

15. Supreme Court nominee _____

EXERCISE 11 _____

Directions: *The following list of terms were taken from the psychology sample textbook chapter Appendix A. Write a brief definition of each. Consult the sample chapter or a dictionary, if necessary.*

1. psychosocial model of health _____

2. psychosomatic medicine _____

3. dysfunctional behavior _____

4. nonadaptive behavior _____

5. posttraumatic stress disorder _____

6. retrospective studies _____

7. prospective studies _____

8. cognitive restructuring _____

9. reappraising stressors _____

10. biofeedback techniques _____

TABLE 20-3 Common Suffixes

Suffix	Sample Word
Suffixes that refer to a state, condition, or quality	
-able	touchable
-ance	assistance
-ation	confrontation
-ence	reference
-ic	aerobic
-ible	tangible
-ion	discussion
-ity	superiority
-ive	permissive
-ment	amazement
-ness	kindness
-ous	jealous
-ty	loyalty
-y	creamy
Suffixes that mean "one who"	
-ee	employee
-eer	engineer
-er	teacher
-ist	activist
-or	editor
Suffixes that mean "pertaining to" or "referring to"	
-al	autumnal
-ship	friendship
-hood	brotherhood
-ward	homeward

SUMMARY

One of the easiest and most practical ways of determining the meaning of an unknown word is to study carefully how the word is used in the sentence, paragraph, or passage in which it is found. The context—the words around an unknown word—frequently contains various types of clues that help you figure out the meaning of the unknown word. There are four basic types of context clues that are useful in determining the meaning of words in factual material. These types of clues are described in the following list:

> *Definition:* A brief definition or synonym of an unknown word may be included in the sentence in which the word is used.

Example/illustration: Writers may explain their words and ideas by giving specific, concrete examples of them. When an example is given to illustrate or explain a new term or concept, it is sometimes possible to figure out the meaning of an unknown word from the example.

Contrast: The meaning of an unknown word can sometimes be determined from a word or phrase in the context that has the opposite meaning.

Logic of the passage: The meaning of an unknown word can sometimes be determined through reasoning or applying logic to the content of the sentence or paragraph.

Learning word parts—prefixes, roots, and suffixes—is a system of vocabulary learning. This approach enables you to figure out the meaning of an unknown word by analyzing the meanings of its parts. Tables of common prefixes, roots, and suffixes were presented in the chapter.

PART SEVEN

Reading Efficiency Techniques

Most adults, including college students, are inefficient readers: They do not make the best possible use of their reading time, and they do not apply skills that would enable them to read faster. They read all types of material at the same rate, and they are always careful to read everything. Many adults have the capacity to read twice as fast as they usually read.

The purpose of this part of the book is to discuss situations in which you could read faster and to present techniques that will enable you to do so. Chapter 21 discusses the factors that affect how fast you read and then suggests reading rates for four different categories of reading. You are given an opportunity to measure your own reading rate for each category. Finally, the chapter offers suggestions on how to read faster.

Chapter 22 considers situations in which it is not necessary to read everything and offers specific techniques for selective reading. The chapter suggests a procedure for *skimming*—getting an overview, or general picture, of an article—and a procedure for *scanning*—rapidly looking through material to locate a particular piece of information.

21

Improving Your Reading Rate and Flexibility

> **Use this chapter to:**
> 1. *Find out how fast you read and how your rate compares to that of other college students.*
> 2. *Learn how to adjust your rate to suit your purpose and the material you are reading.*
> 3. *Find out how to increase your overall reading rate.*

Reading rate, the speed at which you read, is measured in words per minute (wpm). Do you read 100 wpm, 200 wpm, 300 wpm, 400 wpm? At what rate should you be reading? Are you a fast or a slow reader? You should be able to read at 100, 200, 300, and 400 wpm; you should be both a fast *and* a slow reader. These answers may seem strange or even contradictory, but they are nevertheless true. Your reading rate should change in different situations and with different types of reading material. There are a number of variables that determine what your reading rate should be on any particular printed page. The purpose of this chapter is to present these variables that affect reading rate and to show you how to adjust, or vary, your reading rate to deal with them. In this chapter you will also measure your reading rate and learn how to increase it.

FACTORS THAT INFLUENCE READING RATE

There are literally hundreds of factors that influence how fast you read. These variables also affect your comprehension of what you read. Factors that influence both reading rate and comprehension can be divided into three general categories: text characteristics, reader characteristics, and reader's purpose. *Text characteristics* are the features of the printed material that influence how easy or difficult it is to read. The skills and traits of a person that determine or affect rate and comprehension are called *reader characteristics. Reader's purpose* refers to the reason the material is read and the level of comprehension needed.

Text Characteristics

The way writers write, the words they use, how they put words together, and how clearly they can express ideas all contribute to how easy it is to read a passage and how fast it can be read.

EXPERIMENT _____

Try the following experiment. First, read each of the following passages:

PASSAGE 1

War is usually thought of as a political conflict. However, there are many causes of this political conflict. It may arise from economic problems. Or it may stem from conflicts between racial or ethnic groups. Cultural differences between countries may also contribute to political conflict. Individual personalities of leaders are also involved in wars. To study war, then, we must study many different fields such as economics, history, and psychology.

PASSAGE 2

In studying the fourteen theories of the origins of war which follow, the reader will discover that while war is typically regarded as a political phenomenon, it springs not only from political events, but from economic motives, from ethnic and racial conflict, from cultural and anthropological differences, from individual personalities and sometimes from psychopathology. A comprehensive study of the causes of war necessarily carries one into the literatures of politics, economics, history, philosophy, psychiatry, social psychology, anthropology, psychology and other pertinent fields of study. In keeping with the central concept of this book, then, this chapter seeks not to present a single comprehensive theory of the causes of war, but a comparative and comprehensive review of the several principal theories.

–Jones, *The Logic of International Relations*, p. 397

Which passage seemed easier? The passages are approximately the same length, but they differ greatly in many other features—primarily characteristics that contribute to difficulty. Passage 1 is written at a fourth-grade level, while Passage 2 is at a college level.

Look again at each passage; what features of the writing make Passage 1 easier or Passage 2 more difficult? Try to list below as many differences as you can:

Passage 1   *Passage 2*

_____   _____

_____   _____

_____   _____

_____   _____

There are a great many differences between those two passages. Some of the obvious differences are:

1. Passage 1 uses short, relatively simple sentences. The words are short; the vocabulary is easy. The passage contains clear examples, and the terms are clearly defined.
2. In Passage 2, the sentences are longer and more complex. The words are longer and more difficult. The passage is more detailed and complicated, and words with specialized, technical meanings are used.

Linguists, people who study language, could list many other differences between the two passages. Very technical or subtle features of language, called linguistic variables, have been found to affect how easily a passage may be understood. Linguistic variables include the total number of syllables, the number of times a word is repeated, and the arrangement of words within a sentence. However, some variables have a greater effect than others and are more useful to note; these are sentence length, vocabulary difficulty, and the sophistication of the concepts being discussed.

Sentence Length: A passage with very long sentences can make reading more difficult and will force you to read more slowly. Try reading the following sentence; notice how the length of the sentence seems to hold you back and slow you down.

> Caught in global recession and inflation, forced by Washington to revalue their currency in a direction injurious to their prosperity, and once again conscious of their vulnerability to foreign economic decisions, the Japanese also saw domestic capital flow out to lucrative investment opportunities elsewhere.

> —Jones, *The Logic of International Relations,* p. 99

Vocabulary: A passage with difficult or unfamiliar vocabulary can have the same effect—understanding becomes difficult or impossible, and your rate of reading is extremely slow. Try the following:

> The liberal-cynical criminologist is skeptical about the perfectability of crime control efforts, and locates criminogenic forces in the basic structure and institutions of society, but he still retains a belief in the continued viability of American society in its present form.

> —Barlow, *Introduction to Criminology,* p. 26

Ideas and Concepts: In addition to these mechanical features of language, ideas and concepts also affect difficulty. Even when written in fairly simple language, an article may discuss complicated ideas or follow a sophisticated line of reasoning. In the following sample, you will notice that, although the language used is clear and direct, a difficult concept is discussed.

> The whole universe may have an overall curvature. If it is negatively curved, it is open-ended and extends without limit; if it is positively curved, it closes in on itself. The surface of the earth, for example, forms a closed curvature; so that if you travel along a geodesic, you come back to your starting point.

Similarly, if the universe were positively curved, it would be closed; so that if you could look infinitely into space through an ideal telescope, you would see the back of your own head! (This is assuming that you waited a long enough time or that light traveled infinitely fast.)

–Hewitt, *Conceptual Physics*, p. 587.

While you can do nothing to change the characteristics of writing that affect difficulty, you can change how you approach the writing. You can deliberately slow down if you encounter a passage with long, complicated sentences or an article that presents difficult concepts or complicated arguments. Or you can deliberately speed up when you find a passage with simple, unsophisticated vocabulary. In other words, you can *adjust* your rate to the characteristics of the reading material.

Reader's Characteristics

A second set of factors that influences how fast you are able to read and how well you comprehend is related to you, the reader. Here is only a partial list of the many things about you that affect your reading speed.

Your Vocabulary Level: If your general reading vocabulary level is high, you will not encounter many words that you do not know, and your speed will be unaffected. On the other hand, if your reading vocabulary is weak and you meet several unknown words in every paragraph, you will find that you lose speed as you pause to look for context clues to their meaning.

Your Comprehension Ability: Your level of skill in understanding sentences and paragraphs will affect your rate. If you have trouble locating the core parts of a sentence or cannot identify the topic, main idea, and details of a paragraph, then your rate will suffer as you spend time looking for and understanding these elements.

Your Physical State: How you feel physically affects both rate and comprehension. If you are extremely tired, or just recovering from the flu, you will not be able to perform at your peak level. Concentration may become a problem, or you may not be able to force yourself to stay awake. If you are hungry, or if the room is extremely hot or cold, your reading performance may also be affected.

Your State of Mind: Just as your physical state can affect your reading rate, so can your mental or emotional state. If you are depressed or worried, you may not be able to concentrate easily; if you are excited or anxious about something, your mental state may not be conducive to effective reading.

Your Interest in the Material: Your interest in what you are reading influences how fast and with what degree of comprehension you read. If you are reading about a topic that interests you, you are likely to read faster and with more understanding than if you are reading about a subject in which you have little or no interest.

Your Background Knowledge: The amount of knowledge you have of a topic partially determines how well you will be able to read about it. Suppose you are assigned to read a passage taken from the middle of an introductory botany textbook. If you have completed a course in botany, the passage will probably be understandable and easy enough to read. On the other hand, if you have never studied botany, the passage will be extremely difficult and confusing; it will be necessary to read very slowly, and you might have to stop to look up any unfamiliar terms and concepts.

Reader's Purpose

Your purpose for reading is an important factor related to both rate and comprehension. If you are reading a magazine article for enjoyment, your purpose is different from when you are reading a textbook chapter to prepare for an exam. If you are paging through the newspaper, your purpose differs from your purpose when you are reading a poem for your English literature class.

Your reading rate is determined partly by your purpose for reading. There are four basic types of reading, ranging from an extremely slow analysis to an extremely rapid overview of the material. Each type is related to a specific kind of material, has a definite purpose, and is done at a certain speed. These are summarized in Table 21-1.

TABLE 21-1 Types of Reading

Method of Reading	Range of Speed	Purpose in Reading	Types of Material
Analytical	Under 100 wpm	Detailed comprehension: analysis, evaluation, critique	Poetry, argumentative writing
Study-reading	150–250 wpm	High comprehension and high recall	Textbooks, library research
Casual reading	250–400 wpm	Moderate comprehension of main ideas, entertainment, enjoyment, general information	Novels, newspapers, magazines
Accelerated reading	Above 600 wpm	Overview of material, rapid location of a specific fact	Reference material, magazines, novels, nonfiction

DEVELOPING YOUR READING FLEXIBILITY

As you can see from Table 21-1, no one should have just one reading rate. Instead, your reading rate should vary according to *what* you are reading and *why* you are reading it. Adjusting your rate in response to the material and to your purpose for reading is called *reading flexibility*.

Learning to adjust your rate according to style, content, and purpose will require a conscious effort at first. If you are now in the habit of reading everything at the same pace, as most college students are, then you will need to force yourself to make an assessment of the particular reading material before deciding how fast you can read it. When you use the technique of prereading, you are only a small step away from adjusting your rate. By prereading, you familiarize yourself with the overall content and organization of the material. You may also include, as part of your prereading, a step in which you pay particular attention to the overall difficulty of the material. While prereading, you will sample enough of the actual writing to be able to assess the level of complexity of both the language and the content.

Deciding how much to speed up or slow down for a particular article is a matter of judgment. You will find through experience that you will be able to judge how much you can afford to alter your speed. It is not important to know precisely how much to increase your speed. Rather, the important thing is to develop the skill of *flexibility*. Here is a step-by-step procedure you can follow that will help you build the habit of varying your reading rate.

1. Choose a time and place for reading that will help rather than hinder your concentration. Choose a time when you are alert and your state of mind is conducive to study.
2. Preread the material. As you preread, assess the difficulty of both the writing style and the content. Are there a lot of difficult words? Are the sentences long and complicated? How factual is the material? How much background information do you have on the subject?
3. Define your overall purpose for reading. Your purpose will determine the level of comprehension and the degree of retention that you require. Are you reading for enjoyment, looking up facts, or reading a text chapter to prepare for an exam?
4. Decide what rate would be appropriate for reading this particular material.
5. After you've finished the first page of the reading material, stop and evaluate. Are you understanding and remembering what you are reading? Can you summarize the ideas in your own words?

MEASURING YOUR READING FLEXIBILITY

You now realize that the type of material you read and how you approach it determine, in part, your reading rate. Most students want to know whether they are fast or slow readers, or above or below average. Also, you can measure your reading flexibility if various types of materials are used and the purpose for reading each is defined.

Before beginning to measure your rate for each type of reading listed on the chart in Table 21-2, you will need to know how to figure out your words per minute, which is the unit of measurement used in computing reading rate.

How to Compute Words per Minute (wpm)

1. After you have chosen a passage in a book or article, count the total number of words in any three lines. Divide the total by three and round it off to the nearest whole number. This will give the average number of words per line.
2. Count the number of lines in the article or book by counting the number of lines on one page and multiplying that number by the total number of pages. Multiply the number of words per line by the total number of lines. This will give you a fairly accurate estimate of the total number of words.
3. Time yourself as you read, using a watch with a second hand. Record both minutes and seconds of your starting time (for example, 4:20 18). Start reading when the second hand of the clock reaches twelve. Record your finishing time. Subtract your starting from your finishing time.
4. Divide your total reading time into the total number of words. To do this, round off the number of seconds to the nearest quarter of a minute and then divide. For example, if your total reading time was 3 minutes and 12 seconds, round it off to 3.25 minutes and then divide. Your answer will be your words-per-minute score.

The following example illustrates computation of words per minute.

Total number of words on 3 lines: 23
Divide by 3 and round off: $23 \div 3 = 7\%= 8$
Number of lines in article: 120
Multiply number of words per line by number of lines:
$8 \times 120 = 960$ (total words)

    Subtract finishing time 1:13 22
      from starting time 1:05
                       8 minutes 22 seconds

Round off to nearest ¼ minute: 8½ minutes
Divide time into total number of words:
    $960 \div 8.5 = 112$ + a fraction (your reading rate)

TABLE 21-2   Reading Rate

Method of Reading	Average Speed	Your Speed (wpm)
Analytical	Below 100 wpm	_____
Study-reading	150–250 wpm	_____
Casual reading	250–400 wpm	_____
Accelerated	Above 600 wpm	_____

Measuring Your Analytical Reading Rate

1. Select a poem or a passage from a complicated essay in an English textbook, or choose an extremely detailed description of a process from another of your texts, or pick a discussion of a controversial issue that you plan to analyze carefully.
2. Estimate the number of words, read the material, time yourself, and compute your words-per-minute score. Record your wpm in the chart in Table 21-2.
3. Check your comprehension; could you now write a paper analyzing and reacting to what you read?

Measuring Your Study-Reading Rate

Choose a passage from one of your textbooks that you have not read but expect will be assigned. Assume that you will have to pass an exam on the material later in the course. Then follow steps 2 and 3 given above.

Measuring Your Casual Reading Rate

Choose a passage of several pages from a novel you are reading or select several pages from a magazine article that interests you. Timing yourself, read it only for enjoyment or general information. Then compute your wpm, and fill in the chart in Table 21-2.

Measuring Your Accelerated Reading Rate

Choose a magazine article on a subject that interests you. It should be at least one page in length. Assume that you are in a hurry and do not have time to read the entire article but that you want to know what major ideas the article contains. Quickly read through the article, reading certain portions and skipping others. Try to read less than half of the material. Time yourself as you read, compute your wpm score, and record it in Table 21-2.

Interpreting Your Results

If your reading rate was nearly the same for each type of reading, then you do not vary your speed according to purpose and type of material. Review the suggestions on page 350 for developing your reading flexibility, then deliberately speed up or slow down as you read various types of material.

If each of your rates was below average, this suggests that you are a slow reader. When students learn that their rate is low, their first impulse is to work on improving their reading speed. Usually, however, this approach is ineffective. A slow reading rate is more often a symptom than a cause. A slow rate is to reading as chills and fever are to a cold. The chills and fever are not the cause of the cold; rather they are symptoms that let you know you have a cold. Similarly, a slow reading rate suggests that something else is wrong. Usually, the problem is comprehension—you are having difficulty understanding what you read. If your reading rate is slow, do not simply try to read faster. Instead, work on the cause—comprehension skills. Focus on developing the comprehension skills presented in Part Three of this text.

SUGGESTIONS FOR READING FASTER

To read faster, you must improve your capacity to process information rapidly. Instead of thinking about your eyes and how they move, concentrate on getting information quickly from the printed page. Reading faster involves understanding ideas and how they interrelate.

By working through this book, you have learned numerous skills and techniques that have improved your comprehension. Many techniques that improve comprehension also improve rate. Reading faster is often a combination of pushing yourself to higher reading speeds on different types of materials and learning and applying several new techniques. The following suggestions will help you to read faster.

Avoid Roadblocks to Reading Efficiency

There is a group of poor reading habits that are carryovers from when you first learned to read. These are (1) moving your head as you read, (2) moving your lips as you read, and (3) using your finger or pen to keep your place on the line. Each of these habits can slow you down and contribute to poor comprehension.

Moving Your Head: When children learn to read, they have difficulty moving only their eyes straight across a line of print. Because of this lack of eye control, many children move their heads from left to right as they proceed across the line. While this habit may be necessary for children, it is not for adults with adequate visual control. Some adults, however, have never eliminated the habit. Moving the head rather than just the eyes prevents adult readers from reading at even a normal reading rate and also creates strain and muscular fatigue. Ask someone to check to see if you move your head while reading; this person should check when you are not consciously thinking about this problem.

If you have this habit, it is probably a very old one that will require effort to overcome. One of the easiest ways to break it is to sit with your elbow up on your desk with your hand cupping your chin. If you start to move your head, you will feel your hand and forearm move, and this will remind you to correct the habit.

Moving Your Lips: Lip movement while reading silently is also a carryover from beginning reading experiences. Most students are taught to read orally first. Later on, when making the change from mostly oral to mostly silent reading in second or third grade, many children move their lips. Eventually, when the changeover is completed, lip movement should be eliminated. For some students, however, this habit hangs on. For an adult, lip movement limits rate improvement. The average adult rate of speech (pronouncing words out loud) is 125 words per minute, while the average adult rate for silent reading is 250 to 300 words per minute. You can see that moving your lips can really slow your silent reading down—by as much as half. However, there is one situation in which lip movement may be appropriate. When you are reading something that is extremely difficult or complicated, you may find that moving your lips or even whispering aloud as you read helps you to understand the material.

Young children are sometimes broken of the habit of lip movement by having them hold a pencil horizontally between their lips as they read. When their lips move, the pencil wiggles or drops. This technique is not appropriate for adults, but you may wish to try a more sophisticated version. Sit in a position so that part of your hand or your fingers touch your lips. If you move your lips while reading, you will feel the movement on your hand or fingers.

Keeping Your Place on the Line: Another bad habit left over from childhood reading is keeping your place on a line of print by moving your finger or a pen, pencil, or index card across the line as you read. Children are sometimes allowed to do this because they lack the eye control to keep their eyes from jumping from line to line or to move their eyes straight across one line smoothly. For adults, however, this habit results in a very slow word-by-word reading.

The solution to this problem is simple—tightly grasp the book with both hands. This will prevent you from following across the line with your finger or another object. Be careful you don't cheat and slide your thumb down the margin as a guide to where you are on the page. If you have tried unsuccessfully to control this habit, an eye exam is advisable. Inability to keep one's place on the line is one symptom of a need for corrective lenses.

Preread to Familiarize Yourself with the Material

In Chapter 5 you learned that prereading is a means of improving your comprehension by becoming familiar with the organization and content of material before you begin to read it. In addition to improving your comprehension, prereading increases your reading speed. Because prereading enables you to anticipate the flow of ideas, you will find yourself able to read the material more rapidly.

Try to Eliminate Regressions

As your eyes move across a line, they normally proceed from left to right. Occasionally, instead of moving to the next word, your eyes move backward, or regress, to a word in the same line or in a line already read. Regressions (backward movements) scramble word order, thus creating confusion that slows your pace. Although even very good readers make regressions, your rate and comprehension will improve if you can reduce the number of regressions. The following suggestions will help you eliminate or reduce regressions.

1. Be conscious of the tendency to regress, and force yourself to continue reading. Do not allow yourself to regress until you have finished a sentence. Then, if the meaning is still unclear, reread the entire sentence.
2. If you frequently regress to a word or phrase on a previous line, you might try sliding a 5″ × 8″ index card down the page as you read. Use the card to cover the lines you have finished reading. This technique will help break the habit of regression because when you look back, the line will be covered.

3. Although it is not a good habit to form, try guiding your eye movement by using a pen or your finger to force yourself continually forward. Move your finger across each line at a speed with which your eyes can keep pace. The forward motion of your finger or pen will guide your eye and force it along in a left-to-right pattern.

Read in Meaning Clusters

Most college students read word by word, looking at each word and then moving to the next one. A more efficient way to read is to combine words that naturally go together. Try not to think of a sentence as a string of single words. Instead, think of it as several word clusters, or phrases. Look at the following sentence:

The math instructor told her class about the quiz.

"The" does not convey any meaning by itself. While "math" does have meaning, it is intended to describe the next word, "instructor." Rather than reading the first three words separately, try to think of them together as a meaningful phrase—"the math instructor." The remainder of the sentence could then be read as two additional phrases: "told her class" and "about the quiz."

The following brief paragraph has been divided into meaningful word groups separated by slashes. Read the paragraph; as you read, try to see and think of each cluster as a unit of thought rather than as two or three separate words.

In order / to protect themselves / against loss / drivers purchase / liability insurance. / There are / two types of / liability insurance. / Bodily injury liability / provides payment / if you / are injured / in an accident. / Property damage liability / covers you / when your car / damages the property / of others.

Notice that words that make sense together are grouped together. Words are grouped with the words they explain or modify.

To see if you can group words into meaningful clusters, divide the following paragraph with slashes. The first line has been done for you.

The United States / has changed / in the past one hundred years / from an agricultural economy / to an industrial economy / and has become / the world's first / service economy. What does the term /service mean? There is no /widely accepted definition /in marketing. In fact, /there is no clear distinction /between those firms /that are part of a marketing channel /for products /and those firms /that market services. Restaurants are often classified /as food distributors /because they compete with supermarkets, / but restaurants /also provide services to customers.

–Kinnear and Bernhardt, *Principles of Marketing*, p. 654

Once you begin reading in word clusters, you will find that meaning falls into place more easily, thus enabling you to read somewhat faster.

Learn to Pace Yourself

An established method of improving your reading rate is *pacing*, which requires maintaining a preestablished rate. Pacing means pushing yourself to read faster than your normal speed while maintaining your level of comprehension. There are numerous ways to pace yourself in order to increase your speed; among the most common methods are:

1. *Use an index card.* Slide a 3″ × 5 ″ card down the page as you read, moving it so that it covers up lines as they are read. This technique will force you along and keep you moving rapidly. Move the card down the page at a fixed pace, and try to keep up while reading. How fast you move the card will depend on the size of print and the length of the line, and will then vary for each new piece of material you read. At first you will need to experiment to find an appropriate pace. Try to move at a pace that is slightly uncomfortable and that you are not sure you can maintain.
2. *Use your hand or index finger, or a pen or pencil.* Use your hand or index finger, pen or pencil in the same manner as the index card. Using your hand does not completely obstruct your view of the page and allows you to pick up clues from the layout of the page (to see that a paragraph is ending, that a graphic example is to follow, and so on).
3. *Use a timer or clock.* Start by measuring what portion of a page you can read in a minute. Then set a goal for yourself: Determine how many pages you will attempt to read in a given period of time. Set your goal slightly above what you measured as your current rate. For example, suppose in a particular book you can read half a page in a minute. You might set as your goal to read five pages in nine minutes (forcing yourself to read a little more than a half page per minute). The next day, try to read five pages in eight or eight and a half minutes. Use an alarm clock or timer to let you know when you have used up your time.

EXERCISE 1 _____

Directions: *Select a magazine or newspaper article that you are interested in or a section of a paperback you are reading. Using one of the pacing techniques described in this section, try to increase your current reading speed by approximately 50 wpm. Record your results in the space provided.*

Article title: _____

Estimated number of words: _____

Finishing time: _____

Starting time: _____

Reading time: _____

Words per minute: _____

Estimated level of comprehension: _____

Use Rereading to Build Speed

Although rereading is not an effective way to learn, it is an effective method of building your reading speed. Rereading at a slightly faster pace prepares you for reading new material faster. Rereading gets you moving at a faster rate and serves as a practice or "trial run" for reading new material faster.

To reread for speed increase, use the following steps:

1. Select an article or passage and read it as you normally would for careful or leisure reading.
2. Time yourself and compute your speed in words per minute after you finish reading.
3. Take a break (five minutes or so). Then reread the same selection. Push yourself to read faster than you read the first time.
4. Time yourself and compute your speed once again. You should be able to reread the selection at a faster rate than you read it initially.
5. Read a new selection, pushing yourself to read almost as fast as you *re*read the first selection.

EXERCISE 2 ————————————————

Directions: *Choose two magazine or newspaper articles that you are interested in reading. Follow the preceding steps for rereading to build speed. Record your results below.*

ARTICLE 1

Title: _____

Estimated number of words: _____

First reading
    Time: _____

    Words per minute: _____

Second reading
    Time: _____

    Words per minute: _____

ARTICLE 2

Title: _____

Estimated number of words: _____

First reading
    Time: _____

    Words per minute: _____

SUMMARY

Reading rate is influenced by three factors: text characteristics, reader's characteristics, and reader's purpose. Text factors refer to the features of language that determine the difficulty of what you read. These include sentence length, vocabulary, and complexity of ideas.

Reader's factors refer to those characteristics, skills, and habits that affect reading rate which you, the reader, have developed. Among the most important variables are your vocabulary level, level of comprehension, physical and mental state, interest in the material, and familiarity with the subject.

While both writer's and reader's factors directly influence your rate, a third major factor also determines how fast you read—your purpose for reading. depending on the amount and type of information you must retain, your reading rate should fluctuate widely. The ability to adjust your reading rate as determined by the type of material and your purpose for reading is called *reading flexibility*.

This chapter focused on the development of reading flexibility. It established four categories of reading and provided four different reading situations for measuring your rate and flexibility. Finally, general suggestions for reading faster were offered.

22

Skimming and Scanning

Use this chapter to:

1. *Learn to adjust your rate to what you are reading and your purpose for reading it.*
2. *Learn techniques for skimming and scanning.*

Can you think of any situation in which it would not be necessary to read every word on a printed page? Consider the telephone directory. Have you ever read all the words on any page of it? The answer is obvious; each time you look up a phone number, your read selectively, picking out only the information you need and skipping everything else. Think of other types of printed material that you read the same way. List them below:

_____   _____

_____   _____

_____   _____

_____   _____

Your responses might have included bus schedules,
listings, theater schedules, want ads, and dictionaries
There are many types of printed material that
ough, beginning-to-end, careful reading. This chapte
in which you can afford to skip material as well a
which it is not necessary to read everything. The
systematic approach to help you decide what to rea

WHEN DON'T YOU HAVE TO READ E

Before you begin to read selectively, you
there is nothing sacred about the printed word.

think that anything that appears in print must be true, valuable, and worth reading. Actually, the importance and value of printed information are affected by whether you need to learn it or whether you can use it in a practical way. Depending on the kind of material and your purpose for reading it, many times you may need to read only some parts and skip over others. You might read selectively when:

1. *A high level of comprehension is not needed.* If you are not trying to remember a major portion of the facts and details, then you might concentrate on reading only main ideas. This method of reading only main ideas is called *skimming*. Specific techniques for skimming are presented later in the chapter.

2. *You are searching for specific information.* If you are looking up the date of a historical event in your history text, you would skip over everything in the chapter except the exact passage that contains the information. This technique of skipping everything except the specific information for which you are looking is called *scanning*. Practice in scanning techniques is included later in the chapter.

3. *You are familiar with what you are reading.* In a college chemistry course, for example, you might find that the first few chapters of your text are very basic if you have already studied high school chemistry. You could afford to skip basic definitions and explanations and examples of principles that you already know. Do not, however, decide to skip an entire chapter or even large sections within it; there just may be some new information included. You may find that more exact and detailed definitions are given or that a new approach is taken toward a particular topic.

4. *The material does not match your purpose in reading.* Suppose, in making an assignment in your physics text, your instructor told you to concentrate only on theories, laws, and principles presented in the chapter. As you begin reading the chapter, you find that the first topic discussed is Newton's law of motion, but the chapter also contains a biographical sketch of Newton giving detailed information about his life. Since your purpose in reading the chapter is to focus on theories, laws, and principles, it would be appropriate to skip over much of the biographical information.

TYPES OF MATERIAL TO SKIP

Just as there are situations when it is appropriate to skip over information, there are also various types and styles of writing in which it is possible to skip information. Some writers include many examples of a particular concept or principle. If, after reading two or three examples, are sure that you understand the idea being explained, just quickly the remaining examples. Unless they present a new aspect or int of view, skip over them.

ters provide detailed background information before leading on of the intended topic. If a chapter starts out by summing that was covered in a chapter you just read last ecessary to read this information again carefully review.

EXERCISE 1 _____

Directions: *Each of the following items suggests a reading situation and describes the material to be read. After reading each item, decide whether the reader should (a) read the material completely; (b) read parts, and skip other parts; or (c) skip most of the material.*

1. Your history instructor has assigned each student to read a historical novel for the purpose of getting a realistic picture of what life was like and how people lived during a certain period. As you are reading, you come to a detailed two-page description of the type of gowns southern women wore to a particular party. How should you read these two pages? _____

2. You are doing research for a sociology term paper on the world population explosion. You are looking for information and statistics on recent population trends. You have located several books from the 1940s on the topic of population growth in the United States. How would you read these books? _____

3. Your nursing instructor has just returned a test on a chapter describing the nursing process. She indicates that the class's overall performance on this test was poor and suggests that the chapter be reviewed. You received a grade of 79 on the test. How should this chapter be reread? _____

4. Your biology professor has assigned a number of brief outside readings along with the chapters in your regular textbook. He has put them on reserve in the college library for the use of all his classes. This is the only place they can be used. He did not say whether you would be tested on them. How would you read them? _____

5. You have just attended English class, where your instructor discussed Milton's *Paradise Lost*. During his discussion he made numerous references to Dante's *Inferno*. You have never read this second work but think it's important to know something about it. How would you read it? _____

SKIMMING TECHNIQUES

As you know, the term *skimming* refers to the pro_____ main ideas within a passage and simply glancing at t_____ material. Skimming is used to get an overall pictur_____ become generally familiar with the topics and idea_____ the gist of a particular work. Usually skimming is a_____ skimming is all that you intend to do with the articl_____ read it more completely later. You are willing to se_____ the article, giving up a major portion of the details_____

At this point, you may be thinking that skin_____ the technique of prereading. If so, you are correc_____ a form of skimming. To be more precise, there_____ ming: *preread skimming*, *skim-reading*, and *re_____ skimming assumes that you plan to read the en_____

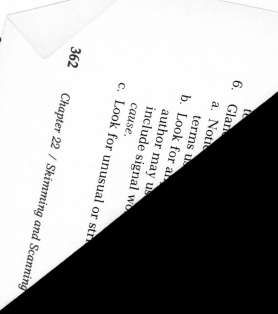

6. Glan_____
   a. Not_____
   terms u_____
   b. Look for a_____
   author may u_____
   include signal wo_____
   cause.
   c. Look for unusual or st_____

that you are prereading as a means of getting ready to read. Skim-reading refers to situations in which skimming is the only coverage you plan to give the material. Review skimming assumes you have already read the material and are going back over it as a means of study and review.

Prereading has already been discussed in Part Two, Chapter 5. Methods of review after reading are part of the reading-study systems, such as SQ3R, discussed in Part Four, Chapter 12. Therefore, this chapter will focus on skim-reading techniques.

DEMONSTRATION OF SKIMMING

The sample passage in Figure 22-1 has been included to demonstrate what skimming is like. The parts of the passage that should be read while skimming appear in color print.

The passage is taken from a sociology text on courtship and marriage. It appears at the end of a chapter that discusses masculine and feminine roles and conflicts. The article is included not as part of the chapter, but as an additional reading selected to give a perspective on or interpretation of the topic discussed in the chapter itself. Since the article is not factual and not part of the text itself, skimming it for main ideas is appropriate.

How to Skim-Read

Your purpose in skimming is to get an overall impression of the content of a reading selection. The technique of skimming involves selecting and reading those parts of the selection that contain the most important ideas and merely glancing at the rest of the material. Below is a step-by-step procedure to follow in skimming for main ideas.

1. Read the title. If the piece is an article, check the author, publication date, and source.
2. Read the introduction. If it is very long, read only the first paragraph completely. Read the first sentence of every other paragraph. Usually the first sentence will be a statement of the main idea of that paragraph.
3. Read any headings and subheadings. The headings, when taken together, form an outline of the main topics that are covered in the material.
4. Notice any pictures, charts, or graphs; these are usually included to emphasize important ideas, concepts, or trends.
5. If you do not get enough information from the headings or if you are working with material that does not have headings, read the first sentence of each paragraph.
    ce at the remainder of the paragraph.
    e any italicized or boldface words or phrases. These are key
    ed throughout the selection.
    y lists of ideas within the text of the material. The
    e numerals, such as (1), (2), (3), in the list or may
    rds such as *first*, *second*, *one major cause, another*

    king features of the paragraph. You may

It's Really the Men Who Need Liberating

Mary Calderone

. . . I am particularly concerned about the hostility now fermenting between men and women. Just when men and women have the opportunity to mean more to each other than ever before, and when the world, the society and that entity known as the family need them *together,* they are exploding apart.

Men and women are deeply uneasy with and about each other; they circle each other warily, fencing and feinting; their visual contacts are sidewise, not direct; they are mistaking bodily for interpersonal intimacy. There is little trust between them.

One reason for this may be that women have come so far, so fast. In the span of my own lifetime, women have achieved rights and freedoms undreamed of in the previous century: rights of franchise, of property ownership, of guardianship of children; freedoms in education, professions, occupations, recreation, movement, dress, behavior. Imagine that at 15 I was wearing long black stockings for swimming, and felt daring when I rolled them below the knees!

By contrast, in this same period, males, who have always had the rights, have achieved far fewer freedoms. Only recently have they begun to emerge from their age-old stereotyped grooves of earning, governing and fighting, and from their compulsively fixed patterns of masculinity in dressing, professions, rec-

reation and life-style. That these were grooves and patterns they had themselves designed made them no less confining, but it did make breaking out of them all the more fearful a process. As men have begun to emerge from these stereotypes, doubtfully and hesitantly, they have found that in leaving the security of their old shells, they are that much more exposed and vulnerable to the incomparably more secure and liberated females.

A few years ago at a meeting of about 100 professionals in counseling and family life, I asked the men to sit in the rear and listen while the women gave me a series of adjectives on the theme "What I would like to see men become 20 years from now." For a half hour the women discussed the qualities they desired, then they faced the men. At first, the men were defensive about adjectives they termed predominantly "feminine," such as tender, gentle, empathic, nurturing, artistic. But the women convinced them that these were desirable qualities that would enhance men's own evolution as individuals. By the time the meeting ended the men admitted that the women had listed qualities that they would like t... but felt they wer... velop... woul... ety... mar... of...

Adapted by permission of the author from Mary Calderone, "It's Really the Men Who Need Liberating," Guest Editorial, *Life* 69 (4 September 1970). Dr. Calderone is a cofounder of SIECUS, the Sex Information and Education Council of the U.S., and has been its Executive Director for the fourteen years of its existence.

FIGURE 22-1   Example of Skimming

364

FIGURE 22-1 (Continued)

Chapter 22 / Skimming and Scanning

claims made by women against their own subjugation and exploitation by males over the centuries and in the present, the bald fact is that hostility and vengefulness of half a population against the other half is never what is needed at any moment in history, but most especially in this one.

What *is* needed, then, in the relationships of the sexes to each other? I would say primarily a joint realization from the very earliest years that participation in all life processes relates to being human rather than to being sexual. Therefore it is not so much competitiveness or aggressiveness or submission or exploitation of either sex by the other that is at issue, as the opportunities each one of us, being human, can find to enjoy and be enjoyed by, help and be helped by, stimulate and be stimulated by members of the sex that is not ours as well as of the one that is.

Women simply cannot run this world alone. But then, neither can men! Together they can do it, and much, much better than it is being run at present. Together, both as individuals and as the two sexual collectivities, they can help and support each other in the free choices to be made as *both* sexes find out that love and sex, jobs and families, work and play, world concerns and self concerns are not mutually exclusive. They are points in the life continuum that deserve and can receive different emphases at different epochs or moments in that life—without being at the expense of either man or woman.

"His" and "Hers" should not divide the world, which is *ours*. There is no need for any lifelong choice of a role or an occupation. Either sex should be free to come and go across frontiers that exist only as we ourselves choose to establish them. . . .

Freedom to choose what and how to be, as male or female—by knowing what the choices are and balancing one's own good, one's partner's or associate's good and the common good—this is what each sex should make possible *for* the other sex, not wrest violently *from* the other sex. Women will have to make the first gestures on behalf of men's liberation, for at this moment men are still entrapped in their own centuries-old power play. But women can afford such generosity, for women have forged ahead of men at other, deeper levels. The obligation is on us, as women, to ease the way for men to those deeper levels of relationships where power is powerless and the truest satisfactions as human beings are to be found.

Then the power questions won't matter at all, nor even exist anymore.

notice a series of dates, many capitalized words, or several large-
figure numbers.

7. Read the summary or last paragraph.

EXERCISE 2 _____

Directions: *Skim each of the following selections. Then summarize each article in the space provided.*

Selection 1: *"To Lie or Not to Lie? The Doctor's Dilemma"*

_____

_____

_____

Selection 2: *"Aging and Death"*

_____

_____

_____

Selection 3: *"A Good Word for Bad Words"*

_____

_____

_____

1. **TO LIE OR NOT TO LIE? THE DOCTOR'S DILEMMA**

   –Sissela Bok

   Should doctors ever lie to h⸻
   recovery or to conceal the ⸻
   government, and other li⸻
   often seem dwarfed by gr⸻
   news or to uphold a pror⸻
   promote the public inter⸻

   What should docto⸻
   coming for a routine pl⸻
   with his family who, tl⸻
   have a form of cancer⸻
   Is it best to tell him th⸻
   he is ill, or minimize⸻
   least conceal the tru⸻

   Doctors confro⸻
   see important reaso⸻
   such lies differ sha⸻

Studies show that most doctors sincerely believe that the seriously ill do not want to know the truth about their condition, and that informing them risks destroying their hope, so that they may recover more slowly, or deteriorate faster, perhaps even commit suicide. As one physician wrote: "Ours is a profession which traditionally has been guided by a precept that transcends the virtue of uttering the truth for truth's sake, and that is 'as far as possible do no harm.'"

Armed with such a precept, a number of doctors may slip into deceptive practices that they assume will "do no harm" and may well help their patients. They may prescribe innumerable placebos, sound more encouraging than the facts warrant, and distort grave news, especially to the incurably ill and the dying.

But the illusory nature of the benefits such deception is meant to bestow is now coming to be documented. Studies show that, contrary to the belief of many physicians, an overwhelming majority of patients do want to be told the truth, even about grave illness, and feel betrayed when they learn that they have been misled. We are also learning that truthful information, humanely conveyed, helps patients cope with illness: helps them tolerate pain better, need less medication, and even recover faster after surgery.

Not only do lies not provide the "help" hoped for by advocates of benevolent deception; they invade the autonomy of patients and render them unable to make informed choices concerning their own health, including the choice of whether to *be* a patient in the first place. We are becoming increasingly aware of all that can befall patients in the course of their illness when information is denied or distorted.

Dying patients especially—who are easiest to mislead and most often kept in the dark—can then not make decisions about the end of life: about whether or not to enter a hospital, or to have surgery; about where and with whom to spend their remaining time; about how to bring their affairs to a close and take leave.

Lies also do harm to those who tell them: harm to their integrity and, in the long run, to their credibility. Lies hurt their colleagues as well. The suspicion of deceit undercuts the work of the many doctors who are scrupulously honest with their patients; it contributes to the spiral of litigation and of "defensive medicine," and thus it injures, in turn, the entire medical profession.

Sharp conflicts are now arising. Patients are learning to press for answers. Patients' bills of rights require that they be informed about their condition and about alternatives for treatment. Many doctors go to great lengths to provide such information. Yet even in hospitals with the most eloquent bill of rights, believers in benevolent deception continue their age-old practices. Colleagues may disapprove but refrain from remonstrating. Nurses may bitterly resent having to take part, day after day, in deceiving patients, but feel powerless to take a stand.

There is urgent need to debate this issue openly. Not only in medicine, but in other professions as well, practitioners may find themselves repeatedly in straits where serious consequences seem avoidable only through deception. Yet the public has every reason to be wary of professional deception, for such practices are peculiarly likely to become ingrained, to spread, and to erode trust. Neither in medicine, nor in law, government, or the social sciences can there be comfort in the old saw, "What you don't know can't hurt you."

2. AGING AND DEATH

–James Geiwitz

Grow old along with me!
The best is yet to be,
The last of life, for which
*   the first was made,*

–Robert Browning

Aging and death are two subjects that are generally avoided in conversation. When they come up, an uneasy atmosphere develops. Growing old generally elicits bad jokes at best, and death is discussed in euphemisms—"passed away," "kicked the bucket," "the late————."

Why do Americans have such strong negative reactions to growing old and to dying? Perhaps the fear of death is understandable, since what happens next is totally unknown, and uncertainty is always a little frightening. But why do millions of Americans dye their hair, have "face-lifts" and other cosmetic surgery, and otherwise spend so much time, energy, and money on the effort to keep looking young?

AGING: PSYCHOLOGICAL ASPECTS

Some of the reasons the American culture is so youth-oriented have to do with its rapidly changing, super-industrial status. In some cultures, particularly in the past, the wisdom of the "elders" was highly valued. They had experience: They knew what was likely to happen and what to do in a variety of situations. In our culture, the elders know about things that no longer exist. Often they are bewildered about events. Old people are no longer respected for their wisdom; they are "out of date."

Ironically, it is the super-industrial cultures that have the most old people. Advances in medical science have doubled the percentage of United States citizens over the age of 65 in this century alone. At the same time, our society has pressed to make earlier retirements possible and, in some industries, required.

Retirement means an abrupt change in habits. For some people, it is an unhappy switch from an active, productive life into what feels like uselessness. The daily r———— f a job disappears, leaving the retired person plenty of spar———————— Some people are unable to seek out new frier———————————— women, disabled by the physic——————— the loss of income that comes ————— leave their homes and move i—————— home. No longer able to direc———— dependent on other people. 7———— been taken away: What they————— all be decided for them. So———— A person may spend day af———— with only brief periods of ————— the elderly person may be———— are increasing numbers ————— alleviate these problems————— new activities or jobs th————— a valuable part of the h————

368

Chapter 22 / Skimming and S

It is important to realize that the changes we face at retirement *can* be dealt with, just like changes at any other time of life. For many people, retirement is an opportunity, a chance to do things they never had time to do before. As you might expect, people who adjusted well to life before retirement are the best adjusted after retirement. But in both youth and age, adjustment is an active process. The people who are happiest in retirement are those who seek out new activities, like gardening and volunteer social work, to replace the ones no longer available to them. They also seek out social companions who share their interests, instead of sitting in sullen isolation, lamenting the deaths of friends and how no one visits them anymore. They may even join the Gray Panthers, a radical political organization for old people that lobbies for the rights and benefits of the elderly: improved bus service, tax reforms, new health laws.

AGING: BIOLOGICAL ASPECTS

Biologically, aging may be defined as a decline in the ability of the body to avoid or fight off the effects of accidents, disease, and other types of stress. Thus, most people die of a disease, not "natural causes." There is good evidence that each of us has an alloted time in life that can be shortened by disease or accident, but not lengthened. Medical science has increased the *average* lifespan in many countries by saving the lives of infants and young people, but it has had little effect among the very old. For example, if all cancer (a prime killer of the elderly) were eliminated, the average lifespan would increase by only 1.5 years.

It is very difficult to distinguish between "pure" aging and the effects of various chronic diseases that often come with age. These diseases include arthritis—inflammation of the joints, causing pain and decreased dexterity and mobility—and arteriosclerosis—hardening and thickening of the arteries. Arthritis makes it hard for the victim to move around and to do certain things. Arteriosclerosis causes increased blood pressure, which may cause headaches and generally poor circulation. Poor circulation, in turn, makes adjustment to cooler temperatures more difficult; and poor blood circulation to the brain may result in some problems in processing information.

A classic study of *healthy* men between the ages of 65 and 91 compared their physical and mental abilities to those of another group of men, average age 21. The older men proved as fit as the younger men on a number of variables. Measures of blood flow to the brain and oxygen consumption during exercise did not differ between groups. The older subjects were superior in non-timed tests of intelligence, such as vocabulary, and poorer in tests requiring speed or involving reaction time. The reaction-time tests showed the most marked results. By and large, however, there were very few differences between the healthy old men and healthy young men. This indicates the validity of a definition of aging as increasing susceptibility to diseases, diseases which may cause many of the symptoms we often incorrectly attribute to aging itself.

Of course, many physical changes are directly related to aging. Hair may become gray (or disappear altogether); the skin wrinkles; the senses become less acute and the bones more brittle, making accidents more likely and more serious. There is some evidence that pain becomes less painful, so not all changes are for the worse. And contrary to popular myth, people up to and even over 80 years old are capable of enjoying sexual intercourse—and many do.

DEATH AND DYING

Death and dying are sad, depressing subjects to most of us. No matter how prepared we are, or however strongly we may believe in a life after death, the loss of a close friend or relative is painful. The bereaved—those who have lost a loved one to death—are often faced with serious problems of adjustment, including coping with loneliness, sorrow, and the simple tasks of day-to-day living. There is a funeral, a will to be read and executed, expressions of sympathy to be accepted and responded to. These institutionalized aspects of the mourning period may help, as Freud once suggested, to spread the grief over several days. But soon they are over, and then comes the crying, the depression, the difficulty in sleeping, concentrating, and remembering, the lack of appetite for food and for life—the most common symptoms in a study of over 100 people who had lost a husband or wife.

During the period of bereavement, which often lasts a year or two, grief at least slightly affects the person's ability to function. For someone who has lost a spouse, the probability of a fatal illness, accident, or suicide is slightly higher during this period; these symptoms may be related to others, such as heavy drinking.

But what is death like for the person who is dying? From interviews with over 200 dying patients, one psychiatrist identified five attitudes experienced by these patients, often but not always in sequence (Kübler-Ross, 1970). *Denial* is usually the first stage. The patient says, in effect, "No! Not me!" Patients even choose to ignore obvious symptoms instead of openly confronting their own fears. This stage is followed by *anger:* The patient demands, "Why me? Why now?"

In the third stage, called *bargaining*, the patient seeks for a pardon or at least a postponement. Often he or she tries to make a bargain, secretly or openly, with God or "fate" or even Satan. One woman's bargain was "If I can only be allowed to live to see my son marry. . . ." She managed to get the hospital staff to teach her self-hypnosis to control the pain so that she could attend her son's wedding.

The fourth stage is *depression*, which develops as the patient realizes the loss of everything and everybody he or she loves is close at hand. This "preparatory" sorrow is probably necessary for the final stage, *acceptance*. In this fifth and last stage, the patient usually weans himself away from the world, desiring less and less contact with an increasingly small number of close friends. Acceptance was perhaps best expressed by Stewart Alsop, the noted journalist, just before he died: "A dying man needs to die as a sleepy man needs to sleep, and there comes a time when it is wrong, as well as useless, to resist."

One of the msot important points brought out in Kübler-Ross's studies is the dying person's need to talk about his or her fears and feelings about death. In fact, Kübler-Ross believes that if we were more open in thinking and talking about our deaths throughout our lives, we would live fuller lives and die with much less trauma and struggle. Death is, after all, one of the inescapable facts of human experience, and should be allowed to take a less fearsome and more accepted position in our daily lives.

3.   **A GOOD WORD FOR BAD WORDS**

   –*Time* magazine

   Zurich, Switzerland's largest city, installed an obscenity hot line in the late '70s. Subscribers to the service received a code name and a secret telephone number. At any hour of the day or night, for about a dollar a minute, they could talk to four men and four women who cheerfully listened to obscenities. That service reflects well enough the changing nature of profanity. It is not socially approved—an approved profanity is no profanity at all—but more and more tolerated and even encouraged. Movies and greeting cards are filthier than ever. Graffiti are the subject of scholarly tomes, and many forms of therapy goad patients into relieving their frustration by letting loose expletives. As all scholars know, many successful men are prominent cursers, from George Washington to Dodger Manager Tommy Lasorda, who unfurled 144 obscenities in a brief pep talk to his team last year [1980].

   All to the good, says psychologist Chaytor Mason, who thinks it is time that cursing got the (expletive deleted) credit it deserves. Like most theorists of swearing, Mason regards foul language as a valuable safety valve that helps society function without too much frustration. Mason, a professor at the University of Southern California's Institute of Safety and Systems Management, has found that people under hypnosis never swear (no stress, no swearing) and that in patients suffering from depression, a barrage of profanity is often a sign of recovery. "Profanity is the essence of the human being," he says. "Like scratching, it releases tension, and like sex, it's one of those very personal, satisfying acts."

   Among grandiose claims for gutter language, Mason's may rank only third. The silver medal goes to one William Dwight Whitney, a nineteenth-century Yale philologist who thought that human speech evolved out of primitive cursing—the angry yawps and yelps of early man. The gold medal winner is Sigmund Freud, who once suggested that cursing was the beginning of civilization. "The first human being who hurled a curse instead of a weapon against his adversary," Freud once remarked, "was the founder of civilization."

   Not all cussing is so glorious, of course. Mason thinks the movies are overdoing it nowadays because "it sells." Obsessive profanity can be a sign of schizophrenia, he says, especially if a person has always been excessively restrained. Conformists in dead-end jobs often use harsh swear words. "Moderates who use milder words a small amount of the time usually are, on the whole, pretty happy."

   But too little swearing is as bad as too much, he says. Used judiciously, four-letter words can salvage self-esteem and save one's ego from extermination. "The person using them," says the professor, "is proving that at least he has a mastery over something, if only his own mouth. He is verbally hitting below the belt. It's a way of feeling powerful when one feels helpless. Show me a person who never swears, and I'll show you a person who is unduly afraid of people. There are times when we all have to get down and get earthy."

Women, for example, are swearing more and fainting less: "Historically, men never permitted or taught women to swear, so when they became upset, their blood pressure would drop and they'd faint." Swearing even has a role to play in romance. A man or woman might swear early in a relationship as a test of affection. And during sexual intercourse, says Mason, "a woman may want her partner to talk dirty so she can temporarily become another person who is emotionally unrestrained."

Children almost automatically go through a swearing period, he says, using the magic words as a form of pre-adult swagger or to test the limits of their freedom at home. Though parents may bridle, Mason thinks they should actually guide their young in swearing, telling them which words are appropriate and where to use them. Reason: if parents swear but children are not allowed to, the lesson is that parents teach a code they do not live by. As a result, children often give up confiding in parents and start leading the familiar double life of angel at home and delinquent elsewhere.

Mason thinks World War II was the great watershed in American cursing. In 1939 Clark Gable's line in *Gone with the Wind*, "Frankly, my dear, I don't give a damn," had the nation gasping. But the wartime draft taught millions of youngsters, and later their friends and families, the foul and aggressive language of the barracks. Now, says Mason, damn and hell are virtually useless as swearwords. Even fouler and more powerful expressions too are losing their ability to shock. He suggests, rather lamely, that Americans will rise to the challenge by inventing new shocking expressions to meet a national need.

Not so, says Reinhold Aman, an admitted sewer mouth who edits *Maledicta*, a scholarly magazine about insults and swearing. Aman thinks Americans have nearly used up their patrimony of high-shock expressions and will not be able to create new ones. His suggestion: restore the florid insults and curses long common in rural America and also start using foreign expressions. "Europe, Asia and Africa make up an inexhaustible reservoir of foul language with tremendous shock value," he says, offering several unprintable examples. For those who cannot bring themselves to use the "dirty dozen" or so foul expressions left to most Americans, he suggests his own training regimen. Since most U.S. dirty words stress *f*, *sh*, *k*, *p*, *t*, *s* and *x* sounds, make up harmless combinations, such as "shexing" and "oh fex." This, he reasons, will let off steam, puzzle many and offend none.

Aman agrees with Mason that there is no point in trying to stop swearing. One sign that they are correct is the fate of Curseaholics Anonymous, an anti-swearing group founded in Cambridge, Mass., last June. Its 24-hour hot line was so swamped with foulmouthed calls from offended swearers that the group disbanded in July.

SCANNING TECHNIQUES

Scanning is a method of selective reading that is used when you are searching for a particular fact or the answer to a question. Scanning can best be described as a looking rather than a reading process. As you look for the information you need, you ignore everything else. When you finish scanning a page, the only thing you should know is whether it contained the information you were looking for. You should *not* be able to recall topics, main ideas, or details presented on the page. You already use the technique of scanning daily: you regularly scan telephone books, television listings, and indexes. The purpose of this section is to help you develop a rapid, efficient approach for scanning.

Use the following step-by-step procedure to become more skilled in rapidly locating specific information:

1. State in your mind the specific information you are looking for. Phrase it in question form if possible.
2. Try to anticipate how the answer will appear and what clues you might use to help you locate the answer. If you are scanning to find the distance between two cities, you might expect either digits or numbers written out as words. Also, a unit of measurement, probably miles or kilometers, will appear after the number.
3. Determine the organization of material: it is your most important clue to where to begin looking for information. Especially when you are looking up information contained in charts and tables, the organization of the information is crucial to rapid scanning.
4. Use headings and any other aids that will help you identify which sections might contain the information you are looking for.
5. Selectively read and skip through likely sections of the passage, keeping in mind the specific question you formed and your expectations of how the answer might appear. Move your eyes down the page in a systematic way. While there are various eye movement patterns, such as the "arrow pattern" (straight down the middle of the page) or the "Z pattern" (zigzagging down the page), it is best to use a pattern that seems comfortable and easy for you.
6. When you reach the fact you are looking for, you will find that the word or phrase will stand out, and you will notice it immediately.
7. When you have found the needed information, carefully read the sentences in which it appears in order to confirm that you have located the correct information.

EXERCISE 3 _____

Directions: *Scan each paragraph or passage to locate the answer to the question stated at the beginning of each.*

1. *Question:* In what unit is energy measured?

    Passage:

    Work is done in lifting the heavy ram of a pile driver, and, as a consequence, the ram acquires the property of being able to do work on a body beneath when it falls. When work is done in winding a spring mechanism, the spring acquires the ability to do work on an assemblage of gears to run a clock, ring a bell, or sound an alarm. And when a battery is charged, it may in turn do the work of a wound spring. In each case, something has been acquired. When work is done on an object, something is given to the object, which, in many cases, enables it do work. This "something" may be a physical separation of attracting bodies; it may be a compression of atoms in the material of a body; or it may be a rearrangement of electric charges in the molecules of a body. This something that enables a body to do work is called *energy*. Like work, energy is measured in joules. It appears in many forms, which we will discuss in subsequent chapters. We shall give attention here to the two forms of mechanical energy: potential energy and kinetic energy.

–Hewitt, *Conceptual Physics*, p. 82

2. *Question:* What was Hitler's promise?

Passage:

In September the United States requested, and Hitler and Mussolini agreed to, a big-power crisis conference at Munich. Included were the two Fascist leaders and the premiers of Britain and France (but not of the Soviet Union), who met to discuss the Czech crisis and how war might be averted. At Munich the democratic leaders took Hitler at his word that he would make no further demands if given the Sudetenland, and the Allies abandoned Czechoslovakia to its fate. Prime Minister Chamberlain returned to London with the wishful declaration that he had achieved "peace in our time," on the grounds of Hitler's promise that this was "the last territorial claim which I have to make in Europe." These are now remembered as some of the most tragic statements in diplomatic history.

–Jones, *The Logic of International Relations*, p. 54

3. *Question:* How do rural theft rates compare with suburban rates?

Passage:

Published national data do give us some idea of the dimensions of the theft problem, at least from the standpoint of the criminal justice system. In 1984, burglary, larceny-theft, and motor vehicle theft accounted for 10,608,473 (around 90 percent) of the 11,881,755 Index offenses reported by the FBI. Arrests numbered 1,846,500, or around 80 percent of total arrests for Index offenses. All three offenses showed steady increases during the 1960s, with burglary and larceny continuing to climb, though more slowly, during the 1970s. Motor vehicle theft tapered off and remained fairly stable, with a rate of around 450 recorded incidents per 100,000 population. The published national data indicate other characteristics of these three Index offenses: (1) rural rates are substantially below those found in both cities and suburbs; (2) suburban rates have been increasing faster than have large city rates; and (3) of those offenses reported, less than 20 percent are cleared by arrest. . . .

–Barlow, *Introduction to Criminology*, p. 209

4. *Question:* Why was an Irish militia supposedly formed?

Passage:

Revolution in America also brought drastic changes to Ireland. Before 1775, that unhappy island, under English rule, had endured centuries of religious persecution, economic exploitation, and political domination. During the war, however, Henry Gratton (1746–1820) and Henry Flood (1732–91), two leaders of the Irish Protestant gentry, exploited English weakness to obtain concessions. An Irish militia was formed, supposedly to protect the coasts against American or French attacks. With thousands of armed Irishmen behind them, the two leaders resorted successfully to American methods. In February 1782, a convention in Dublin, representing 80,000 militiamen, demanded legislative independence, which the English Parliament subsequently granted. An Irish legislature could now make its own laws, subject to veto only by the English king. Ireland thus acquired a status denied the American colonies in 1774.

–Wallbank et al., *Civilization Past and Present*, Vol. 2, p. 533

5. *Question:*   How does the cost of in-home retailing compare with suburban rates?

Passage:

In-home retailing involves the presenting of goods to customers in a face-to-face meeting at the customer's home or by contacting the customer by telephone. This solicitation can be done without advance selection of consumers or follow-ups based upon prior contact at stores, or by phone or mail. The well-known Tupperware party fits in this category. Here a person has a social gathering where everyone knows a sales presentation will be made. Besides Tupperware, the largest companies operating in this type of retailing are Avon (cosmetics), Electrolux (vacuum cleaners), Amway (household products), World Book (encyclopedia and books), Shaklee (food supplements), Home Interiors and Gifts (decorative items), L. H. Stuart (jewelry and crafts), Stanley Home Products (household products), and Kirby (vacuum cleaners). Despite the great cost savings of having no store and no inventory, labor costs make this form of retailing expensive. Expenses are estimated to average about 50 percent of sales, compared to about 26 percent for all retailing.

–Kinnear and Bernhardt, *Principles of Marketing*, p. 388

6. *Question:*   What agreement was violated when West Germany was incorporated into NATO?

Passage:

Far from accepting the role of antagonist in world politics and in the strategic arms race, the Kremlin seeks to defend its island of socialism from capitalist encirclement. Bolstering their traditional fears of exposed borders, the Soviets have experienced overt attempts by Japan and the West to bring down their power. Japanese and American landings in Siberia at the close of the First World War, shortly after the Bolshevik Revolution of 1917, were historic signals of the need to maintain rigorous defense against the capitalist industrialized states. More recently, American efforts after the Second World War to influence Soviet policy in Eastern Europe through atomic monopoly have accentuated the need for vigilance. NATO in particular, and the string of anti-Soviet alliances in general, added further to the need. Incorporation of West Germany into NATO in apparent violation of the Potsdam Agreement of 1945 was the ultimate sign of American intentions of maintaining anti-Soviet tension throughout Europe; the Kremlin responded by forming the Warsaw Pact. Soviet arms policy, far from being the cause of the balance of terror, is a response to the capitalist (specifically American) political and strategic threats.

—Jones, *The Logic of International Relations,* p. 387

7. *Question:* What race of inmates are victimized in prisons?

Passage:

In Bowker's view, racial and ethnic group victimization is the most significant and widespread. It used to be that the minority black inmates were the object of victimization, but now it appears that in many prisons it is the whites, especially the middle-class whites, who are victimized by black inmates. Leo Carroll's (1974) research at a New England state prison confirms the direction of interracial aggression, as does a more recent study of Stateville, the Illinois penitentiary at Joliet. In Stateville, James Jacobs (1977) found four highly cohesive gangs whose reputation and power dominated interracial contacts and radiated throughout the prison. The Black P. Stone Nation, the Devil's Disciples, and the Vicelords are black gangs; the Latin Kings is made up of Hispanic inmates. Their exploitation of other prisoners is extensive.

—Barlow, *Introduction to Criminology,* p. 465

8. *Question:* What is a spiff?

Passage:

Manufacturers often sponsor *contests* with prizes like free merchandise, trips, and plaques to dealers who reach certain specified sales levels. Additionally, they may get free *merchandise allowances* or even *money bonuses* for reaching sales performance goals. Once in a while, there is a sweepstakes, where "lucky" dealers can win substantial prizes. For example, Fisher-Price Toys had great success with a sweepstakes that gave cooperating dealers a chance to win a trip to Puerto Rico. These types of programs may also be directed at in-store sales personnel for their individual sales performances. A direct payment by a manufacturer to a channel member salesperson is called a *spiff.* This is very common at the consumer level for consumer durables and cosmetics, and at the wholesale level for beer and records. Another version of a spiff is when retailers pay their salespeople to push certain items. Clearly, this practice makes it possible for consumers to be deceived by a salesperson attempting to earn *push money.* As a result, these types of payments are controversial.

—Kinnear and Bernhardt, *Principles of Marketing,* p. 495

9. *Question:* What were the objectives of the New Deal?

Passage:

In the 1932 elections, Franklin D. Roosevelt, only the third Democrat to be elected to the presidency since 1860, overwhelmed

Hoover by assembling a coalition of labor, intellectuals, minorities, and farmers. The country had reached a crisis point by the time he was to be inaugurated in 1933, and quick action had to be taken in the face of bank closings. Under his leadership, the New Deal, a sweeping, pragmatic, often hit-or-miss program, was developed to cope with the emergency. The New Deal's three objectives were relief, recovery, and reform. Millions of dollars flowed from the federal treasury to feed the hungry, create jobs for the unemployed through public works, and provide for the sick and elderly through such reforms as the Social Security Act. In addition, Roosevelt's administration substantially reformed the banking and stock systems, greatly increased the rights of labor unions, invested in massive public power and conservation projects, and supported families who either needed homes or were in danger of losing the homes they inhabited.

–Wallbank et al., *Civilization Past and Present*, Vol. 2, p. 781

10. *Question:* Why does the tide come in rapidly at the Bay of Fundy?

Passage:

Ocean tides are complicated because of the presence of interfering land masses and friction with the ocean bottom. Because of these complications, the tides break up into smaller "basins of circulation," where a tidal bulge travels around the basin like a circulating wave that travels around a small basin of water when it is tilted properly. There is always a high tide someplace in the basin, although at a particular locality it may be hours away from an overhead moon. In midocean the variation in the water level— the range of the tide—is usually a meter or two. This range varies in different parts of the world; it is greatest in some Alaskan fjords and is most notable in the basin of the Bay of Fundy, between New Brunswick and Nova Scotia in southeast Canada, where tidal differences sometimes exceed 15 meters. This is largely due to the ocean floor, which funnels shoreward in a V-shape. The tide often comes in faster than a person can run. Don't dig clams near the water's edge at low tide in the Bay of Fundy!

–Hewitt, *Conceptual Physics*, p. 134

SUMMARY

Many adults feel that it is important to read every word on a printed page. This mistaken notion is often responsible for a slow, inflexible rate of reading. Actually, there are many types of material that do not require a thorough, beginning-to-end, careful reading. There are also many situations in which reading everything is not necessary—situations in which selective reading (reading some parts and skipping others) is more appropriate. It is effective to read selectively in situations in which you need only main ideas, you are looking for a specific fact or answer to a question, you are highly familiar with the content of the material, or the material contains information that does not relate to your purpose for reading. Finally, there are certain types of material and styles of writing in which it is possible to skip information.

In situations where it is appropriate to read selectively, the techniques of skimming and scanning are useful. Skimming is a process of reading only main ideas and simply glancing as the remainder of the material. There are three basic types of skimming: preread skimming, skim-reading, and review skimming. The type of skimming used depends on the reader's purpose. Scanning is a method of selective reading that is used when searching for a particular fact or answer to a question.

Sample Textbook Chapter

Health, Stress, and Coping
(from Zimbardo, *Psychology and Life*)

14

Health, Stress, and Coping

It started out like most school days for the big-city college teacher—only bleaker. He was late because he had overslept, having set the clock-radio alarm to 7:00 P.M. instead of 7:00 A.M. (a Freudian wishful fantasy, no doubt); but he was still tired. He hadn't gone to sleep until almost 2:00 A.M., and he hadn't slept well—he had been worrying all night about his promotion decision, due to be handed down today by the senior faculty.

He skipped breakfast, checked to see if his socks were the same color, fly zipped, gathered his lecture notes together, and raced down the four flights of stairs to head off another parking ticket. He had already been tagged for over $200 worth, and he was determined not to get stung again; but with alternate street parking from 8:00 A.M. and overcongested traffic, it was a Mission Impossible situation.

7:58 and counting. But where was his car? He couldn't remember where he had parked it, because every night it was parked on a different street. He gambled on 71st Street—and lost. Running down 68th Street, he was just in time to see a police officer approaching his car. Too late; in an instant the ticket was issued and he owed the city another $15.00.

Outrage slowly turned to anger as he drove away and nearly ran a pedestrian down at the corner (she deserved to be frightened for walking so slowly). They exchanged obscenities. In no time he was stuck in the morning traffic jam in the tunnel—horns honking, exhaust fumes building up, tempers boiling.

Eleven minutes late to class, he begged departing students to return. Most did so resentfully. The lecture went badly; he couldn't concentrate or get his emotions under sufficient control. He felt guilty for having forced the class to stay and promised himself to give a dynamite lecture tomorrow to make up for today's disaster (but that would mean working late again, and he was tired already).

During office hours, he had some doughnuts and coffee, and smoked a few cigarettes. His research assistant told him she had to leave school to work full-time because her father had died and she must support her family. She cried over the loss of her father and her education. He was distressed at the loss of his only reliable graduate assistant. He took some aspirin for the headache that got progressively worse during endless student counseling.

Afternoon mail a mixed bag. First letter told him his research article had been accepted for publication in a prestigious journal. Joy! Second letter told him he was overdrawn again at the bank—and it was ten days before payday. He wouldn't borrow from his kid brother again; too humiliating. What could he sell? He began to feel overwhelmed, depressed. There was no way out!

Finally he was invited into the Chairman's office. He wished he had not already finished his last pack of cigarettes. "We all respect the kind of work you've been doing . . . *but (but! but!)* some people feel you need more time to mellow . . . too brash."

Depressed: "I don't deserve it; I'm not any good."

Angry: "They're all wrong."

Result: more depressed; headache built up between his eyes. He gulped down a stiff drink from the bottle he kept in his desk.

Later in the day, he forgot to keep his doctor's appointment to check on the headaches and chest pain he'd been having. He got some candy bars and a soft drink from the vending machine, ignoring his secretary's pointed remarks about the extra weight he was gaining. Then he lost his temper with her for not finishing the typing he had given her yesterday. She cried and he apologized. He decided to call it a day.

He got stuck in the evening rush-hour traffic, as usual; but finally he got home—or, almost. He drove up 69th, down 70th, up 71st, down 72nd—in search of the elusive 10 × 4 feet of unoccupied asphalt in which to bury his car. The day ended like any other day—only much bleaker.

his account of the activities of one college professor is far removed from the serene life we imagine to exist in the "Ivory Tower" of academia. This stress-filled life-style is propelling this teacher—and many like him in other lines of work—away from well-being and toward illness. The choices he makes about eating, drinking, smoking, exercise, and commuting, as well as decisions regarding work and achievement, combine to create an unhealthy pattern of living that could be lethal. Even before this unhealthy life-style shortens the teacher's expected life span, it will spawn a variety of negative physical and psychological consequences that diminish the quality of his life. Moreover, because "no person is an island unto him or herself," as this teacher's stress builds, it spills over, negatively affecting the lives of those with whom he interacts. Thus he becomes a source of stress as well as its target.

In this chapter, we will see psychologists playing dual roles as scientists and advocates for health. As scientists engaged in one of psychology's newest research areas—health psychology—they investigate the ways in which psychological and social processes contribute to the development, treatment, and prevention of illness. As advocates, they are willing to apply their research findings and recommend strategies to help people get well and stay healthy. Moreover, they are able to utilize their methodological skills in the evaluation of medical and psychological interventions designed to promote health.

►Health and Health Psychology

Health refers to the general condition of the body and mind in terms of their soundness and vigor. It is not simply the absence of illness or injury, but is more a matter of how well all the body's component parts are working. "To be healthy is to have the ability, despite an occasional bout of illness, to live with full use of your faculties and to be vigorous, alert, and happy to be alive, even in old age" (Insel & Roth, 1985, p. xvii).

The development of modern health care has rested largely on the biomedical model, which incorporates a dualistic conception of mind and body. The body alone—its changes and its pathology—has been the basis for the diagnosis and treatment of illness; the mind has been viewed as the province of philosophers and priests, not physicians. However, in recent years there has been a profound rethinking about the mind-body rela-

Table 14.1 *Take Care of Yourself*

Research indicates that people who practice seven simple health habits feel better, have fewer illnesses, and are less likely to miss work or school because of health problems (Belloc & Breslow, 1972). How well are *you* following these basic rules for good health?

1. Do not smoke cigarettes.
2. Get some regular exercise.
3. Use alcohol moderately or not at all.
4. Get seven or eight hours of sleep nightly.
5. Maintain proper weight.
6. Eat breakfast.
7. Do not eat between meals.

tionship. It is now recognized that the state of the body is linked in important ways to the state of the mind. For example, there is substantial research evidence that the mind can influence susceptibility and resistance to disease, apparently because of the physiological links between the brain, nervous system, and the immune system (Ornstein & Sobel, 1987).

In one set of studies, laboratory rats were subjected to stressful events. For some rats, the stress was uncontrollable; there was nothing they could do to change it. For other rats, the stress was under their control, because they learned to terminate the stressor by turning a wheel. This difference in the psychological factor of control was of critical importance. Although both groups of rats received exactly the same number of stressful events, the rats who lacked control showed decrements in their immune functioning. (Maier, 1984)

Psychological and social factors play a significant role in physical health, and the understanding of this point is leading to the development of a *biopsychosocial* model of health and illness. For example, a person is more likely to stay well if he or she practices good health habits, such as those listed in **Table 14.1;** but what determines whether these habits are carried out? They are certainly influenced by the person's beliefs and attitudes, cultural values, and the practice of these habits by family or friends. Psychological factors have also been clearly demonstrated to have a place in the development of many major illnesses (including heart disease, cancer, and stroke), as well as in such disorders as ulcers, high blood pressure, infectious diseases, migraine, low back pain, dermatitis, obesity, asthma, and diabetes. Furthermore, good health practices, such as those listed in Table 14.1, have been correlated with lower mortality rates (see **Figure 14.1**).

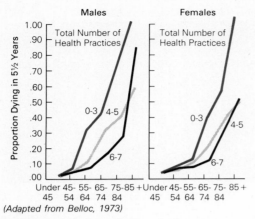

Males   Females

Total Number of Health Practices

Total Number of Health Practices

Proportion Dying in 5½ Years

1.00 .90 .80 .70 .60 .50 .40 .30 .20 .10 .00

0-3   4-5

6-7

0-3   4-5

6-7

Under 45- 55- 65- 75-85+   Under 45-55- 65- 75- 85 +
45   54 64 74 84   45   54 64 74 84

(Adapted from Belloc, 1973)

Figure 14.1 *Health Practices and Mortality*
Adults who followed most or all of the good health practices listed in Table 14.1 were found to be in better health than adults who followed few or none of the practices. A five and one-half year follow-up indicated a correlation between the health practices and longevity. The more of the seven practices followed, the lower were mortality rates at each age level.

The acknowledgment of the importance of psychological factors in health has spurred the growth of health psychology. **Health psychology** is devoted to understanding psychological influences on the way people stay healthy, the reasons they become ill, and the way they respond when they do get ill (Taylor, 1986). There are several different areas of concern for health psychologists: (a) health promotion and maintenance; (b) prevention and treatment of illness; (c) causes and correlates of health, illness, and dysfunction; and (d) improvement of the health care system and health policy information (Matarazzo, 1980).

There are several other fields that have focused on the study of psychology and medicine. How is health psychology related to them? *Behavioral medicine* had its origins in the psychological tradition of behaviorism (see chapter 1). As such, it dealt with overt health behaviors and the conditions that modified or maintained them. However, it has expanded beyond those early behaviorist boundaries. In addition to studying covert, as well as overt, behaviors, it draws on many other disciplines besides psychology, including immunology, neuroanatomy, epidemiology, anthropology, sociology, pharmacology, and public health (Miller, 1983). Thus, behavioral medicine is more an *interdisciplinary* field, whereas health psychology involves primarily the single discipline of psychology. Another related area is *psychosomatic medicine,* which, like health psychology, focuses on the rela-

tionship between psychological and somatic (bodily) processes; however, this area has developed within the field of psychiatry.

Other relevant disciplines in the social sciences are *medical sociology* and *medical anthropology,* which are also concerned with studying health and illness. The difference between them and health psychology lies in the unit of analysis. For psychology, the unit is the *individual;* for sociology, it is the larger *group;* and for anthropology, it is the *culture.* Thus, for instance, a medical sociologist might study the structure of a hospital or develop proposals for modifying its operation in order to provide better health care (Cockerham, 1978). A medical anthropologist might be concerned about cultural differences in the definition of health and illness, or cultural rituals for the treatment of disease (Foster & Anderson, 1978).

All of these medical fields are related to health psychology and share with it a reliance on the biopsychosocial model. However, health psychology has some unique contributions to make to our understanding of health and illness. In the following sections, we will get an overview of these contributions by looking at each of the major areas of health psychology.

Health Promotion and Maintenance

The first area focuses on the ways in which people can stay well and healthy and the methods that can be used to encourage such healthy behaviors. For example, it has been well established that regular exercise is an important factor in promoting and maintaining health. In particular, major improvements in health are gained from such exercises as bicycling, swimming, running, or jumping rope. These *aerobic* exercises are characterized by high intensity, long duration, and high endurance; and they lead to increased fitness of the heart and respiratory systems, improvement of muscle tone and strength, and many other health benefits. However, most people do not engage in such exercise in any consistent way. Researchers are now exploring the questions of who exercises regularly and why, as well as trying to determine what programs or strategies are most effective in getting people to start exercising and *continue* exercising (Dishman, 1982). One clear finding has been that people are more likely to exercise regularly if it is easy and convenient to do so. This is one reason why many companies are now providing exercise equipment, aerobics classes, or jogging tracks for their employees to use during their work breaks.

490   Chapter 14   Health, Stress, and Coping

Joseph Matarazzo

Other examples of health-promoting behaviors are immunizations for childhood diseases and paying attention to diet (eating foods low in cholesterol and fats, eating regular meals, avoiding sugary snacks) and dental hygiene (brushing teeth regularly, using dental floss, having regular check-ups). Health psychologists must find ways to educate people about such health habits and motivate them to practice and maintain these habits. Psychologists have studied principles for changing attitudes and modifying behavior (as we shall see in chapter 17) and have applied these principles to techniques for therapy and for social change. Clearly, they can also apply them to the promotion of health.

Prevention and Treatment of Illness

Prevention of illness means to eliminate or reduce the risk that people will get sick. The prevention of illness in the 1980s poses a much different challenge than it did at the turn of the century (Matarazzo, 1984). In 1900 the primary cause of death was infectious disease. Health practitioners at that time launched the "first revolution" in American public health. Through the use of research, public education, the development of vaccines, and changes in public health standards (such as waste control and sewage), they were able to eradicate, or substantially reduce, such diseases as influenza, tuberculosis, polio, measles, and smallpox.

Today the primary cause of death is *life-style* (see **Table 14.2**). Smoking, being overweight, eating foods high in cholesterol, drinking too much alcohol, driving without seat belts, and leading stressful lives—all of these factors play a major role in heart disease, cancer, strokes, cirrhosis, accidents, and suicide (see the **Close-up** on preventing AIDS on p. 492). It is estimated that almost half of the deaths in the United States are the result of life-style factors, a statistic that led the U.S. Surgeon

General to call for a "second revolution" in American public health (U.S. Department of Health, Education, and Welfare, 1979). In his report on the health of the nation, then-Secretary of Health, Education and Welfare Joseph Califano remarked:

> We are killing ourselves by our own careless habits. We are killing ourselves by carelessly polluting the environment.
>
> We are killing ourselves by permitting harmful social conditions to persist—conditions like poverty, hunger and ignorance—which destroy health, especially for infants and children.
>
> You, the individual, can do more for your own health and well-being than any doctor, any hospital, any drug, any exotic medical device. (1979, p. viii)

Table 14.2 Major Causes of Death and Associated Risk Factors, United States, 1977

Cause	Percentage of Deaths	Risk Factor
Heart Disease	37.8	Smoking, hypertension, elevated serum cholesterol, diet, lack of exercise, diabetes, stress, family history
Malignant Neoplasms (cancer)	20.4	Smoking, worksite carcinogens, environmental carcinogens, alcohol, diet
Stroke	9.6	Hypertension, smoking, elevated serum cholesterol, stress
Accidents Other Than Motor Vehicle	2.8	Alcohol, drug abuse, smoking (fires), product design, handgun availability
Influenza and Pneumonia	2.7	Smoking, vaccination status
Motor Vehicle Accidents	2.6	Alcohol, no seat belts, roadway design, vehicle engineering
Diabetes	1.7	Obesity
Cirrhosis of the Liver	1.6	Alcohol abuse
Arteriosclerosis	1.5	Elevated serum cholesterol
Suicide	1.5	Stress, alcohol and drug abuse, gun availability

(Adapted from Harris, 1980)

Close-up *Life-style Factors in Preventing AIDS*

One of today's most frightening diseases is AIDS. Unheard of until a few years ago, it is now an epidemic; over 25,000 persons in the United States are known to have contracted AIDS, and, of these, about half have died. It is estimated that 1.5 million people are infected with the AIDS virus (although they may not yet be aware of it) and that all of them are capable of spreading the virus to others (U.S. Public Health Service, 1986).

AIDS is an acronym for Acquired Immune Deficiency Syndrome. The AIDS virus is known by several scientific names: HIV (Human Immunodeficiency Virus), HTLV-III (Human T-Lymphotropic Virus), or LAV (Lymphadenopathy Associated Virus). This virus attacks the white blood cells (T-Lymphocytes) in human blood, thus damaging a person's immune system and weakening his or her ability to fight other diseases. The person then becomes vulnerable to infection by a host of other viruses and bacteria, which can cause such life-threatening illnesses as cancer, meningitis, and pneumonia. The AIDS virus can be passed from one person to another primarily in one of two ways: (a) the exchange of semen and blood during sexual contact, and (b) the sharing of intravenous drug

needles and syringes used for "shooting" drugs.

At the present time, *THERE IS NO CURE FOR AIDS.* Also, at the present time, *THERE IS NO VACCINE TO PREVENT AIDS.*

Who is at risk? *Everyone.* Although the initial discovery of AIDS in the United States was in the male homosexual community, the disease has spread. AIDS is being found among heterosexuals as well as homosexuals and among women, as well as men. It is predicted that AIDS will increase and spread throughout the general population, in just the same way as other sexually transmitted diseases like syphilis and gonorrhea—but with much more devastating consequences to the affected individuals and society. Given the escalating number of AIDS cases, the anticipated additional burden on the health care system will be unprecedented.

The only way to protect oneself from being infected with AIDS is to change those *lifestyle* factors that put one at risk. Basically, this means making changes in patterns of sexual behavior. The safest approach is either to abstain from sexual activity or to be faithful to one (noninfected) partner, who is also monogamous. However, where multiple sexual partners are involved, then the *only* way to prevent infection by the AIDS

virus is to: (a) be tested for AIDS, and (b) practice "safe sex"—that is, use condoms during sexual contact.

At this time, *prevention* is the only protection against AIDS—and it is our only hope for stopping the AIDS epidemic.

For further information about AIDS, see Coates et al., 1984; Nungesser, 1986, and Temoshok et al., 1987. You can also call these toll-free telephone hotlines: Public Health Service AIDS Hotline (800/342-AIDS), Nationally Sexually Transmitted Diseases Hotline (800/221-7044).

This second revolution involves the necessity for Americans to modify their behavioral choices, which clearly have more effect on well-being and longevity than biological and genetic makeup or their exposure to viruses and bacteria. The American government has become increasingly involved in establishing national goals for the prevention of

disease and the protection and promotion of health (see **Table 14.3**).

What are prevention strategies in the "war on life-style"? One approach is to change or eliminate poor health habits. Programs to help people quit smoking, lose excess weight, or reduce alcohol intake are examples of this strategy.

492   Chapter 14   Health, Stress, and Coping

A major study to prevent heart disease was conducted in three towns in California. The goals of the study were (a) to persuade people to reduce their cardiovascular risk via changes in smoking, diet, and exercise; and (b) to determine which method of persuasion was more effective. In one town a two-year campaign was conducted through the mass media, using television, radio, newspapers, billboards, and mailed leaflets. The second town received the same two-year media campaign plus a personal instruction program on modifying health habits for high-risk individuals. The third town served as a control group and received no persuasive campaign. How successful were the campaigns in modifying life-style? The results showed that the townspeople who had gotten only the mass-media campaign were more knowledgeable about the links between life-style and heart disease, but they showed only modest changes in their own behaviors and health status. However, in the town where the media campaign was supplemented with personal instruction, people showed more substantial and long-lasting changes in their health habits, particularly reduced smoking. (Farquhar et al., 1984; Maccoby et al., 1977)

Thus, the good news is that life-style factors *can* be modified. The bad news is that: (a) it is difficult and expensive to do so, and (b) mass media campaigns are not as effective in changing some health behaviors as had been hoped. They may, however, contribute to long-term changes in social attitudes that support life-style changes.

Another approach to prevention is to keep people from developing bad health habits in the first place. It is not easy to get people to stop a behavior that is well established, so it may be more effective in the long run to discover how to keep them from

getting started. This issue is clearly illustrated by the habit of smoking, which has enormous societal costs and has been called the single greatest cause of preventable death in the United States. The severe economic costs to the nation associated with smoking are estimated to be nearly $54 billion a year, according to a team of five leading health economists quoted in the *Washington Post* (April 21, 1987). Their figures are as follows:

Direct Medical Costs	$23.3 billion
Salary Losses per Year	9.3
Lifetime Earning Losses of Smokers who Died in 1984	21.1
Total	$53.7 billion

In 1980 a total of 270,269 deaths were attributed to smoking—resulting in 3.9 million person-years lost. Smoking behavior is notoriously hard to change, despite a wide variety of programs and therapies (Leventhal & Cleary, 1980). Because smoking often starts in adolescence, some psychologists have tried to tackle the problem by studying ways to persuade teenagers *not* to try cigarettes. The programs that seem to be most successful provide antismoking information in formats that appeal to adolescents, portray a positive image of the nonsmoker as independent and self-reliant, and use peer group techniques—popular peers serve as nonsmoking role models—and instruction in ways to resist peer pressure (Evans et al., 1978). The principles developed from campaigns to teach people to "just say no" can be used to prevent the onset of drug use and other addictive behaviors.

Unlike prevention, *treatment* focuses on helping people adjust to their illnesses and recover from them. Pain is an aspect of many illnesses and injuries, and there are many psychological techniques of pain control, such as biofeedback, hypnosis, relaxation, and distraction (see our earlier discussion in chapter 5, p. 181). In addition to pain, emotional distress may be aroused by various medical procedures. Some people may be afraid of a dentist's drill or get upset at the idea of having surgery.

Table 14.3 *Fifteen Specific, Measurable Objectives for Producing Better Health for Americans by 1990*

A. Preventive Health Services
1. Control of high blood pressure
2. Family planning
3. Pregnancy and infant health
4. Immunization
5. Sexually transmitted diseases

B. Health Protection
6. Control of toxic agents
7. Occupational safety and health
8. Accident prevention and injury control
9. Fluoridation and dental health
10. Surveillance and control of infectious diseases

C. Health Promotion
11. Smoking and health
12. Misuse of alcohol and drugs
13. Nutrition
14. Physical fitness and exercise
15. Control of stress and violent behavior

(From Matarazzo, 1984)

Researchers have found that patients who show the best recovery from surgery are those who received complete information before their operations. This information prepared the patients for the aftereffects of the surgery, both physical and emotional, and gave them a greater sense of psychological control. Patients who received sufficient preoperative information showed better postoperative adjustment on a number of indexes: they experienced less psychological distress, they did not need as many narcotics to control pain, and they were able to leave the hospital sooner. (Janis, 1958; Johnson, 1983)

Often a treatment regimen, which might include medications, dietary changes, prescribed periods of bed rest and exercise, and follow-up procedures (such as return check-ups, rehabilitation training, or chemotherapy), will be established for patients. Inducing them to stick to these treatment plans (a problem known as patient adherence or compliance) is a major issue for health care professionals and health psychologists. The communication between patient and practitioner is an important factor in patient adherence (and is also a factor in the rise of malpractice litigation). When practitioners communicate clearly, make sure that their patients understand what has been said, act courteously, and convey a sense of caring and supportiveness, patients will be more satisfied with their health care and will be more likely to adhere to the prescribed treatments (DiMatteo & DiNicola, 1982). Compliance-gaining strategies developed by social psychologists (described in chapter 17) help overcome the lack of cooperation between patients and practitioners.

Type A people are always in a hurry, are unable to relax, and strive intensely for achievement.

Causes and Correlates of Health, Illness, and Dysfunction

Health psychologists are also interested in the *causes* (etiology) of illness and injury. Clearly, bad health habits are important causal factors, as noted earlier; however, personality or individual behavioral styles may also play a causal role.

A great deal of research attention has focused on a particular behavioral style called the **Type A behavior syndrome** that contributes to the chances of coronary heart disease. Type A people are always in a hurry, unable to relax, and are abrupt in their speech and gestures, frequently interrupting to finish what someone else is saying. They are highly competitive, insist on "going it alone," strive intensely for achievement, show a high level of hostility and impatience, and engage in compulsive activity. Some of these characteristics are valued in our society, but this is a very *dysfunctional* behavioral style. Type A businessmen, for example, are stricken with coronary heart disease more than twice as often as men in the general population (Friedman & Rosenman, 1974; Jenkins, 1976). In fact, many studies have shown that people manifesting the Type A behavior syndrome are at significantly greater risk for *all* forms of cardiovascular disease (Dembroski et al., 1978; Haynes & Feinleib, 1980). Unfortunately, Type A behavior patterns are now being seen among college and high-school students, and even among children in grade school (Thoresen & Eagleston, 1983).

Men have been much more likely than women to develop the Type A syndrome, evidently because our society has encouraged and reinforced those traits as essential for success in a competitive business enterprise (see **Close-up:** *The Masculine Gender Role Is Hazardous to Your Health,* p. 495). Alas, as more women enter top-level business positions, we are seeing more Type A behavior emerging among females, although there are twice as many Type A men under fifty who currently have coronary heart disease than Type A women of similar age. By contrast, among people who are clearly *not* Type A, the chances of such disease are equally low in both sexes.

Can Type A behaviors be modified to reduce the risk of heart disease? According to recent research, the answer is yes. When post-heart-attack patients were involved in an extensive 3-year program of counseling and behavior modification techniques, they showed fewer Type A behaviors, and they had a lower rate of repeat heart attacks (Friedman et al., 1984).

Health Care System and Health Policy Formation

A final focus of health psychology is on the delivery of health care. Health institutions, the health professionals who staff them, and the health policies that guide them have all been the focus of research. For example, studies have found distinct patterns in the use of health services. Social class is an important factor—the poor are more likely to be ill, but they have less money to spend on health care. Those who are poor are more likely to see a physician only for emergencies and not for any regular or preventive care, and they usually get treated in clinics rather than private offices (Herman, 1972). Other studies have found differences between eth-

"The Masculine Gender Role Is Hazardous to Your Health"

It has long been known that men, as a group in our society, die younger than women. In 1980, the average life span for males was about eight years shorter than that for females. In addition, there are striking sex differences in many of the major causes of death. As can be seen in the table, the death rate for males exceeds that for females for several types of disease. Moreover, the ratio of males to females is extremely large for homicide, suicide, and accidents. Analyses of this sex differential show clearly that the primary cause is *life-style*—even more than biological factors. More specifically, it is the behaviors which are learned as part of the masculine gender role that put males at greater risk (Harrison, 1978). "Each of these causes of death is linked to behaviors which are encouraged or accepted more in males than in

Major Causes of Death (1980 Data)

	Percentage of All Deaths	Ratio of Males to Females (as a percentage)
Heart Disease	38.3	1.2
Cancer	20.9	1.2
Cerebrovascular Disease	9.6	.7
Accidents	5.3	2.6
Pulmonary Disease (asthma, bronchitis, emphysema)	2.8	2.3
Influenza and Pneumonia	2.7	1.1
Diabetes Mellitus	1.8	.7
Cirrhosis, Liver Disease	1.5	1.9
Arteriosclerosis	1.5	.7
Suicide	1.4	3.4
Homicide	1.2	3.8
Certain Causes in Infancy	1.1	1.4

(U.S. National Center for Health Statistics, 1984)

females: using guns, drinking alcohol, smoking, working at hazardous jobs, and seeming to be fearless. Thus, the behaviors of males in our society make a major contribution to their elevated mortality" (Waldron, 1976, p. 2).

---

nic groups in the interpretation of their symptoms and their readiness to seek medical treatment (Zola, 1973).

Providing health care can be enormously challenging and rewarding; however, dealing with pain, illness, and death can be so emotionally stressful that practitioners run the risk of "burnout." **Burnout** is a syndrome of emotional exhaustion, depersonalization, and reduced personal accomplishment. Health practitioners begin to lose their caring and concern for the patients, and may come to treat them in detached and even dehumanized ways. As they do so, they begin to feel bad about themselves and worry that they are failures. Burnout is correlated with greater absenteeism and turnover, impaired job performance, poor relations with coworkers, family problems, and poor personal health (Maslach, 1982).

Several social and situational factors affect the occurrence and level of burnout—and, by implication, suggest ways of preventing or minimizing it. For example, the quality of the patient-practitioner interaction is greatly affected by the number of patients for whom a practitioner is providing care; The greater the number, the greater the cognitive, sensory, and emotional overload. Another factor is the amount of direct contact with patients. Longer work hours in continuous direct contact with patients is correlated with greater burnout, especially when the nature of the contact is very difficult and upsetting (patients who are dying or who are verbally abusive). The emotional strain of such prolonged contact can be eased by a work schedule that provides chances for a practitioner to withdraw temporarily from such high-stress situations, while doing some other kind of work.

Health and Health Psychology **495**

Issues of stress and coping have long been a central, core topic of health psychology. "Stress affects the lives of all people, everywhere. It is a cause of illness and accidents, producing stress in the victims and those who must care for them. Stress affects personality, modifying our perceptions, feelings, attitudes, and behavior, and it reaches beyond its immediate victims to affect the political, social, and work organizations whose activities they direct and carry out. . . . Growth and survival are very much related to . . . success in coping with stress" (Warshaw, 1979, p. 3).

In the remaining sections of this chapter, we will look at what psychologists mean by *stress*. Within this broad area of basic research and application, three general questions are of major concern to health psychologists: How does stress affect us physically and psychologically? How do common stressors in our society affect our health? How can we cope with stress more effectively?

▶ The Concept of Stress

It should be obvious from the *Opening Case* why stress has been called a "disease of civilization." The rapid pace of our lives, overcrowded living conditions, too many demands on our time, interferences with our personal ambitions, and frustrating job conditions all contribute to the modern stress equation; but would we be better off without stress? That would be a life without challenge—no difficulties to surmount, no new fields to conquer, no reason to sharpen our wits or improve our abilities. Stress is an unavoidable part of living, because every organism faces challenges from its environment and from its own needs. These challenges are "problems" it must solve if it is to survive and thrive.

Stress is the pattern of specific and nonspecific responses an organism makes to stimulus events that disturb its equilibrium and tax or exceed its ability to cope. The stimulus events include a large variety of external and internal conditions that collectively are called stressors. A **stressor** is a stimulus event that places a demand on an organism for some kind of adaptive response. The stress response is composed of a diverse combination of reactions on several levels, including physiological, behavioral, emotional, and cognitive changes.

No doubt you have observed that some people experience one stressful event after another and do not break down, while others are seriously upset by even low-level stress. This happens because the effect of most stressors is not a direct one, but is determined partly by other conditions. These conditions are known as **moderator variables**—variables that change the effect of a stressor. The cognitive appraisal and evaluation of a stressor is one such moderator variable—is it viewed as a threat or a challenge? The resource that is available to deal with that stressor is another moderator variable. All of these elements of the stress process—stressors, stress, cognitive appraisal, resources, and stress response—are diagrammed in **Figure 14.2.**

The Role of Cognitive Appraisal

Before a stress response begins, a demand on the organism (stressor) must be recognized on some level and evaluated. **Cognitive appraisal** plays a central role in defining the situation—what the demand is, how big a threat it is, what resources one has for meeting it, and what strategies are appropriate. Some stressors, such as bodily injury or finding one's house on fire are seen as threats by almost anyone, but many other stressors can be defined in various ways, depending on our overall life situation, the relation of this particular demand to our central goals, our competence for dealing with it, and our assessment of our competence. The situation that causes acute distress for me may be all in a day's work for you.

Our appraisal of a stressor and of our resources for meeting it can be as important as the actual stressor in determining our conscious experience, what coping strategies we will see as appropriate, and how successful we will be. If we define a stressor as too much for us to deal with, we create a self-fulfilling prophecy: we are likely to fail even if objectively we are capable of dealing adequately with the demand. Doctors have long known that a patient's attitude can be as important as the physical condition in determining the course of the illness (see *Close-up*, p. 498).

Cognitive appraisal may define a stressor as an interesting new challenge that will be fun to test oneself against instead of as a threat. The experience may be one of exhilaration, of being "psyched up," anticipating achievement and increased self-esteem. Such a positive reaction to a stressor has been called **eustress** (*eu* means "good").

Richard Lazarus, a pioneer in recent stress research, has distinguished between two stages in our cognitive appraisal of demands. He uses the term **primary appraisal** for the primary evaluation of the seriousness of a demand. It starts with

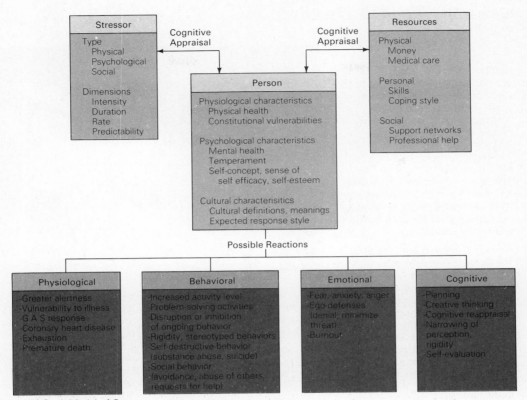

Figure 14.2 *A Model of Stress*
This chart summarizes the main relationships discussed in this chapter. Cognitive appraisal of the stress situation influences and is influenced by the stressor itself and the physical, social, and personal resources available for dealing with it. The person, embodying a unique combination of physiological, psychological, and cultural characteristics, reacts to threat in various possible ways, including physiological, behavioral, emotional, and cognitive responses, some adaptive and some maladaptive or even lethal.

the questions: What's happening? Is this thing good for me, stressful, or irrelevant? If the answer is *stressful,* an individual appraises the potential impact of the stressor by determining whether harm has occurred, or is likely to, and whether action is called for. Once a person decides something must be done, **secondary appraisal** begins. The person evaluates the personal and social resources that are available to deal with the stressful circumstance and the action that is needed (Lazarus, 1966). Then, as coping responses are tried, appraisal continues; if the first ones don't work and the stress persists, new responses are initiated. **Chronic stress** is defined as a state of arousal, continuing over time, in which demands are perceived by an individual as greater than the inner and outer resources available for dealing with them (Powell & Eagleston, 1983).

Physiological Stress Reactions

In chapter 4 we learned that the brain developed originally as a center for more efficient coordination of action. *Efficiency* meant flexibility of response to changing environmental requirements and also a quicker, often automatic response. One set of brain-controlled physiological stress responses occurs when an organism perceives an external threat (a predator, for example). Instant action and extra strength may be needed if the organism is to survive; a whole constellation of automatic mechanisms has evolved that meet this need. Another set of physiological stress reactions occurs when the danger is internal, and the stability and integrity of the organism are threatened by invading microbes or other disease agents that upset the normal physiological processes.

Close-up   *Voodoo Deaths*

Captivating to the imagination are the sudden voodoo deaths described in anthropological reports. There are many documented cases in which healthy people who believed that they had transgressed sacred laws or had been the subjects of curses have died soon afterward. The following is an account of behavior observed in one tribe when a man discovered that a bone was being pointed at him in a certain way by an enemy.

He stands aghast, with his eyes staring at the treacherous pointer, and with his hands lifted as though to ward off the lethal medium, which he imagines is pouring into his body. His cheeks blanch and his eyes become glassy and the expression of his face becomes horribly distorted. . . . He attempts to shriek but usually the sound chokes in his throat, and all that one might see is froth at his mouth. His body begins to tremble and the muscles twist involuntarily. He sways backwards and falls to the ground, and after a short time appears to be in a swoon; but soon after he writhes as if in mortal agony, and, covering his face with his hands, begins to moan. . . . From this time onwards he sickens and frets, refusing to eat and keeping aloof from the daily affairs of the tribe. Unless help is forthcoming in the shape of a countercharm . . . his death is only a matter of a comparatively short time. (Basedow, 1925, cited in Cannon, 1942, p. 172)

Other reports tell of healthy people succumbing to sudden death upon discovering that they have transgressed against the supernatural world by eating for-

bidden food. In one case, the expectation of death—and hence the death itself—was delayed until long after the fateful act.

A young traveler, visiting a friend, was served a dish containing fowl. He asked if it was wild hen, a delicacy banned for the young, and ate it only when assured that it was not. A few years later, the friend admitted laughingly that it had, in fact, been wild hen. The young man began to tremble and within twenty-four hours was dead. (Pinkerton, 1814)

Reports such as these were thoroughly analyzed by the respected physiologist Walter Cannon (1942), who became convinced of the reality of the phenomenon, though, at the time, such reports were generally greeted with skepticism by sophisticated Westerners.

Two explanations for the "sudden death" phenomenon associated with extreme fright and feelings of hopelessness were advanced. According to Cannon's theory (1957), oversecretion of epinephrine could im-

pair the capillary walls, allowing a passage of fluid to the surrounding tissues; the resulting reduction in the volume of the circulating blood could send the organism into a state of shock, leading to deterioration of the heart and nerve centers. Another researcher, who observed sudden death in wild rats placed under extreme, frightening stress, found that overstimulation of the parasympathetic nervous system was responsible (Richter, 1957). More recently, an anthropologist studying Australian aborigines has found evidence that victims of sorcery may actually die from dehydration when family and friends withdraw all life-support systems, including water (Eastwell, 1984).

Today we not only recognize the reality of the close interdependence of psychological and physiological processes, but are identifying the precise mechanisms by which emotions, attitudes, and beliefs can lead to physiological reactions that can become illness-inducing or life-threatening (see Lachman, 1983).

498

Emergency Reactions to External Threats

In the 1920s Walter Cannon, a Harvard University physiologist, outlined the first scientific description of the way animals and humans respond to external danger. He found that a sequence of activity was triggered in the nerves and glands to prepare the body for combat and struggle—or for running away to safety. Cannon called this basic dual stress response the **"fight-or-flight" syndrome.**

At the center of this primitive stress response is the *hypothalamus*, which, as we have seen, is involved in a variety of emotional responses. The hypothalamus has sometimes been referred to as the "stress center" because of its twin functions in emergencies: (a) it controls the autonomic nervous system, and (b) it activates the pituitary gland.

The autonomic nervous system (described briefly in chapter 4) regulates the activities of the body's organs. In conditions appraised as stressful, breathing becomes faster and deeper, heart rate increases, blood vessels constrict, and blood pressure rises. In addition to these internal changes, muscles open the passages of the throat and nose to allow more air into the lungs, while also producing facial expressions of strong emotion. Messages go to smooth muscles to stop certain bodily functions, such as digestion.

Another function of the autonomic nervous system during stress is to "get the adrenaline flowing." It signals the inner part of the adrenal glands, the adrenal medulla, to release two hormones, epinephrine and norepinephrine, which, in turn, signal a number of other organs to perform their specialized functions. The spleen releases more red blood corpuscles (to aid in clotting if there is an injury), while the bone marrow is stimulated to make more white corpuscles (to combat infection). The liver is stimulated to produce more sugar, which builds up body energy. It is believed that epinephrine (also called adrenaline) plays a more important role in fear reactions (and flight) while norepinephrine (also called noradrenaline) is more associated with rage reactions (and fight).

The pituitary gland responds to signals from the hypothalamus by secreting two hormones vital to the stress reaction. The **thyrotrophic hormone (TTH)** stimulates the thyroid gland which, in turn, makes more energy available to the body. The **adrenocorticotrophic hormone (ACTH)** stimulates the outer part of the adrenal glands, the adrenal cortex, resulting in the release of a group of hormones called *steroids*, which are important in metabolic processes and in release of sugar into the blood from the liver. ACTH also signals various organs of the body to release about thirty other hormones, each of which plays a role in the body's adjustment to this "call to arms." A summary of this physiological stress response is shown in **Figure 14.3.**

Figure 14.3 *The Body's Response to Stress*

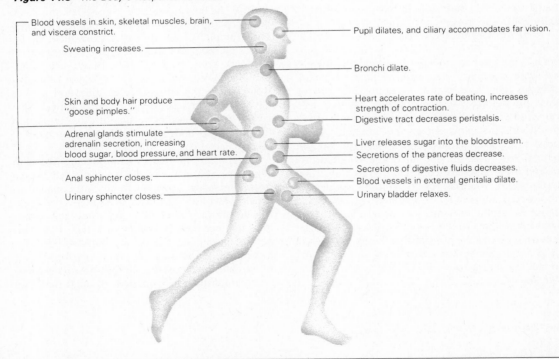

- Blood vessels in skin, skeletal muscles, brain, and viscera constrict.
- Sweating increases.
- Skin and body hair produce "goose pimples."
- Adrenal glands stimulate adrenalin secretion, increasing blood sugar, blood pressure, and heart rate.
- Anal sphincter closes.
- Urinary sphincter closes.
- Pupil dilates, and ciliary accommodates far vision.
- Bronchi dilate.
- Heart accelerates rate of beating, increases strength of contraction.
- Digestive tract decreases peristalsis.
- Liver releases sugar into the bloodstream.
- Secretions of the pancreas decrease.
- Secretions of digestive fluids decreases.
- Blood vessels in external genitalia dilate.
- Urinary bladder relaxes.

A firefighter undergoes a physiological response to stress so that he or she can endure the physical strain.

It is obvious, then, that many bodily processes are activated by danger signals. Now let's consider their adaptive significance in two different stressful situations. When a call comes into a firehouse, the fire fighters respond with the physiological components of the stress response. Muscles tense, breathing speeds up, heart rate increases, adrenaline flows, extra energy becomes available, and the fire fighters become less sensitive to pain. They will need these responses in order to endure the physical strain of battling a potentially destructive, sometimes lethal, disaster. These built-in capacities to deal with *physical* stressors by mobilizing the body's active response systems have been valuable throughout the ages.

Now consider people working on a crisis "hot line," taking calls from potentially suicidal strangers. These workers undergo the same physiological stress responses as a result of the *psychological* stressors they face. In contrast to the fire fighters, their physiological response is not adaptive, because no physical activity is being demanded that might use the extra energy and strength. They must, instead, try to stay calm, concentrate on listening, and make thoughtful decisions. Unfortunately, these skills are not enhanced by the stress response, so what has developed in the species as an adaptive preparation for dealing with external danger is not the most adaptive pattern for dealing with many modern-day sources of stress. In fact, recurring or chronic arousal that is not dealt with by appropriate physical activity may, in time, lead to malfunctioning. (See also "The Way We Act" in *The Best of Science*.)

The General Adaptation Syndrome

The first modern researcher to investigate the effects of continued severe stress on the body was Hans Selye, a Canadian endocrinologist. Selye studied stressors that threatened the physical functioning of the body rather than stressors, like predators, that required behavioral responses. According to Selye's theory of stress, there are many kinds of stressors (including all diseases and many other physical and psychological conditions), but all call for adaptation by an organism to maintain or regain its integrity and well-being. (This is another aspect of homeostasis, mentioned in chapter 11.)

In addition to responses that are specific to a particular stressor (such as constriction of the blood vessels in response to cold), there is a characteristic pattern of *nonspecific* adaptational physiological mechanisms that occurs in response to continuing threat by almost any serious stressor. Selye called this pattern the **general adaptation syndrome (GAS).** He found a characteristic sequence of three stages in this syndrome: an alarm reaction, a stage of resistance, and a stage of exhaustion (Selye, 1956). These stages are diagrammed in **Figure 14.4:** "The General Adaptation Syndrome."

The *alarm reaction* consists of the physiological changes by which a threatened organism immediately moves to restore its normal functioning. Whether the stressor is physical (such as inadequate food, loss of sleep, disease, bodily injury) or psychological (such as loss of love or personal security), the alarm reaction consists of the same general pattern of bodily and biochemical changes. For example, people suffering from different illnesses all seem to complain of such symptoms as headache, fever, fatigue, aching muscles and joints, loss of appetite, and a general feeling of being unwell. Unlike the emergency mobilization for behavioral action against an external danger, discussed in the preceding section, the alarm reaction mobilizes the body's defenses for restoration of inner balance.

If exposure to the stress-producing situation continues, the alarm reaction is followed by the *stage of resistance*, in which an organism appears to develop a resistance to the stressor. Even though the disturbing stimulation continues, the symptoms that occurred during the first stage disappear, and the physiological processes that had been disturbed during the alarm reaction appear to return to normal. This resistance to the stressor seems to be accomplished, in large part, through increased

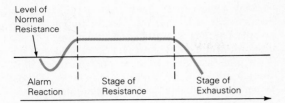

Figure 14.4 *The General Adaptation Syndrome*
On exposure to a stressor, the body's resistance is diminished until the physiological changes of the alarm reaction bring it back up to the normal level. Then, if the stressor continues, the defensive changes "overshoot" in the stage of resistance and the bodily signs characteristic of the alarm reaction virtually disappear; resistance to that stressor rises above normal, but is less to other stressors. Following prolonged exposure to the stressor, adaptation breaks down; in the stage of exhaustion, signs of the alarm reaction reappear, but now the stressor effects are irreversible, and the individual becomes ill and may die. (From Selye, 1974, p. 39)

secretions from the anterior pituitary and the adrenal cortex (ACTH and *cortin,* respectively).

Although there is *greater* resistance to the original stressor during this second stage, there is *reduced* resistance to other stressors. Even a weak stressor may now produce a strong response if it comes when the body's resources are engaged in resisting an earlier, more potent stressor. Some people find they get irritated more easily when getting over a cold, for example. General resistance to disease is reduced in this stage of resistance even though adaptation to the specific noxious agent is improved.

If exposure to the injurious stressor continues too long, a point is reached where an organism can no longer maintain its resistance. It then enters the third phase of Selye's general adaptation syndrome—the *stage of exhaustion*. The anterior pituitary and the adrenal cortex are unable to continue secreting their hormones at the increased rate. This means that the organism can no longer adapt to the chronic stress. Many of the symptoms of the alarm reaction now begin to reappear. If the stressor continues, destruction of bodily tissues, and even death, may occur.

The concept of the general adaptation syndrome has proven valuable to explain disorders that had baffled physicians. Within this framework, many disorders can be viewed as the results of the physiological processes involved in the body's long-continued attempts to adapt to a perceived dangerous stressor. The value of additional ACTH and cortisone in treating some of these diseases can also be understood: such treatment evidently helps the

anterior pituitary and the adrenal cortex maintain the body's resistance to the stressor.

On the other hand, because Selye was a physician, and because his research focused on reactions to physical stressors among experimental animals, such as laboratory rats, his theory has had little to say about the importance of *psychological* aspects of stress in the case of human beings. In particular, Selye's critics believe he overstated the role of nonspecific, *systemic* factors in the production of stress-induced illness. (*Systemic* refers to the whole body as a system, not specific parts.) In work on animals, of course, there was no place for recognizing the importance of cognitive appraisal in human stress reactions, where the perceived *meaning* of a situation determines which physiological reactions occur (Lazarus, 1974; Mason, 1975). Selye himself came to examine similar concepts in his later writings (Selye, 1974). In any case, he is still recognized as the pioneering explorer of stress reactions; his insights and research have led to the creation of a whole new field of study.

Stress and Disease

Selye's original theory emphasized that the stress response occurs as a reaction to various stressors, including illness. The theory also shows how a long-continued stress reaction can itself lead to illness. In fact, stress is now believed to be a contributing factor in more than half of all cases of disease (Pelletier & Peper, 1977). For example, hypertension, a disease that increases the risk of heart attack and premature death, is a stress-related disease.

There are three ways in which stressors can be causal factors in illness. First, long-continued severe stress or chronic arousal resulting from perceived threat can, in time, lead to physiological malfunctioning and illness. In the case of the hotline workers, the emergency physiological arousal for dealing actively with perceived threat was not adaptive when action was not called for. This is true of most psychological stressors, yet the physiological arousal is automatic and keeps occurring anyway whenever people are anxious, feel threatened, or feel pressured. It is their personal appraisal of a situation, and not its objective reality, that matters.

Psychosomatic ("mind/body") **disorders,** also called *psychophysiologic disorders,* are physical disorders in which emotions and thought processes are believed to play a central role. Psychosomatic disorders are often called **diseases of adaptation,** because they have their roots in attempts to adapt to stressors. Stress-induced peptic ulcers or high blood pressure are classic examples of diseases of adaptation, although not all cases of these two disorders are induced by stress. Many disorders can have their origin in either physical or psychological factors or a combination of the two. For a chronic psychological stressor to lead to a physical disorder, a person must have a constitutional vulnerability in a particular bodily system and an ineffective style of dealing with a stressful situation. The person must be either unaware of the chronic emotional arousal or convinced that there is no better way to cope with the difficult situation.

Stressors can also cause illness when the complex physiological mechanisms of the general adaptation syndrome fail to function appropriately and themselves produce diseases. Defensive processes that normally are adaptive are used to excess or used unnecessarily; the body overreacts or reacts inappropriately to foreign invaders or other stressors that may threaten its stability. How does the body know which "invaders" are potentially harmful? The body does *not* always know, and sometimes it makes errors; sometimes, in fact, it responds to stimuli that are actually benign. Allergic reactions are the clearest example of this response. Ragweed pollen has no direct harmful effects on the body; we are best off ignoring its presence. For some people, however, ragweed pollen (or various other allergens) sets off an allergic response involving inflammation of nasal tissues and, often, a total body general adaptation syndrome. Allergies are true diseases of adaptation: if the body did not evaluate the stressor as a danger and create an unnecessary stress response, there would be no disease.

There is a third way in which stress is implicated in illness. The continuing process of adaptation, depleting an organism's store of adaptation energy and cumulatively damaging organ systems, can result in eventual illness. Each of us has a limited reserve of energy which can be used to adapt to stressors. When it has been exhausted, we can no longer fight stressors and will be overcome by disease. This is why all organisms eventually reach the "stage of exhaustion" in the general adaptation syndrome if the stressor is not removed. Although a person may lead an active, healthy life, successfully coping with specific stressors as they arise, each experience of stress uses up some adaptation energy. The thing to do, Selye argued, is to use our adaptation energy wisely, rather than squandering it by responding to civilization's "false alarms" that might better be ignored.

Selye believed that aging itself is primarily the result of loss of "adaptation energy" and of damage to organ systems incurred during a lifetime of stress responses. In his view, our bodies do not age at an even rate, according to some predetermined biological process. Rather, death occurs for each of us when our "weak link" gives out (assuming no special disease or accident). The "weak link" is determined partly by genetic vulnerability and partly by the stressors each of us has faced. It should be recognized that Selye's explanation of aging is far from complete, given the complexity of the aging process and the other causal factors involved (Timiras, 1978). However, there is general agreement that long-continued, severe stress hastens aging, and that reductions in severe stress can contribute to a longer and healthier life span.

Psychological Stress Reactions

Our physiological stress reactions are automatic and predictable, built-in responses over which we normally have no conscious control. Not so our psychological reactions. They are learned and are

The need for a bubble helmet illustrates how little we know about controlling allergies—the immune system's overreaction to harmless particles of pollen, dust, and animal dander.

heavily dependent on our perceptions and interpretations of the world and of our capacity for dealing with it. They include behavioral, emotional, and cognitive aspects.

Behavioral Patterns

The behavior of a person under stress depends in part on the level of stress experienced. *Mild stress* activates and intensifies biologically significant behaviors, such as eating, aggression, and sexual behavior. Mild stress makes an organism more alert; energies are focused and performance may improve. Positive behavioral adjustments may occur, such as becoming better informed, becoming vigilant to sources of threat, seeking protection and support from others, and learning better attitudes and coping skills.

Continued unresolved stressors, such as those that beset the harried professor in our *Opening Case*, can accumulate to become more severe with time, causing maladaptive behavioral reactions such as increased irritability, poor concentration, lessened productivity, and chronic impatience. However, any of those stressors occurring only occasionally, or seen as within a person's capacity to control, causes no problem.

Moderate stress typically disrupts behavior, especially complex behavior requiring skilled coordination. Giving a speech or playing in a recital are familiar examples. For some people, overeating is a typical behavioral response to moderate levels of stress. Aggressive behavior can also occur, especially in response to frustration (we will learn more about the link between frustration and aggression in chapter 18). Moderate stress may also produce repetitive, stereotyped actions, such as pacing in circles or rocking back and forth. These repetitive responses have mixed effects. They are *adaptive* by reducing a high level of stressor stimulation and lessening an individual's sensitivity to the environment. At the same time, they are *nonadaptive* by being rigid and inflexible, and in persisting even when the environmental situation makes other responses more appropriate.

Severe stress inhibits and suppresses behavior and may lead to total immobility, as in the case of the dogs that learned helplessness after being shocked where no escape was possible (p. 268). It has been argued that immobility under severe stress may be a defensive reaction, representing "an attempt by the organism to reduce or eliminate the deleterious effects of stress . . . a form of self-therapy" (Antelman & Caggiula, 1980).

Emotional Aspects

The stress response includes a variety of emotional reactions ranging from exhilaration, in the cases where the stressor is seen as an exciting, manageable challenge, to the far more common negative emotions of irritation, anger, anxiety, discouragement, and depression. Most stress is acutely uncomfortable, producing only negative emotions and efforts to lessen the discomfort in direct or indirect ways.

Stressful life changes involving the loss or separation from friends and loved ones are frequent forerunners of *depression*. Being left behind when important others die or move away seems more likely to result in depression than a similar separation caused by one's own action (Paykel, 1973). Experiencing a cluster of stressful events is another predictor of emotional depression. We will examine the emotional reactions involved in depression when we review affective disorders in chapter 15.

Rape victims, survivors of plane crashes, combat veterans, and others who have experienced extremely traumatic events may react emotionally with a **posttraumatic stress disorder.** This reaction is characterized by involuntary reexperiencing of the traumatic event(s)—especially the original feelings of shock, horror, and fear—in dreams or "flashbacks." In addition, victims experience an emotional numbing in relation to everyday events, associated with feelings of alienation from other people. Finally, the emotional pain of this reaction can result in an increase of various symptoms, such as sleep problems, guilt about surviving, difficulty in concentrating, and an exaggerated startle response (see *Close-up,* p. 504.)

The emotional responses of posttraumatic stress can occur in an acute form immediately following a disaster and can subside over a period of several months. It can also persist, becoming a chronic syndrome called the **residual stress pattern** (Silver & Wortman, 1980). These emotional responses can also be delayed for months or even years. Clinicians are still discovering veterans of World War II and the Korean War who are displaying residual or delayed posttraumatic stress disorders (Dickman & Zeiss, 1982).

This delayed posttraumatic stress syndrome has been a special problem in the case of Vietnam war veterans (Blank, 1982). The problems of many of these former soldiers seemed to be made worse by feelings that they had been rejected by an unsympathetic American public and betrayed by their

Close-up *The Aftershock of Rape*

Two college women who had been sexually assaulted describe some of the enduring psychological dynamics generated by that extremely stressful episode.

Shock

Alice: I was in shock for a pretty long time. I could talk about the fact that I was a rape victim, but the emotions didn't start surfacing until a month later.

Beth: During the first two weeks there were people I had chosen to tell who were very, very supportive; but after two weeks, it was like, "Okay, she's over it, we can go on now." But the farther along you get, the more support you need, because, as time passes, you become aware of your emotions and the need to deal with them.

Denial

Alice: There is a point where you deny it happened. You just completely bury it.

Beth: It's so unreal that you don't want to believe that it actually happened or that it can happen. Then you go through a long period of fear and anger.

Fear

Alice: I'm terrified of going jogging. [Alice had been jogging when she was raped.] I completely stopped any kind of physical activity after I was raped. I started it again this quarter, but every time I go jogging I have a perpetual fear. My pulse doubles. Of course I don't go jogging alone any more, but still the fear is there constantly.

Beth: I've experienced some really irrational thoughts. I was home at Christmas riding in the car with my Dad—my Dad!— and the guy who attacked me was about 21 years old—and yet I got really afraid all of a sudden of my Dad. It's just something you have to work out. There's not anything anybody can do.

Betrayal and Loneliness

Alice: There's also a feeling of having all your friends betray you. I had a dream in which I was being assaulted outside my dorm. In the dream, everyone was looking out their windows—the faces were so clear—every one of my friends

lined up against the windows watching, and there were even people two feet away from me. They all saw what was happening and none of them did anything. I woke up and had a feeling of extreme loneliness. Sometimes you just feel like there's nobody around.

Beth: I still feel very lonely [4 months later]. I didn't have any close friends when I got here. [Beth was raped at the start of her freshman year.] I felt betrayed by my family and friends from high school because they weren't here.

(Excerpted from the *Stanford Daily,* February 2, 1982, with permission. For a systematic analysis of psychological and social issues involved in rape, see Cann et al., 1981.)

---

government, and that they had spent important years of their lives in a wasted effort (Thienes-Hontos et al., 1982).

In a study of Vietnam veterans with combat experience, called the "Forgotten Warrior Project" (Wilson, 1980), it was found that:

1. *Their suicide rate was 23 to 33 percent higher than the national average.*
2. *Of those who had been married when they left the United States, 38 percent were divorced within six months after returning.*
3. *The rate of hospitalization for alcoholism or drinking problems was high and increasing.*
4. *About half of them still had some emotional problems related to adjustment to civilian life.*

Cognitive Effects

Once a stressor has been interpreted as threatening to one's well-being or self-esteem, a variety of intellectual functions may be adversely affected. In general, the greater the stress, the greater the reduction in cognitive efficiency and the interference with flexible thinking.

Because attention is a limited resource, a focus on the threatening aspects of a situation and on one's arousal reduces the amount of attention available for effective coping with the task at hand. Memory is affected too, because short-term memory is limited by the amount of attention given to new input, and retrieval of past relevant memories depends on smooth operation of the use of appropriate retrieval cues. Similarly, stress may interfere with problem solving, judging, and decision making by narrowing perceptions of alternatives and by substituting stereotyped, rigid thinking for more creative responding (Janis, 1982a).

A chronic feeling of threat can also be carried into ordinary situations, as happens when highly test-anxious students carry their anxiety into class discussions too. Finally, there is evidence that a high level of stress impairs children's intellectual development.

To test the hypothesis that stress affects competence and intelligence, researchers developed a stress index based on such variables as family problems and physical disorders. Stress indexes were calculated for over 4000 7-year-old children, and each child's intelligence was tested. The higher the stress index, the lower was the child's IQ. This was particularly true for children with eye problems and for lower-class black children. Children who were held back a year or were assigned to special education classes also showed greater intellectual deficits. The researchers concluded that the stress variables combined to influence the performance measured by the IQ test both in the immediate testing situation and also more generally, through interaction with other personal and social factors. (Brown & Rosenbaum, 1983)

Sources of Stress

Stress is a recurring problem. Naturally occurring changes are an unavoidable part of the lives of all of us. People close to us get sick, move away, die. We get new jobs, leave home, start college, succeed, fail, begin romances, get married, break up. In addition to the big life changes, there are also "life's little hassles"—frustrating traffic jams, snoring roommates, and missed appointments. Unpredictable, catastrophic events will occur for some of us, and for others, chronic societal problems will be important sources of stress.

Major Life Stressors

Sudden changes in our life situation are at the core of stressful life events for many of us. They may make it harder for us to act effectively or may make us physically ill. Even events that we welcome may require major changes in our routines and adaptation to new requirements; this, too, can be stressful.

The influence of major life changes on subsequent mental and physical health has been a source of considerable research. It started with the development of the Social Readjustment Rating Scale (SRRS), a simple scale for rating the degree of adjustment required by the various life changes that many people experience, including both pleasant and unpleasant changes. The scale was developed by asking adults, from all walks of life, to identify, from a list, all the life changes that applied to them and rate the amount of readjustment required by comparing each to marriage, which was arbitrarily assigned a value of 50 *life change units* (LCU). Researchers then calculated the total number of life change units an individual had undergone during that period, using it as a measure of the amount of stress the individual had experienced (Holmes & Rahe, 1967). A modification of this scale for college students is shown in **Table 14.4.**

Many studies have found that life change intensity, as measured by this scale, rises significantly before the onset of an illness. Life stress has been related to sudden cardiac death, tuberculosis, multiple sclerosis, diabetes, complications of pregnancy and birth, chronic illness, and many minor physical problems. It is believed that life stress increases a person's overall susceptibility to illness (Holmes & Masuda, 1974); but illness is itself a major stressor. As expected, LCU values are also high during an illness and for some time thereafter (Rahe & Arthur, 1977).

An improvement in measuring the effects of life events is provided in the Life Experiences Survey (LES), which has two special features. First, it provides scores for both increases *and* decreases in change, rather than increases only, as in the original scale. Second, its scores reflect individual assessments of the events and their desirability. For example, the death of an unloved spouse who left a big inheritance might be rated as quite desirable. Thus this scale goes beyond a mere count of the number of remembered life changes to measure the personal significance of each change (Sarason et al., 1978).

One problem with studies relating stressful life events to subsequent illness is that they tend to be *retrospective*. That is, both the stress measures and the illness measures are obtained by having subjects recall prior events. This presents an opportunity for distortion in memory to bias the results. For example, subjects who are sick may be more likely to remember past stressors than subjects who are well. More recently, however, *prospective* (looking ahead) studies have had similar findings. Life change scores on the *LES* have been obtained, and negative scores have been found to be significantly correlated with physical symptoms reported six months *later* (Johnson & Sarason, 1979). The message again is clear—too many stressful life events are bad for your health.

The Concept of Stress 505

Table 14.4 *Student Stress Scale*

The Student Stress Scale represents an adaptation of Holmes and Rahe's Social Readjustment Rating Scale. Each event is given a score that represents the amount of readjustment a person has to make in life as a result of the change. People with scores of 300 and higher have a high health risk. People scoring between 150 and 300 points have about a 50–50 chance of serious health change within two years. People scoring below 150 have a 1 in 3 chance of serious health change. Calculate your score each month of this year and then correlate those scores with any changes in your health status.

Event	Life Change Unit
Death of a Close Family Member	100
Death of a Close Friend	73
Divorce Between Parents	65
Jail Term	63
Major Personal Injury or Illness	63
Marriage	58
Fired from Job	50
Failed Important Course	47
Change in Health of Family Member	45
Pregnancy	45
Sex Problems	44
Serious Argument with Close Friend	40
Change in Financial Status	39
Change of Major	39
Trouble with Parents	39
New Girl- or Boyfriend	38
Increased Workload at School	37
Outstanding Personal Achievement	36
First Quarter/Semester in College	35
Change in Living Conditions	31
Serious Argument with Instructor	30
Lower Grades than Expected	29
Change in Sleeping Habits	29
Change in Social Activities	29
Change in Eating Habits	28
Chronic Car Trouble	26
Change in Number of Family Get-togethers	26
Too Many Missed Classes	25
Change of College	24
Dropped More than One Class	23
Minor Traffic Violations	20
My Total	_____

Life's Little Hassles

Life is filled with low-level frustrations. Your pencil breaks during an exam, you get stuck in traffic, or you forget to set your alarm clock for an important appointment. To what extent do these minor irritations pile up to become stressors that play havoc with your health? The answer is to a bigger extent than you might imagine.

A psychiatrist distributed 100 questionnaires to the faithful waiting for the 7:12 A.M. ''bullet'' train from Long Island into Manhattan. From the 49 completed questionnaires returned, it was determined that these average commuters had just gulped down their breakfast in less than 11 minutes, if at all; were prepared to spend 3 hours each day in transit; and in 10 years had logged about 7500 hours of rail time—assuming two-week vacations and no time off for illness. Two thirds of the commuters believed their family relations were im-

506 *Chapter 14 Health, Stress, and Coping*

paired by their commuting. Fifty-nine percent experienced fatigue, 47 percent were filled with conscious anger, 28 percent were anxious, and others reported headaches, muscle pains, indigestion, and other symptoms of the long-term consequences of beating the rat race in the city by living in the country. (F. Charaton, personal communication, Spring, 1973)

In another study, when a group of 100 white, middle-class, middle-aged men and women kept track of their daily hassles over a one-year period (along with a record of major life changes and physical symptoms), a clear relationship emerged between hassles and health problems: the more frequent and intense the hassles people reported, the poorer was their health, both physical and mental (Lazarus, 1981). This is only a correlational finding, however; the causal relationships are not clear.

Catastrophic Events

Dining and dancing in a beautiful setting on a Friday evening sounds like a prescription for relieving the stress of a hard week of work. Unfortunately it became, instead, a prescription for a disaster, creating great stress, when, in 1982, two aerial walkways collapsed into the lobby of a hotel in Kansas City, Missouri. Immediately affected were the 2000 people who were attending a tea dance, more than 300 of whom were killed or injured. Also experiencing stress were 1000 rescue workers, who worked more than 10 hours just to get through the rubble to all the victims. Another 5000 people were less directly affected: workers at the hotel, personnel at hospitals in the area, and friends and families of victims (Gist & Stolz, 1982). No count could be made of those who were affected in the immediate community and to television viewers across the nation, as people tried to deal with the senselessness of the event and the anxieties it created about the possibility of other such disasters elsewhere.

People's reactions when disaster strikes go through stages from shock to acceptance.

Research on the physical and psychological effects of catastrophic events has been prolific. However, it has followed a rather different research tradition from the one used in studies of personal stressors, and there is no scale assessing the relative impact of different kinds of natural disasters.

Researchers have found that five stages occur predictably in people's responses to disasters:

Typically, there is a period of shock and even "psychic numbness," during which people cannot fully comprehend what has happened. The next phase involves what has been called "automatic action"; people try to respond to the disaster and may behave adaptively, but with little awareness of their actions and poor later memory of the experience.

In the next stage, people often feel great accomplishment and even a positive sense of communal effort for a shared purpose. Also in this phase, people feel weary and are aware that they are using up their reserves of energy. During the next phase, they experience a letdown; their energy is depleted and the impact of the tragedy is finally comprehended and felt emotionally. An extended period of recovery follows, as people try to rebuild and to adapt to the changes brought about by the disaster. (Cohen & Ahearn, 1980)

Knowledge of these typical reaction stages provides a model that is helpful in predicting people's reactions when disaster strikes, enabling rescue workers to anticipate and help victims deal with the problems that arise. Responses to such varied events as floods, tornadoes, airplane crashes, and factory explosions have all been shown to fit this model of disaster reactions.

Chronic Societal Sources of Stress

What of environmental stressors that are part of the ongoing circumstances of life: overcrowding, economic recession, fear of nuclear war? What cumulative effect do such stressors have on us?

For today's children, the threat of nuclear war is a major source of stress. Studies of the nuclear fears of children since the mid-1960s have shown that children know and care about the threat of nuclear war and have a high degree of uncertainty about their own future. One of the early researchers concluded, "The profound uncertainty about whether or not mankind has a foreseeable future exerts a corrosive and malignant influence upon important development processes in normal and well-functioning children" (Escalona, 1965). Although this particular survey did not refer to the bomb or nuclear war, 70 percent of the children sampled mentioned spontaneously that their future would include nuclear weapons and destructive war.

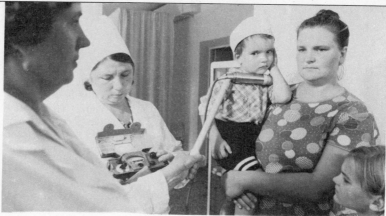

Twentieth-century technology has brought new frustrations into the lives of many people. The threat of nuclear war looms large in the minds of children as well as adults throughout the country. And chemical contamination of the environment has created a great deal of stress for individuals.

More recently, some psychiatrists made a detailed analysis of the attitudes of 1000 students in several parts of the country (Beardslee & Mack, 1983). They found a general disquiet and uneasiness about the future, with many students deeply disturbed. For example, a 10-year-old school child wrote to President Reagan:

> I am 10 years old. I think nuclear war is bad because many innocent people will die. The world could even be destroyed. I don't want to die. I don't want my family to die. I want to live and grow up. Please stop nuclear bombs. (Yudkin, 1984, p. 24)

Studies since 1983 have found a significant increase in the expression of fear, helplessness, and anger toward the adult generation, with many young people questioning whether it is worthwhile working hard to prepare for a future that they do not expect to have (Hanna, 1984; Yudkin, 1984).

Adults, too, are worried about nuclear disaster, but they are also affected by the more immediate problems of employment and economic security. Many stress-related problems increase when the economy is in a downswing. Admission to mental hospitals, infant mortality, suicide, and deaths from alcohol-related diseases and cardiovascular problems all increase (Brenner, 1976).

Psychologists found that unemployed men reported more symptoms, such as depression, anxiety, and worries about health than did those who were employed. Because these symptoms disappeared when they were subsequently reemployed, the researchers argued that the symptoms had been the results of being unemployed, rather than being indicators of more disturbed workers who had been particularly likely to lose their jobs. (Liem & Rayman, 1982)

The pollution of our environment creates psychological stress as well as physical threats. The chemical miracles of our modern technology have led to unexpected contamination of whole areas where people have had to be evacuated, as at Love Canal, near Buffalo, New York, and Times Beach, Missouri. The malfunctioning and consequent release of radioactive steam at the Three Mile Island nuclear power plant in 1979 and the 1986 explosion of the Russian nuclear power factory in Chernobyl provided dramatic examples of environmental stressors. Those living in the area experienced considerable stress from fears about the immediate and long-term health consequences. In addition, widespread stress was experienced by citizens in other parts of the world, worried about other possible nuclear accidents. One consequence of the American nuclear accident was the U.S. Court of Appeals' decision to recognize the *legal status* of psychological stress as a necessary part of the environmental impact survey that must be carried out before the plant could be reopened.

Environmental sources of stress, as well as the others considered in this section, arise out of our imperfect human capacity to solve all the problems of a complex society. Such problems are not simply technological, but also political and psychological. Many modern day stressors will require solutions not at the individual level, but through cooperation

508 *Chapter 14 Health, Stress, and Coping*

within communities and even across nations. The clearest example of this international concern for combating shared environmental stressors is the "acid rain" pollution that is harming the Canadian environment, in part caused by emissions from factories in the United States.

Coping Strategies

If living is inevitably stressful, and if too much stress can disrupt our lives, and even kill us, we need to learn how to cope so that we can survive. **Coping** refers to attempts to meet environmental demands in order to prevent negative consequences (Lazarus & Folkman, 1984). There are many different coping techniques, some of which will be more effective than others for a given person in a given situation.

Because animals in the wild must adapt biologically to their environment, their mechanisms for coping are coded in their genes and limited by the slow timetable of evolutionary processes. Human beings have a tremendous potential for adapting not only biologically, over generations, but psychologically, within a lifetime—even within a short period of time if they decide they want to change.

In this final section of the chapter, we will look at a variety of strategies that people use to reduce the amount of stress they experience and to lessen its harmful effects. Some strategies are ones that most of us use naturally and habitually, whereas others are special techniques that can be learned. Some strategies are individual ones, to be done "on one's own"; in contrast, social strategies depend on the presence of other people.

Problem-focused Versus Emotion-focused Coping

Coping strategies can be grouped into two main types, depending on whether the goal is to *deal with the problem* (problem-focused) or to *lessen the discomfort of it* (emotion-focused). Several subcategories of these two basic approaches are shown in **Table 14.5.**

The first main approach includes any strategy to deal *directly* with the stressor, whether through overt action or through realistic problem-solving mental activities. We face up to a bully or run away; we try to win him or her over with bribes or other incentives. Taking martial arts training or notifying the "proper authorities" are other approaches that may prevent a bully from continuing to be a threat. In all these strategies, our focus is on the *problem* to be dealt with and on the agent that has induced the stress. We acknowledge the "call to action," we appraise the situation and our resources for dealing with it, and we undertake a response that is appropriate for removing or lessening the threat.

In the second approach, we do not look for ways of changing the stressful situation; instead we try to change our feelings and thoughts about it. This coping strategy is called *emotion regulation*. It is a remedial, rather than a problem-solving strategy, because it is aimed at relieving the emotional impact of stress to make us feel better, even though the threatening or harmful stressor is not changed. Relying on this approach, people may take alcohol or tranquilizers—and these may work for a while. On occasion, haven't you dealt with an unpleasant event by using consciously planned distractions such as going to a party or watching TV? Some-

Table 14.5 *Taxonomy of Coping Strategies*

Problem-focused Coping Change stressor or one's relationship to it through direct actions and/or problem-solving activities	Fight (destroy, remove, or weaken the threat)
	Flight (distance oneself from the threat)
	Seek options to fight or flight (negotiating, bargaining, compromising)
	Prevent future stress (act to increase one's resistance or decrease strength of anticipated stress)
Emotion-focused Coping Change self through "activities" that make one feel better but do not change the stressor	Somatically focused activities (use of drugs, relaxation, biofeedback)
	Cognitively focused activities (planned distractions, fantasies, thoughts about oneself)
	Unconscious processes that distort reality and result in intrapsychic stress

(Lazarus, 1975)

times, we confront our fears by ''whistling a happy tune'' or with laughter (see *Close-up,* p. 511). However, this approach to coping has its drawbacks.

> *One research study compared depressed and nondepressed middle-aged people over a one-year period. It was found that those who were depressed were using appraisals and coping patterns that created problems and perpetuated their depression. They were just as likely as the nondepressed to feel that something could be done about the situations they faced, and even to focus on problem solutions, but they diverged in their tendency to accentuate the negative. They worried more about not being stronger, wished they could change themselves and/or the situation, kept putting off action until they had more information, and spent more time seeking emotional support for their feelings of distress. What emerged was an indecisive coping style that was likely to promote a sense of personal inadequacy—which, in turn, was a source of more depression. (Coyne et al., 1981)*

The ego defense mechanisms discussed in chapter 12 (such as repression, denial of reality, and rationalization) are familiar emotion-regulating approaches. Undertaken unconsciously to protect us from the pain of inner anxieties, they enable us to appraise situations in less self-threatening ways. They lead to coping strategies that are essentially aimed at self-protection rather than at solving problems. At times, however, they cause us to distort reality and, when overused, can lead to maladaptive coping.

Altering Bodily Reactions

''Stress equals tension'' for many people. This often means tight muscles, high blood pressure, constricted blood vessels in the brain, and chronic oversecretion of hormones. Fortunately, many of these tension responses can be controlled by a variety of techniques—some ages old, some quite new.

Relaxation

Relaxation through meditation has ancient roots in many parts of the world. For centuries in Eastern cultures, ways to calm the mind and still the body's tensions have been practiced. Today Zen discipline and Yoga exercises from Japan and India are part of daily life for many people both there and, increasingly, in the West. In our own culture, a growing number of people have been attracted to workshops and therapy in relaxation training and to various forms of meditation.

Just as stress is the nonspecific response of the body to any demand made on it, there is growing evidence that complete relaxation is a potent antistress response. The *relaxation response* is a condition in which muscle tension, cortical activity, heart rate, and blood pressure all decrease and breathing slows. There is reduced electrical activity in the brain, and input to the central nervous system from the outside environment is lowered. In this low level of arousal, recuperation from stress can take place. Four conditions are regarded as necessary to produce the relaxation response: (a) a quiet environment, (b) closed eyes, (c) a comfortable position, and (d) a repetitive mental device. The first three lower input to the nervous system, while the fourth lowers its internal stimulation (Benson, 1975).

Progressive relaxation is a technique that has been widely used in American psychotherapy. Designed by Edmund Jacobson (1970), the approach teaches people alternately to tense and relax their muscles. In this way they learn the experience of relaxation and discover how to extend it to each specific muscle. After several months of daily practice with progressive relaxation, people are able to achieve deep levels of relaxation. The relaxation response can also be produced by hypnosis. The beneficial effects of these relaxation training methods extend beyond the time when people are actively practicing them. For example, in one study hypertensive patients who learned to lower their blood pressure by relaxing continued to have lower blood pressure when they were asleep (Agras et al., 1980).

Biofeedback

Biological feedback, or *biofeedback,* was described briefly in chapter 8. Sophisticated recording devices and computers make it possible to provide this feedback by detecting small changes in a body process, amplifying them, and indicating they are present by means of a visual or auditory signal which is ''on'' whenever the change is occurring. Paradoxically, although individuals do not know how they do it, concentrating on the desired result in the presence of this signal produces change in the desired direction. Biofeedback is a self-regulatory technique being used for a variety of special applications, such as control of blood pressure, relaxation of forehead muscles (involved in tension headaches), and even overcoming extreme blushing. This method is also being used to induce nonspecific general relaxation (Birbaumer and Kimmel, 1979).

It's Not So Stressful When I Laugh

For decades the *Reader's Digest* has carried a feature of jokes entitled "Laughter, the Best Medicine." Is it? What is the relationship between laughter and stress? There are several lines of evidence to suggest that humor is used by children to handle stressful home life; that professional comedians and comedy writers tend to come from family backgrounds filled with tension, and that laughter may be good therapy for certain kinds of illness.

A longitudinal study examined the development of humor in young children during the first six years of their lives.

The elementary-school-age children who laughed most were those who had been exposed to "tough and potentially hazardous situations" and whose mothers had withheld help in solving problems. In contrast, children who had been "babied" and protected from conflict had a less developed sense of humor. (McGhee, 1979)

This finding supports the view of Freud (1905/1960) that humor may develop as a means of coping with stressful situations or anxiety-arousing circumstances.

Humor as a "coping mechanism" is also revealed in two studies in which professional comedians and comedy writers were interviewed. Most professional humorists tended to be funny as children and continued this style of relating to people into adulthood (Fry & Allen, 1975). Their childhood typically showed a pattern of early stress and poor home adjustment. Their early lives were "marked by suf-fering, isolation, and feelings of deprivation. Humor offered a relief from their sufferings and a defense against inescapable panic and anxiety" (Janus, 1975, p. 174).

Carol Burnett, for example, had parents who were both alcoholics and fought frequently. She describes using humor as a way of gaining strength rather than "buckling under" in her tension-filled home. Humor created a playful state of mind for her as a child, deflected her attention away from its source onto the role of child-as-comedian, and dissipated some of the hostile feelings.

If a stressful childhood can promote the development of humor, maybe laughter can work to reduce adult stress. Norman Cousins, former editor of *The Saturday Review,* used such reasoning to help himself recover from a serious illness. He was hospitalized for a rare disease of the connective tissue, which is crippling and from which he was told he would not recover. Working with a cooperative physician, he checked out of the hospital and into a hotel room where for several months he supplemented massive injections of ascorbic acid (vitamin C) with a steady diet of old *Candid Camera* films and other belly-laugh-inducing movies. He completely recovered from his "incurable illness."

Fifteen years later, a high-pressure schedule of travel, speaking, and deadlines led to a heart attack and a diagnosis of damaged heart muscle and congested coronary arteries. Cousins was able to avoid a bypass operation by again confidently taking charge of his own recovery. Following a regimen of diet, gradually increasing exercise, writing, amateur photography, and *humor,* he was able to resume full-time work less than a year after his attack (Cousins, 1979, 1983). Allen Funt, the genius behind *Candid Camera,* is currently involved in a project to make available to patients funny scenarios from his library of classics and then to evaluate their effectiveness in coping with illness (from a personal communication, April 1987).

Modifying Cognitive Strategies

A powerful way to handle stress more adaptively is to change our evaluations of stressors and our self-defeating cognitions about the way we are dealing with them. We need to find a different way to think about a given situation, our role in it, and the causal attributions we make to explain the undesirable outcome.

Reappraising Stressors

The close connection between cognitive appraisal and the degree of autonomic nervous system arousal has been demonstrated in studies where the cognitive appraisal was systematically varied.

> When subjects watched an upsetting film showing vivid circumcision rites in a primitive tribe, they were less physiologically aroused when the film had a sound track that either denied the dangers or discussed them in an intellectual, detached way. (Speisman et al., 1964)
>
> In another study, subjects viewing a film of an industrial accident were less aroused if they were "emotionally inoculated" by being warned in advance that it was coming and given a chance to imagine the threatening scenes beforehand. As shown in Figure 14.5, this cognitive preparation, which gave them an opportunity to rehearse mentally both the stressful episode and their coping responses to it, was more successful than relaxation training in lowering arousal. (Folkins et al., 1968)

Learning to think differently about certain stressors, to relabel them, or to imagine them in a less threatening (perhaps even funny) context are forms of cognitive reappraisal that can reduce stress.

Restructuring Cognitions

Another way of managing stress better is intentionally changing what we are telling ourselves about stress and our handling of it. Such messages can lead to both cognitive restructuring and more effective coping. For example, depressed or insecure people often tell themselves that they are no good, that they'll do poorly, and—if something goes well—that it was a fluke.

Meichenbaum (1977) has proposed a three-phase process to intentionally change this self-fulfilling cycle. In Phase 1, people work to develop a greater awareness of their actual behavior, what instigates it, and what its results are. One of the best ways of doing this is to keep daily logs. By helping people redefine their problems in terms of their causes and results, they can increase their feelings of control.

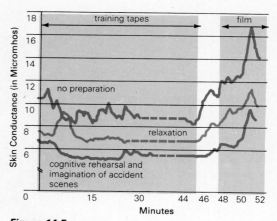

Figure 14.5
Stress induced by highly arousing films can be lowered to some extent by relaxation training. "Emotional inoculation" through cognitive rehearsal of the stressful scenes lowers the stress response even more. (Adapted from Folkins et al., 1968)

In Phase 2, they begin to identify new behaviors that negate the maladaptive, self-defeating behaviors—perhaps smiling at someone, offering a compliment, or acting assertively. In Phase 3, after adaptive behaviors are being emitted, individuals appraise their consequences, avoiding the former internal dialogue of put-downs. Instead of telling themselves "I was lucky the professor called on me when I happened to have read the text," they will say, "I'm glad I was prepared for the professor's question. It feels great to be able to respond intelligently in that class."

In sum, this approach means initiating responses and self-statements that are incompatible with previous defeatist cognitions. The people realize that they are changing and taking full credit for it—which promotes further successes. **Table 14.6** gives examples of the new kinds of self-statements that help at different stages in dealing with stressful situations.

Supportiveness of the Environment

Life in societies is the most powerful weapon in the struggle for life. . . . Thus it was that thousands of years before humans appeared, association [of animals in social units] was preparing the way for human society. (Chapin, 1913, p. 103)

We all cope with stress as individuals, but for a lifetime of effective coping and for the continued success of our species, it is necessary for us to band together with our families, friends, and neighbors (at home and throughout our small planet). Isola-

512 *Chapter 14 Health, Stress, and Coping*

Table 14.6 *Examples of Coping Self-Statements*

Preparation
I can develop a plan to deal with it.
Just think about what I can do about it. That's better than getting anxious.
No negative self-statements, just think rationally.

Confrontation
One step at a time; I can handle this situation.
This anxiety is what the doctor said I would feel: it's a reminder to use my coping exercises.
Relax; I'm in control. Take a slow deep breath. Ah, good.

Coping
When fear comes just pause.
Keep focus on the present; what is it I have to do?
Don't try to eliminate fear totally; just keep it manageable.
It's not the worst thing that can happen.
Just think about something else.

Self-reinforcement
It worked; I was able to do it.
It wasn't as bad as I expected.
I'm really pleased with the progress I'm making.

(Adapted from Meichenbaum, 1975)

tion can lead to inadequate coping and is itself the cause of much stress. Much contemporary research points to the improvement in coping that can come from being part of a social support network and from living and working in a healthy environment.

Social Support Networks

Social support refers to the resources provided by other persons (Cohen & Syme, 1985). These resources can include material aid, socioemotional support (love, caring, esteem, sympathy, sense of group belonging), and informational aid (advice, personal feedback, information). The persons who can provide these resources for an individual are those with whom he or she has significant social relationships—such as family members, friends, coworkers, and neighbors.

There is now a sizable body of evidence showing that the presence of social support makes people less vulnerable to stress. When people have other people they can turn to, they are better able to handle job stressors, unemployment, marital disruption, serious illness, and other catastrophes, as well as their everyday problems of living (Gottlieb, 1981; Pilisuk & Parks, 1986).

Nearly 7000 adults were surveyed in 1965 to determine their health and health-related behaviors, as well as other background factors and the extent of their social relationships. From this information a social network index was computed for each person, based on the number and importance of social contacts in the person's life. Mortality (death rate) data were then collected for a 9-year period on 96 percent of this original sample.

The social network index was significantly correlated with overall death rate and also with cause of death. For every age group and both sexes, there were more deaths among people who had few social contacts than among those with many connections. This effect was independent of their health status at the time of the initial survey and independent of their socioeconomic status. Furthermore, those who were socially isolated had been more likely to engage in poor health behaviors (smoking, drinking, overeating, irregular eating, inadequate sleep). Nevertheless the extent of their social contacts still predicted their mortality over and above the effects of any or all of these poor health practices. In fact, most of the deaths occurred among those who lacked social and community ties. It is clear that lack of a social support system increases one's vulnerability to disease and death. (Berkman & Syme, 1979)

Other studies have found that socially unconnected people engage in more maladaptive ways of thinking and behaving than do those who share their concerns with other people (Silberfeld, 1978). *Decreases* in social support in family and work environments are related to *increases* in psychological maladjustment. This negative relationship was found even when the researchers looked at groups who had the same *initial* levels of support, maladjustment, and life change (Holohan & Moos, 1981).

Structure of the Physical Environment

Like the harried professor in our *Opening Case*, many of us are often coping with a succession of frustrating, stressful events—too often in ways that increase our stress still further. We need to give more thought to changing our unhealthy, stress-

Coping Strategies 513

inducing *environments,* as well as developing more effective and satisfying behavior patterns.

In a study of residential care programs for the elderly, more cohesive, supportive groups developed where the environment provided such simple amenities as lounges and seating arrangements that were well grouped for conversation (Moos & Lemke, 1984). Likewise, the physical structure of a college dormitory influences the social climate among the students.

> *In one study, residents in dormitories with long corridors of many rooms had more difficulty developing a social support network than residents in dormitories with short corridors. The smaller areas helped define small friendship groups, while the extended areas created a greater sense of impersonality. (Baum & Valins, 1979)*
>
> *When the students on the long corridors felt that their living conditions were crowded, they developed coping patterns to deal with conflict situations that differed from the patterns developed by those living in short-corridor dormitories. On an experimental task in which it is possible either to cooperate or to compete, the residents of short corridors tended to be more cooperative. The students on the long corridors tended to be either more competitive or more likely to withdraw. (Baum et al., 1982)*

In addition to the physical structure of the environment, its social and psychological dimensions can be critically important in increasing or decreasing stress. For example, the perceived freedom of choice to either enter or not enter a particular environment may determine whether a person will adapt successfully to it. As we saw in chapter 2, elderly women who chose to go into a retirement home lived longer, as a group, than those who entered feeling they had no choice (Ferrare, 1962). Moreover, when residents of retirement homes felt that they had more choice and control over their environment, their health improved and they engaged in more activities (Rodin, 1983). Such research findings have important implications for policies and programs in institutional settings.

Stress Control and Your Mental Health

The harried professor in our *Opening Case* experienced many stressors, but several choices he had made contributed to his stress level and lack of good health—to eat poorly, to live in an overcrowded and noisy city, to own a car, to work at a competitive job, and to spend more than he earned. What choices are *you* making? Are they producing stress that is damaging to your health and well-being?

Instead of waiting for stress or illness to come and then reacting to it, we need to set goals and structure our lives and life-styles in ways most likely to bring us what we really want. The following ideas are presented as guidelines to encourage a more active role in taking charge of your own life and in creating a more positive psychological environment for yourself and others.

1. Look for the causes of your behavior in the current situation or in its relation to past situations, and *not* just in some defect in yourself. Understand the *context* of your behavior.

2. Compare your reactions, thoughts, and feelings with those of other comparable individuals in your current life environment so that you can gauge the appropriateness and relevance of your responses.

3. Have several close friends with whom you can share feelings, joys, and worries. Work at developing, maintaining, and expanding your social support networks.

4. Don't be afraid to risk showing others that you want to be their friend or even to give and accept love. Don't let rejection deter you from trying again—after "cleaning up your act."

5. Never say bad things about yourself, such as *stupid, ugly, uncreative, a failure.* Look for sources of your unhappiness in elements that can be modified by future actions—what can you do differently next time to get what you want?

6. Always take full credit for your successes and happiness (and share your positive feeling with other people).

7. Keep an inventory of all the things that make you special and unique, those qualities you have to offer others. For example, a shy person can offer a talkative person the gift of being an attentive listener. Know your sources of personal strength and the coping resources available to you.

8. When you feel you are losing control over your emotions (hyperexcited or depressed), distance yourself from the situation by: (a) physically leaving it; (b) role-playing the position of some other person in the situation or conflict; (c) projecting your imagination into the future to gain temporal perspective on what seems like an overwhelming problem now; or (d) talking to someone who is sympathetic.

9. Don't dwell on past misfortunes or sources of guilt, shame, and failure. The past is gone and thinking about it keeps it alive in memory. Nothing you have said or done is new under the sun.

514   Chapter 14   Health, Stress, and Coping

10. Remember that failure and disappointment are sometimes blessings in disguise, telling you that your goals are not right for you or saving you from bigger letdowns later on. Learn from every failure experience. Acknowledge it by saying, "I made a mistake," and move on.

11. If you see someone you think is troubled, intervene in a concerned, gentle way to find out if anything is wrong and if you can help or get help. Often, listening to a friend's troubles is all the therapy needed, if it comes soon enough. Don't isolate the "stranger" and be tolerant of deviance—but, of course, respect your own need for personal safety as well.

12. If you discover you cannot help yourself or the other person in distress, seek the counsel of a trained specialist in your student health department. In some cases a problem that appears to be a psychological one may really be physical, as with glandular conditions.

13. Assume that anyone can be helped by an opportunity to discuss his or her problems openly with a mental health specialist; therefore, if you do go to one, there is no need to feel stigmatized.

14. Develop long-range goals; think about what you want to be doing five, ten, twenty years from now and about alternative ways of getting there. Always try to enjoy the process of getting there too; "travel hopefully" and you will arrive eventually and be more fulfilled.

15. Take time to relax, to meditate, to enjoy hobbies and activities that you can do alone and by means of which you can get in touch with yourself.

16. Think of yourself not as a passive object to which bad things just happen, but as an active agent who at any time can change the direction of your entire life. You are what you choose to be and you are seen by others in terms of what you choose to show them.

17. Remember that, as long as there is life, there is hope for a better life, and as long as we care for one another, our lives will get better.

▶ ## Summary

▶ Health refers to more than the absence of illness or injury; it is concerned with the general soundness and vigor of the mind and body. The growing awareness of the role of psychological and social factors in physical health has led to the development of a biopsychosocial model of health and illness.

▶ Health psychology is devoted to understanding the influence of psychological factors on health, illness, and responses to illness. Behavioral medicine is an interdisciplinary field which focuses on overt health behaviors and the conditions that affect them. Psychosomatic medicine, which, like health psychology, studies the relationship between psychological factors and physical health, developed within the field of psychiatry. In the study of health and illness, medical sociology focuses on the group and medical anthropology focuses on the culture.

▶ The concerns of health psychology include the promotion and maintenance of health, the prevention and treatment of illness, and the study of the causes and correlates of health, illness, and dysfunction.

▶ Prevention of illness refers to reducing the risk that people will become ill. Today, prevention often focuses on changes in life-style, such as change or elimination of poor health habits. Treatment is concerned with helping people adjust to their illnesses and recover.

▶ Health psychologists study not only poor health habits as causes of illness, but also the influence of personality and individual behavioral styles, such as Type-A behavior syndrome, on health and illness. Type-A behavior is a competitive, hard-driving, hostile behavioral pattern associated with high risk for coronary heart disease. Most common in men, it is now being seen more in women and even in adolescents and children.

▶ Stress is the pattern of reactions an organism makes in response to stressors, stimulus events that tax its ability to cope.

▶ We do not react directly to a stressor, but to our perception and interpretation of it; thus our cognitive appraisal is a moderator variable: it moderates (changes) the effect of the stressor. Other moderator variables are our inner and outer resources for dealing with a stressor and our attitudes and coping patterns.

▶ Cognitive appraisal defines the demand; primary appraisal determines whether the demand is stressful, while secondary appraisal evaluates the available personal and social resources and the appropriate action. In chronic stress, demands over time are perceived as greater than resources.

▶ Physiological stress reactions are automatic mechanisms facilitating swift emergency action. They are regulated by the hypothalamus and include many emergency body changes, carried out through the action of the autonomic nervous system and the pituitary gland. They lessen sensitivity to pain and provide extra energy for fight or flight. They are useful to combat physical stressors, but can be maladaptive in response to psychological stressors, especially when stress is severe or chronic.

Summary 515

- The general adaptation syndrome is a three-stage pattern of physiological defenses against continuing stressors that threaten internal well-being. Following the alarm reaction, there is a stage of resistance in which psychological defenses are activated until adaptive resources fail in the stage of exhaustion.

- Psychosomatic diseases are physical diseases caused by chronic physiological stress reactions to perceived threats. Other diseases of adaptation occur when normal adaptive responses become excessive or are inappropriate. The "wear and tear" on the body brought about by continuing responses to stress is considered to be a factor in aging.

- Psychological stress reactions include behavioral, emotional, and cognitive elements. Mild stress can enhance performance and even be experienced as pleasant (eustress). Moderate stress disrupts behavior and may lead to repetitive, stereotyped actions. Severe stress suppresses behavior.

- Emotional stress reactions include irritation, anger, and depression. Posttraumatic stress disorders are emotional stress reactions that follow acutely stressful experiences, sometimes occurring months or years after the experience and including many behavioral, physiological, and emotional symptoms.

- Cognitive stress reactions include a narrowing of attention; rigidity of thought; and interference with judgment, problem solving, and memory.

- Psychological stressors are more common than physical stressors for most of us. Major life changes, even pleasant ones, can be stressful, as can the accumulation of everyday "hassles." Catastrophic events can be sources of severe stress, as can long-term environmental problems.

- Two basic coping strategies to deal with perceived threat are (a) treating the problem itself in some way (problem-focused coping), and (b) lessening the discomfort and anxiety we are feeling (emotion-focused coping).

- We can learn to manage stress better through: (a) changing health-threatening physiological reactions (relaxation and biofeedback), and (b) changing our cognitive strategies.

- Those most vulnerable to stress are individuals who lack a social support network and are in life situations in which they feel they have no control. Building and participating in positive social support groups is health promoting.

Sample Textbook Chapter

Homeostasis II: Temperature Regulation (from Curtis, *Biology*)

CHAPTER 38

Homeostasis II: Temperature Regulation

For life forms, the seeming wastelands of the deserts and the poles represent great extremes of hot and cold. Yet, in fact, measured on a cosmic scale, the temperature differences between them are very slight. Life exists only within a very narrow temperature range. The upper and lower limits of this range are dictated by the nature of biochemical reactions, which sustain life and which are all extremely sensitive to temperature change.

Biochemical reactions take place almost entirely in water, the principal constituent of living things. The slightly salty water characteristic of living tissues freezes at −1 or −2°C. Molecules that are not immobilized in the ice crystals are left in such a highly concentrated form that their normal interactions are completely disrupted. In Chapter 8, we saw that, as temperature rises, the movement of molecules increases and the rate of biochemical reactions goes up rapidly. In fact, it is a convenient generalization that the rates of most biochemical reactions about double for every 10°C increase in temperature. The upper temperature limit for life is apparently set by the point at which proteins begin to lose their functional three-dimensional conformation (a process known as denaturation). Once denaturation occurs, enzymes and other proteins whose function depends on a specific shape are inactivated. As a consequence of this restriction to a very narrow tem-

38–1
Temperature regulation involves behavioral responses, as well as physiological and anatomical adaptations. Here a jackrabbit seeks shelter from the Arizona sun in the shade of a mesquite tree. Note the large ears, which are highly vascularized.

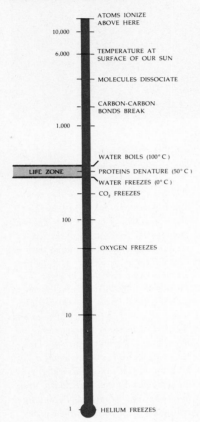

38–2

Life processes can take place only within a very narrow range of temperature. The temperature scale shown here is the Kelvin, or absolute, scale. Absolute zero (0 K) is equivalent to −273.1°C, or −459°F, and is the temperature at which all molecular motion ceases.

ATOMS IONIZE ABOVE HERE

10,000

6,000 — TEMPERATURE AT SURFACE OF OUR SUN

MOLECULES DISSOCIATE

CARBON-CARBON BONDS BREAK

1,000

WATER BOILS (100°C)

LIFE ZONE — PROTEINS DENATURE (50°C)

WATER FREEZES (0°C)

CO_2 FREEZES

100

OXYGEN FREEZES

10

1 — HELIUM FREEZES

perature range, living organisms must either find external environments that range from just below freezing to between 45 and 50°C, or they must create suitable internal environments. (However, there are exceptions: cyanobacteria have been found in hot springs at 85°C, and recently bacteria have been discovered in the superheated waters of submarine vents, where heat escapes through fissures in the earth's crust. In the laboratory, these bacteria metabolize and multiply at temperatures of about 100°C. The special adaptations that make this possible are not yet known.)

The ways in which temperature requirements are met—and, in particular, the internal regulation of temperature, another example of homeostasis—are the subject of this chapter. Before going into the details of these processes, however, it is worth taking a moment to consider what excellent temperature regulators most mammals are. One of the simplest and most dramatic demonstrations of this capacity was given some 200 years ago by Dr. Charles Blagden, then secretary of the Royal Society of London. Dr. Blagden, taking with him a few friends, a small dog in a basket, and a steak, went into a room that had a temperature of 126°C (260°F).* The entire group remained there for 45 minutes. Dr. Blagden and his friends emerged unaffected. So did the dog. (The basket had kept its feet from being burned by the floor.) But the steak was cooked.

PRINCIPLES OF HEAT BALANCE

Water balance, as we saw in the preceding chapter, requires that the loss of water through urine, sweat, and respiration equal the water ingested. Similarly, maintaining a constant temperature depends on heat gains equaling heat losses. For living organisms there are two primary sources of heat gain: one is the radiant energy of the sun; the other is the heat generated by exothermic chemical reactions in an organism (Figure 38–3).

Heat Transfer

Heat is lost by transfer to a cooler body. If the two bodies are in direct contact, the movement of heat is called *conduction*. Conduction of heat consists of the direct transfer of the kinetic energy of molecular motion, and it always occurs from a region of higher temperature to a region of lower temperature. Some materials are better heat conductors than others. When you step out of bed barefoot on a cool morning, you probably prefer to step on a wool rug than on the bare floor. Although both are at the same temperature, the rug feels warmer. If you touch something metal, such as a brass doorknob, it will feel even cooler than the wood floor. These apparent differences in temperature are actually differences in the speed at which these different types of materials conduct heat away from your body. The doorknob, like all metals, is an excellent conductor, and wood is a better heat conductor than wool.

Water is a better conductor than air. You are quite comfortable in air at 21°C (70°F) but may be uncomfortable in water at the same temperature. Fat and air are poor conductors and so can serve as insulators. Animals that need to conserve heat are typically insulated with either fur or feathers, which trap air, or with fat or blubber.

---

*   A Celsius to Fahrenheit temperature conversion scale can be found in Appendix B at the back of the book.

733   CHAPTER 38 *Homeostasis II: Temperature Regulation*

(a)

(b)

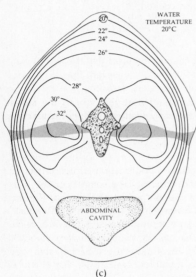

WATER
TEMPERATURE
20°C

20°
22°
24°
26°
28°
30°
32°

ABDOMINAL
CAVITY

(c)

38–3

Heat sources. (a) Within the wintering hive, bees maintain their temperature by clustering together in a dense ball; the lower the temperature, the denser the cluster. The clustered bees produce heat by constant muscular movements of their wings, legs, and abdomens. In very cold weather, the bees on the outside of the cluster keep moving toward the center, while those in the center move to the colder outside periphery. The entire cluster moves slowly about on the combs, eating the stored honey, which is their energy source. The photograph shows the upper half of an opened wintering hive. (b) Mound-building birds incubate their eggs in large compost heaps. The parent birds start by digging a pit, 3 meters wide and 1 meter deep, and raking plant litter into it. Following the spring rains,

when the litter begins to decompose, the birds cover the fermenting heap with a layer of sand up to a meter in depth. The female lays her eggs in this mound, which is heated from beneath by the chemical reactions in the litter. The male regulates the temperature of the eggs by scraping away the sand around them to expose them to air or sun or piling up warm sand around them at night. The entire cycle from the beginning of mound building until the last egg hatches takes about a year. (c) Muscular activity and chemical ractions are also sources of internal heat. This diagram shows the temperatures in a cross section of a 70-kilogram big-eye tuna. The heat is produced by metabolism, particularly in the hard-working, red, myoglobin-containing muscle tissue, indicated in light color.

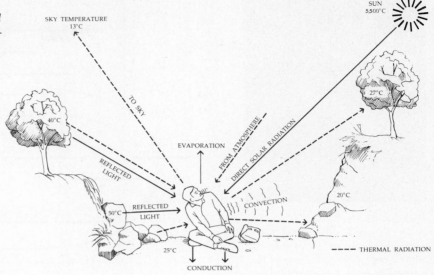

38–4
Heat exchanges between a mammal and its environment. The core body temperature of the man is 37°C. The air temperature is 30°C and there is no wind movement.

Conduction in fluids (air or water) is always influenced by *convection*, the movement of air or water in currents. Because both air and water become lighter as they get warmer, they move away from a heat source and are replaced by colder air or water, which again moves away as it warms.

Radiation is the transfer of energy by electromagnetic waves in the absence of direct contact, as between the sun and an organism. The energy may be transferred as light or heat, depending on the wavelength of the radiation (see Figure 10–3 on page 212). Light energy falling on an object is either absorbed as heat or reflected. Dark objects absorb more than light-colored ones.

Another route of heat exchange is by evaporation. As we saw in Chapter 2, every time a gram of water changes from a liquid to a gas, it takes more than 500 calories away with it. Many organisms, including ourselves, have exploited this property of water as a means for rapid adjustment of the heat balance. These routes of heat transfer are summarized in Figure 38–4.

Size and Temperature

Heat is transferred into or out of any object, animate or inanimate, across the body surface, and transfer of heat, like diffusion of gases, is proportional to the surface area exposed. The smaller the object, as we saw in Chapter 5, the larger its surface-to-volume ratio. Ten pounds of ice, separated into individual ice cubes, will melt far faster than the equivalent volume in a solid block. For the same reason, it is much more difficult for a small animal to maintain a constant body temperature than it is for a large one.

735   CHAPTER 38 *Homeostasis II: Temperature Regulation*

(a)

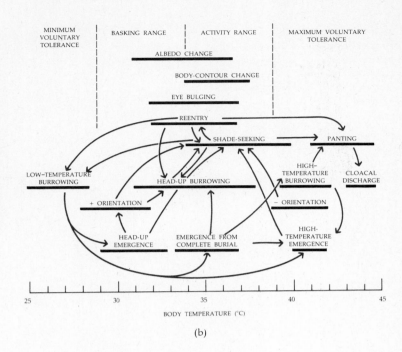

(b)

38-5

In laboratory studies, the internal temperature of reptiles was shown to be almost the same as the temperature of the surrounding air. It was not until observations were made of these animals in their own environment that it was found that they have behavioral means for temperature regulation. By absorbing solar energy, reptiles can raise their temperature well above that of the air around them. (a) Shown here is a horned lizard (often but not accurately known as a horned toad) that, having been overheated by the sun, has raised its body to allow cooling air currents to circulate across its belly. (b) This chart is based on field studies of the behavior of a horned lizard in response to temperature fluctuations. Changes in albedo (whiteness) are produced by pigment changes in the epithelial cells. Albedo changes affect the reflection versus absorption of light rays.

"Cold-blooded" and "Warm-blooded"

In common parlance, animals are often characterized as "cold-blooded" and "warm-blooded." This fits in with everyday experience: a snake is usually cold to the touch, and a living bird feels warm. Actually, however, a "cold-blooded" animal may create an internal temperature for itself that is warmer than that of a "warm-blooded" one. Another approach is to classify animals as ectotherms and endotherms. Ectotherms are warmed from the outside in, and endotherms are warmed from the inside out. These categories correspond approximately but not completely with "cold-blooded" and "warm-blooded." As we saw in Figure 38-3c, a large fish, such as a tuna, which is considered "cold-blooded," generates a considerable amount of metabolic heat. Finally, animals may be characterized as poikilotherms and homeotherms. A *poikilotherm* (from the Greek word *poikilos*, meaning "changeable") has a variable temperature, and a *homeotherm*, a constant one. These terms are generally used as synonymous with "cold-blooded" and "warm-blooded," though again the correspondence is not perfect. Fish that live deep in the sea, where the temperature of the water remains constant, have a body temperature far more constant than a bat or a hummingbird, whose temperatures, as we shall see, fluctuate widely depending on their state of activity. Nevertheless, poikilotherm and homeotherm are the most widely accepted terms and are those that we shall use in the rest of this discussion.

POIKILOTHERMS

Most aquatic animals are poikilotherms, with their temperatures varying with that of the surrounding water. Although the metabolic processes of such animals gen-

736   SECTION 6 BIOLOGY OF ANIMALS

erate heat, it is usually quickly dissipated, even in large animals. In most fish, for example, heat is rapidly carried from the core of the body by the bloodstream and is lost by conduction into the water. A large proportion of this body heat is lost from the gills. Exposure of a large, well-vascularized surface to the water is necessary in order to acquire enough oxygen, as you will recall from Chapter 35. This same process rapidly dissipates heat, so fish cannot maintain a body temperature significantly higher than that of the water. They also cannot maintain a temperature lower than that of the water, since they have no means of unloading heat.

In general, large bodies of water, for the reasons we discussed in Chapter 2, maintain a very stable temperature. At no place in the open ocean does the temperature vary more than 10°C in a year. (By contrast, temperatures on land may vary annually in a given area by as much as 60 to 70°C.) Because water expands as it freezes, ice floats on the surface of the water, insulating the water so that life continues beneath the surface of the ice. In shallower water, where greater temperature changes occur, fish seek an optimal temperature, presumably the one to which their metabolic processes are adapted. However, because they can do almost nothing to make their own temperature different from that of the surrounding water, they can be quickly victimized by any rapid, drastic changes in water temperature.

Terrestrial reptiles—snakes, lizards, and tortoises—are also poikilotherms, but they can often maintain remarkably stable body temperatures during their active hours, even though ambient temperatures vary. By careful selection of suitable sites, such as the slope of a hill facing the sun, and by orienting their bodies with a maximum surface exposed to sunlight, they can heat themselves rapidly (as rapidly as 1°C per minute), even on mornings when the air temperature, as on deserts or in the high mountains, may be close to 0°C. As soon as their body temperatures go above the preferred level, lizards move to face the sun, presenting less exposed surface, or they seek shade. By such behavioral responses, lizards are able to keep

38–6
Observed metabolic rates of mammals. Each division on the abscissa represents a tenfold increase in weight. The metabolic rate of very small mammals is much higher than that of larger mammals, owing principally to their greater surface-to-volume ratios.

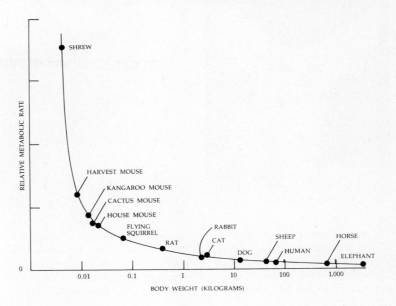

their temperatures oscillating within a quite narrow range. At night, when their body temperatures drop and they become sluggish, these animals seek the safety of their shelters. There they will not become immobilized in an exposed position, where they would be vulnerable to predators.

HOMEOTHERMS

Homeotherms are animals that maintain a constant body temperature despite fluctuations in their environment, and most maintain a body temperature well above that of their surroundings. Among modern organisms, only birds and mammals are true homeotherms. All homeotherms are endotherms, with the oxidation of glucose and other energy-yielding molecules within body cells as their primary source of heat. In terms of energy requirements, their cost of living is high: the metabolic rate of a homeotherm is about twice that of a poikilotherm of similar size at similar temperature. In short, homeotherms pay a high price for their independence. Also, the smaller the size, the higher the price. Small homeotherms have a proportionally larger heat budget than large ones, because of surface-to-volume ratios (see Figure 38–6).

Because it is heated from within, a warm-blooded mammal is warmer at the core of its body than at the periphery. (Our temperature usually does not reach 37°C, or 98.6°F, until some distance below the skin surface.) Heat is transported from the core to the periphery largely by the bloodstream. At the surface of the body, the heat is transferred to the air, as long as air temperature is less than body temperature. Temperature regulation involves increasing or decreasing heat production and increasing or decreasing heat loss at the body surface.

(a)

(b)

(c)

38–7
The size of the extremities in a particular type of animal can often be correlated with the climate in which it lives. (a) The fennec fox of the North African desert has large ears that help it to dissi-

pate body heat. (b) The red fox of the eastern United States has ears of intermediate size, and (c) the Arctic fox has relatively small ears. Like all mammals, these foxes are homeotherms, animals

that maintain a constant internal temperature despite variations in external temperature.

738   SECTION 6 BIOLOGY OF ANIMALS

The Mammalian Thermostat

The remarkable constancy of temperature characteristic of humans, and many other animals as well, is maintained by an automatic system—a thermostat—in the hypothalamus. Like the thermostat that regulates your furnace, the thermostat in the hypothalamus receives information about the temperature, compares it to the set point of the thermostat, and, on the basis of this comparison, initiates appropriate responses. Unlike your furnace thermostat, however, the hypothalamic thermostat receives and integrates information from widely scattered temperature receptors. Also, rather than just controlling an on-off switch, the hypothalamic thermostat has a variety of responses at its command, as summarized in Figure 33-13 on page 669.

Under ordinary conditions, the skin receptors for hot and cold are probably the most important sources of information about temperature change. However, the hypothalamus itself contains receptor cells that monitor the temperature of the blood flowing through it. As some interesting experiments have demonstrated, information received by these hypothalamic receptors overrides that from other sources. For example, in a room in which the air is warmer than body temperature, if the blood circulating through a person's hypothalamus is cooled, he or she will stop perspiring, even though the skin temperature continues to rise.

The elevation of body temperature known as fever is due not to a malfunction of the hypothalamic thermostat but to its resetting. Thus, at the onset of fever, an individual typically feels cold and often has chills; although the body temperature is rising, it is still lower than the new thermostat setting. The substance primarily responsible for the resetting of the thermostat is a protein released by the white blood cells in response to a pathogen. The adaptive value of fever, if any—and we can only presume that there is one—is a subject of current research. One possibility, supported by some evidence, is that it creates an environment inhospitable to pathogens. Another is that it stimulates the release of a substance important in immunological reactions.

Regulating as Body Temperature Rises

In mammals, as the body temperature rises above its thermostat setting, the blood vessels near the skin surface are dilated, and the supply of blood to the skin increases. If the air is cooler than the body surface, heat can be transferred from the skin to the air. Heat can also be lost from the surface by the evaporation of saliva or perspiration. Some animals—dogs, for instance—pant, so that air passes rapidly over their large, moist tongues, evaporating saliva. Cats lick themselves all over as the temperature rises, and evaporation of their saliva cools their body surface. Horses and human beings sweat from all over their body surfaces. For animals that dissipate heat by water evaporation, temperature regulation at high temperatures necessarily involves water loss, which, in turn, stimulates thirst and water conservation by the kidneys. Dr. Blagden and his friends were probably very thirsty.

Regulating as Body Temperature Falls

When the temperature of the circulating blood begins to fall below the thermostat setting, blood vessels near the skin surface are constricted, limiting heat loss from the skin. Metabolic processes increase. Part of this increase is due to increased muscular activity, either voluntary (shifting from foot to foot) or involuntary (shivering). Part is due to direct stimulation of metabolism by the endocrine and

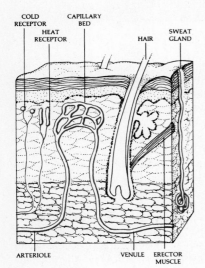

38-8

Cross section of human skin showing structures involved in temperature regulation. In cold, the arterioles constrict, reducing the flow of blood through the capillaries, and the hairs, each of which has a small erector muscle under nervous control, stand upright. Beneath the skin is a layer of subcutaneous fat that serves as insulation, retaining the heat in the underlying body tissues. With rising temperatures, the arterioles dilate and the sweat glands secrete a salty liquid. Evaporation of this liquid cools the skin surface, dissipating heat (approximately 540 calories for every gram of H_2O).

COLD RECEPTOR CAPILLARY BED
HEAT RECEPTOR   HAIR   SWEAT GLAND

ARTERIOLE   VENULE   ERECTOR MUSCLE

739   CHAPTER 38 *Homeostasis II: Temperature Regulation*

(a)

(b)

38–9

(a) *Dogs unload heat by panting, which involves short, shallow breaths. When it is hot, a dog pants at a rate of about 300 to 400 times a minute, compared with a respiration rate of from 10 to 40 times a minute in cool surroundings. Evaporation of water from the tongue, unlike evaporation from the skin, does not result in the loss of salt or other important ions. (b) Elephants, lacking sweat glands, wet down their thick, dry skins with mud or water. They also unload heat by flapping their ears, which are highly vascularized.*

nervous systems. Adrenaline stimulates the release and oxidation of glucose. Autonomic nerves to fat increase its metabolic breakdown. In some mammals, though apparently not in humans, the thyroid gland increases its release of thyroxine, the thyroid hormone. Thyroxine appears to exert its effects directly on the mitochondria.

Most mammals have a layer of subcutaneous fat that serves as insulation. Homeotherms also characteristically have hair or feathers that, as temperature falls, are pulled upright by erector muscles under the skin, trapping air, which insulates the surface. All we get, as our evolutionary legacy, are goose pimples.

Meeting Energy Costs

As we noted previously, maintaining a constant temperature adds significantly to an animal's energy budget. Birds, in particular, have high metabolic requirements. Although comparatively small, they maintain a higher body temperature—40 to 42°C—than most mammals. Also, unlike many other small homeotherms, they spend much of their time exposed. Flight compounds their problems. To fly, birds must keep their weight down, and so they cannot store large amounts of fuel. Because of this and the high energy requirements of their way of life, birds need to eat constantly. A bird eating high-protein foods, such as seeds and insects, commonly consumes as much as 30 percent of its body weight per day. Bird migrations are dictated not so much by a need to seek warmer weather as by a need for longer days with more daylight hours for feeding themselves and their young.

Cutting Energy Costs

Less energy is consumed by a sleeping animal than by an active one. Bears, for example, nap for most of the winter, living on fat reserves, permitting their temperature to drop several degrees, and keeping their energy requirements down.

Turning down the thermostat saves more fuel. Some small animals have different day and night settings. A hummingbird, for instance, has an extremely high rate of fuel consumption, even for a bird. Its body temperature drops every evening when it is resting, thereby decreasing its metabolic requirements and its fuel consumption.

740   SECTION 6 BIOLOGY OF ANIMALS

38–10

Heat conservation measures. (a) Hibernation saves energy by turning down the thermostat. This dormouse has prepared for hibernation by storing food reserves in body fat. (b) Note the heat-conserving reduction in surface-to-volume ratio in this hibernating chipmunk. (c) Many small animals, such as these penguin chicks, huddle together for warmth. Huddling decreases the effective surface-to-volume ratio. A few of the chicks have lifted their heads from the warmth of the huddle to observe the photographer at work.

(a)

(b)

Hibernation, which comes from *hiber,* the Latin word for "winter," is another means of adjusting energy expenditures to food supplies. Hibernating animals do not stop regulating their temperatures altogether—like the hummingbird, they turn down their thermostats. Hibernators are mostly small animals, including a few insectivores, hamsters, ground squirrels, some South American opossums, some bats, and a few birds, such as the poor-will of the southwestern United States. In these animals, the thermostat is set very low, often close to that of the surrounding air (if the air is above 0°C). The heartbeat slows; the heart of an active ground squirrel, for instance, beats 200 to 400 times a minute, whereas that of a hibernating one beats 7 to 10 times a minute. The metabolism, as measured by oxygen consumption, is reduced 20 to 100 times. Apparently, even aging stops; hibernators have much longer life spans than similar nonhibernators. However, despite these profound physiological changes, hibernators do not cease to monitor the external environment. If the animals are exposed to carbon dioxide, for example, they breathe more rapidly, and those of certain species wake up. Similarly, animals of many species wake up if the temperature in their burrows drops to a life-threatening low of 0°C. Hibernators of some species can be awakened by sound or by touch.

Arousal from hibernation can be rapid. In one experiment, bats kept in a refrigerator for 144 days without food were capable of sustained flight after 15 minutes at room temperature. As indicated, however, by the arousals at 0°C, the arousal is a process of self-warming rather than of collecting environmental heat. Breathing becomes more regular and then more rapid, increasing the amount of oxygen available for consumption; subsequently, the animal "burns" its stored food supplies as it returns to its normal temperature and the fast pace of a homeothermic existence.

(c)

741   CHAPTER 38 *Homeostasis II: Temperature Regulation*

ADAPTATIONS TO EXTREME TEMPERATURES

We rely mainly on our technology, rather than our physiology, to allow us to live in extreme climates, but many animals are comfortable in climates that we consider inhospitable or, indeed, uninhabitable.

Adaptations to Extreme Cold

Animals adapt to extreme cold largely by increased amounts of insulation. Fur and feathers, both of which trap air, provide insulation for Arctic land animals. Fur and feathers are usually shed to some extent in the spring and regrow in the fall.

Aquatic homeotherms, such as whales, walruses, seals, and penguins, are insulated with fat (neither fur nor feathers serve as effective insulators when wet). In general, the rate of heat loss depends both on the amount of surface area exposed and on temperature differences between the body surface and the surroundings. These marine animals, which survive in extremely cold water, can tolerate a very great drop in their skin surface temperature; measurements of skin temperature have shown that it is only a degree or so above that of the surrounding water. By permitting the skin temperature to drop, these animals, which maintain an internal temperature as warm as that of a person, expend very little heat outside of their fat layer and so keep warm—like a diver in a wet suit.

Numerous animals similarly permit temperatures in the extremities to drop. By so doing, they conserve heat. The extremities of such animals are actually adapted to live at a different internal temperature from that of the rest of the animal. For example, the fat in the foot of an Arctic fox has a different thermal behavior from

38–11
Aquatic mammals, such as this bull fur seal, have a heavy layer of fat beneath the skin that acts, in effect, like a diver's wet suit, insulating them against heat loss. On land, they have a problem unloading heat. One way they do it is by keeping their fur moist; another is by sleeping, which, in some species, reduces heat production by almost 25 percent.

that of the fat in the rest of its body, so that its footpads are soft and resilient even at temperatures of −50°C. Also, for many of these animals, particularly those that stand on the ice, this capacity is essential for another reason. If, for example, the feet of an Arctic seabird were as warm as its body, they would melt the ice, which might then freeze over them, trapping the animal until the spring thaws set it free.

Countercurrent Exchange

In many Arctic animals, the arteries and veins leading to and from the extremities are juxtaposed in such a way that the chilled blood returning from the legs (or fins or tail) through the veins picks up heat from the blood entering the extremities through the arteries. The veins and arteries are closely apposed to give maximum surface for heat transfer. Thus the body heat carried by the blood is not wasted by

38–12

The principle of countercurrent heat exchange is illustrated by a hot-water pipe and a cold-water pipe placed side by side. In (a), the hot water and cold water flow in the same direction. Heat from the hot water warms the cold water until both temperatures equalize at 5. Thereafter, no further exchange takes place, and the outflowing water in both pipes is lukewarm. In (b), the flow is in opposite directions (that is, it is countercurrent), so that heat transfer continues for the length of the pipes. The result is that the hot water transfers most of its heat as it travels through the pipe, and the cold water is warmed to almost the initial temperature of the hot water at its source.

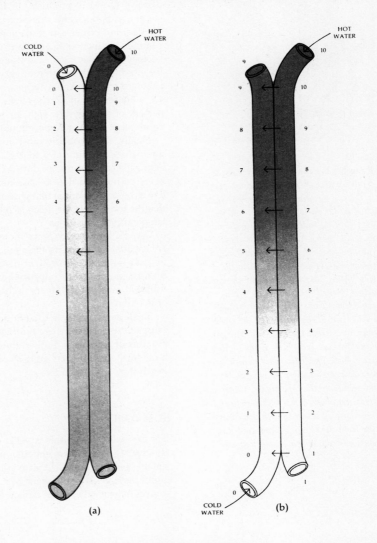

(a) (b)

743   **CHAPTER 38** *Homeostasis II: Temperature Regulation*

being dissipated to the cold air at the extremities. Instead it serves the useful function of warming the chilled blood that would otherwise put a thermal burden on the body. This arrangement, which serves to keep heat in the body and away from the extremities, is, of course, another example of countercurrent exchange.

Adaptations to Extreme Heat

We are efficient homeotherms at high external temperatures, as Dr. Blagden's experiment showed. Our chief limitation in this regard is that we must evaporate a great deal of water in order to unload body heat, and so our water consumption is high. The camel, the philosophical-looking "ship of the desert," has several advantages over human desert dwellers. For one thing, the camel excretes a much more concentrated urine; in other words, it does not need to use so much water to dissolve its waste products. In fact, we are very uneconomical with our water supply; even dogs and cats excrete a urine twice as concentrated as ours.

Also, the camel can lose more water proportionally than a person and still continue to function. If a human loses 10 percent of body weight in water, he or she becomes delirious, deaf, and insensitive to pain. If the loss is as much as 12 percent, the person will be unable to swallow and so cannot recover without assistance. Laboratory rats and many other common animals can tolerate dehydration of up to 12 to 14 percent of body weight. Camels can tolerate the loss of more than 25 percent of their body weight in water, going without drinking for as long as an entire week in the summer months, three weeks in the winter.

Finally, and probably most important, the camel can tolerate a fluctuation in internal temperature of 5 to 6°C. This tolerance means that it can store heat by letting its temperature rise during the daytime (which the human thermostat would never permit) and then release heat during the night. The camel begins the next day at below its normal temperature—storing up coolness, in effect. It is estimated that the camel saves as much as 5 liters of water a day as a result of these internal temperature fluctuations.

Camels' humps were once thought to be water-storage tanks, but actually they are localized fat deposits. Physiologists have suggested that the camel carries its fat in a dorsal hump, instead of distributed all over the body, because the hump, acting as an insulator, impedes heat flow into the body core. An all-over fat distribution, which is decidedly useful in Arctic animals, would not be in inhabitants of hot climates.

Small desert animals usually do not unload heat by sweating or panting; because of their relatively large surface areas, such mechanisms would be extravagant in terms of water loss. Rather, they regulate their temperature by avoiding direct heat. Most small desert animals are nocturnal, like the earliest mammals, from which they are descended.

SUMMARY

Life can exist only within a very narrow temperature range, from about 0°C to about 50°C, with few exceptions. Animals must either seek out environments with suitable temperatures or create suitable internal environments. Heat balance requires that the net heat loss from an organism equal the heat gain. The two primary sources of heat gain are the radiant energy of the sun and cellular metabolism. Heat

38–13
By facing the sun, a camel exposes as small an area of body surface as possible to the sun's radiation. Its body is insulated by fat on top, which minimizes heat gain by radiation. The underpart of its body, which has much less insulation, radiates heat out to the ground cooled by the animal's shadow. Note also the loose-fitting garments worn by the camel driver. When such garments are worn, sweat evaporates off the skin surface. With tight-fitting garments, the sweat evaporates from the surface of the garment instead, and much of the cooling effect is lost. The loose robes, which trap air, also serve to keep desert dwellers warm during the cold nights. Other adaptations of the camel to desert life include long eyelashes, which protect its eyes from the stinging sand, and flattened nostrils, which retard water loss.

is lost by conduction, the transfer of thermal energy from one object to another; by radiation via electromagnetic waves; and by evaporation.

Animals that take in energy primarily from the outside are known as ectotherms; animals that rely on internal energy production are known as endotherms. Most ectotherms are poikilotherms, animals whose internal temperature fluctuates with that of the external environment. Most endotherms are homeotherms, animals that maintain a constant internal temperature.

In mammals, temperature is regulated by a thermostat in the hypothalamus that senses temperature changes in the circulating blood and triggers appropriate responses. As body temperature rises, blood vessels in the skin dilate, increasing the blood flow to the surface of the body. Evaporation of water from any body surface increases heat loss.

As body temperature falls, energy production is increased by increased muscular activity (including shivering) and by nervous and hormonal stimulation of metabolism. Homeotherms in cold climates are usually insulated by subcutaneous fat and fur or feathers.

Energy can be conserved by setting the thermostat lower. Some small homeotherms, such as hummingbirds, have different day and night settings. Others, hibernators, make seasonal adjustments.

Adaptations to extreme cold principally involve (1) insulation by heavy layers of fat and fur or feathers, and (2) countercurrent mechanisms for conserving heat within the body. Adaptations to extreme heat are largely water conservation measures and also include many behavioral responses.

QUESTIONS

1. Distinguish among the following terms: endotherm, ectotherm, poikilotherm, and homeotherm.

2. Compare the surface-to-volume ratio of an Eskimo igloo with that of a California ranch house. In what way is the igloo well suited to the environment in which it is found?

3. Compare hibernation in animals with dormancy in plants. In what ways are they alike? In what ways are they different?

4. Plants, as well as animals, are warmed above air temperature by sunlight, and plants cannot actively seek shade. Why might the leaves in the sunlight at the top of an oak tree be smaller and more extensively lobed (more fingerlike) than the leaves in the shady areas lower on the tree?

5. In terms of temperature regulation, what is the advantage of having temperature monitors that are located externally, as on the outside of a building or in the skin? Why is it also important to monitor the internal temperature? Which should be the principal source of information for your thermostat?

6. Diagram a heat-conserving countercurrent mechanism in the leg of an Arctic animal.

Answer Key

Note: Answers are given for odd-numbered items only. A complete key appears in the *Instructor's Manual.* Answers are not included in this key for exercises that require lengthy or subjective response or the underlining or marking of passages.

PART ONE
Succeeding in College

Chapter 1
How to Succeed

EXERCISE 2

1. Identify and jot down areas (topics, periods) of weakness; look for patterns, such as type of questions missed; find out where questions were taken from (text or lecture); use as a review for final exam.
3. Review procedures before attending lab; underline key steps in lab manual.

EXERCISE 3

1. Talk with instructor and ask for copies of any materials distributed; talk with classmates.
3. Organize materials in a looseleaf notebook by chapter topic.

Chapter 2
Managing Your Time

EXERCISE 2

1. His choices include
   a. reducing work hours; seeking financial aid if needed
   b. settling for less than a B average in some courses
   c. asking another family member to accept additional household responsibilities
   d. dropping one or more courses
3. Mark's plan has two faults. First, he should not leave the most difficult assignment, that requiring the greatest amount of concentration, until last. Second, he should not schedule his study of subjects according to likes or dislikes. Instead, he should select them according to the difficulty and type of assignment given.
5. Evaluate his study plan according to the suggestions given in the section "Building a

Time Schedule." He should rearrange his schedule so as to follow the scheduling suggestions presented on pages 2–20.

Chapter 3
Becoming a More Successful Learner: Principles of Learning and Memory

EXERCISE 1

1. Approximately 23 percent
3. Although taking the notes would serve as a form of rehearsal, without further review you can expect your recall to be fairly poor.

EXERCISE 2

1. Responses may include lighting, heating, colors of walls, clock ticking, traffic in street, noise in corridor, feeling of watch on wrist.
3. Number Seven Theory: information is grouped
5. It took longer than twenty seconds to reach the phone, or the person did not group the numbers together and could not remember each separately.

EXERCISE 3

1. Rote learning
3. Recoding
5. Recoding

EXERCISE 4

1. The group that paraphrased used recoding. Underlining is repetition (rote learning) of existing information. Rote learning alone is an inefficient learning strategy.
3. The film recodes and enables students to make elaborations.

EXERCISE 5

1. Retrieval
3. Encoding and storage
5. Retrieval

EXERCISE 6

1. (a) She used only rote learning; (b) she was not able to concentrate; (c) she did not select what was important to learn.
3. The student did not selectively attend to the quiz announcement.
5. Selective attention
7. He is providing elaborative rehearsal.

EXERCISE 7

1. Categorization (group into political, economic, etc.), association (associate with particular wars), elaboration
3. Think of an instructor who exemplifies each feature.
5. Draw a graph that shows the relationship between price and quantity. Visualize stacks of dollar bills and piles of an item of variable demand.
7. Elaborate on each problem type by anticipating variations. Study similarities and differences among problem types. Determine and learn distinctive characteristics of each problem type.
9. Intent to remember: establish what is important to know about each stage; categorization: organize information into a chart by stage and type of development; elaboration: compare and contrast, think of examples at each stage.

PART TWO
Techniques for Effective Reading

Chapter 4
Improving Concentration and Managing Stress

EXERCISE 1

1. You already have associations built up for sleep and relaxation that will make studying more difficult.
3. Your attention will be divided; at least part of the time you will be listening to and thinking about the tape.
5. The snack bar is probably very busy during lunch hours and will be too distracting.
7. You are in an unfamiliar environment, and getting down to studying will be more difficult than in your own environment.

EXERCISE 6

1. Pressure and stress increase at the end of the quarter, possibly affecting her health.
3. The student should develop and follow a time schedule or routine to enable her to stay caught up on reading, to finish papers ahead of schedule, and to study for final exams. The student should pay extra attention to her health, including diet and exercise, when she feels pressured.

Chapter 5
Prereading

EXERCISE 1

1. T
2. F
3. F
4. T
5. F
6. T
7. T
8. T
9. F
10. T

EXERCISE 2

1. The text contains a collection of articles written by different authors as well as reports of studies done on individuals.
3. The section is organized chronologically, or in order of occurrence in time.
5. b
7. The graph suggests that the relationship of price to production of various types of goods is an important topic in the chapter. The cartoon indicates that a key concept in economic systems is cost as it is influenced by consumer choice. The picture tells us that currency as a means of exchange of goods is topic addressed in the chapter.

Chapter 6
Strategies for Active Reading

EXERCISE 4

1. What are the aids that help merge files? How do they function?
3. How are electromagnetic waves produced?
5. What sociological factors are related to delinquency? How are they related?
7. What has been the influence of "experts" on child-rearing practices?
9. How are physical characteristics inherited?

EXERCISE 5

1. What are the three branches of philosophical analysis?
3. How has the treatment of conflict changed?
5. How does empathetic listening differ from deliberative listening?
7. To read data from a disk, what does the operating system need to know?
9. What are the three categories of poor nutritional states?

EXERCISE 8

1. Analysis: must be able to solve probability problems
Approach: practice solving sample and end-of-chapter problems; make up own problems and solve them.
3. Analysis: select important ideas; develop questions; consider controversial issues
Approach: list key topics and important points; predict essay question and prepare outline answer

EXERCISE 10

a. conduction: the movement of heat between two bodies in direct contact
    convection: transfer of heat through fluids (air or water)
    radiation: transfer of energy by electromagnetic waves without direct contact

b. A poikilotherm has a variable body temperature whereas a homeotherm has a constant one. *Examples:* poikilotherm—lizards; homeotherm—dogs

c. Radiant energy from the sun and the heat generated by exothermic chemical reactions

d. Heat transfer occurs more rapidly in smaller organisms.

PART THREE
Comprehension Skills

Chapter 7
Understanding Sentences

EXERCISE 1

1. S
3. N
5. N
7. S
9. S

EXERCISE 2

	Subject	Verb	Object
1.	sister	took	car
3.	textbook	contains	exercises
5.	storage, processing, retrieval	are	—
7.	companies	issue	warranties
9.	audit	is required	—

EXERCISE 3

1. C
3. C
5. C
7. S   the Cuban economy . . . sugar
9. S   they fall . . . air

EXERCISE 7

	Core Parts	Crossed Out
1.	industrialization—made	in the nineteenth century
3.	we—perceive	then
5.	graphite—is made	on the other hand; like sheets of paper

EXERCISE 8

Core Parts

1. steel—is
3. cause—cannot be determined

5. man—has been puzzled and exasperated; teaching—has been an attempt
7. human beings—have; they—amble, stride, jog, sprint
9. anthropologists—have accumulated

EXERCISE 9

1. Multiple personality is caused by stress.
3. Some individuals do not grieve because of personality factors or particular situations.
5. The Soviet Union is more willing and able to deliver arms faster than the United States.

EXERCISE 11

1. French involvement, American involvement
3. Compute adjusted gross and taxable income; consult a tax table
5. Hearings are held; presidential review

EXERCISE 12

1. industry—displaced
3. Crimes—are
5. currency and things—are termed

EXERCISE 13

1. Brenner has done research linking mental illness to the state of economy.
3. Women are moving toward economic equality with men due to their growing importance in the work force.
5. Americans earn their living differently in the twentieth century than prior to it.

Chapter 8
Understanding the Paragraphs

EXERCISE 1

1. b
3. c
5. a
7. c
9. b

EXERCISE 2

1. Innovative solutions to energy conservation
3. Emotional responses and information processing
5. Pattern recognition
7. Limitation of computers or human instructions for computers
9. Gross national product

EXERCISE 3

1. Second sentence
3. Third sentence
5. First sentence
7. Second sentence
9. Third sentence

EXERCISE 4

1. b, c, e
3. a, b, c, d

5. a, b, c, d, e
7. a, c, d, e
9. a, b, e

EXERCISE 5

1. Topic: taste
   Main idea: Taste is poorly developed in humans.
   3. Topic: theory
   Main idea: A theory is at first an idea, then a hypothesis, and finally a verified explanation.
5. Topic: formal organization
   Main idea: Formal organizations make it possible for members of our complex society to work together.
7. Topic: government expenditures
   Main idea: The two types of government expenditures are direct purchases and transfer payments.
9. Topic: information explosion or revolution in communications
   Main idea: The information explosion, along with cultural change, has produced a society in which the young influence adults and societal standards.

EXERCISE 6

1. Topic: growth of Congress
   Main idea: As the United States increased its population and number of States, Congress grew correspondingly.
3. Topic: probability experiments
   Main idea: Probability experiments involve trials and outcomes.
5. Topic: conflict in speech making
   Main idea: There are numerous ways to establish conflict in a speech.
7. Topic: hearing loss or stimulation deafnes'
   Main idea: Temporary hearing loss can occur from a single exposure to loud sounds, and permanent loss can occur from frequent exposure.
9. Topic: growth of plant life
   Main idea: Plant life on earth evolved slowly, over the course of a billion years.

Chapter 9
Following Thought Patterns in Textbooks

EXERCISE 4

1. Description
3. Description or fact—statistic
5. Fact—statistic
7. Example
9. Fact—statistic

EXERCISE 5

1. Cause-effect
3. Contrast
5. Enumeration

EXERCISE 6

1. Enumeration
3. Cause-effect
5. Cause-effect
7. Definition
9. Definition

PART FOUR
Textbook Reading Skills

Chapter 10
Textbook Aids to Learning

EXERCISE 2

1. b
3. b

EXERCISE 3

Texts 3, 5, 8, and 10 may be outdated.

EXERCISE 4

1. Textbooks should present the field of biology as a source of pleasure and excitement.
3. Molecular genetics
5. Part I deals with subcellular and cellular life, Part II with organisms, and Part III with populations.

EXERCISE 6

1. Careful reading, active rehearsal, goal setting, controlling distractions, time management
3. Before reading the chapter
5. Yes. He refers to it as a "unique journey": he mentions enjoying "the discovery of learning" and "the most incredible phenomenon in the entire universe—the human mind."

EXERCISE 7

1. It is divided into three sections: the unity of life, energetics, and genetics.
3. To relate or apply chapter content to issues or practical situations.

EXERCISE 8

1. b
3. a
5. c

EXERCISE 9

Figure 10-2

1. To show four alternative constitutional amendment processes.
3. (a) Two-thirds vote by Congress followed by conventions held by three-fourths of the states; (b) national constitutional convention requested by legislatures of two-thirds of the states followed by ratification by legislatures of three-fourths of the states.

Figure 10-7
1. To compare sales volume, profit margin, and new product addition at various states of the product life cycle.
3. Between the growth and maturity stages.
5. As sales volume declines the need for new product profit peaks.

Figure 10-8
1. Political expenditures (total and per voter) from 1952 to 1980.
3. Total and per voter expenditures have steadily increased.

EXERCISE 10
1. b

Chapter 12
Study-Reading for Academic Disciplines

EXERCISE 4
Psychology chapter: vocabulary review step, underline step
Biology chapter: record step or outline step

PART FIVE
Classroom Performance Skills

Chapter 14
Note-taking Techniques

EXERCISE 3
Recall clues: Freud's psychoanalytic theory, association, repression, suppression, trauma, interpretation of dreams, three parts of personality.
Questions: What is free association? What is repression? What is suppression? What is trauma? How can dreams be interpreted? What are the three parts of the personality? What does each do?

Chapter 17
Taking Exams

EXERCISE 1
1. 1, 15, 5, 50, 4; other similar time plans may be correct.

EXERCISE 2

1.	less	T
3.	only	F
5.	most	T
7.	all	T
9.	better	F

EXERCISE 3

	Topic	Limiting word(s)	Key Word
1.	trend	long-term effects	

	Topic	Limiting word(s)	Key Word
3.	Industrial Revolution	one effect	explain
5.	War of 1812	events	describe
7.	textbook chapter	approach	describe
9.	lecturer	techniques	summarize

PART SIX
Vocabulary Development

Chapter 19
Expanding Your Vocabulary

VOCABULARY QUIZ
1. Answers will vary.
3. A photoreceptor in the retina of the eye.
5. No
7. Answers will vary. *Example:* My uncle is a credit to our family.

EXERCISE 1
1. obscure
3. Answers will vary: *Webster's New World Dictionary* lists seventy.
5. addenda
7. best, favorable, earliest part or stage, highest quality
9. failing, weakness, foible, vice

EXERCISE 2
1. distressed, despondent, disheartened, sorrowful, grief-stricken
3. explaining, discussing, describing, arguing, debating, illustrating
5. excellent, praiseworthy, pleasing, superior, laudable

EXERCISE 4
Biology chapter: conduction, convection, radiation, poikilotherm, homeotherm, countercurrent mechanisms, hibernators, endotherm, ectotherm . . .

Chapter 20
Using Context and Word Parts

EXERCISE 1
The underlined parts should be
1. a form of government in which the people effectively participate
3. an essential fatty acid necessary for growth and skin integrity in infants
5. able to reach comfortably to the tips of all the other fingers

EXERCISE 2
1. close, dependent
3. negative emotional experience
5. fears

EXERCISE 3

1. strong, forceful
3. delay, put off
5. banished, excluded from a group

EXERCISE 4

1. brought back into favor
3. curses, expressions of abhorrence
5. struck out, removed

EXERCISE 5

The underlined parts should be as follows (context clues are given in parentheses):

1. The principle that the powers of government should be separated and put in the care of different parts of government (definition)
3. Amble, stride, job, and sprint (example-illustration)
5. Ranging from treatment as innocents to being tolerated as fools to persecution as witches (example-illustration).

EXERCISE 6

1. a. Added to
   b. Authenticity, sense of reasonableness, or correctness
   c. Mentioning, referring to
   d. Not able to satisfy
   e. Eagerly
3. a. Provide a source of income
   b. Charitable gifts
   c. Distribute
   d. Expenses, costs

EXERCISE 7

1. Not normal; deviant
3. Not logical or reasonable
5. Unchangeable, not able to reverse

EXERCISE 8

1. Below standard, unacceptable
3. Communication over distance by radio, telephone, television, etc.
5. Taking effect on a specified date in the past
7. Not part of the required course of study
9. To transfer or introduce blood into a vein
11. Dishonest or incorrect use
13. Tiresome, lacking variety
15. Having several syllables

EXERCISE 9

1. Belief in only one God
3. Historical record, narrative
5. Process of carrying or removing goods from one country to another

7. Orderly process of reasoning about the unknown
9. Competent in many features; able to change or adapt
11. The proportion of deaths to total population of a region
13. Loud, noisy
15. Belonging to a corporation

EXERCISE 10

1. Using force to intimidate or control
3. Belief in comfort and pleasure as highest goals or values
5. Not able to pass; blocked
7. Not touchable
9. Questioning, examining
11. Condition of being flustered (nervous, befuddled)
13. Out of regard or respect for
15. One who is nominated to an office

EXERCISE 11

1. Psychological development of an individual in relation to his or her social environment
3. Disordered or impaired functioning
5. Following injury or resulting from it
7. Looking forward in time
9. A new appraisal or evaluation

PART SEVEN
Reading Efficiency Techniques

Chapter 22
Skimming and Scanning

EXERCISE 1

1. c
3. a
5. b

EXERCISE 2

1. Doctors have a responsibility to be open and honest with their patients.
3. The article describes the change in attitudes toward the use of profanity and discusses the uses of profanity.

EXERCISE 3

1. Joules
3. Rural rates are lower.
5. Costs are higher.
7. White
9. Relief, recovery, and reform

References

American Heritage Dictionary of the English Language. Boston: Houghton-Mifflin, 1978.

Tom Anselmo et al.. *Thinking and Writing in College*. Boston: Little, Brown, 1986.

Hugh D. Barlow. *Introduction to Criminology*. Boston: Little, Brown, 1984.

Sylvan Barnet and Hugo Bedau. *Current Issues and Enduring Questions*. NY: St. Martins Press, 1987.

Lois Berman and J. C. Evans. *Exploring the Cosmos*. Boston: Little, Brown, 1986.

Bernard C. Campbell. *Humankind Emerging*. Scott, Foresman, 1985.

Roger Chisholm & Marilu McCarty. *Principles of Economics*. Glenview, IL: Scott, Foresman, 1981.

James Coleman et al. *Abnormal Psychology and Modern Life*. Glenview, IL: Scott, Foresman, 1984.

Elliot Currie & Jerome H. Skolnick. *America's Problems: Social Issues and Public Policy*. Boston: Little, Brown, 1984.

Helena Curtis. *Biology*. NY: Worth Publishers, 1983.

Bowman O. Davis et al. *Conceptual Human Psychology*. Columbus, OH: Charles E. Merrill, 1985.

Randall C. Decker. *Patterns of Exposition 6*. Boston: Little, Brown and Company, 1978.

Raymond A. Dumont and John M. Lannon. *Business Communications*. Boston: Little, Brown, 1985.

Douglas Ehninger et al. *Principles and Types of Speech Communication*. Glenview, IL: Scott, Foresman, 1986.

Peter K. Eisinger et al. *American Politics: The People and the Policy*. Little, Brown, 1982.

Robert B. Ekelund and Robert D. Tollison. *Economics*. Boston: Little, Brown, 1986.

Ross J. Eshleman and Barbara G. Cashion. *Sociology: An Introduction*. Boston: Little, Brown, 1985.

Barbara Schneider Fuhrmann. *Adolescence, Adolescents*. Boston: Little, Brown, 1986.

Martin J. Gannon. *Management: An Organizational Perspective*. Boston: Little, Brown and Company, 1977.

E. Thomas Garman et al. *Personal Finance*. Boston: Houghton Mifflin. 1985.

Paul G. Hewitt. *Conceptual Physics*. Boston: Little, Brown, 1985.

Michael C. Howard, *Contemporary Cultural Anthropology*. Boston: Little, Brown, 1986.

Walter S. Jones. *The Logic of International Relations*. Boston: Little, Brown, 1985.

Thomas C. Kinnear and Kenneth L. Bernhardt. *Principles of Marketing*. Glenview, IL: Scott, Foresman, 1986.

Robert L. Lineberry. *Government in America*. Boston: Little, Brown, 1986.

Marilu Hurt McCarty. *Dollars and Sense: An Introduction to Economics*. Glenview, IL: Scott, Foresman, 1985.

Donald L. Macmillan. *Mental Retardation in School and Society*. Boston: Little, Brown, 1982.

Charles D. Miller and Vern H. Heeren. *Mathematical Ideas*. Glenview, IL: Scott, Foresman, 1986.

Frederic S. Mishkin. *The Economics of Money, and Financial Markets*. Boston: Little, Brown, 1986.

Sydney B. Newell. *Chemistry*. Boston: Little, Brown and Company, 1977.

Robert C. Nickerson. *Fundamentals of Structured Cobol*. Boston: Little, Brown, 1984.

John and Erna Perry. *Face to Face: The Individual and Social Problems*. Boston: Little, Brown, 1976.

Hal B. Pickle and Royce L. Abrahamson. *Introduction to Business*. Glenview, IL: Scott, Foresman, 1986.

Adele Pillitteri. *Maternal-Newborn Nursing*. Boston: Little, Brown, 1985.

Adele Pillitteri. *Nursing Care of the Growing Family*. Boston: Little, Brown and Company, 1976.

Henry L. Roediger III et al. *Psychology*. Boston: Little, Brown, 1987.

Andrew D. Szilagyi, Jr. and Marc J. Wallace, Jr. *Organizational Behavior and Performance*. Glenview, IL: Scott, Foresman, 1987.

Barbara Upton with John Upton. *Photography* Boston: Little, Brown, 1985.

Robert A. Wallace. *Biology: The World of Life*. Glenview, IL: Scott, Foresman & Co., 1987.

T. Walter Wallbank et al. *Civilization Past and Present*. Vol. 2. Glenview, IL: Scott, Foresman, 1987.

Gary Wasserman. *The Basics of American Politics.* Boston: Little, Brown, 1985.

Richard L. Weaver II. *Understanding Inter-Personal Communication.* Glenview, IL: Scott, Foresman, 1987.

Burton Wright and John P. Weiss. *Social Problems.* Boston: Little, Brown, 1980.

Philip G. Zimbardo. *Psychology and Life.* Glenview, IL: Scott, Foresman, 1985.

Endnotes

CHAPTER 7
1. Mishkin, *The Economics of Money, Banking, and Financial Markets,* p. 51.
2. Nickerson, *Fundamentals of Structured Cobol,* p. 8.
3. Perry and Perry, *Face to Face: The Individual and Social Problems,* p. 63.
4. Garmen et al., *Personal Finance,* p. 367.
5. Pillitteri, *Maternal-Newborn Nursing,* p. 312.
6. Campbell, *Humankind Emerging,* p. 45.
7. Campbell, p. 1.
8. MacMillan, *Mental Retardation in the School and Society,* p. 34.
9. Campbell, p. 45.
10. Campbell, p. 118.
11. Campbell, p. 119.
12. Campbell, p. 120.
13. Jones, *The Logic of International Relations,* p. 29.
14. Coleman and Butcher, *Abnormal Psychology and Normal Life,* p. 160.
15. Currie and Skolnick, *America's Problems; Social Issues and Public Policy,* p. 188.
16. Jones, p. 314.
17. Jones, p. 5.
18. Barlow, *Introduction to Criminology,* p. 422.
19. Chisholm and McCarty, *Principles of Economics,* p. 138.
20. Jones, p. 248.
21. Currie and Skolnick, p. 206.
22. Currie and Skolnick, p. 294.

CHAPTER 10
1. Roediger et al., *Psychology,* p. A6.
2. *American Heritage Dictionary of the English Language,* p. 380.

CHAPTER 20
1. Newell, *Chemistry,* p. 17.
2. Newell, p. 41.
3. Campbell, *Humankind Emerging,* p. 3.
4. Campbell, p. 107.
5. Wasserman, *The Basics of American Politics,* p. 25.
6. Wasserman, p. 8.
7. Newell, p. 43.
8. Pillitteri, *Nursing Care of the Growing Family,* p. 280.
9. Newell, p. 45.
10. Campbell, p. 21.
11. Gannon, *Management: An Organizational Perspective,* p. 20.
12. Decker, *Patterns of Exposition 6,* p. 9.
13. MacMillan, *Mental Retardation in the School and Society,* p. 5.
14. Campbell, p. 189.
15. Wasserman, p. 33.
16. Newell, p. 388.
17. Campbell, p. 16.
18. Wasserman, p. 87.
19. MacMillan, p. 11.

continued from page iv

Henry L. Roediger III et al., *Psychology*. Copyright © 1987 by Henry L. Roediger III, J. Philippe Rushton, Elizabeth D. Capaldi, and Scott G. Paris. Reprinted by permission of Little, Brown and Company.

Roget's International Thesaurus, 4th ed. by Robert L. Chapman. Copyright © 1977 by Harper & Row, Publishers Inc. Reprinted by permission of Harper & Row.

Hans Selye, M.D., *Stress Without Distress*. Copyright © 1974 by Hans Selye, M.D. Reprinted by permission of Harper & Row.

"The Aftershock of Rape," excerpted from the *Stanford Daily*, February 2, 1982. Reprinted by permission.

Andrew D. Szilagyi, Jr., and Marc J. Wallace, Jr., *Organizational Behavior and Performance*. Copyright © 1987 by Scott, Foresman and Co., Inc. Reprinted by permission of the publisher.

"A Good Word for Bad Words" in *Time*, 14 December, 1981. Copyright © 1981 by Time Inc. All rights reserved. Reprinted by permission.

Robert A. Wallace, *The World of Life*. Copyright © 1987 by Scott, Foresman and Co., Inc. Reprinted by permission of the publisher.

Walter T. Wallbank et al., *Civilization Past and Present*, Vol. 2. Copyright © 1987 by Scott, Foresman and Co., Inc. Reprinted by permission of the publisher.

Gary Wasserman, *The Basics of American Politics*. Copyright © 1985 by Little, Brown and Co. (Inc.) Reprinted by permission.

Richard L. Weaver III, *Understanding Interpersonal Communication*. Copyright © 1987 by Scott, Foresman and Co., Inc. Reprinted by permission of the publisher.

Philip G. Zimbardo, *Psychology of Life*, 12th ed. Copyright © 1988 by Scott, Foresman and Co., Inc. Reprinted by permission of the publisher.

Index